A BIOGRAPHICAL DICTIONARY OF
DARK AGE
BRITAIN

SEABY'S BIOGRAPHICAL DICTIONARIES:

A Biographical Dictionary of *The Byzantine Empire* Nicol (in preparation)
A Biographical Dictionary of *Dark Age Europe* James (forthcoming)
A Biographical Dictionary of *Ancient Egypt* David and David (forthcoming)

A biographical dictionary of

DARK AGE BRITAIN

England, Scotland and Wales
c. 500–c. 1050

Ann Williams,
Alfred P. Smyth
and
D. P. Kirby

LONDON

© Ann Williams, Alfred P. Smyth and David Kirby 1991
First published 1991

Typeset by Setrite Typesetters
Printed by Biddles Ltd., Guildford, England.

for the publishers
B A Seaby Ltd
7 Davies Street
London W1Y 1LL

Distributed by
B T Batsford Ltd
PO Box 4, Braintree, Essex CM7 7QY

A CIP Catalogue record
for this book is available
from the British Library

ISBN 1 85264 047 2

Contents

Preface

The period covered in this book begins in about AD 500, when southern Britain was emerging from Roman rule, and ends in the middle of the eleventh century, by which time the kingdoms of the English, Scots and Welsh were fully formed. The English entries include no-one whose career fell mainly in the reign of Edward the Confessor, though some people recorded in the volume died in the 1050s. There is a precedent for ending the 'Old English' period in 1042, rather than 1066, in Dorothy Whitelock's edition of *English Historical Documents*, volume I. It would be illogical to discuss the career of Harold II without including that of William I and the difficulties of separating the early Norman from the late English period would mean the inclusion of both. Such coverage would have produced a much longer and more unwieldy volume; King Edward and his contemporaries have therefore been left for a future compilation. Gruffudd ap Llywelyn, who became king of Gwynedd in 1039, however, is included, as is Macbeth, who died in 1057.

This volume does not cover Ireland, whose wealth of source material presents special problems and deserves a work to itself. But Irishmen and women who settled in Britain are included, such as **Kentigerna** of Loch Lomond and the abbots of Iona. Similarly, most Vikings who came only as visitors, however notorious, have been excluded, whereas those Scandinavians who established themselves in the Danelaw and in Scotland and the Isles have been included. A list of Pictish kings of the period is supplied among the genealogies.

The entries are arranged alphabetically, except that the Old English character *æsc* (Æ, æ) has been treated as two letters; thus **Áed** is preceded by **Æbbe** but followed by **Ælfwine**. People who share the same name, with no distinguishing bye-name, appear in chronological order by date of death, or (where this is not known) the date of their last known appearance in the sources. Chronological tables for the main events in English, Scottish and Welsh affairs provide a cross-reference, so that the people in the alphabetical entries can be placed in their chronological context. The genealogies fulfil a similar purpose; these have been provided for the most important or complex families. An asterisk has been used to mark the first occurrence of a name within an entry for which a separate entry has been supplied.

Some explanation for the name-forms used in this book should be given. Consistent spelling of names is not to be expected in medieval or indeed early modern writers. Names are easily garbled in transmission, especially when they are based on language unfamiliar to the recipient; and conventional spellings themselves change with time. For English names, the forms used in the annual volumes of *Anglo-Saxon England* (published by the Cambridge University Press) have been adopted. Even so, absolute consistency has not been possible. The few Old English names still in use at the present day appear in their modern forms, for example, **Alfred** and **Edgar**. The form **Athelstan** has been used in preference to *Æthelstan*, though in all other names of this type, Old English *æsc* has been used. Some modern spellings are so entrenched that it would be pedantic not to use them; thus, St **Chad** rather than *Ceadda*. Variant spellings have been included where appropriate, in brackets, and, where they are very different from the standard form, they are cross-referenced; hence, **Kenelm** St *see* **Cynehelm**. A particular problem arose with the first element *Beorht-* and its variants *Briht-* and *Byrht-*. In such cases the form in which the individual name most commonly occurs has been used; thus, **Beorhtwulf**, king of Mercia, **Brihtheah**, bishop, and **Byrhtnoth**, ealdorman. Scandinavian names appear in their Old Norse form, except for King **Cnut** whose name retains its traditional anglicized spelling.

In the case of Scottish names, the original Gaelic or Old Irish forms have been preserved for the period prior to *c*. 850, and after that time (which coincides with the establishment of the dynasty of Kenneth Mac Alpín) anglicized forms are given. So, for the earlier Gaelic period we have **Domnall** and **Cináed** while for later Scottish kings we have **Donald** and **Kenneth**. For Welsh personal names, modern rather than earlier forms have generally been used, but some earlier spellings (e.g. **Riderch** for **Rhydderch**) do occur.

The dates given for individuals derive from primary source material, which is variable in the amount of detail it provides. Birth-dates are hardly ever recorded, though they can sometimes be inferred from the age at death, where this is known. Such dates appear in the body of the text but not the entry headings. Death-dates are more common, but sometimes the day is known (from obituary lists) but not the year; if this is the case the information similarly appears in the body of the entry but not the heading. Dates in the headings refer to tenure of office with the death date if it is different (and available). For many people, only approximate dates can be supplied, and for some only a *floruit* is known.

Genealogical tables have been constructed to show relationships and lines of descent between individuals where this seemed helpful. In some areas and periods, however, this is not feasible, and so regnal lists have been drawn up. This applies particularly to the English kings of the sixth and seventh centuries. We have tended here to give traditional dates as found, for example, in Stenton's works, since the chronology is still problematical and subject to constant revision. Asterisks in the tables and lists indicate an entry in the main listing.

A wide-ranging work of reference of this nature invariably demands that judgements on complex historical issues have to be made on the part of each individual co-author, working to a format which cannot allow for conflicting scholarly opinions to be assessed fully. The short list of references which accompanies each entry should allow the reader to pursue the subject more fully.

Of the three co-authors, Dr Ann Williams has been responsible for the Anglo-Saxon entries, Dr Alfred P. Smyth for the Scottish, and Dr D.P. Kirby for the Welsh.

We have drawn upon the help and advice of many friends and colleagues in the construction of this dictionary; special gratitude is accorded to Professor G W S Barrow (Department of Scottish History, University of Edinburgh) and Professor A A M Duncan (Department of Scottish History, University of Glasgow) for help and advice with the Scottish entries, and to Professor R Geraint Gruffydd (Centre for Advanced Welsh and Celtic Studies, University College of Wales, Aberystwyth) for kindly reading and commenting on a number of the Welsh entries. Thanks are also due to Margaret Smyth for her help with proof-reading the Scottish entries. All three authors wish to express their profound thanks to Paula Turner of B. A. Seaby Ltd. for correcting several errors at the proofing stage and for seeing the work so conscientiously through the press. Any errors which still remain are our own responsibility.

ANN WILLIAMS   NOVEMBER 1990
ALFRED P. SMYTH
D.P. KIRBY

Glossary

Ætheling (OE). A member of the royal kindred; the sons or brothers of the reigning king, from whom the next ruler was chosen.

Bretwalda (OE). Literally 'ruler of Britain'; the overlord of the southern English in the period before the unification of England.

Burh (OE). Literally 'a fortified site'; a walled town or fortress, also a fortified manor house.

Cild (OE). Literally 'a young person'; used to indicate high rank in the tenth and eleventh centuries.

Computus (Latin, *computare*, to reckon, count). The study of mathematical topics; specifically, to determine the date of Easter.

Ealdorman (OE). From *ealdor*, 'lord', *mann*, 'man'; the governor of a province (see Shire). Replaced by the title 'earl' in the eleventh century.

Familia (Latin). The family or household of a bishop.

Geld (OE). Literally 'money, tax'; a tax or tribute, payable in money, levied by the English kings of the tenth and eleventh centuries; *Danegeld* was the tribute paid to Viking armies, *heregeld* ('army-tax'), the tax raised to pay the royal fleet and its crews from 1012–51. (See also Hide.)

Geneat (OE). A mounted retainer, of free but not noble status.

Gleeman (OE). An entertainer; a jester or singer.

Hearthtroop (OE *heorthwerod*). The personal following of a lord.

Heriot (OE *heregeatu*). The render, in arms and armour, paid at death by a retainer to his lord (see also Thegn).

Hide (OE *hid, hida*). From the seventh century, the standard unit for the assessment of tax and tribute; notionally, the amount of land which would support one family.

Housecarl (ON *huskarl*). A retainer, of noble status; introduced into England in the time of Cnut; synonymous with Thegn.

Hundred (OE *hund*). Subdivision of a Shire (qv), with fiscal, judicial and military functions; notionally a hundred households or hides (qv).

Leech (OE *laece*). A physician, doctor.

Letter-close. A private letter, sent sealed or otherwise fastened so that the contents could not be read without breaking the seal or fastening; as opposed to 'letter-patent', a public document, which could be opened and read without destroying the seal.

Lith, lithsmen (ON *lith*). A company of men in the following of a lord; specifically the crews of the royal fleet maintained by the English kings from 1012–51.

Minster (Latin *monasterium*) (OE *mynstre*). In the Anglo-Saxon period, used both for monasteries, with monks following a communal rule (regulars) and for communities of priests with parochial functions (seculars). In modern terminology, 'minster' is used only for the latter, to describe the 'mother-churches', whose priests served the inhabitants of the district dependent upon the church (its parish). Minster parishes were larger than those of later centuries.

Morning-gift (OE *morgen gifu*). The gift, usually of land, made by a husband to his wife after the consummation of marriage.

Gleeman (OE). An entertainer; a jester or singer.

Oblate (Latin *oblatus*, offered). A child offered to God by being placed in a monastery, with the intention that it should enter religion.

Patricius (Latin). Literally 'noble-(man)'; in eighth-century Northumbria, used to distinguish the highest-ranking layman in the king's service and perhaps equivalent to the Frankish 'mayor of the palace', the controller of the royal household.

Reeve (OE *gerefa*). Administrative officer, in charge of the management of an estate, and of the district dependent upon that estate. The sheriff (*scir-gerefa*), who emerges in the tenth century is the king's representative in the Shire (qv).

Scriptorium (Latin). The writing office of ecclesiastical communities, where manuscripts were produced; the royal scriptorium was a primitive Chancery.

Seax (OE). A one-edged knife or sword, from which the Saxons took their name.

Seneschal (Latin, *seniscalcus*, OE *discthegn*). The steward of a household; his main charge was provisioning.

Ship-soke (OE). Unit of three hundred hides (qv), often attached to bishoprics, and charged with the provision of a ship and its crew to the national fleet in tenth and eleventh century England.

Shire (OE *scir*). Literally, 'office, official charge'; area of administration. In seventh- and eighth-century Wessex, each shire was entrusted to an ealdor-man (qv). The term and the institution were exported to England north of the Thames in the tenth century, when the West Saxon kings became kings of England.

Thegn (OE). Literally 'boy, young man, servant'; a man of noble status, having (in Wessex) a wergeld (qv) of 1200s as opposed to the 200s wergeld of a non-noble free man or peasant. In tenth- and eleventh-century England, the nobility were graded according to their heriots (qv); in descending rank, ealdormen, king's thegns, median thegns (that is, thegns who were not directly king's men).

Wergeld (OE). Literally 'man-price'; the sum of money paid by the kin of a killer as compensation to the kin of the man he killed. By the tenth century, the wergeld had become a means of assessing legal rights and judicial fines; a thegn's wergeld was 1200s, that of a non-noble free man or peasant was 200s.

Witan, witenagemot (OE). Literally, 'the wise; the assembly of the wise'; the king's councillors, who had the right and duty to advise him.

Chronological Table: England

c 400–c. 600.	The period of the English settlement of Britain.
449	Traditional date for the landing of Hengest in Britain.
477	Ælle lands in Sussex.
c. 500–50	Establishment of the kingdom of Wessex.
547–59	Ida king in Bernicia.
577	Battle of Dyrham: Cuthwine and Ceawlin take the British cities of Gloucester, Cirencester and Bath.
590–604	Pontificate of Gregory the Great.
593–617	Æthelfrith king of Bernicia and Northumbria.
596	Gregory despatches Augustine to Britain.
597	Augustine lands in Kent and is received by King Æthelberht.
604	Æthelfrith seizes Deira; exile of Edwin.
617	Battle of the River Idle; Rædwald of East Anglia kills Æthelfrith; Edwin becomes king.
617–33	Edwin king of Northumbria.
c. 625	Edwin marries Æthelburh, daughter of Æthelberht; Paulinus leads Kentish mission to Northumbria.
627	Edwin baptized by Paulinus.
628	Penda of Mercia defeats the West Saxons at Cirencester.
633	Battle of Hatfield Chase; Edwin killed by Cadwallon of Gwynedd and Penda of Mercia. Cadwallon killed by Oswald at the battle of 'Heavenfield' (nr Hexham).
634–42	Oswald king of Northumbria.
634	Aidan comes from Iona to convert Northumbria; Lindisfarne founded.
634–51	Aidan bishop of Northumbria.
642	Battle of *Maserfeld* (Oswestry); Oswald killed by Penda of Mercia.
642–70	Oswiu king of Northumbria.
651	Oswine of Deira killed by Oswiu. Death of Aidan and succession of Finán. Cuthbert enters Melrose.
655	Battle of the River *Winwæd*; Penda killed by Oswiu. Mercia ruled from Northumbria for three years.
658	Mercian rebellion in favour of Wulfhere, son of Penda.
658–75	Wulfhere king of Mercia.
661	Death of Finán and succession of Colmán as bishop of Northumbria.
664	Synod of Whitby. Colmán returns to Ireland, and Wilfrid made bishop. Plague reaches England and kills many, including Archbishop Deusdedit. Cuthbert becomes prior of Lindisfarne.
668	Wigheard, archbishop-elect, dies at Rome. Pope Vitalian consecrates Theodore archbishop.
668–90	Archiepiscopate of Theodore.
669	Theodore and Hadrian reach Canterbury. Chad bishop of Mercia.
670–85	Ecgfrith king of Northumbria.
672	First synod of the English Church at Hertford.
674	Benedict Biscop founds Monkwearmouth.

675–704	Æthelred king of Mercia.
678	Wilfrid driven from Northumbria by Ecgfrith.
679	Battle of the River Trent; Æthelred of Mercia defeats Ecgfrith.
680	Bede enters Monkwearmouth.
681	Foundation of Jarrow; Bede is one of the new brethren.
684	Ecgfrith raids Ireland.
685	Cuthbert bishop of Lindisfarne; battle of *Nechtanesmere*; Ecgfrith killed fighting against the Picts. Wilfrid bishop of Ripon.
685–705	Aldfrith king of Northumbria.
687	Death of Cuthbert on the Inner Farne.
688–716	Ceolfrith abbot of Jarrow.
688–726	Ine king of Wessex.
689	Death of Benedict Biscop.
690–726	Wihtred king of Kent.
690	Death of Theodore. Wilfrid driven from Northumbria by Aldfrith.
698–721	Eadfrith, scribe of the Lindisfarne Gospels, bishop of Lindisfarne.
705–16	Osred king of Northumbria.
706	Synod of the River Nidd; Wilfrid restored to his property.
709/10	Wilfrid dies at Oundle.
716–57	Æthelbald king of Mercia.
722	Boniface appointed bishop; preaches in Germany and cuts down sacred oak at Geismar.
731	Bede completes the *Ecclesiastical history of the English people*.
732	Boniface archbishop of Mainz.
735	Death of Bede. York becomes an archiepiscopal see; Ecgberht is the first archbishop of York.
754	Death of Boniface.
757	Æthelbald is murdered at Seckington; civil war in Mercia.
757–86	Cynewulf king of Wessex.
757–96	Offa king of Mercia.
765–92	Archiepiscopate of Jænberht at Canterbury.
768	Charlemagne becomes king of the Franks.
776	Battle of Otford; Kent throws off Mercian control.
781	Alcuin joins the court of Charlemagne.
786	Cynewulf killed by the ætheling Cyneheard. Ecgberht is driven from Wessex and takes refuge with Charlemagne; Beorhtric is king of Wessex and marries Offa's daughter, Eadburh. Papal legation to England.
787	Synod of Chelsea; see of Lichfield raised to status of archbishopric and the province of Canterbury is divided; Hygeberht, archbishop of Lichfield, consecrates Ecgfrith king of the Mercians.
792	Death of Archbishop Jænberht. Æthelheard archbishop of Canterbury.
793	Vikings sack Lindisfarne.
796	Deaths of Offa and Ecgfrith.
796–821	Cœnwulf king of Mercia.
800	Pope Leo III crowns Charlemagne emperor of the Romans.
802–39	Ecgberht king of Wessex.
803	Synod of *Clofesho*; Lichfield demoted from archbishopric.
805–32	Wulfred archbishop of Canterbury.

814	Death of Charlemagne; Louis the Pious emperor and king of the Franks.
821–3	Ceolwulf I king of Mercia.
823	Ceolwulf is deposed; Beornwulf becomes king of Mercia.
825	Ecgberht of Wessex defeats and kills Beornwulf at the Battle of *Ellendun* (Wroughton). Æthelwulf, son of Ecgberht, conquers Kent.
830	Wiglaf becomes king of Mercia.
835	Vikings attack Sheppey.
836	Ecgberht defeated by Vikings at Carhampton.
838	Battle of Hingston Down; Ecgberht defeats the Britons of Dumnonia and their Viking allies.
839–58	Æthelwulf king of Wessex.
840	Death of Louis the Pious, emperor and king of the Franks. Civil war in Frankia.
843	Æthelwulf defeated by Vikings at Carhampton. Treaty of Verdun; the Frankish empire is divided between the sons of Louis the Pious. Charles the Bald becomes king of western Frankia (France).
851	Æthelwulf defeats a Viking army at the battle of *Aclea*. His son Athelstan wins a sea-battle against the Vikings off Sandwich.
852–74	Burgred king of Mercia.
853	Joint Mercian and West Saxon attack on Wales. Burgred marries Æthelwulf's daughter, Æthelswith.
855–56	Æthelwulf's pilgrimage to Rome.
856	Æthelwulf marries Judith, daugther of Charles the Bald.
858–60	Æthelbald king of Wessex; he marries his stepmother, Judith.
860–65	Æthelberht king of Wessex.
865–71	Æthelred I king of Wessex.
865	Arrival of the 'Great Army' of Ivarr the Boneless and Halfdan in England.
867	Ælle of Northumbria killed by Vikings.
869	Edmund of East Anglia killed by Vikings.
870–71	Viking assault on Wessex; Æthelred and Alfred win the battle of Ashdown, but lose the battle of Basing. Æthelred dies of wounds and is buried at Wimborne. Guthrum and the 'summer army' join Halfdan.
871–99	Alfred king of Wessex.
874	Vikings occupy Repton. Burgred driven from Mercia and goes to Rome. Ceolwulf II king of Mercia.
876	Vikings under Halfdan settle Northumbria.
877	Viking occupation of eastern Mercia.
878	Guthrum occupies Chippenham; Alfred driven into the Somerset marshes, where he fortifies Athelney. Alfred wins the battle of Edington. Guthrum accepts baptism and establishes peace with Alfred by the Treaty of Wedmore.
879–90	Guthrum king in East Anglia.
c. 879	Death of Ceolwulf II of Mercia.
c. 884	Æthelred of Mercia marries Æthelflæd, daughter of Alfred.
886	Alfred takes London.
892–95	Viking raids in Wessex; contained by Alfred.
899	Death of Alfred.
899–924	Edward the Elder king of Wessex.
900	Rebellion of the ætheling Æthelwold.

903	Æthelwold killed at the battle of the Holme.
910	Battle of Tettenhall; Danes of York are defeated by Edward the Elder. Ragnall becomes king of York.
911	Death of Æthelred, Lord of Mercia.
911–18	Æthelflæd Lady of the Mercians.
914	Ragnall attacks Bamburgh. First battle of Corbridge.
917	Æthelflæd takes Derby. Edward storms Tempsford. Submission of the Danes of Northampton. Danes of East Anglia and Essex submit to Edward.
918	Leicester submits to Æthelflæd. York offers submission to Æthelflæd, but her death at Tamworth ends negotiations. The second battle of Corbridge.
919	Ragnall regains York. Edward the elder deprives Ælfwynn of authority in Mercia.
920	Death of Ragnall; Sigtrygg Caech king of York.
924	Deaths of Edward the Elder and his son Ælfweard.
924–39	Athelstan king of Wessex.
926	Sigtrygg Caech marries Eadgyth, Athelstan's sister. Hugh the Great marries Eadhild, Athelstan's half-sister.
927	Death of Sigtrygg Caech; Athelstan seizes York.
928	Henry the Fowler, king of Germany, asks for an English bride for his son Otto; Edith sent to Germany as Otto's wife.
934	Athelstan campaigns in Scotland.
937	Battle of *Brunanburh*; Athelstan defeats Constantine III of Scotland and Olafr Gothfrithson of Dublin.
939	Death of Athelstan; Olafr Gothfrithson takes York.
940–46	Edmund king of Wessex.
940	Olafr sacks Tamworth and seizes the Five Boroughs (Leicester, Derby, Nottingham, Lincoln and Stamford).
941	Death of Olafr Gothfrithson; Olafr Sigtryggson king of York.
942/43	Dunstan abbot of Glastonbury.
943	Olafr Sigtryggson driven from York; Edmund seizes the Five Boroughs.
946	Edmund murdered at Pucklechurch.
946–55	Eadred king of Wessex.
947	Eirikr Bloodaxe becomes king of York.
948	Eirikr is driven out by Eadred; Olafr Sigtryggson returns.
952	Eirikr's second rule in York. Archbishop Wulfstan of York arrested on the orders of Eadred.
954	Eirikr killed on Stainmore; Northumbrians submit to Eadred.
955	Æthelwold re-founds Abingdon. Death of Eadred.
955–59	Eadwig king of Wessex.
956	Eadwig quarrels with Dunstan and expels him from England; Dunstan goes to Ghent.
957	Edgar, Eadwig's brother, becomes king of Mercia.
959–75	Edgar king of Wessex and England.
961	Dunstan becomes archbishop of Canterbury; Oswald is made bishop of Worcester.
963	Æthelwold becomes bishop of Winchester.
964	Marriage of Edgar and Ælfthryth.
971	Oswald archbishop of York.
973	Edgar consecrated king of the English at Bath. Expedition to Chester; Edgar receives the submission of the Norse and British kings.

975	Death of Edgar.
975–78	Edward the Martyr king of England.
978	Murder of Edward the Martyr at Corfe, Dorset.
978–1016	Æthelred II king of England.
979	Æthelred consecrated at Kingston-on-Thames.
980	Viking raids begin again with attack on Southampton.
984	Death of Æthelwold.
988	Death of Dunstan.
991	Olafr Tryggvason defeats an English army at Maldon; Ealdorman Byrhtnoth is killed.
992	Death of Oswald.
993	Olafr Tryggvason sacks Bamburgh and defeats an English army in Lindsey.
994	Olafr Tryggvason and Swein Forkbeard of Denmark harry Kent. Olafr comes to terms with Æthelred and accepts baptism; he returns to Norway.
996	Wulfstan bishop of London.
997–1001	Vikings raid England.
1001	Treachery of Pallig; extensive raids in the south-west.
1002	Æthelred marries Emma, sister of Richard II of Normandy. Massacre of St Brice's Day; murder of Danish merchants and settlers in England. Wulfstan becomes bishop of Worcester and archbishop of York.
1003	Invasion of Swein Forkbeard; Exeter sacked.
1003–7	Swein Forkbeard campaigns in England.
1007	Eadric Streona ealdorman of Mercia.
1009	Thorkell the Tall arrives with the 'immense raiding-army'.
1009–12	Thorkell's army campaigns in England.
1010	Battle of Ringmere; Thorkell defeats the East Anglians under Ulfkell Snilling.
1012	Canterbury sacked; Archbishop Ælfheah martyred in the Danish camp at Southwark. Thorkell tries to prevent his murder; the army disperses, and Thorkell enters the service of King Æthelred.
1013	Swein Forkbeard arrives in England. The English magnates submit to him, and Æthelred is driven out; he flees to Normandy.
1014	Swein dies, 2 February. The Danes choose Cnut as king, but the English magnates send to Æthelred in Normandy. Æthelred returns and Cnut is driven out.
1015	Murder of the northern leaders, Sigeferth and Morcar, by Eadric Streona, on Æthelred's orders. The ætheling Edmund marries Sigeferth's widow, and receives the submission of the north. Cnut attacks Wessex and is joined by Eadric Streona.
1016	Cnut takes Northumbria. Æthelred dies on 23 April and Edmund Ironside becomes king. He wins the battle of Sherston, but is defeated by Cnut at the battle of Ashingdon. They divide England, Cnut taking the north and Edmund Wessex. Edmund dies on 30 November.
1016–35	Cnut king of England.
1017	Thorkell the Tall earl of East Anglia; Eadric Streona murdered on Cnut's orders. Cnut marries Emma.
1018	Agreement at Oxford; Cnut accepted as king.

1018/19	Cnut goes to Denmark; he becomes king on the death of his brother, Haraldr.
1020	Godwine earl of Wessex.
c. 1023	Leofric earl of Mercia.
1027	Cnut's pilgrimage to Rome.
1028	Norway conquered by the Danes.
1030	Olafr Helgi killed at the battle of Stiklastadir.
1035	Magnus Olafson throws off Danish suzerainty of Norway. Death of Cnut.
1035–40	Harold I king of England.
1035	Harold appointed regent with support from Leofric of Mercia. Emma holds Winchester for Harthacnut, with support of Godwine. Harthacnut campaigns against Magnus Olafson.
1036	Murder of the ætheling Alfred by Harold and Earl Godwine. Emma flees to Bruges.
1037	Harold becomes full king.
1040	Death of Harold. English magnates send for Harthacnut.
1040–2	Harthacnut king of England.
1041	Heavy tax imposed on England. Men of Worcester refuse to pay; Worcestershire is harried on Harthacnut's orders. Edward the Confessor arrives in England, and is accepted by Harthacnut as his heir.
1042	Death of Harthacnut; Edward the Confessor becomes king.

Chronological Table: Scotland

c. 407	Withdrawal of Roman army from Britain.
409	Zosimus reports Britons to have expelled Roman officials and to have organized their own defences against Saxons.
c. 450	Alleged migration of Cunedda and his sons from Manaw of Gododdin to north Wales.
c. 460	Coroticus (Ceretic) of Strathclyde, recipient of letter from St Patrick who was then evangelizing in northern Ireland.
c. 500–50	*Floruit* of Saint Ninian.
c. 525–50	Angles establish coastal territory of Bernicia centred on Bamburgh (formerly British fortress of *Din Guoaroy*).
563	Arrival of Columba in Scotland.
563–583	Exploration in North Atlantic by Cormac Ua Liatháin from base in the Western Isles. Exploration of the Northern Isles, Faroes and Iceland by Brendan of Clonfert from a base on the Garvellachs in Firth of Lorn.
570	Death of Gildas, British historian.
c. 570–90	Urien rules British kingdom of Rheged.
c. 570–612	*Floruit* of Saint Kentigern.
574	Columba ordains Áedán mac Gabhráin king of Scots Dál Riata.
575	Convention of Druim Cett (Co. Derry). Attended by Columba and Scots king, Áedán mac Gabhráin.
c. 580	*Floruit* of Riderch Hen, king of the Strathclyde Britons, friend of Kentigern and Columba.
c. 585	Death of Bruide mac Maelchon, king of Picts.
c. 585–89	Columba founds Durrow.
c. 590	Urien of Rheged slain while besieging Northumbrian Angles at Lindisfarne.
593–617	Æthelfrith king of Northumbria.
597	Death of Columba.
c. 600	Northern Britons led by the Gododdin slaughtered in unsuccessful attack on Angles at Catterick.
603	Áedán mac Gabhráin invades Northumbria: defeated by Æthelfrith at *Degsastan*.
c. 608	Death of Áedán mac Gabhráin, king of Scots.
617	Martyrdom of Donnán and his community on Eigg.
617–33	Edwin king of Northumbria. Eanfrith, Oswald, and Oswiu, sons of Æthelfrith of Northumbria, in exile among the Scots and Picts.
c. 625	Alleged foundation of Abernethy by Kildare nuns under patronage of Nechtán king of the Picts.
c. 627	Roman mission of Paulinus to Northumbrian Angles.
629–42	Domnall Brecc king of Scots.
634	Oswald victorious over Cadwallon in battle near Hexham.
634–42	Oswald king of Northumbria.
634–51	Bishop Aidan rules Northumbrian Church from Lindisfarne.
637	Battle of Mag Rath in Ulster. Scottish Dál Riata loses control of territory on Irish mainland.
638	Northumbrian assault on Edinburgh: Anglian conquests extend northwards to Forth.

642	Domnall Brecc, king of Scots, slain by Strathclyde Britons in battle of Strathcarron.
642–70	Reign of Oswiu in Bernicia and (from 655) over all Northumbria.
c. 651	Cuthbert enters Melrose.
651–60	Bishop Finán rules Northumbrian Church from Lindisfarne.
652	Death of Abbot Ségéne of Iona, friend of Oswald of Northumbria.
653–57	Talorgen son of Eanfrith, king of Picts.
660–64	Bishop Colmán rules Northumbrian Church from Lindisfarne.
660–80	Anglian conquest of British kingdom of Rheged.
664	Synod of Whitby.
669	Wilfrid described as bishop of Northumbrians and of Picts under Oswiu's dominion. Death of Abbot Cumméne of Iona who wrote *Miracles of Columba*.
c. 670	Adomnán arrives at Iona.
670	Death of Oswiu of Northumbria.
670–85	Ecgfrith king of Northumbria.
672	Picts depose Drest from kingship. Pictish army massacred by Ecgfrith.
672–93	Bruide son of Bili, king of Picts.
673	Máelrubai founds Applecross. Evangelization of Picts of north-west Scotland.
679	Adomnán succeeds Failbe as ninth abbot of Iona.
679–86	Adomnán writes his work on *The Holy Places*.
c. 681	Northumbrians establish Anglian bishopric at Abercorn.
685	Picts under Bruide mac Bili defeat and slay Ecgfrith of Northumbria in battle of Dunnichen Moss (*Nechtanesmere*).
685–705	Aldfrith king of Northumbria.
686	Adomnán's first visit to court of Aldfrith of Northumbria.
687	Death of Saint Cuthbert.
688	Adomnán's second visit to court of Aldfrith of Northumbria.
688–92	Adomnán writing *Life of Columba*.
c. 695–704	Adomnán tries to persuade Picts to adopt Roman usage.
697	Adomnán promulgates *Law of Innocents* (protecting non-combatants in time of war).
c. 700	Bewcastle Cross erected near Anglian frontier with Britons of south-west Scotland.
704	Death of Adomnán.
c. 706–24	Nechtán son of Derile, king of Picts.
711	Picts slaughtered by Northumbrians in plain of Manaw.
c. 712	Ecgbert arrives at Iona and persuades Columban clergy in Scotland to accept Roman usage.
717	Nechtán expels Columban clergy 'across the Spine of Britain'.
722	Death of Máelrubai of Applecross.
c. 725	Irish monks (as reported by Dicuil) now visiting the Faroes from the Northern Isles of Scotland.
729–61	Óengus I, son of Fergus, king of Picts.
c. 731	Pehthelm, Northumbrian bishop, appointed to see of Whithorn.
733	Death of Kentigerna, saint of Loch Lomond.
735	Death of Bede.
747	Death of Cú-Chuimne the Wise of Iona, Latin poet and canonist.

750–52	Teudebur son of Bili, king of Strahtclyde Britons, becomes overlord of Picts.
752	Conquest of Kyle by Eadberht of Northumbria.
756	Death of Bealdhere (Baldred) of Tyninghame.
766–72	Abbot Suibhne rules Iona: Dicuil, Carolingian scholar, may have been his pupil.
c. 780–806	*Book of Kells* begun on Iona and later completed at Kells.
793	First Viking raid on Lindisfarne.
794	First Viking raid on Scottish Isles.
795	Viking devastation on the Isle of Skye and on Iona.
c. 795	Irish monks, as reported by Dicuil, visiting Iceland from February to August.
802	Vikings return to burn Iona.
803	Last mention of Northumbrian bishop of Whithorn.
806	Vikings attack Iona for third time and butcher 68 of the *familia*.
807–14	Abbot Cellach of Iona builds new church at Kells. Iona largely abandoned for more than a century.
c. 811–20	Constantine son of Fergus king of Scots Dál Riata and of Picts. Major new ecclesiastical foundation at Dunkeld.
820–34	Óengus II, son of Fergus, king of Scots Dál Riata and of Picts. Major new ecclesiastical foundation at St Andrews (on site of older church).
825	Torture and martyrdom of Blathmac at the hands of Viking raiders on Iona.
829–31	Diarmait, abbot of Iona, visiting his Scottish *paruchia* (from Kells) with relics of Columba.
839	Major Viking victory over Picts: Eóganán son of Óengus II, king of Scots and Picts, slain in battle. Eclipse of the Scoto-Pictish house of Fergus.
c. 840	Kenneth mac Alpín succeeds to kingship of Dál Riata.
c. 847	Kenneth mac Alpín king of Scots and Picts.
849	Division of relics of Saint Columba between church of Kells in Ireland and church of Kenneth mac Alpín (? at Dunkeld).
c. 850	Danish attacks on Norwegian colonists in Northern and Western Isles.
c. 850–57	*Floruit* of Ketil Flatnose, ruler of Hebrides.
c. 855	Beginnings of Viking earldom on Orkney under Sigurd I the Powerful.
858–62	Donald I king of Scots: the laws of Dál Riata promulgated at Forteviot.
866–67	Danish conquest of Northumbria: English Bernicia survives as satellite of Danish York.
866–69	Campaign of Olaf the White of Dublin against Picts.
870–71	Olaf the White and Ivarr sack Dumbarton.
870–90	Migration of Hebridean and Caithness Norsemen to Iceland under leadership of Aud the Deep Minded and others of Ketil Flatnose's kin.
872	Artgal, king of Strathclyde Britons, slain at the instigation of Constantine I of Scotland.
874–75	Halfdan, king of Northumbrian Danes, attacks Picts and Strathclyde Britons.
877	Constantine I, king of Scots, slain by Danes.
889	Expulsion of Giric, king of Scots, and of Eochaid son of Rhun, king of the Strathclyde Britons.

900–43	Constantine II king of Scots.
c. 900	*Floruit* of Torf Einar, first historical Viking Earl of Orkney.
900	Scots annexe Strathclyde: migration of Strathclyde British aristocracy to North Wales.
903	Norse Grandsons of Ivarr plunder Dunkeld 'and all Scotland'.
904	Ivarr, grandson of Ivarr, defeated and slain by the Scots in Strathearn.
906	Constantine II and Bishop Cellach of St Andrews pledge themselves at Scone to uphold the rights of the Scottish Church.
c. 911	Ragnall, grandson of Ivarr, captures York and confiscates church land in Bernicia.
914	First battle of Corbridge: Ragnall victorious over Scots and Bernicians.
918	Scandinavian York and Dublin reunited under the Grandsons of Ivarr. Second battle of Corbridge between Ragnall and Constantine II in which Vikings lose many men. First mention of the office of *Mórmaer* ('High Steward') in the Scottish kingdom.
919	Edward the Elder, having annexed Mercia, occupies Manchester in Northumbria.
920	Constantine II of Scotland, Ragnall of York, the Bernician Angles, and Strathclyde Britons, all enter into treaty with Edward the Elder.
927	Gothfrith grandson of Ivarr, succeeds to York kingship. Athelstan, king of Wessex, invades Northumbria and Gothfrith seeks aid of Constantine II and Owen of Strathclyde. Treaty at Penrith between Athelstan and Scottish rulers.
934	Olafr Gothfrithsson succeeds to kingship of Norse Dublin. Scots rejoin the Dublin alliance and Athelstan invades Scotland as far as Dunnottar.
937	Battle of Brunanburh: Constantine II of Scotland, Olafr Gothfrithsson of Dublin, and Owen of Strathclyde, defeated by Athelstan of Wessex.
939	Death of Athelstan. Olafr Gothfrithsson captures York.
941	Olafr Gothfrithsson sacks St Bealdhere's church at Tyninghame in (Bernician) Lothian. Death of Olafr Gothfrithsson who is succeeded in York kingship by his cousin, Olafr Cuaran.
943–54	Malcolm I king of Scots.
943–52	Constantine II of Scotland in retirement as monk at St Andrews.
945	Edmund invades Cumbria (? = Strathclyde and Cumbria) and 'grants' it to Malcolm king of Scots. Olafr Cuaran returns to his Dublin throne.
947	Eirikr Bloodaxe, exiled king of Norway, welcomed at York by Archbishop Wulfstan.
948	Eadred of Wessex invades Northumbria and forces York Danes to expel Eirikr Bloodaxe. Malcolm I of Scotland plunders 'the English as far as the Tees': Olafr Cuaran reunites kingdoms of York and Dublin. Eirikr Bloodaxe and his warband withdraw to Orkney.
c. 950–970	*Floruit* of Catroe, Picto-Scottish saint.
952	Olafr Cuaran finally abandons his York throne. Eirikr

	Bloodaxe returns to York for second reign.
954	Slaying of Eirikr Bloodaxe on Stainmore: end of Viking rule in Northumbria. Wessex kings rule to the Scottish border.
954–62	Indulf king of Scots: Edinburgh occupied and Lothian annexed by Scots.
963	Death of Fothad mac Brain, 'scribe and bishop of the Scottish Isles': resurgence of Christianity among Norse colonists in Hebrides.
965	Duncan, abbot of Dunkeld, slain in battle fought between rival contenders for Scottish crown.
966–1005	Breakdown of alternating succession to the Scottish kingship. Successful attempt by descendants of Constantine I to exclude descendants of his brother Áed from the kingship.
971	Kenneth II king of Scots plunders England as far as Stainmore.
973	Kenneth II of Scotland, and Malcolm, king of Strathclyde-Cumbria, enter into treaty with Edgar, king of England, at Chester.
980	Olafr Cuaran resigns his Dublin kingship and becomes monk at Iona.
c. 985	Icelandic sons of Njál join in Norse raid on Hebrides and the Clyde estuary (as described in Njáls Saga).
c. 985	Eirikr the Red discovers and colonizes Greenland with help of Hebridean Norsemen.
986	Danish marauders attack Hebrides. Iona attacked on Christmas night: abbot and fifteen of his community slain.
989	Gothfrith Haroldsson, king of Hebrides, slain by men of Dál Riata.
c. 995	Leif Eiriksson, later explorer of North America, visiting in Hebrides.
995	Olafr Tryggvason forcibly converted Earl Sigurd the Stout of Orkney.
1005–34	Malcolm II king of Scots.
1006	Unsuccessful raid by Malcolm II on Durham.
1014	Earl Sigurd the Stout of Orkney defeated and slain while fighting against the army of Brian Boru at Clontarf.
1018	Battle of Carham: Malcolm II of Scotland allied with Owen the Bald of Strathclyde victorious over English of Bernicia.
1031–32	Invasion of Scotland by Cnut who forced Malcolm II (and perhaps Macbeth) to submit.
1034–40	Duncan I king of Scots.
c. 1035	Earl Thorfinn II of Orkney won decisive victory at Tarbat Ness over the Scottish ruler Karl Hundason (? Macbeth) after which Caithness and Ross remained firmly in Norse hands.
c. 1037	Rögnvaldur Brúsason returned to the Orkneys from Norway and shared Orkney earldom with his uncle Thorfinn II.
1040–57	Macbeth king of Scotland.
c. 1042	Thorfinn II earl of Orkney led Viking raid on western England.
1045	Crinan abbot of Dunkeld slain by Macbeth.
1046	Rögnvaldur earl of Orkney slain by his uncle Earl Thorfinn II.
c. 1046–75	Arnór Earls' Poet, Icelandic court poet to Norse earls of Orkney.
1050	Macbeth king of Scotland and Thorfinn II earl of Orkney undertake two independent pilgrimages to Rome.
c. 1052	Thorolf first Norse bishop of Orkney established there by Earl

	Thorfinn II. Decline of Viking paganism in Northern Isles.
1054	Siward earl of Northumbria invades Scotland in unsuccessful attempt to depose Macbeth and place Malcolm Canmore on Scottish throne.
1057	Macbeth slain in battle at Lumphanon. Malcolm III Canmore the victor.
1057–58	Lulach king of Scots in opposition to Malcolm III Canmore.
1058–93	Malcolm III Canmore king of Scotland.
c. 1065	Death of Thorfinn II, earl of Orkney at Birsay.

Chronological Table: Wales

429	First visit of Germanus, bishop of Auxerre, to Britain.
431	The deacon Palladius sent to the Scots who believe in Christ.
c. 450	Possible *floruit* of St Patrick. Cunedda establishes the First Dynasty of Gwynedd. Possible *floruit* of Vortigern and the coming of the Saxons.
c. 490	*Floruit* of Ambrosius Aurelianus.
c. 500	The battle of Mount *Badon*. Possible *floruit* of Arthur.
c. 500−40	Gildas writes the *De Excidio Britanniae* (*The Ruin of Britain*).
c. 549	The death of Maelgwn, king of Gwynedd.
c. 570	*Floruit* of Urien of Rheged.
c. 600	Possible date of the battle of *Catraeth*.
c. 615	The death of Selyf, king of Powys, in the battle of Chester.
c. 625	The death of Cadfan, king of Gwynedd.
633	Cadwallon, king of Gwynedd, slays Edwin in the battle of Hatfield.
634	Cadwallon slain by Oswald in the battle of Heavenfield.
642	*Floruit* of Cynyddylan of Powys. The death of Oswald in the battle of *Maserfeld*.
655	The withdrawal of Cadafael, king of Gwynedd, on the eve of the battle of the *Winwæd* in which Penda, king of the Mercians, was slain.
682	Probable date of the death of Cadwaladr, king of Gwynedd.
768	Elfoddw, 'archbishop' of Gwynedd, induces the Church in Wales to accept the Roman dating of Easter.
809	The death of Elfoddw, 'archbishop' of Gwynedd.
825	The accession of Merfyn as king and the establishment of the Second Dynasty of Gwynedd.
844	The death of Merfyn, king of Gwynedd.
c. 855	The death of Cyngen, king of Powys, in Rome.
856	Rhodri the Great, king of Gwynedd, slays the Viking leader, Horm.
877	Rhodri, king of Gwynedd, driven out of his kingdom by the Vikings.
878	The slaying of Rhodri, king of Gwynedd, by the Saxons.
c. 885	Asser of St David's visits Alfred, king of the West Saxons, and agrees to spend six months of each year in his service.
c. 885−93	The kings of South Wales submit to Alfred.
893	Anarawd, king of Gwynedd, submits to Alfred, king of the West Saxons, and Asser completes his *Life of King Alfred*.
916	The death of Anarawd, king of Gwynedd.
927	Morgan, king of Gwent and Glywysing, and Hywel Dda, king of Deheubarth, submit to Athelstan, king of the West Saxons, at Hereford.
942	The death of Idwal, king of Gwynedd.
950	The death of Hywel Dda, king of Deheubarth.
952	The sons of Idwal, Iago and Ieuaf, ravage Dyfed twice.
954	The sons of Idwal, Iago and Ieuaf, ravage Ceredigion.
973	Iago, king of Gwynedd, and his nephew, Hywel, among the kings who submitted to Edgar, king of Wessex, at Chester.

974	The death of Morgan, king of Gwent and Glywysing.
983	The death of Hywel, king of Gwynedd.
988	The death of Owain, king of Deheubarth.
999	The death of Maredudd, king of Deheubarth. The death of Morgenau, bishop of St David's.
1018	Llywelyn ap Seisyll slew Aeddan ap Blegywryd.
1023	Death of Llywelyn ap Seisyll, king of Gwynedd.
1033	Death of Rhydderch ab Iestyn, king of Deheubarth.
1039	Death of Iago ab Idwal, king of Gwynedd, and the accession of Gruffudd ap Llywelyn ap Seisyll.
1044	Gruffudd ap Llywelyn slew Hywel ab Edwin, king of Deheubarth.
1055	Gruffudd ap Llywelyn slew Gruffudd ap Rhydderch, king of Deheubarth.
1055 – c. 1060	Gruffudd ap Llywelyn established himself also in Morgannwg and as the ruler of all Wales.
1056	Gruffudd ap Llywelyn swore to be a loyal sub-king of Edward the Confessor.
1062 – 63	Harold, earl of Wessex, invaded the territory of Gruffudd ap Llywelyn: the assassination of Gruffudd on 5 August 1063.

Genealogical and Regnal Tables

*Æthelberht 580/93–616/18

*Eadbald 616/8–40

*Eorcenberht 640–64

*Ecgberht 664–73

*Hlothhere 673–85

Eadric 684–86

Mul 687

Oswine 688–90

*Wihtred 690–725

*Æthelberht 725–62

Eanmund *c.* 762–*c.* 764

Heahberht *c.* 764–*c.* 785

Ealhmund *c.* 784

*Eadberht Præn 796–8

Note: Multiple kingship was practised in Kent; only the main line is shown here: see Yorke 1990: 33

Table I. Kings of Kent c. 580–798

*Rædwald *c.* 599–*c.* 625

Eorpwald

Ricberht

*Sigeberht 630/1–*c.* 635

Ecgric

*Anna *d. c.* 654

*Æthelhere *d.* 655

Æthelwold 655–63

Ealdwulf 663–713

*Ælfwald 713–49

Beonna 749

Æthelred

*Æthelberht *d.* 794

Eadwald

Athelstan

Æthelweard

*Edmund 855–69

Table II. Kings of East Anglia c. 599–869

*Cynegils 611–43

*Cenwealh 643–72

*Seaxburh 672–3

Æscwine 674–6

*Centwine 676–85

*Cædwalla 685–88

*Ine 688–726

Æthelheard 726–40

Cuthred 740–56

Sigeberht 756–7

*Cynewulf 757–86

*Beorhtric 786–802

Note: *The chronology of the kings before Cynegils is very difficult*
to establish; see the discussion in Yorke 1990: 130ff.

Table III. *Kings of Wessex 611–802*

*Penda *c.* 626–55

*Peada (Middle Anglia) 655–56

*Wulfhere 658–75

*Æthelred 675–704

*Coenred 704–9

*Ceolred 709–16

Ceolwald 716

*Æthelbald 716–57

Beornred 757

*Offa 757–96

*Ecgfrith 796

*Coenwulf 796–821

*Ceolwulf I 821–3

*Beornwulf 823–6

Ludeca 826–7

*Wiglaf 827–*c.* 38

Wigmund *c.* 838–40

*Beorhtwulf 840–52

*Burgred 852–74

*Ceolwulf II 874–79

Table IV. *Kings of Mercia *c.* 626–879*

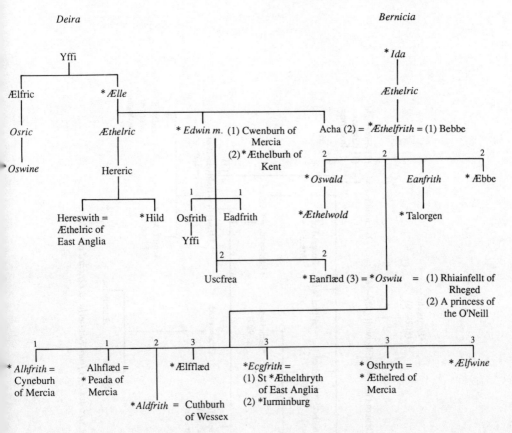

Table V . *Kings of Northumbria in the seventh century*
Numbers indicate which children were borne by which wives; the reigning kings appear in italics

*Eadwulf 705	*Æthelred 774–79; 790–96
*Osred 705–16	*Ælfwald 779–88
*Coenred 716–18	*Osred 788–90
*Osric 718–29	*Osbald 796
*Ceolwulf 729–37	*Eardwulf 796–?810
*Eadberht 737–58	*Eanred ?810–?41
*Oswulf 758–59	Æthelred 840/1–48/9
*Æthelwold Moll 759–65	Rædwulf 844
*Alhred 765–74	Osberht 848/9–67
	*Ælle 867

Table VI. *Kings of Northumbria 705–867*

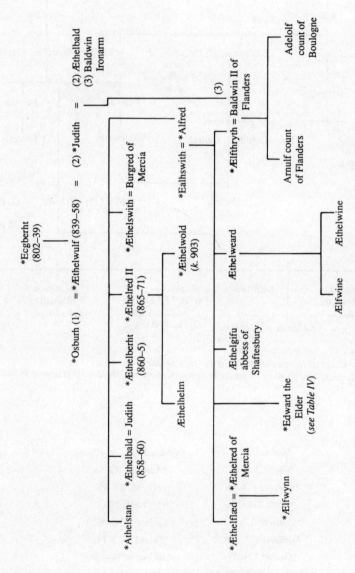

Table VII. The West Saxon kings from Ecgberht to Edward the Elder

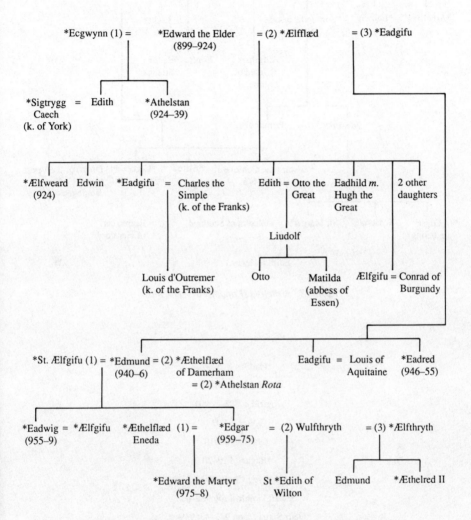

Table VIII. The West Saxon kings from Edward the Elder to Æthelred II.

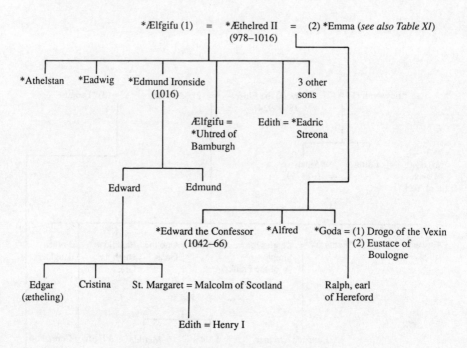

Table IX. Æthelred II and his descendants

*Halfdan 875–77

*Guthfrith *c.* 883–95

Sigfrid *c.* 895–*c.* 901

Knutr *c.* 902

*Halfdan *d.* 910

*Ragnall 910–20

*Sigtrygg Caech 920–27

*Olafr Gothfrithson 939–41

*Olafr Sigtryggson 941–43; 949–52

*Eirikr Bloodaxe 947–48; 952–54

Note: This table is based on Smyth 1975, 1979

Table X. Scandinavian Kings of York 875–954

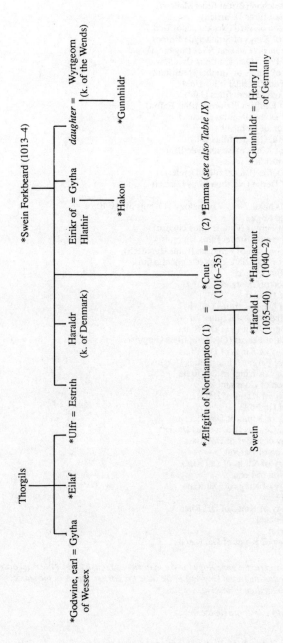

Table XI. The Danish kings of England

1.	*Bruide mac Maelchon (Bridei filius Mailcon)	556–84
2.	*Gartnait (Gartnart filius Domelch)	584–602
3.	*Nechtan grandson of Verb (Nechtu nepos Uerb)	602–21
	See genealogy of Kings of Strathclyde Britons	
4.	Cinioch filius Lutrin (Cinedon filius Lugthreni)	621–31
5.	Gartnait son of Foth (Garnard filius Uuid/Gwid)	631–35
	See genealogy of Kings of Strathclyde Britons	
6.	Bruide son of Foth (Breidei filius Uuid)	635–41
7.	Talorg son of Foth (Talorc filius Uuid)	641–53
8.	*Talorgan son of Eanfrith (Talorcen filius Enfret)	653–57
9.	Gartnait son of Domnall (filius Donuel)	657–63
10.	*Drust (Drest) son of Domnall	663–72
11.	*Bruide son of Bili (Bredei filius Bili)	672–93
	See genealogy of Kings of Strathclyde Britons	
12.	*Taran son of Entifidich	693–97
13.	*Bruide son of Derile (Bredei filius Derelei)	697–706
14.	*Nechtan son of Derile (Necthon filius Derelei)	706–24
15.	*Drust (Drest)	724–29
16.	*Alpín son of Eochaid. No. 21 genealogy of Kings of Dál Riata	726–28
14a	Nechtan (second reign)	728–29
17.	*Óengus I son of Fergus (Onuist filius Urguist)	729–61
18.	*Bruide son of Fergus (Bredei filius Uuirguist)	761–63
19.	*Ciniod (Cinadhon) son of Feredach (filius Uuredech)	763–75
	See genealogy of Dál Riata kings of Cenél Loairn	
20.	Alpín (Elpin filius Uuroid)	776–80
21.	Drust (Drest) son of Talorgan	780
22.	Talorgan son of Drostan	780–82
23.	*Talorgan son of Óengus (filius Onuist)	782
24.	*Conall son of Tadg (Canaul filius Tarl'a)	785–89
	No. 26 genealogy of Kings of Dál Riata	
25.	*Constantine son of Fergus (Castantin filius Uurguist)	789–820
	No. 28 genealogy of Kings of Dál Riata	
26.	*Óengus II son of Fergus (Unuist filius Uurguist)	820–34
	No. 29 genealogy of Kings of Dál Riata	
27.	Drust (Drest) son of Constantine	834–37
	No. H genealogy of Kings of Dál Riata	
28.	Talorgan son of Uuthoil	837
	No. I genealogy of Kings of Dál Riata	
29.	*Eóganán son of Óengus (Uuen filius Unuist)	837–39
	No. J genealogy of Kings of Dál Riata	
30.	Uurad (Ferat) son of Bargoit	839–42
	No. K genealogy of Kings of Dál Riata	
31.	Bruide (Bred) son of Ferat	842
	No. L genealogy of Kings of Dál Riata	
32.	Kineth son of Ferat	842–43
	No. M genealogy of Kings of Dál Riata	
33.	Bruide son of Fochel	843–45
34.	Drust son of Ferat	845–48
	No. O genealogy of Kings of Dál Riata	

It is not possible to construct a genealogy for the majority of Pictish kings either because several dynasties were participating in the kingship or because the earlier stages in the succession may have been determined by matrilinear descent.

Dates for reign-lengths are approximate only.

Table XII. Pictish kings in the historical period

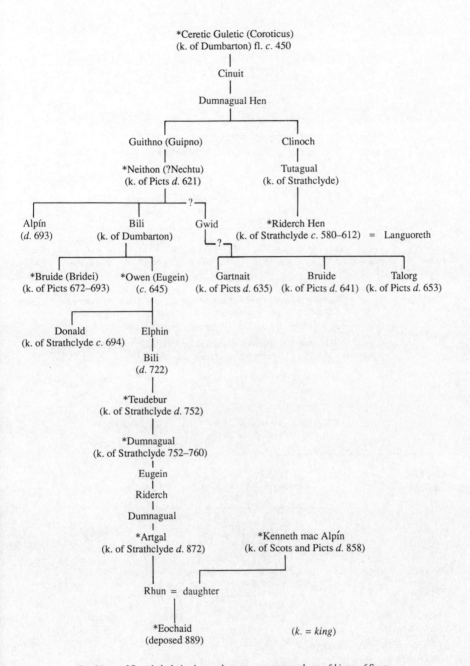

*Ceretic Guletic (Coroticus)
(k. of Dumbarton) fl. *c.* 450

Cinuit

Dumnagual Hen

Guithno (Guipno)   Clinoch

*Neithon (?Nechtu)   Tutagual
(k. of Picts *d.* 621)   (k. of Strathclyde)

                              ─?─

Alpín   Bili   Gwid   *Riderch Hen
(*d.* 693)   (k. of Dumbarton)   (k. of Strathclyde *c.* 580–612) = Languoreth
                                  ─?─

*Bruide (Bridei)   *Owen (Eugein)   Gartnait   Bruide   Talorg
(k. of Picts 672–693) (*c.* 645)   (k. of Picts *d.* 635) (k. of Picts *d.* 641) (k. of Picts *d.* 653)

Donald   Elphin
(k. of Strathclyde *c.* 694)

                  Bili
                  (*d.* 722)

*Teudebur
(k. of Strathclyde *d.* 752)

*Dumnagual
(k. of Strathclyde 752–760)

Eugein

Riderch

Dumnagual

*Artgal   *Kenneth mac Alpín
(k. of Strathclyde *d.* 872)   (k. of Scots and Picts *d.* 858)

Rhun = daughter

*Eochaid   (*k.* = *king*)
(deposed 889)

For kings of Strathclyde in the tenth century see genealogy of kings of Scots.

Table XIII. Kings of the Strathclyde Britons

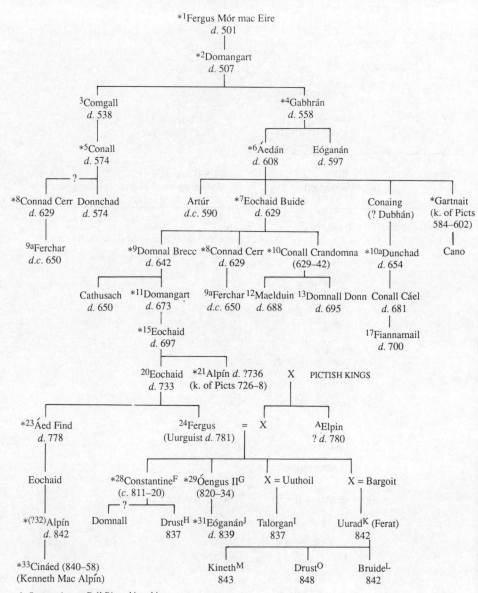

CENÉL GABHRÁIN DYNASTY

Table XIV. Kings of Dál Riata

1 Succession to Dál Riata kingship
25, 26, 27, 30 unplaced
F Succession to Pictish kingship

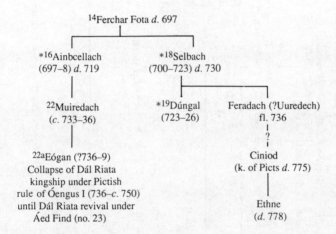

Table XIVa. Kings of Dál Riata: Cenél Loairn Dynasty

Claiming descent from Loarn, the brother of Fergus Mór mac Eirc, ancestor of main line of Dál Riata kings.

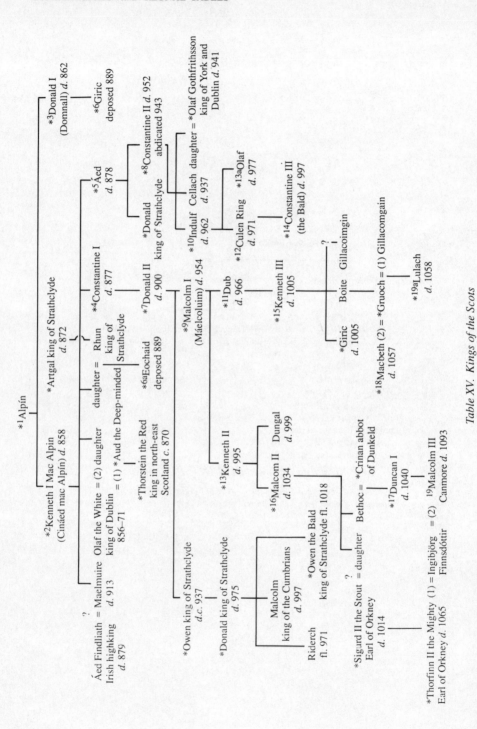

Table XV. Kings of the Scots

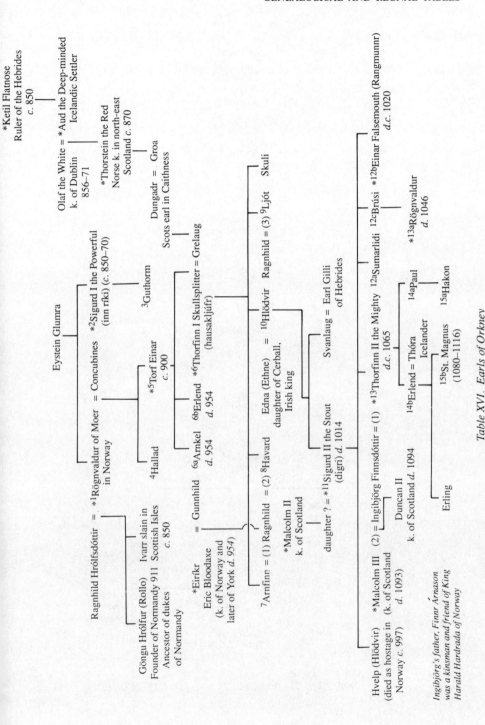

Table XVI. Earls of Orkney

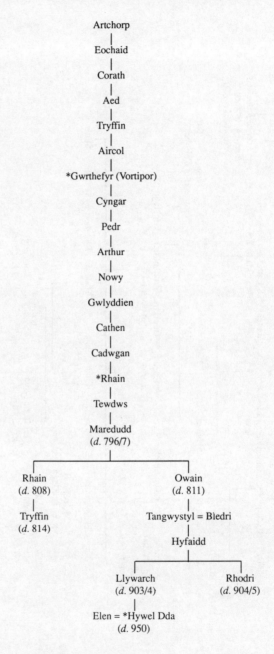

Artchorp
|
Eochaid
|
Corath
|
Aed
|
Tryffin
|
Aircol
|
*Gwrthefyr (Vortipor)
|
Cyngar
|
Pedr
|
Arthur
|
Nowy
|
Gwlyddien
|
Cathen
|
Cadwgan
|
*Rhain
|
Tewdws
|
Maredudd
(*d.* 796/7)

Rhain   Owain
(*d.* 808)   (*d.* 811)
| |
Tryffin   Tangwystyl = Bledri
(*d.* 814) |
                           Hyfaidd

Llywarch   Rhodri
(*d.* 903/4)   (*d.* 904/5)
|
Elen = *Hywel Dda
(*d.* 950)

Table XVII. The traditional descent of the kings of Dyfed

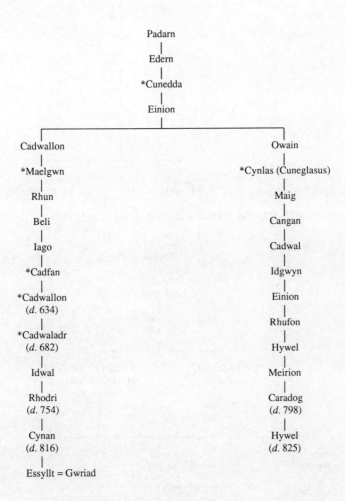

Padarn
|
Edern
|
*Cunedda
|
Einion

Cadwallon	Owain
*Maelgwn	*Cynlas (Cuneglasus)
Rhun	Maig
Beli	Cangan
Iago	Cadwal
*Cadfan	Idgwyn
*Cadwallon (d. 634)	Einion
*Cadwaladr (d. 682)	Rhufon
Idwal	Hywel
Rhodri (d. 754)	Meirion
Cynan (d. 816)	Caradog (d. 798)
Essyllt = Gwriad	Hywel (d. 825)

Table XVIII. The traditional descent of the First Dynasty of Gwynedd

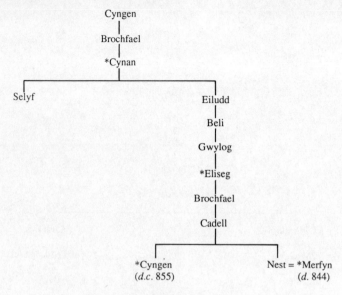

Table XIX. The traditional descent of the kings of Powys

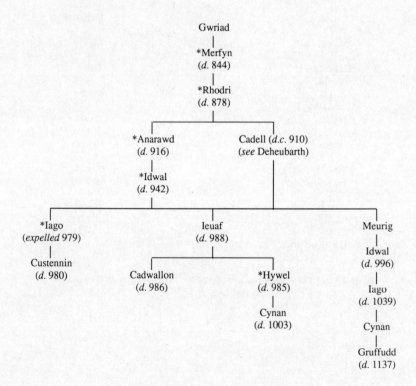

Table XX. The descent of the Second Dynasty of Gwynedd

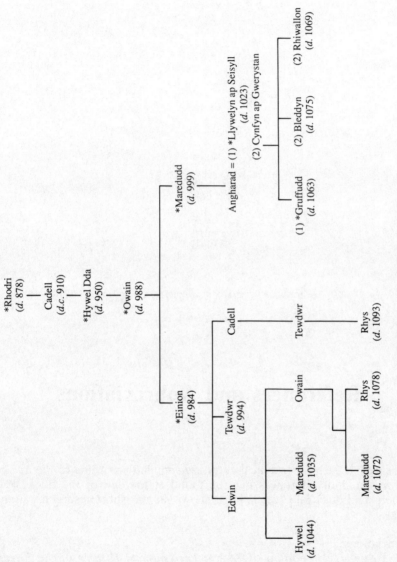

*Rhodri
(d. 878)

Cadell
(d.c. 910)

*Hywel Dda
(d. 950)

*Owain
(d. 988)

*Einion
(d. 984)

*Maredudd
(d. 999)

Angharad = (1) *Llywelyn ap Seisyll
(d. 1023)
(2) Cynfyn ap Gwerystan

(1) *Gruffudd
(d. 1063)

(2) Bleddyn
(d. 1075)

(2) Rhiwallon
(d. 1069)

Cadell

Tewdwr

Rhys
(d. 1093)

Tewdwr
(d. 994)

Edwin

Owain

Maredudd
(d. 1035)

Hywel
(d. 1044)

Rhys
(d. 1078)

Maredudd
(d. 1072)

Table XXI. The descent of the kings of Deheubarth

Tewdrig
|
Meurig
|
Arthrwys
|
Morgan
|
Ithel
|
Rhys
|
Brochfael
|
Gwriad
|
Arthfael
|
Rhys
|
*Hywel
(*d.* 885/6)
|
Owain
|
*Morgan
(*d.* 974)

Table XXII. The traditional ancestry of Morgan ab Owain king of Morgannwg

References and Abbreviations

References to each biographical entry are supplied according to the author-date system. Full references may be found at the end of the book. Page numbers to books and articles are shown in the short reference after a colon.

Abbreviations:

HE refers to the edition of Bede's *Ecclesiastical History of the English People* by Colgrave and Mynors 1969.

ASC refers to the edition of the *Anglo-Saxon Chronicle* by Whitelock, Douglas and Tucker 1961. Cited by year: s.a. = sub anno

A

Abba reeve *d.* after 835

Most wills of the pre-Conquest period are those of the high nobility, and the will of Abba is therefore of interest since he did not come from this exalted group and may even have been a non-noble free man. He was a Kentishman, and a reeve, though of what district is unknown. He left his land (he does not tell us where it lay) to his wife, Heregyth, so long as she remained unmarried; if she re-married, or if she died, it was to pass to his two brothers, Ealhhere and Æthelwold and their heirs. If they had no heirs, the land was to go to Freothemund, whose relationship to Abba is not specified, and then to his sisters' sons. In the event of the whole family dying out, the residual heir was Christchurch Canterbury, in whose archive the will was preserved. Abba lived at a time when Danish raids were becoming more and more frequent, and the likelihood of whole kindreds perishing must have seemed all too possible.

BIBL. Harmer 1914, no. 2: 3-5, 40-2, 72-81

Abbo St, abbot 988−1004

Abbo, a monk of the reformed monastery of Fleury-sur-Loire, came to Ramsey Abbey at the request of St *Oswald to teach in its school. He was one of the most outstanding scholars of the tenth century, a 'most worthy flower of the abbey of flowers'. He was born at Orleans, and entered Fleury as a child oblate. He studied at Rheims and Paris, and rose to become head of Fleury's school, declaring that 'there is nothing in life more pleasant than to learn and to teach'. He spent two years at Ramsey (985−7), where he composed a treatise on grammar, an elegaic poem on the landscape of Ramsey, and various works on astronomy. His most famous pupil was *Byrhtferth of Ramsey, who quotes some of Abbo's ideas in his own *Manual*, and the later reputation of Ramsey as a centre of mathematical studies must be connected with Abbo's teaching. Abbo also wrote a Latin account of the martyrdom of St *Edmund, based on material supplied by St *Dunstan. In 987 he returned to Fleury, of which he became abbot the following year. He participated in the councils of the Frankish church, and served as ambassador to the papal curia on behalf of King Robert. In 1004 he was at the monastery of La Reole in Gascony, whose community was at odds with its reforming abbot. Abbo attempted even there to continue his studies, but was summoned from his books to a riot in the courtyard. He went out to calm the situation, still carrying his pen and notebook, and was stabbed in the side with a lance by one of the excitable Gascons. He was killed at once. The manuscript upon which he was working at the time of his murder has been identified as the prose life of Dunstan, sent to him by Wulfric, abbot of St Augustine's Canterbury, with the request that he translate it into verse.

BIBL. Farmer 1978: 1; Lutz 1977: 41-52, 166-8

Acca St, bishop *d.* 740

Acca was chaplain to St *Wilfrid, and a close friend. It was he who, with Wilfrid's kinsman, Tatberht, commissioned the *Life* of Wilfrid from *Eddius Stephanus. He also supplied *Bede with material for the *Ecclesiastical History* and many of Bede's theological works are dedicated to Acca. He succeeded Wilfrid as abbot of Hexham in 709, which was also a bishopric. In 731, he was expelled from his see; the reasons are unknown, but may have had to do with the deposition of *Ceolwulf king of Northumbria in the same year. He died in 740, and was buried at Hexham, where he was venerated as a saint. The cross erected over his grave is still preserved in the present church.

BIBL. *HE* v, 20: 530-3; Farmer 1978: 1-2

Adomnán abbot of Iona *c.* 624–704

Adomnán, like his kinsman *Columba, was a member of the Irish dynasty of Tír Conaill. Little is known of his early life spent as a monk in Ireland. He may have received part of his monastic education in Brega in Meath, and he is likely to have completed his studies and perhaps held a prominent position at the Columban monastery of Durrow in Offaly. Adomnán joined the community of Iona during the abbacy of *Failbe whose rule began in 669 and he succeeded Failbe as ninth abbot and head of the Columban *paruchia* in 679. Soon after becoming abbot, he began writing his work on *The Holy Places*, an account of the Holy Land which also included information on Egypt, Constantinople and Sicily. Adomnán based this work on information he received from the shipwrecked Frankish bishop, Arculf, who had himself spent nine months in Jerusalem in the early 670s. Adomnán presented a copy of his work on *The Holy Places* to King *Aldfrith of Northumbria whose court he visited in 686 and in 688. On his first visit to Aldfrith he successfully negotiated the release of 60 Irish captives taken prisoner by *Ecgfrith of Northumbria during a raid on the Irish coast in 684. Adomnán's friendship with King Aldfrith may have gone back a long way. Aldfrith had been an exile on Iona in 684 and earlier, as a youth in Ireland, he may have been tutored by Adomnán, perhaps at Durrow. Adomnán's work on *The Holy Places* was later used extensively by *Bede, who may have been present as a boy during Adomnán's visit to Jarrow when the abbot of Iona accepted the Roman customs for the celebration of Easter, abandoning the Celtic rite of his own Columban community.

Adomnán's decision to accept the Roman Easter isolated him from his own community and he spent the remainder of his life trying to persuade his followers in Scotland, Pictland and Ireland to abandon the Celtic tradition relating to Easter practices. During this period also (688–92), he wrote his celebrated *Life of Columba* which provides not only a major source of information on that saint but also on the life of the early Celtic Church. The crowning achievement of Adomnán's career came at the Synod of Birr in 697 when he promulgated his *Law of Innocents* designed to protect non-combatants (the elderly, women and children, and clergy) from the savagery of Dark Age warfare. This Law was binding not only throughout Ireland but also in the kingdoms of the Scots and of the Picts. Its enactment was witnessed by 40 leading churchmen and 51 tribal and provincial kings, including *Bruide son of Derile, king of the Picts, and *Eochaid son of Domangart, king of Scots. Adomnán died among his own community on Iona in his 77th year in 704. He was remembered as a great saint and a great scholar — the confidant of Scottish, Pictish, British, Irish and Northumbrian kings. His relics were translated on Iona into a portable shrine in 727, and his festival was kept on 23 September. Scottish churches and dedications associated with Adomnán extend from Sanda, off the Mull of Kintyre in the south-west, to Forglen in north-east Banffshire, and from Forvie in Aberdeenshire to Inchkeith in the Firth of Forth.

BIBL. Anderson and Anderson 1961: 92-8; Herbert 1988: 47-56; Reeves 1857: 376-8; Smyth 1984: 116-40

Æbbe St, abbess *d*. 683

Æbbe, daughter of King *Æthelfrith of Bernicia, fled to Scotland when her father was defeated and killed in 617 by his rival, *Edwin of Deira. When in 634, her brother *Oswald became king of Northumbria, Æbbe, now converted to Christianity among the Irish, returned to Northumbria and became abbess of Coldingham. The monastery, a double-house for men and women, stood on St Abb's head, which preserves Æbbe's name, and its ruins are still visible. It acquired a dubious reputation. St *Adomnán complained that 'the cells that were built for prayer and for reading have become haunts of feasting, drinking, gossip and other delights; even the virgins who are dedicated to God... spend their time weaving elaborate garments with which to adorn themselves as if they were brides, thus imperilling their virginity, or else to make friends with strange men'. The fire which destroyed the monastery in 686 was attributed to this behaviour.

BIBL. *HE* iv, 19: 292-3; 25: 420-7; Farmer 1978: 116-17

Æbbe St, queen and abbess *d*. 694 *see* **Eafa**

Áed Find king of Scots Dál Riata *c*. 748–78

Áed Find ('the Fair') was of the main Cenél Gabhráin line of Dál Riata. His reign over the Scots marked a temporary recovery from political unrest which had been evident since *c*. 700 and also a return to power of the descendants of *Áedán mac Gabhráin who in the early eighth century had been ousted by the Cenél Loairn. In the more recent past, the kings of Dál Riata had been overshadowed by the Picts under the rule of their powerful king, *Óengus I, when he overthrew Dál Riata in a series of victorious engagements in 736. The exact details of Áed Find's genealogy may not be entirely accurate due to the lack of continuity in Cenél Gabhráin rule in the half century prior to his reign. Áed's father, Eochaid, had died in 733, when Áed may have been too young to succeed, but Áed is reckoned to have assumed the kingship of Dál Riata by 750, at which time we read of the 'decline of the overlordship of Óengus' king of the Picts. Óengus died in 761, and seven years later (768) Áed Find fought a battle in Fortriu in Pictland against Óengus's successor, *Ciniod. In the reign of *Donald I (858–62), the laws of Dál Riata, as defined in the time of Áed Find, were imposed on Scots and Picts alike at Forteviot in Fortriu. Áed's other nickname was that of *Airechtech* ('of the assemblies') which would again suggest a reputation for law-giving and good rule.

BIBL. Anderson 1922, vol. 1: 248-9; Anderson 1973: 189-90; Smyth 1984: 179, 181-2, 188

Áed son of Kenneth, king of Scots 877–8

Áed succeeded his brother *Constantine I and was slain in the first year of his reign by his rival first cousin, *Giric, in a battle at Strathallan. Yet Giric failed to pass the Scottish kingship to his descendants, and it was the progeny of Áed and his brother Constantine who shared the Scottish crown until the end of the tenth century.

BIBL. Anderson 1922, vol. 1: 357

Áedán mac Gabhráin king of Scots Dál Riata 574–608

Áedán was one of the greatest warlords in the British Isles during the early Middle Ages, dominating political and military events in northern Britain and campaigning from the Orkneys to the Isle of Man and from Ulster to Northumbria. Áedán's mother was probably a British princess, and he may have been a grandson of Dumnagual or Dyfnwal Hen, king of the Strathclyde Britons. One of his queens was also from a British royal house and yet another may have been Pictish. But Áedán himself was of Irish lineage, being a great-grandson of *Fergus Mór the founder of the Dál Riata dynasty. While clearly acknowledged as the son of *Gabhrán in the Old Irish genealogies, there is an alternative tradition which claims that Áedán was one of twin sons born to Eochaid mac Muiredaig, king of Leinster, and his queen, Feidelm, during their exile in Dál Riata. Áedán, this story relates, was one of those twins substituted for a daughter born to Gabhrán at the same time.

On the death of Áedán's predecessor, *Conall son of Comgall, in 574, the succession seems to have been disputed between Áedán and his kinsmen, resulting in the slaying of one of Conall's sons 'and many other allies of the sons of Gabhrán' in Kintyre. This strife may not have pleased *Columba, who according to *Adomnán originally preferred Áedán's brother, Eóganán, as candidate for the kingship of Dál Riata. Columba however did play a central role in Áedán's election. We are informed by Adomnán that Columba anointed Áedán at his inauguration, while other traditions show Columba acting as *anamchara*, or spiritual director, to the Scots king. Both Áedán and Columba attended the Convention of Drumceat (Druim Cett) in Co. Derry in 575. At this meeting an agreement was worked out between Áedán, king of Scots Dál Riata, and the Irish highking, Áed mac Ainmerech. Although the Scots ruler was allowed to collect tribute from his Irish territories in Ulster, he was still obliged to supply military service to his Irish overlord for the lands which he ruled in Ulster.

Áedán led an expedition against the Orkneys in 580, those islands then being under Pictish overlordship and still pagan at that time. Two years later we find him attacking the Isle of Man (or less likely the British kingdom of Manaw Gododdin in Lothian). Áedán seems to have ousted an Ulster king from Man at this time. Adomnán describes a battle which Áedán fought against the Miathi c. 590 in which the Scots king won an empty victory and lost two of his sons. Adomnán shows Columba praying for Áedán's victory. The Miathi — or ancient *Mæatæ of Classical* writers — ruled a territory which may have once extended from Angus and the Mearns to Stirling, and south of the Forth to the Antonine Wall. Áedán's expansion east of the Grampians is also vouched for in sources which associate him with the Forth and with his granting of a fort to St Berach at Aberfoyle, in Perthshire. Áedán may have been the father of *Gartnait, a king of the Picts who died in 602. His intrusion into southern Pictish territory inevitably brought Áedán into hostile contact with the Bernician Angles, then ruled by the powerful *Æthelfrith. In 598, two of Áedán's sons — Domangart and Bran — were assassinated by the Northumbrians under circumstances which are unknown. The Scots king may have been trying to expand south of the Forth at the expense of those Britons of Manaw Gododdin who had recently been overrun by the Bernicians. Early British records suggest hostility between Áedán and the Northern Britons of Strathclyde and Gododdin. Or it may be as *Bede pointed out, that Áedán feared Æthelfrith's advance towards the Forth. At any rate, in 603, Áedán led a great army of Scots from Dál Riata, together with more distant Irish allies, against the Northumbrians. He suffered a defeat at *Degsastan*, but the English also incurred heavy losses. As a result of this abortive expedition, the Scots did not renew their interest in Lothian until the early tenth century. Áedán may have abdicated or he may have been deposed after the debacle at *Degsastan*, but he lived for a few years after that defeat, dying in his middle or late seventies on 17 April, most likely in 608.

BIBL. Anderson 1922, vol. 1: 74-97, 122-6; Anderson 1973: 145-56; Bannerman 1974: 80-90; Duncan 1975: 43-4; Smyth 1984: 30, 95-8, 116

Ælberht (Æthelberht) archbishop of York 767—80

Ælberht was a relative of *Ecgberht, archbishop of York, his predecessor in office, and entered the York community as a boy. He rose to become head of the school, which reached its height under his governance. His most famous pupil, *Alcuin, left a glowing testimony to Ælberht's life, character and teaching. Like *Benedict Biscop, Ælberht travelled extensively, collecting books for York's library. After the death of Ecgberht in 766, Ælberht was elected archbishop. He enriched the church with splendid decoration, including an altar to St Paul 'in the spot where *Edwin the warrior-king was baptized', and built a new basilica in honour of the Holy Wisdom (a most unusual dedication in western Christendom). He retired from his see in old age, in favour of another pupil, *Eanbald.

BIBL. Godman 1982: lx-xxiii, 109—29

Ælfflæd St, abbess 654—713

Ælfflæd was born in 654 to *Eanflæd, daughter of *Edwin and wife of

*Oswiu of Northumbria. Her birth coincided with her father's victory at the battle of the *Winwæd*, and as a thankoffering, the child was vowed to God. She was entrusted as an oblate to her kinswoman *Hild, first at Hartlepool and then at Whitby. There she was joined, in 670, by her mother, and when Hild died in 680, Ælfflæd and Eanflæd became joint abbesses. It was in their time that the anonymous Whitby *Life* of St *Gregory the Great was composed. Unlike Hild, who favoured Celtic customs, Eanflæd and Ælfflæd supported the Roman style and were friends and supporters of St *Wilfrid. Indeed it was largely due to Ælfflæd's support at the Synod of the River Nidd in 706, where she testified to the will of her half-brother *Aldfrith, that Wilfrid regained his Northumbrian possessions. It is not surprising that Wilfrid's biographer, *Eddius, should praise Ælfflæd as 'comforter and best counsellor of the whole province'. She was also a close friend of St *Cuthbert, and was instrumental in persuading him to accept the bishopric of Lindisfarne. In 704, on her mother's death, she became sole abbess of Whitby, and died in 713.

BIBL. *HE* iii, 24: 290-1; iv, 26: 428-31; Colgrave 1927: 128-33; Colgrave 1940: 230-9; Farmer 1978: 128

Ælfflæd abbess *d.* after 850

Ælfflæd was the daughter of *Ceolwulf I, the last known king of Mercia who could claim descent from the royal line. She married Wigmund son of *Wiglaf, king of Mercia, to whom she bore the future saint, *Wigstan. It was Wigstan who persuaded her not to accept the suit of Beorhtfrith son of King *Beorhtwulf. Ælfflæd was heir to the personal property of both her father and his brother *Cœnwulf, neither of whom left male heirs. Cœnwulf's heiress was his daughter *Cwœnthryth, abbess of Winchcombe, who died after 827, and by the mid-eighth century, Ælfflæd was disposing of Winchcombe's property, presumably as abbess. Her marital career illustrates the value of royal heiresses. She may have been the mother of *Ceolwulf II of Mercia.

BIBL. Levison 1946: 249-59

Ælfflæd queen *d.* after 920

Ælfflæd, daughter of Æthelhelm, ealdorman of Wiltshire, was the second wife of King *Edward the Elder. She bore him eight children, including two sons, Ælfweard, who was briefly king of Wessex in 924, but died the same year, and Edwin, who died in 933 (see *Athelstan). Her six daughters include *Eadgifu, who married Charles the Simple, king of the Franks, Eadhild, who married Hugh the Great of Neustria, Edith, wife of Otto of Saxony, the future Emperor, and Ælfgifu, who married Conrad of Burgundy. Ælfflæd commissioned the gold embroideries now in the Treasury of Durham Cathedral. They were made for Frithestan, bishop of Winchester (909−31) and presented to St *Cuthbert's shrine by Ælfflæd's stepson, Athelstan. Ælfflæd retired to Wilton, where she died. Her husband had re-married (see *Eadgifu) by 920.

BIBL. Yorke 1988b: 70-3

Ælfflæd noblewoman *d.* 1000−2

Ælfflæd, daughter of Ælfgar, ealdorman of Essex, married *Byrhtnoth, who succeeded to her father's ealdordom in 956. Both she and her husband were benefactors of Ely Abbey. After her husband was killed at the battle of Maldon in 991, she presented the church of Ely with a tapestry depicting his deeds, now unfortunately lost. Her will survives, disposing of a large estate in Essex, Suffolk, Hertfordshire and Cambridgeshire. Her sister *Æthelflæd was the wife of King *Edmund.

BIBL. Whitelock 1930, no. 15: 38-43, 141-46; Sawyer 1968, no. 1486

Ælfgifu St, queen *d.* 944

St Ælfgifu was the first wife of *Edmund of Wessex, and mother of the future kings, *Eadwig and *Edgar. She was a benefactor of Shaftesbury Abbey, where she died, and where her cult developed.

BIBL. *ASC* s.a. 955; Farmer 1978: 128

Ælfgifu queen *d.* after 966

Ælfgifu, wife of King *Eadwig, was the sister of *Æthelweard, ealdorman of the Western Provinces, and thus a descendant of King *Æthelred I. The marriage of Ælfgifu and Eadwig was regarded by some as within the prohibited degrees, and was dissolved on these grounds by Archbishop *Oda in 958. As a result, some sources regard her as a concubine rather than a wife, notably those connected with SS *Dunstan and *Oswald. The houses connected with St *Æthelwold, however, regard her marriage as legitimate, and at the New Minster, Winchester, she is commemorated as Eadwig's queen. In her will she remembered the New Minster and also the Old Minster, Winchester and Abingdon Abbey, both refounded by Æthelwold. This difference of ecclesiastical opinion, and the fact that more irregular unions passed without notice, suggests that her marriage was dissolved for political, rather than religious, reasons. She survived into the reign of her brother-in-law, *Edgar, who addressed her as 'kins-woman' in two charters granting her lands in Buckinghamshire and Oxfordshire; both are dated 966. Her will mentions her brothers, Ælfweard and Æthelweard, and her sister Ælfwaru, and includes the bequest of a necklace to Edgar's queen, *Ælfthryth.

BIBL. Yorke 1988b: 76-80 Sawyer 1968, nos. 737-8, 1484

Ælfgifu wife of King Æthelred II, *d.* before 1002

Ælfgifu, daughter of *Thored, ealdorman of Northumbria, and wife of *Æthelred II is a shadowy figure, best remembered in her children. She bore Æthelred six sons: *Athelstan, Ecgberht, *Edmund, Eadred, *Eadwig and Edgar, and three daughters: Edith, who married *Eadric Streona, ealdorman of Mercia, Ælfgifu, who married *Uhtred, ealdorman of Bamburgh, and an unnamed girl who became abbess of Wherwell.

The Athelstan who fell in battle against the Danes at Ringmere in 1010, and who is described as *thes cinges athum* (which could mean either son- or brother-in-law) was probably Ælfgifu's brother.

BIBL. Barlow 1970: 28-9; *ASC* s.a. 1010

Ælfgifu of Northampton *d. c.* 1040

Ælfgifu of Northampton was the daughter of *Ælfhelm, ealdorman of Northumbria and grand-daughter of the 'noble lady' *Wulfrun, foundress of Wolverhampton. In 1006 her father was murdered by *Eadric Streona on the orders of King *Æthelred II and her brothers blinded. In *c.* 1013, she married *Cnut, son of *Swein of Denmark, to whom she bore two sons, Swein and *Harold. Her association with Cnut survived his second marriage with *Emma of Normandy, which does not seem to have been preceded by a divorce from Ælfgifu. In 1030, she became regent of Norway for her son Swein; her energy in carrying out her duties caused Norwegians to compare subsequent bad patches in their history favourably with 'Ælfgifu's time'. She and her son were expelled from Norway by King Magnus, just before Cnut's death in 1035. Her second son, Harold, seized the English kingdom, and ruled till his death in 1040. Ælfgifu's subsequent fate is unknown and the date of her death is not recorded.

BIBL. Campbell, M 1971: 66-79

Ælfheah the Bald St, bishop 935−51

Ælfheah the Bald was one of the earliest movers of the monastic reform movement, which transformed the English church in the tenth century. He seems to have begun his career in the household of King *Athelstan, and was promoted to the bishopric of Winchester in 935. The episcopal see (the Old Minster) was, and remained for many years, a house of secular priests, but Ælfheah is said to have been a monk, though where, and to whom, he made his profession is nowhere recorded. He may have been a kinsman of *Dunstan, who entered his *familia* and made his monastic profession to him. Another product of Ælfheah's nurture was St *Æthelwold, who as bishop of Winchester promoted the cult of Ælfheah.

BIBL. Yorke 1988b: 66-8; Farmer 1978: 14

Ælfheah ealdorman 959−70

Ælfheah was the son of *Ealhhelm, ealdorman of Mercia. In 956 he became seneschal (*discthegn*) to King *Eadwig, who promoted him to the ealdordom of Hampshire in 959. Ælfheah was a close friend of *Ælfsige, bishop of Winchester, who appointed him guardian of his young son Godwine. In his will Ælfheah made bequests to the sons of King *Edgar and Queen *Ælfthryth, and addresses the latter as *gefætheran* ('gossip'), which denoted the relationship between parents and godparents and suggests that he was godfather to one of the young æthelings. He was addressed as 'kinsman' by the kings *Eadred, Eadwig and Edgar, and probably belonged to a collateral branch of the royal kindred. His wife Ælfswith, whom he had married before 940, was a lady of some importance and a landholder in her own right. Their sons were Ælfweard and *Godwine; the latter became ealdorman of Lindsey.

BIBL. Williams 1982; Sawyer 1968: no. 1485

Ælfheah (Alphege) St, archbishop of Canterbury 1005×12

Ælfheah is said to have made his monastic profession at Deerhurst,

Gloucestershire, and to have lived some time as a hermit until *Dunstan made him abbot of Bath. In 984 he succeeded *Æthelwold as bishop of Winchester. He was one of the envoys who arranged the truce between *Æthelred II and *Olafr Tryggvason in 994. He became archbishop of Canterbury in 1005. When in 1011 the 'immense raiding-army' of *Thorkell the Tall stormed Canterbury, Ælfheah was the most eminent of those taken prisoner. His steadfast refusal to allow a ransom to be paid for him so enraged the Viking host that, fortified with 'southern wine', they murdered him on 19 April 1012. The murder, which took place in the Viking camp at Southwark, is graphically described in the contemporary *Anglo-Saxon Chronicle*:

'They pelted him with bones and ox-heads and one of them struck him on the head with the back of an axe, so that he sank down with the blow, and his holy blood fell on the ground and so he sent his holy soul to God's kingdom.'

He was buried in St Paul's, London, and venerated as a martyr. In 1023, his remains were translated to Canterbury by King *Cnut, much against the wishes of the Londoners, and only the presence of the royal housecarls, who lined the route and escorted the body, prevented a riot.

BIBL. *ASC* s.a. 1012; Brooks 1984: 283-5

Ælfhelm ealdorman 993–1006

Ælfhelm, son of *Wulfrun, was a Mercian nobleman, the brother of *Wulfric Spot. In 993 he was appointed ealdorman of Northumbria by *Æthelred II, but in 1006 he fell foul of the king and was murdered, on Æthelred's orders, by *Eadric Streona. His sons, Wulfheah and Ufegeat, were blinded, but his daughter *Ælfgifu of Northampton survived to become the wife of King *Cnut and mother of King *Harold I.

BIBL. Sawyer 1979: x/iii; Hart 1975: 258-9

Ælfhere ealdorman 956–83

Ælfhere was the son of *Ealhhelm, ealdorman of Mercia. In 956, he was appointed to his father's ealdordom by King *Eadwig, and in the reign of *Edgar was premier ealdorman. His brother *Ælfheah held the ealdordom of Hampshire from 959 to 970, and two other brothers, Eadric and Ælfwine, were prominent king's thegns. The family was related to that of the West Saxon kings, and one of the most powerful in the kingdom. Ælfhere's rivalry with *Æthelwine of East Anglia brought the country to the brink of civil war on Edgar's death in 975, when he supported the claims of *Æthelred II, son of Queen *Ælfthryth, against those of Æthelwine's candidate, *Edward the Martyr, son of Edgar's first wife, *Æthelflæd Eneda. Ælfhere was also hostile to St *Oswald, bishop of Worcester, and a close friend of Æthelwine, an enmity which earned him the venom of St Oswald's biographer, *Byrhtferth of Ramsey, who described him as 'the blast of the mad wind which came from the western territories'. He has been regarded as the leader of the 'anti-monastic' party who attacked the reformers and their religious foundations in the years following Edgar's death, but the issue was not 'reform' as such, but political control. Ælfhere's objection was to the great liberty of Oswaldslow, consisting of 300 hides belonging to the bishopric of Worcester, which was established by Edgar as an episcopal immunity in the heart of Mercia, from which the ealdorman's powers were excluded. Oswald's foundations, notably Winchcombe, got short shrift from Ælfhere, but he was a benefactor of Glastonbury, and of Abingdon, and appears to have been on good terms with St *Æthelwold. When Edward the Martyr was murdered at Corfe in 978, it was Ælfhere who translated the king's body to Shaftesbury in the following year. Since Edward's murder was carried out by the 'nobles and chief men' of Queen Ælfthryth, Ælfhere's motives have been called in question, but no source implicates him in the king's death. He remained the premier ealdorman during the first years of Æthelred II, and on his death in 983 was succeeded by his brother-in-law *Ælfric cild. He was buried at Glastonbury.

BIBL. Williams 1982

Ælfhun bishop 1002/4−?13

Ælfhun, abbot of Milton Abbas, Dorset, succeeded *Wulfstan as bishop of London some time between 1002 and 1004. He received the body of the martyred *Ælfheah of Canterbury in 1012 and had it interred in St Paul's Cathedral. He was accused of trying to steal the body of St *Edmund, which was brought to London for safe-keeping in his time, and placed in the church of St Gregory. In 1013, when *Swein of Denmark was triumphantly rolling up the provinces of England, Ælfhun was entrusted with conducting the young æthelings, the sons of *Æthelred and *Emma, to their maternal kin in Normandy. He seems to have died there, for his successor was consecrated on 16 February 1014.

BIBL. Whitelock 1975

Ælfric ealdorman 982−1016

Ælfric was appointed ealdorman of Hampshire by *Æthelred II in 982. His reputation is poor; he is said to have bribed the king to bestow the abbacy of Abingdon on his brother, Edwin, and to have encroached on the liberties of that house. In 992, he was one of the leaders of a fleet which intercepted the raiding-force of *Olafr Tryggvason; Ælfric was accused not only of deserting the fleet on the eve of battle, but also of warning Olafr of the English approach. It was perhaps this action which led to the blinding of his son, Ælfgar, in the following year, but Ælfric himself remained in office, and after the death of *Æthelweard of the Western Shires in c. 998, he was premier ealdorman. In 1003 he was commanding the English host again, against *Swein of Denmark,

'but he was up to his old tricks. As soon as they were so close that each army looked upon the other, he feigned himself sick, and began retching to vomit, and said that he was taken ill, and thus betrayed the people he should have led; for, as the saying goes, "When the leader weakens the whole army is very much hindered". When Swein saw that they were irresolute, and that they all dispersed, he led his army to Wilton and they ravaged and burnt the borough, and he betook him then to

Salisbury and from there back to the sea, to where he knew his wave-coursers were.'

From 1006, Ælfric is overshadowed by *Eadric Streona as the villain of the *Chronicle*'s tale. Whether either of them were really guilty of all the crimes of which they were accused is a moot point. Ælfric died valiantly enough, fighting for King *Edmund against *Cnut at the battle of Ashingdon in 1016.

BIBL. *ASC* s.a. 1003; Keynes 1980: 157, 177, 205-6, 213-14; Hart, 1975; 266-7

Ælfric archbishop of Canterbury 995–1005

Ælfric began his career as a monk of Abingdon and became in turn abbot of St Albans, bishop of Ramsbury and finally archbishop of Canterbury in succession to *Sigeric. His will is extant, disposing of land in Kent, Middlesex, Buckinghamshire, Berkshire, Oxfordshire and Gloucestershire. Its bequests illuminate the hardships caused by the Danish invasions of his time, and the measures taken to combat them. Ælfric remitted the debts owed to him by the people of Kent, Middlesex and Surrey, which were probably incurred to meet the Danegelds of 994 and 1002; he also left a ship to each of the shires of Kent and Wiltshire, presumably to meet such royal demands for ships as occurred in 1008. He bequeathed to his lord, King *Æthelred, 'his best ship and the sailing-tackle with it, and 60 helmets and 60 coats of mail' to equip its quota of warriors. Ælfric also regained the estate of Monks' Risborough, Buckinghamshire, which Sigeric had sold to pay the demands for tribute in 994, and restored it to Christchurch. The statement in the 'F' version of the *Anglo-Saxon Chronicle* that he expelled the secular clerks from Christchurch and replaced them with monks is probably fabricated.

BIBL. Brooks 1984: 257-60, 283

Ælfric the Homilist abbot 1005–c. 1010

'The greatest prose stylist of the Old English period', Ælfric, was educated at the Old Minster, Winchester, under St *Æthelwold. In 987 he moved to the monastery at Cerne Abbas, Dorset, founded by *Æthelmær son of *Æthelweard, ealdorman of the Western Provinces, and there became master of the novices. It was here that he wrote the *Catholic Homilies*, dedicated to *Sigeric, archbishop of Canterbury, and the *Lives of the Saints*, dedicated to Ealdorman Æthelweard. His work as a school-master also produced a Latin grammar and the *Colloquy*, a series of Latin dialogues between master and pupil aimed at teaching fluency in Latin conversation. He also translated *Genesis* into English at the request of Æthelweard, who later commissioned a translation of the book of *Joshua*. In 1005 Æthelmær founded a second monastery at Eynsham, Oxfordshire, of which Ælfric became abbot. Here he composed a Latin life of his old master Æthelwold, a monastic customary based upon Æthelwold's *Regularis Concordia*, and a treatise *On the Old and New Testaments*, for a layman, Sigeweard. Of all his works, the *Catholic Homilies* are perhaps the most famous. Two series were written, intended not only for his own

11

use, but as preaching material for others, both in monastic communities, and for secular churches. Like the *Lives of the Saints*, they could also be used for private devotional reading. Unlike his contemporary Archbishop *Wulfstan, Ælfric took no part in secular politics. It is as a scholar and a teacher that he is remembered. His relationship with his patrons, lay and ecclesiastical, shows the close ties of friendship which existed between the great nobles and the ecclesiastical reformers of the tenth century.

BIBL. McGatch 1977

Ælfric cild ealdorman 983−5

Ælfric cild was a rich nobleman from the east midlands; his land lay in Northamptonshire and Huntingdonshire, and he was a benefactor of Peterborough Abbey. He married the daughter of *Ealhhelm, ealdorman of Mercia, and was closely associated with her brother *Ælfhere, ealdorman of Mercia, whom he succeeded in office. In 985 he was banished, for unspecified reasons. His son *Ælfwine was killed at the battle of Maldon in 991, fighting in the hearthtroop of Ealdorman *Byrhtnoth.

BIBL. Scragg 1981: 108

Ælfric Puttoc archbishop of York 1023−51

Ælfric Puttoc, ('Kite', 'bird of prey'), succeeded *Wulfstan as archbishop of York in 1023. Little is known of his career until 1035, when he seems to have supported *Harthacnut against *Harold I in the succession dispute on the death of *Cnut. When Harthacnut became king in 1040, it was Ælfric who incited him to dig up his half-brother's body and throw it into the Thames. He also accused Earl *Godwine and Bishop *Lyfing of complicity in Harold's murder of the ætheling *Alfred, as a result of which Lyfing was deprived of his bishopric of Worcester, which was given to Ælfric. In 1041, however, Lyfing was re-instated. Ælfric seems, apart from these episodes, to have played a greater part in local than national affairs. In 1026, he went in person to Rome to collect his pallium, the first archbishop of York to do this, although the archbishops of Canterbury has been accustomed to collect their pallia from Rome since 927. He began the building of a refectory and dormitory in the minster of Beverley, completed by Archbishop Ealdred (1060−9) and translated the relics of *John of Beverley into a new shrine. He died in 1051, and was buried at Peterborough.

BIBL. Cooper 1970: 14-18

Ælfsige bishop 951−8

Ælfsige succeeded *Ælfheah the Bald as bishop of Winchester in 951. Unlike his predecessor, Ælfsige was not a monk, but a married man; in his will he refers to his wife ('my kinswoman') and his son ('my young kinsman'). In the time of *Eadwig, Ælfsige was the senior bishop, which is probably why he was chosen to replace Archbishop *Oda of Canterbury, when the latter died on 2 June 958. He set out for Rome to collect his pallium, but his retinue met such hard weather crossing the Alps in the early winter that Ælfsige died of the cold. His will appoints his friend, Ealdorman *Ælfheah, as guardian of his son, who must have been a small child, for he is the 'Godwine of Worthy, Bishop Ælfsige's son' who fell in battle against the Danes in 1001.

BIBL. Brooks 1984: 237-8; Sawyer 1968: no. 1491; *ASC* s.a. 1001

Ælfthryth daughter of King Alfred *d.* after 918

The youngest daughter of King *Alfred, Ælfthryth, married Baldwin II, count of Flanders, and bore him two sons, Arnulf I of Flanders, and Adelolf, count of Boulogne. She is last heard of in 918, when she gave Lewisham to the abbey of Blandinium, Ghent.

BIBL. Stenton 1971: 344

Ælfthryth queen 964–1002

Ælfthryth was the daughter of a Devonshire magnate, *Ordgar. She married *Æthelwold, ealdorman of East Anglia, and, after his death in 962, became the second wife of King *Edgar, who made her father ealdorman of Devon. She was a major patron of the monastic reform movement, and a particular friend of St *Æthelwold, of whose house at Ely she was a benefactor. She played a key role in Æthelwold's re-foundation of Peterborough Abbey, for it was she who persuaded the king to grant him the site of the ruined church. The prominent role assigned to the queen in the *Regularis Concordia* (generally assumed to be from Æthelwold's pen) may reflect this alliance of queen and bishop, as may the decoration of the *Benedictional of St Æthelwold*, which contains 'the earliest European representation of the coronation of the Virgin as Queen of Heaven'. Ælfthryth was the particular patron of the English nunneries, founding Wherwell (where she eventually retired) and Amesbury, and endowing Barking. Æthelwold's Old English translation of the Rule of St Benedict, adapted for the use of nuns, may have been intended for Ælfthryth and her houses. When Edgar died in 975, Æthelwold supported Ælfthryth's claims for the succession of her son, *Æthelred II, against that of *Edward the Martyr, son of Edgar's first wife, *Æthelflæd Eneda. Edward, however, succeeded, but was murdered in 978, at Corfe, Dorset. He was visiting his half-brother and stepmother at the time, and the crime was attributed to Ælfthryth's supporters. Later historians, from the twelfth century onwards, have implicated the queen in her stepson's killing, but no contemporary sources accuse her. She dominated the early years of her son's reign, though her influence declined after *c.* 983. She did not, however, retire from public life until 999. The first wife of Æthelred II, *Ælfgifu, is a shadowy figure, and it seems to have been his mother who reared his children; in his will, the eldest son *Athelstan refers to 'my grandmother, Ælfthryth, who brought me up' and in 990–2, she was a witness in a lawsuit relating to land in Berkshire, in company with one Æfic, described as the æthelings' seneschal (*para æthelinga discten*). A little later she gave written testimony to the conditions upon which her husband, Edgar, had granted Taunton to Bishop Æthelwold; a rare example of an early letter from an English queen. She died in 1002.

BIBL. Keynes 1980: 164-74, 181-2; Yorke 1988b: 81-6; Sawyer 1968: nos. 1242, 1454

Ælfwald king of East Anglia 713—49
Apart from the fact that *Felix dedicated the *Life* of St *Guthlac to him, nothing is known of Ælfwald of the East Angles, except that he had a sister, Ecgburh, who was abbess of an unidentified monastery. Ælfwald wrote a letter of encouragement to St *Boniface, promising him the prayers of seven (unspecified) monasteries.

BIBL. Colgrave 1956: 15-16

Ælfwald St, king of Northumbria 779—88
Ælfwald, son of *Oswulf, became king of Northumbria in 779, after the expulsion of *Æthelred. His rule was not unopposed; in 779/80 his *patricius* Beorn was burnt by *Osbald and Æthelheard, who seem to have been adherents of Æthelred, and Ælfwald himself was murdered by his own *patricius*, Sicga, on 23 September 788. His body was carried to Hexham, where he was venerated as a saint, and a great light was seen shining over the spot where he was murdered, probably Chesters on the Wall, where a church was built in honour of St *Cuthbert and St *Oswald. Cuthbert's old community of Lindisfarne, however, do not seem to have joined in the celebrations, for they gave Christian burial to Ælfwald's slayer, Sicga, in 793, despite the fact that he died a suicide. It was also the Lindisfarne monks who harboured Osbald when he was exiled in 796. Ælfwald's sons Ælf and Ælfwine were murdered by Æthelred in 791. They were perhaps too young to succeed in 788, for *Osred became king on Ælfwald's death.

BIBL. Rollason 1983; Kirby 1974b; Thacker 1981

Ælfweard bishop 1035—44
Ælfweard is described as a kinsman of King *Cnut; since he was promoted to the abbacy of Evesham by Cnut's opponent *Æthelred II, this can scarcely have been a blood relationship and Ælfweard was probably related to Cnut's English wife, *Ælfgifu of Northampton. He came from the same part of the kingdom, for he gave land in Northamptonshire and Cambridgeshire to Ramsey Abbey, the house where he made his monastic profession. He was made abbot of Evesham in 1014 (or perhaps 1016), and his connections with Cnut enabled him to mitigate some of the effects of the Danish conquest in the west; Evesham was placed under the personal protection of Cnut's second wife and queen, *Emma. It was Cnut who promoted Ælfweard to the bishopric of London in 1035. It might be expected that he would have supported *Harold I, son of *Ælfgifu of Northampton, in the succession dispute which arose on Cnut's death in the same year; Harold's party included Earl *Leofric, one of Evesham Abbey's patrons. In 1040, however, Ælfweard was one of the emissaries sent to Denmark to invite Harold's rival *Harthacnut to accept the kingdom of England.

Ælfweard continued to hold Evesham after his appointment to London.

He rebuilt the shrine of St *Ecgwine and stocked the library with books. He also purchased the relics of the Flemish saint, Odulf, which had been stolen by Viking raiders from their shrine at Stavoren, and brought to London; they were re-installed at Evesham. Less creditably, he removed the relics of St *Osyth from Chich to St Paul's, and was afflicted with leprosy as a punishment. He retired from his bishopric, and, having been refused admission by the ungrateful monks of Evesham, returned to Ramsey, where he died on 25 July 1044.

BIBL. Whitelock 1975

Ælfwine king of Deira *d.* 679

Ælfwine, son of *Oswiu of Northumbria, was killed at the battle of the Trent in 679, at the age of 18. He was under-king of Deira, his brother *Ecgfrith being king of Northumbria. Their sister *Osthryth was the wife of *Æthelred of Mercia, the victor in the battle, and *Bede describes Ælfwine as 'much beloved in both kingdoms'. *Eddius tells how, as the body of the slain king was carried into York, 'all the people with bitter tears tore their garments and their hair'. Ælfwine's death nearly provoked a blood-feud between the Northumbrian and Mercian royal kindreds, which was averted by Archbishop *Theodore, who arranged payment of the wergeld.

BIBL. *HE* iv, 21: 400-1; Colgrave 1927: 50-1

Ælfwine son of Ælfric *d.* 991

Ælfwine son of Ælfric was one of those killed at the battle of Maldon in 991, fighting against the invading force of *Olafr Tryggvason. In the poem written to commemorate the event, he is the first to rally the English force after the death of their leader, Ealdorman *Byrhtnoth:

'Remember all the times that we spoke over our mead
When we boasted together on the hall-benches
Like heroes, thinking of hard battles.
Now men may see which of us is bold.
I will declare my lineage to all:
I was born in Mercia of a mighty kin:
My grandsire Ealhhelm was an ealdorman,
Wise and rich in this world's goods.
The nobles of that nation shall not reproach me
that I left this field where my lord lies dead
to seek my homeland. My grief is greatest:
He was both my kinsman and my lord.'

Ælfwine is described as 'young in years' by the poet, but must have been at least 25; he received a legacy under the will of his maternal uncle, Ealdorman *Ælfheah, who died in 970 or 971. His father *Ælfric *cild*, ealdorman of Mercia, was banished for treason in 985, and both he and *Ælfhere, his predecessor and brother-in-law, had been political opponents of Ælfwine's lord, Byrhtnoth. His mother was probably Æthelflæd daughter of *Ealhhelm ealdorman of Mercia.

BIBL. Scragg 1981: 108, ll.211-224

15

Ælfwold bishop 997–1012/15

The will of Ælfwold, bishop of Crediton, is still extant, and of great interest. It details his heriot, paid to his lord the king, of 'four horses, two saddled and two unsaddled, and four shields and four spears and two helmets and two coats of mail, and 50 *mancuses* of gold'. This more or less corresponds to the heriot of a king's thegn as detailed in *Cnut's Secular Code but Ælfwold also bequeathed to the king a ship of 64 oars 'all ready except for the rowlocks' and adds that 'he would like to prepare it fully in a style fit for his lord if God would allow him'. More peaceful pursuits are indicated by his bequest to the king's uncle, *Ordwulf, of two books, a *Martyrology* and a work by the Carolingian scholar, Hrabanus Maurus.

BIBL. Whitelock 1955, no. 50: 419-30 (Cnut's Secular Code, II, 71, i); no. 122: 536-7

Ælfwynn Lady of the Mercians 918–19

Ælfwynn, daughter of *Æthelred and *Æthelflæd, succeeded her mother as Lady of the Mercians in 918, but at the end of the following year she was 'deprived of all authority in Mercia and taken into Wessex' by her maternal uncle, *Edward the Elder, king of Wessex. Thus Edward completed the subjugation of Mercia to Wessex begun in 911, when on the death of Æthelred he 'succeeded to London and Oxford and all the lands which belonged to them'. Ælfwynn was probably in the early twenties at this time; she was born before 903. Nothing more is known of her.

BIBL. *ASC* s.a. 911, 918-19

Ælle king of Sussex *c.* 477–91

Ælle, founder of the kingdom of Sussex, landed at *Cymenesora* (now under the sea, near Selsey Bill) in 477, and drove the British force which opposed him into *Andredesleah*; this was the great forest which covered much of the Weald, named from the Roman fortress of Pevensey (*Anderida*). A second battle is recorded in 485, and in 491, *Anderida* itself was stormed, and the inhabitants slaughtered. Ælle then vanishes from sight, but *Bede names him as the first Bretwalda (overlord) of the southern English. What historical truth lies behind these traditions of the origins of Sussex is difficult to say. The names of Ælle's three sons, Cymen, Wlencing and Cissa, occur in local place-names; Cymen's name in *Cymenesora* itself (Cymen's shore), Wlencing's in Lancing, and Cissa's in Chichester ('Cissa's ceaster'). It is not, of course, impossible that these places were named after Ælle's sons, but the possibility that the sons' names were extrapolated from existing place-names must also be borne in mind. What connection, if any, Ælle had with later kings of Sussex (the next named is *Æthelwalh) is conjectural.

BIBL. Welch 1978; Welch 1989

Ælle king of Deira ?569–?99

Little is known of Ælle, founder of the Deiran royal line. The *Anglo-Saxon Chronicle* gives him a regnal length of 30 years, but also says that he came to power in 560 and died in 588. *Bede implies that he was reigning at the time of the arrival of St *Augustine in 597, and the *Life* of *Gregory the Great tells us that the English slaves whom Gregory saw in the Roman slave-market at a date between 585 and 590 were subjects of Ælle of Deira. (Gregory's puns on both names are preserved.) Ælle's regnal dates would probably be more reasonably interpreted as *c.* 569–*c.* 599. His successor Æthelric (*c.* 599–604) was probably his son, and may have been the father of Hereric, whose daughter, St *Hild, founded Whitby Abbey. It must have been Æthelric who was ruling Deira when it was conquered by *Æthelfrith of Bernicia in 604. Æthelfrith, in order to legitimize his rule, married Ælle's daughter, Acha, but the male members of her kindred were driven into exile; these included Hereric, and Acha's brother, *Edwin. One brother of Ælle is known; Edwin's uncle, Ælfric, whose grandson, *Oswine, was king of Deira under *Oswiu.

BIBL. *HE* ii, 1: 132-5; Miller 1979a

Ælle king of Northumbria *d.* 867

In 867, Osberht, king of Northumbria, was overthrown by Ælle; both were subsequently killed in the Viking assault of York in the same year. Nothing further is known of them, but Ælle acquired a posthumous reputation in Scandinavian legend as the king who threw *Ragnarr Lothbrok in the snake-pit; a good story and none the worse for being a complete fabrication.

BIBL. Stenton 1971: 247

Æthelbald king of Mercia 716–57

Æthelbald of Mercia claimed descent from Eowa, brother of *Penda. During the reign of *Ceolred of Mercia, he was in exile, but his future greatness was prophesied by his kinsman, St *Guthlac, whose cult Æthelbald promoted when he became king. Though *Bede's Northumbrian sympathies prevent him from including any Mercian rulers in his list of Bretwaldas (overlords), he does let slip that in 731, Æthelbald had authority over all the southern English, and a charter of the king in 736 styles him 'king not only of the Mercians but also of all the provinces which are called by the general name "South English"', and as 'king of Britain'. His supremacy was neither easily obtained nor stable, and he made many enemies. In 746 St *Boniface reproached him for not taking a wife, but instead committing fornication (particularly with nuns) and for seizing the lands of the Mercian church. Such strictures are not uncommon (the elastic marital customs of the English were a constant theme for churchmen) but the nature of Æthelbald's death suggests a fairly serious loss of popularity; he was murdered at Seckington by his own war-band, a terrible (though not unique) breach of the code of fidelity. A period of civil war followed, from which *Offa emerged victorious, and the Mercian supremacy collapsed. Æthelbald's achievement should not, however, be under-rated. His control, if temporary, was real. His coinage, bearing an image of the king in his helmet-crown (*cynehelm*) circulated throughout Mercia and Kent, and a version (without the politically sensitive emblem of the crowned king) was current in Wessex. Æthelbald was buried at Repton, the house where his champion, Guthlac, had been tonsured. The house was closely connected with later Mercian royalty, and extensive excavations have revealed an impressive structure. Æthelbald himself may be represented on the 'Repton Stone', one face of which bears a rider, armed with sword and *seax*, and carrying a shield.

BIBL. *HE* v, 23: 558-9; Sawyer 1968, no. 89 = Whitelock 1955, no. 67: 453-4; Stenton 1971: 203-6; Metcalf 1977; Biddle and Kjølbye-Biddle 1985

Æthelbald king of Wessex 855—60

Æthelbald was the second son of *Æthelwulf of Wessex; his elder brother, *Athelstan, predeceased their father. Æthelwulf resigned the kingdom of Wessex to Æthelbald in 855, when he undertook his pilgrimage to Rome; the third son, *Æthelberht, was made king of Kent. It is possible that Æthelwulf did not intend to return from Rome, but to make his end there, as other kings before him had done. If so, he changed his mind, and not only returned to Wessex, but brought with him a new wife, *Judith, daughter of Charles the Bald, King of the Franks. Æthelbald was unwilling to surrender the kingdom to his father, and had the support of Ealhstan, bishop of Sherborne, and Eanwulf, ealdorman of Somerset. Æthelwulf retired to Kent, where Æthelberht proved more amenable. On his father's death in 858, Æthelbald caused a scandal by marrying his stepmother, Judith. He died in 860 and was buried at Sherborne.

BIBL. Stenton 1971: 245; Keynes and Lapidge 1983: 14-15

Æthelberht king of Kent 580/93—616/18

Æthelberht, son of *Iurminric, is the first king of Kent whose career can be clearly seen, but even then details are few and contradictory. The date of his accession as given in the *Anglo-Saxon Chronicle*, 565, is almost certainly too early, a date between 580 and 593 is more likely. Before he succeeded his father, he married *Bertha, daughter of the Frankish king, Charibert; the date is probably in the late 570s. This Frankish and Christian connection was probably one of the factors in *Gregory the Great's decision to send St *Augustine to Kent to begin the mission to the English. The successful conversion of Kent was followed by that of Essex, whose king, *Sæberht, was the son of Æthelberht's sister Ricula. *Bede describes Æthelberht as Bretwalda (overlord) of the southern English, but adds that even in his lifetime, *Rædwald of East Anglia was 'gaining the ascendancy for his own people'. Æthelberht is the first English king known to have issued a law-code 'after the manner of the Romans'. It survives to provide our earliest glimpse of the structure of early Kentish society. Æthelberht died, according to Bede, 21 years after he had received the faith; probably between 616 and 618. He was buried in the church of SS Peter and Paul (St Augustine's), where his empty tomb may still be seen.

BIBL. *HE* i, 25: 72-7; ii, 5: 148-5; Whitelock 1955, no. 29: 357-9 (Æthelberht's Code); Brooks 1989a

Æthelberht St *see* Æthelred and Æthelberht SS, *d. c.* 664

Æthelberht king of Kent 725–62

Æthelberht, son of *Wihtred, ruled Kent jointly with his brothers, Eadberht and Ealric, and latterly with Eadberht's son Eardwulf. None of them are heard of after 762, and they seem to have been the last of the dynasty founded by Oisc son of *Hengest. A letter of Æthelberht to St *Boniface is extant, asking for his prayers, and sending gifts of two woollen cloaks and a silver drinking-cup lined with gold. In the letter, he reminds Boniface of his friendship with *Bucge his kinswoman, and asks him for a pair of falcons 'quick and spirited enough to attack crows without hesitation'. Apparently few such falcons were available in Kent.

BIBL. Stenton 1971: 206; Talbot 1954: 142-4

Æthelberht archbishop of York *see* **Ælberht** archbishop of York 767–80

Æthelberht St, king of East Anglia *d.* 794

Æthelberht, king of East Anglia, was murdered on the orders of *Offa in 794. Little is known about him, and the motives for his murder are unknown. He was venerated as a saint, but the later tales contain little of value for the reconstruction of his life. The cathedral church of Hereford was dedicated to him.

BIBL. Rollason 1983; Ridyard 1988: 243-7

Æthelberht king of Wessex 860–5

Æthelberht, the third son of *Æthelwulf of Wessex, was made king of Kent in 855, when his father set out on his pilgrimage to Rome. He succeeded to the whole kingdom of Wessex on the death of his brother *Æthelbald in 860.

BIBL. Stenton 1971: 245

Æthelburh St, queen *d.* 647

Æthelburh was the daughter of *Æthelberht of Kent, who in 625 married *Edwin, king of Northumbria. She took with her to the north *Paulinus, to undertake the conversion of Northumbria. She bore Edwin two children, *Eanflæd and Uscfrea. When Edwin was killed in 633, Æthelburh and Paulinus returned to Kent. She took with her her children and also Yffi, the son of her stepson, Osfrith. It seems that King *Oswald of Northumbria, who became king in 934, put pressure on Æthelburh's brother, King *Eadbald, to dispose of Uscfrea and Yffi, as æthelings of a rival Northumbrian royal house. Æthelburh sent them to Frankish Gaul, to the court of King Dagobert, who was a friend of hers. Both died in childhood and were buried in Frankia. Æthelburh herself retired to Lyminge, a monastery which she herself had founded, and became abbess. She died in 647. *Bede, who tells her story, records her pet-name, Tate.

BIBL. *HE* ii, 9: 162-7, 20: 202-7; Farmer 1978: 138

Æthelburh St, abbess, *d*. 664

Æthelburh was one of the saintly daughters of *Anna, king of the East Angles. She retired to become a nun at the Frankish house of Fare-moutiers-en-Brie, where her half-sister Sæthryth was abbess. After Sæthryth's death, Æthelburh succeeded her in office. Her niece Earcongota also entered the community.

BIBL. *HE* iii, 8: 236-41; Farmer 1978: 137-8

Æthelburh St, abbess *d*. 675

Æthelburh was the sister of *Eorcenwald, bishop of London, and possibly related to the Kentish royal dynasty. She was abbess of Barking, which her brother had founded for her. Her cult developed very early, for *Bede, writing in 731, used an early (and now lost) *Life* as the source for his account of Æthelburh's miracles in the *Ecclesiastical History*. She was succeeded as abbess by Hildelith, for whom *Aldhelm composed his treatise on virginity.

BIBL. *HE* iv, 6-9: 354-63; Farmer 1978: 137

Æthelburh queen *fl*. 688-726

Æthelburh was wife and queen of *Ine, king of Wessex (688-726). In 722, when her husband was campaigning in Sussex, she destroyed the fortress of Taunton, which Ine had built in 710; the circumstances are unknown, but a setback in the West Saxon advance against British Dumnonia may be suspected. She is said to have been instrumental in persuading her husband to retire to Rome, and to have accompanied him there.

BIBL. *ASC* s.a. 722; Stubbs 1887, vol. I: 35-6, 39

Æthelburh abbess *fl*. 774/90

Æthelburh, abbess of Withington, Gloucestershire, was the daughter of Alfred, and a kinswoman of King Ealdred of the Hwicce, who gave her the minster of Fladbury, Worcestershire, between 777 and 790. Both churches had been founded by previous kings of the Hwiccian dynasty, Withington by Oshere and Fladbury by Oshere's son, Æthelheard. They are examples of proprietary churches, belonging to the founders' kindred, whose parishes often coincided with the administrative subdivisions of the early kingdoms. Many were double-houses, having communities of nuns accompanied by secular priests with parochial responsibilities, and the abbesses who ruled them were often members of the founding kindred (see *Cwoenthryth). There was a conflict of interest between the lay founders, especially if they were kings, and the episcopal hierarchy, the former wishing to maintain control of their secular administration, the latter concerned about the quality of their clergy and the maintenance of religious standards. It is this kind of foundation of which *Bede complained in his *Letter to *Ecgberht*, archbishop of York, in 734. In the eighth century, attempts were made to bring such foundations under episcopal control, and this is what happened to Withington; Mildred, bishop of

Worcester, in whose diocese it lay, allowed Æthelburh to hold the church for life on condition that when she died, it should pass into the control of the church of Worcester.

BIBL. Sawyer 1968, nos. 62, 1429, 1255; Whitelock 1955, no. 75: 464

Æthelflæd Lady of the Mercians 911−18

Æthelflæd, the first-born child of *Alfred the Great and his Mercian wife *Ealhswith, married Ealdorman *Æthelred of Mercia, probably in 884. She exercised joint rule of Mercia with her husband, who was stricken with illness for many years before his death in 911, and after he died, she ruled alone until her own demise in 918. Between 889 and 899, she and her husband fortified the episcopal city of Worcester, whose revenues they shared with its bishop, *Wærferth. Their chief residence was Gloucester, which developed both as a town and as an administrative centre under their rule. It was at Gloucester that the Mercian council (*witan*) met in 896, probably in the palace of Kingsholm. From 902 the Mercian rulers were threatened by the Viking colonization of the north-west. The Viking settlement of the Wirral under *Ingimund took place, more or less under Mercian control, between 902 and 905, but in the latter year, the settlers attacked Chester. In response to this threat, Æthelflæd fortified the town in 907. The Norse colonies in Cumbria and the north-west were a danger to the Scots and the Strathclyde Britons as well as to Mercia, and Æthelflæd made efforts to ally with the rulers of both nations. She seems also to have been wooing the English rulers of Bamburgh; *Uhtred and *Ealdred, the sons of its lord *Eadwulf, were encouraged to acquire land in the Danish-held east midlands, presumably to motivate them to support West Saxon efforts to reconquer the area. Moreover in 909 the relics of the Northumbrian royal saint, King *Oswald, were translated from Bardney to Gloucester, into a new church dedicated to him, and built by Æthelflæd and Æthelred. Recent excavation has revealed it to be a richly-appointed building, and it is probable that both Æthelred and Æthelflæd were buried there.

The West Saxon onslaught on the Danish settlements began in 910, with the battle of Tettenhall. While her brother, King *Edward, concentrated on East Anglia and the south-east midlands, Æthelflæd turned her attack on the north midlands and the Danish kingdom of York. She ringed Mercia with *burhs* (fortified strongholds) against the Welsh, the Danes, and the Vikings of Dublin; in 910, she constructed the *burhs* at *Sceargeat* (unidentified), Bridgnorth and *Bremesbyrig* (possibly Bromsgrove); in 912, Tamworth and Stafford were fortified; in 914, Eddisbury and Warwick; in 916, *burhs* were built at *Weardburh* (unidentified), Chirbury and Runcorn. To these must be added the *burhs* of Chester and Worcester, already mentioned, and those at Hereford and Gloucester, both constructed before 914.

The battle of Tettenhall crippled the Danish kingdom of York, and laid it open to the attentions of *Ragnall of Dublin. Ragnall's campaigns against Bamburgh, Scotland and the Strathclyde Britons must have occupied much of Æthelflæd's attentions. In 914, a Viking fleet from Brittany

21

ravaged Wales and the Severn estuary, but were driven off by the levies of Hereford and Gloucester. In 917, Æthelflæd's host ravaged Brycheiniog in revenge for the killing of an Abbot Ecgberht (otherwise unknown). Such actions, which are only mentioned by chance, should always be remembered as the background to Æthelflæd's campaigns in the north and east. In 917, she captured Derby, with the help of her brother, who had engaged the Danish forces of the area by occupying and fortifying Towcester. In the following year, she 'peacefully obtained control of the borough of Leicester' while Edward advanced against Stamford. In 918, a faction of the York Danes offered her their allegiance, but in the same year she died, at Tamworth, on 12 June, 'in the eighth year in which with lawful authority she was holding dominion (*anweald*) over the Mercians'. Her deeds are recorded in the 'Mercian Register', a fragment of a lost Mercian chronicle incorporated in the *Anglo-Saxon Chronicle*.

West Saxon sources refer to Æthelred as an ealdorman, but he and his wife exercised the functions of a king, and the term *anweald* used of Æthelflæd's authority is also used of the kingship. Irish sources call her 'queen of the Saxons' and give her husband the title of king. She passed her authority to her only child, her daughter *Ælfwynn, but Edward took advantage of his sister's death to subsume Mercia into Wessex. The *Anglo-Saxon Chronicle*'s account of the reconquest does not mention her exploits. Æthelflæd, though a West Saxon princess, was the last ruler of an independent Mercia. It is possible that she would have acquiesced in this, for she fostered her nephew, *Athelstan, perhaps with the idea of fitting him to be a future king of Mercia. A statue of Æthelflæd, with her fosterling, was erected at Tamworth in the nineteenth century, to commemorate one of the great rulers of the tenth century.

BIBL. Wainwright 1959; Heighway and Bryant 1986

Æthelflæd Eneda wife of King Edgar *d*. before 964
Æthelflæd Eneda was the first wife of King *Edgar and mother of King *Edward the Martyr. Her father Ordmær was a Hertfordshire magnate, perhaps connected with the family of *Athelstan Half-king, ealdorman of East Anglia. Her nickname means 'the white duck'.

BIBL. Hart 1973: 129-30

Æthelflæd of Damerham *d*. before 991
Æthelflæd of Damerham was the daughter of Ælfgar, ealdorman of Essex; her sister, *Ælfflæd, was married to Ealdorman *Byrhtnoth. Æthelflæd herself married, as his second wife, King *Edmund, and after his death in 946, *Athelstan Rota, ealdorman of south-east Mercia. Like her sister and brother-in-law, she was a benefactor of Ely Abbey, and her will is preserved from the Ely archive. It disposes of land in Berkshire, Hampshire, Essex, Hertfordshire, Cambridgeshire and Suffolk.

BIBL. Sawyer 1968, no. 1494; Hart 1975: 283

Æthelfrith king of Bernicia 592–604, king of Northumbria 604–17
Æthelfrith, son of Æthelric and grandson of *Ida, the founder of the Bernician royal line, became king in 592. Though he lived and died a

pagan, he is eulogized by *Bede as 'a very brave king and most eager for glory'. It was probably against Æthelfrith that the great British raid commemorated in the *Gododdin* was launched, in *c.* 600; Æthelfrith's victory over this force, at Catterick, established him as the most powerful king in the north. In 603, he defeated *Áedán mac Grabhràin of Dál Riata at the battle of *Degsastan*, and in *c.* 616 it was the turn of Selyf (Solomon) map *Cynan, king of Powys, to be defeated at the battle of Chester. This engagement was preceded by Æthelfrith's slaughter of the monks of Bangor-is-Coed, who had assembled to pray for a British victory, which Bede regarded as a judgement on the British churchmen for refusing to submit to the authority of St *Augustine. In 604, Æthelfrith seized control of the kingdom of Deira, driving out *Edwin son of *Ælle, the heir, and taking his sister Acha to wife. He was finally ousted by *Rædwald of East Anglia, who espoused Edwin's cause, defeating and killing Æthelfrith at the battle of the River Idle in 617. Æthelfrith's sons fled into exile in Ireland. The eldest, Eanfrith, was probably the son of Bebba, Æthelfrith's queen, who gave her name to the fortress of Bamburgh. *Oswald is known to have been the son of Edwin's sister, Acha; the mother of *Oswiu and his sister *Æbbe is unknown.

BIBL. Kirby 1967: 22-5; Jackson 1969; Miller 1979a

Æthelheard St, archbishop of Canterbury 792–805
    Æthelheard was chosen by *Offa of Mercia as a more amenable successor when *Jænberht, archbishop of Canterbury, died in 792. He was expelled from his see when *Eadberht Præn seized power in Kent after Offa's death in 796, and fled to Mercia. An appeal against his expulsion was sent to Pope Leo III. King *Cœnwulf of London attempted to get the primatial see shifted from Canterbury to London (which was under direct Mercian control), but Pope Leo would have none of it. He excommunicated Eadberht, and insisted on Æthelheard's restitution to Canterbury. In 798, Cœnwulf invaded Kent, captured and mutilated Eadberht, and replaced Æthelheard in his see. A few years later, the archiepiscopal see of Lichfield was abolished at the Synod of *Clofesho*, 803, and Æthelheard regained control of the whole southern province.

BIBL. Brooks 1984: 120-32, 179-80

Æthelhere king of East Anglia *d.* 655
    Æthelhere, brother and successor of *Anna, king of East Anglia, was killed at the battle of the River *Winwæd* in 655. He was fighting in support of *Penda of Mercia against *Oswiu of Northumbria. Why he should have supported Penda, who had killed several kings of his dynasty, is unknown, due to the extreme obscurity of the East Anglian kingdom in this period.

BIBL. *HE* iii, 24: 290-1

Æthelmær ealdorman 977–82
    Æthelmær was one of the ealdormen appointed by *Edward the Martyr; his sphere of authority was Hampshire, which probably included central Wessex in general. His will survives, disposing of land in Wiltshire,

Hampshire, the Isle of Wight, and, oddly enough, Rutland. He was married, with two sons, but neither succeeded him; on his death his earldom went to *Ælfric. He was buried in the New Minster, Winchester, of which he was a benefactor.

BIBL. Hart 1975: 285-6

Æthelmær ealdorman c. 998–1014

Æthelmær, the patron of *Ælfric the Homilist, was the son of Æthelweard, ealdorman of the Western Provinces. He was descended from king *Æthelred I, and therefore of a collateral line of the royal kindred. In the 990s, he was one of King *Æthelred II's seneschals (*discthegnas*), and after his father's death in c. 998, succeeded to his ealdordom. He founded the abbeys of Cerne, Dorset (in 987) and Eynsham, Oxfordshire (in 1005). He retired from public life in 1005, probably into his monastery of Eynsham, but the crisis of 1013, when *Swein of Denmark seized the kingdom, brought him back into the world. When Swein's raiding-force encamped at Bath, it was Æthelmær who led the thegns of the west to submit to him, and give him hostages. He is last heard of in 1014, and probably died soon afterwards. The Ealdorman *Æthelweard banished in 1020 was probably his son-in-law.

BIBL. Campbell 1962: xii-xvi

Æthelmær se greata (the Fat) king's thegn fl. 997–1009

Æthelmær *se greata* (the Fat) has sometimes been confused with the ealdorman of the same name, the son of Æthelweard. The father of Æthelmær the Fat, however, was called Æthelwold; he was also distinguished as 'the Fat', which therefore seems to be a primitive surname rather than a personal nickname. Æthelmær the Fat's son, Æthelweard, was killed by *Cnut in 1017; 'Florence' of Worcester, in his version of this annal, incorrectly identifies his father as the ealdorman.

BIBL. Keynes 1980: 209; Robertson 1956: 387

Æthelmund ealdorman d. 802

Æthelmund, ealdorman of the Hwicce, was killed at the battle of Kempsford by Ealdorman Weohstan and the levies of Wiltshire, in 802. The context is probably the establishment of *Ecgberht as king of Wessex in the same year, after the death of the pro-Mercian king, *Beorhtric. Æthelmund was the son of Ingild, who in 770 was given land in Wiltshire by Uhtred, king of the Hwicce, and the charter recording the grant reveals that Ingild had been an ealdorman in the time of King *Æthelbald. Æthelmund married Ceolburh, who later became abbess of Berkeley, Gloucestershire; she died in 807. Their son Æthelric proved his will before a Synod at *Clofesho* in 804. Genealogical details for laymen are rare in the eighth century, and only the survival of a handful of charters has revealed the existence of this comital family.

BIBL. Sawyer 1968, nos. 59, 139, 146, 1187, Whitelock 1955, nos. 74, 78, 81

Æthelnoth reeve *fl.* first half of the ninth century

Æthelnoth was reeve (*gerefa*) of Eastry, a royal manor and head of one of the *regiones* (administrative districts) into which the kingdom of Kent was divided. The royal manor (the site of the murder in the seventh century of the Kentish æthelings, *Æthelred and Æthelberht) was the centre for the collection of royal dues and food-rent (*feorm*). Æthelnoth's duties were thus not only to administer the estate, but also to collect the king's taxes. His existence is known because he and his wife Gænburh gave their estate at Eythorne, which they had received from King *Cuthred of Kent, to Christchurch, Canterbury.

BIBL. Robertson 1956, no. 3: 4-5, 262-3; Brooks 1989a: 55-74; Sawyer 1968, nos. 41, 1500

Æthelnoth the Good archbishop of Canterbury 1020–38

Æthelnoth, who became archbishop of Canterbury in 1020, was the first monk of Christchurch to be elected to this office. It is only from his time that monks are recorded at Christchurch at all; the various traditions about the transition from secular priests to monastic clergy in the archiepiscopal church are unsatisfactory, and, although it must have taken place between the appointment of Dunstan in 959, and that of Æthelnoth in 1020, the nature and timing of the change are unknown. Æthelnoth was invested with the pallium by Pope Benedict VIII in 1022; the pope also reconsecrated and blessed him, an honour not to be accorded to any subsequent archbishop until Lanfranc, in 1071. In 1023, the body of the martyred *Ælfheah was removed from London to Canterbury; Ælfweard the Tall and Godric, both Canterbury monks, broke open the tomb in St Paul's and removed the relics, with King *Cnut's support. Æthelnoth was the recipient of Cnut's patronage throughout his archiepiscopate, and in the succession dispute after the king's death adhered to the party of *Harthacnut and *Emma; indeed he is said to have refused to crown Harthacnut's rival, *Harold I, which may account for that monarch's seizure of the manor of Sandwich, belonging to Christchurch, just before Æthelnoth's death in 1038. Some of the most splendid manuscripts of the reform movement were produced in the Canterbury scriptorium in Æthelnoth's time. The master scribe and monk, Eadui Basan, was active in the 1020s and 1030s, producing Gospel-Books, psalters and charters of the most consummate workmanship. This was also the time when English missionaries were visiting the Scandinavian lands over which Cnut reigned. Gerbrand, bishop of Zealand, whose name suggests he was of German origin, was consecrated by Æthelnoth, which brought him into dispute with the archbishop of Hamburg-Bremen, who claimed metropolitan authority over Scandinavia. In his later years, Æthelnoth's health seems to have been failing; in 1035, Eadsige, a royal priest, was appointed as his *chorepiscopus*, and eventual successor.

BIBL. Brooks 1984: 255-78, 287-96

Æthelred king of Mercia 675–704

Æthelred, son of *Penda, succeeded his brother *Wulfhere as king of

Mercia in 675. He married the Northumbrian princess *Osthryth, but relations were bad between the two kingdoms. In 679, Æthelred defeated his wife's brother *Ecgfrith at the battle of the Trent, bringing the Northumbrian supremacy to an end. The death in that battle of Ecgfrith's brother, *Ælfwine, nearly provoked a blood-feud. Mercian feeling against the Northumbrian royal house surfaced again in 697, when Osthryth was murdered by the Mercian nobles. From 691–702, Æthelred harboured the exiled *Wilfrid, who had been driven by *Aldfrith from Northumbria. Æthelred seems to have been a pious man; he endowed the bishopric of Worcester, and founded, with his wife, the monastery of Bardney, to which he retired as a monk in 704, leaving his kingdom to his nephew, *Coenred, son of Wulfhere.

BIBL. *HE* iv, 12: 368-9; 21: 400-1; v, 19: 528-9

Æthelred king of Northumbria 774–9; 790–96

Æthelred, son of *Æthelwold Moll, became king of Northumbria after the deposition of *Alhred, who had ousted his father in 765. Æthelred held the kingdom barely five years, before he was driven out in favour of *Ælfwald son of *Oswulf. After the murder of Ælfwald and the expulsion of his successor *Osred in 790, Æthelred returned, to embark upon a general purge of his enemies. In 791, the sons of Ælfwald, Ælf and Ælfwine, were dragged out of sanctuary in the cathedral at York and murdered, and in the next year, Osred, who had attempted to stage a come-back, was betrayed and killed. Æthelred's marriage in the same year with Ælfflæd, daughter of *Offa, king of Mercia, was perhaps an attempt to secure outside help for his regime. The Viking sack of Lindisfarne in 793 was regarded as a punishment for Æthelred's sins; *Alcuin wrote a letter of reproach to him upon this topic. Nevertheless Alcuin did not wholly disapprove of Æthelred, regarding his murder, on 28 March 796, as a crime, and writing approvingly of his retainer Torhtmund, who avenged him by killing his murderer, Ealdred, in 799.

BIBL. Simeon of Durham, *History of the Kings* in Whitelock 1955, no.3: 243-9 Whitelock 1955, no. 193: 775-7; no. 206: 764-5

Æthelred I king of Wessex 865–71

Æthelred I of Wessex, the fourth son of *Æthelwulf, succeeded his brother *Æthelberht in 865. He was immediately confronted with the most dangerous Viking host yet encountered in England; the 'great heathen army (*miccel here*)', commanded by *Ivarr the Boneless. For a full year this host lived off and in East Anglia; in 867 it attacked Northumbria and seized York, killing the Northumbrian kings, *Ælle and Osberht. It then moved on Mercia and occupied Nottingham. The Mercian king, *Burgred, sought West Saxon aid, and the Danes were besieged, but could not be dislodged; in 868 they removed of their own accord to York, and thence to East Anglia again, where, in 869, St *Edmund was killed at Hoxne. In the autumn of 870, they turned to Wessex, establishing themselves in Reading, and killing *Æthelwulf, ealdorman of Berkshire. Eventually they were brought to battle at Ashdown, where Æthelred and his brother *Alfred had the victory.

Despite the slaughter of many of their leaders, the battle was not a decisive defeat for the Danes; a second engagement a fortnight later, at Basing, was a Danish victory. Either in this engagement or in that at Merton early in 871, Æthelred was seriously injured. At Easter, 871, he died and was buried at Wimborne, Dorset. He left two sons, Æthelhelm and *Æthelwold, but Alfred succeeded to the kingdom.

BIBL. Keynes and Lapidge 1983: 16-17

Æthelred Lord of the Mercians c. 883−911

Æthelred, whose antecedents are unknown, came to power in Mercia after the death of *Ceolwulf II. He married *Æthelflæd, daughter of King *Alfred, probably in 884, and in 886 was entrusted by Alfred with the city of London, re-taken from the Danes. The West Saxon orientation of most of the surviving sources has made Æthelred appear as the subordinate of Alfred and his successor, *Edward the Elder, but, though he accepted West Saxon overlordship, Æthelred behaved rather as a king of Mercia than an ealdorman. He issued charters in his own name without reference to the permission of the West Saxons, an act which implies royal authority. His title, 'Lord of Mercia' also indicates a greater distinction, though he is also styled 'ealdorman' on occasions. Æthelred suffered from a debilitating illness for the latter part of his life, and seems to have left the direction of government to his wife, who succeeded him as sole ruler on his death in 911. Edward the Elder diminished her sphere of authority by taking London and Oxford and their dependent regions into his own hand on Æthelred's death.

BIBL. Stenton 1971: 259-60, 266-7, 324

Æthelred II Unræd king of the English 978−1016

Æthelred II, son of *Edgar and *Ælfthryth, was perhaps nine years old on his father's death in 975. His full brother, Edmund, had died, but his elder half-brother, *Edward the Martyr, was still alive, and despite the urging of Æthelred's mother and Bishop *Æthelwold, it was Edward who became king. He was murdered in 978, by a faction close to Ælfthryth, and it took a further year until Æthelred was consecrated king, on 4 May 979. For the first five years of his reign, Æthelred was under the tutelage of his mother and her friends, but the death of Æthelwold in 984, and *Ælfhere of Mercia in 983 ushered in a new set of influences. There followed a period in which the young king reduced the power and privileges of the reformed churches, but by 993 he had repented of this and repudiated his associates. The next decade saw a flowering of reforming zeal and the reorganization of provincial government. The Wantage Code of 997 recognized the distinctive customs of the Danelaw, but also brought the area more closely into royal control. The hereditary ealdordoms which had proven dangerous in the period after Edgar's death were left vacant as their holders died or forfeited their offices. In their place increased authority was vested in high-reeves and sheriffs, whose districts were smaller, and who could be more easily removed or replaced. This same period also saw the reappearance of external threats to England. Raiders from Scandinavia began operating as early as 980, but the battle of

Maldon in 991 ushered in a period of almost annual assaults by large and well-organized armies (see *Olafr Tryggvason, *Swein of Denmark). The military structure of England was overhauled. The fortified towns (*burhs*) were still in existence, and some refurbishment was undertaken; new *burhs* were constructed in some places (like South Cadbury). The main effort was devoted to meeting the invaders at sea. Edgar had maintained a fleet, and the ship-sokes (groups of hundreds for the raising of ships) probably date from his reign. In 1008, Æthelred commanded that 'ships should be built unremittingly over all England, namely, a warship from every three hundred hides and a helmet and a corselet from every ten'. The fleet thus raised was not very successful, and in 1012, Æthelred adopted the expedient of hiring a mercenary fleet of Vikings, under *Thorkell the Tall, who were paid from an annual levy on the whole country, the heregeld. It was perhaps Æthelred who reorganized the heriot dues, renders in arms and armour made at death to the king from his ealdormen and thegns, in order to provide more effective equipment for the royal levies.

That all these efforts were not, in the end, successful, seems to result from problems of leadership. The only leader praised by the *Anglo-Saxon Chronicle* is *Ulfkell Snilling of East Anglia; otherwise the vicissitudes of the English are attributed to the cowardice and treachery of their commanders (see *Ælfric, *Eadric Streona). Towards the end of the reign, political dissension within the royal family itself exacerbated the problem. Æthelred married twice. His first wife, *Ælfgifu, bore him six sons but was never crowned queen. In 1002, he was married again, to the sister of Duke Richard II of Normandy, *Emma. The purpose of the marriage was to draw the duke away from his Scandinavian allies, who were using Normandy as a base to attack England, but the birth of two sons to a reigning queen threatened the position of the elder æthelings. Moreover Æthelred's marriage to Emma was followed by the massacre of St Brice's Day (3 November) 1003, in which 'all the Danish people who were in England' were ordered to be slain 'because the king had been told that they wished to deprive him of his life by treachery'. The massacre affected Danish merchants and recent settlers, not the Anglo-Danish families of the Danelaw, but it cannot have endeared the king to his northern subjects. When in 1013 Swein of Denmark landed in the mouth of the Humber, the Danelaw submitted to him without a fight, and it was only when he crossed Watling Street that he began to harry the countryside. By Christmas the whole nation had accepted him as king, and Æthelred fled to Normandy. On Swein's death on 2 February 1014, the English nobles repudiated his son *Cnut, and sent to Æthelred, declaring, revealingly, that 'no lord was dearer to them than their rightful lord, if only he would govern his kingdom more justly than he had done in the past'. Æthelred promised, via his son *Edward, that he 'would remedy each one of the things that they all abhorred', and returned in triumph, driving Cnut out of the country.

In 1015, two of the leading thegns of the Danelaw, *Sigeferth and *Morcar, were murdered at Oxford on the king's orders. The ætheling *Edmund, perhaps alarmed by the prominence given to his half-brother in the negotiations of 1014, promptly married the widow of Sigeferth, against his father's will, and received the submission of the Danelaw. When Cnut returned to the assault in the same year, the English force was divided; the north rallied to Edmund and the south to Eadric Streona. In the battles of 1015–16, armies refused to move against the Danes unless the king himself would lead them, but Æthelred was already too ill. The reconciliation between Edmund and his father came too late to save the situation, and Æthelred died on St George's Day (23 April) 1016, 'after a life of much hardship and many difficulties'. His opprobrious nickname, *unræd* ('ill-advised') is recorded only much later. In assessing his reputation it must be remembered that our chief source for his reign, the *Anglo-Saxon Chronicle*, was composed after the Danish victory (between 1016 and 1023) and this disaster casts its shadow over Æthelred's earlier years and obscures his positive achievements.

BIBL. Keynes 1980

Æthelred and Æthelberht SS *d. c.* 664

Æthelred and Æthelberht were the sons of Eormenred, brother of *Eorcenberht, king of Kent. When in 664 Eorcenberht was succeeded by his son *Ecgberht, the æthelings were murdered on their cousin's orders, presumably to forestall any claims on the kingship. Their sister *Eafa, wife of *Merewalh, king of the Magonsæte, demanded the blood-price, and forced Ecgberht to grant her land at Minster-in-Thanet, where she founded a monastery. The æthelings were buried at Eastry, but their remains were translated to Wakering, Essex, where they were venerated as saints. In the tenth century, their relics were moved to Ramsey.

BIBL. Rollason 1983: 1-22; Farmer 1978: 11

Æthelric of Bocking thegn *d.* before 999

Æthelric of Bocking, an Essex thegn who perhaps fought in the battle of Maldon, 991, was accused of complicity in a plot to receive *Swein of Denmark as king, presumably during the time when Swein was operating in alliance with *Olafr Tryggvason in 991–4. Though the charge was laid as early as the archiepiscopate of *Sigeric (*d.* 994), Æthelric was neither cleared of it nor punished for it. After he died, his widow Leofwynn brought his heriot to King *Æthelred II, his lord, at Cookham, Berkshire. The king, however, refused to validate Æthelric's will, one of whose clauses bequeathed the manor of Bocking to the archbishopric of Canterbury. Leofwynn secured the help of the archbishop, *Ælfric, by offering him her morning-gift, and Ælfric bribed the king to allow the will to stand.

BIBL. Whitelock 1955, no. 121: 535-6

Æthelswith queen *d.* 888

Æthelswith, daughter of *Æthelwulf of Wessex, married *Burgred king of Mercia in 853. She died at Pavia in 888 on her way to Rome. Her finger-ring, a fine example of ninth-century metalwork, is preserved in the British Museum (MLA AF 458).

BIBL. *ASC* s.a. 888; Keynes and Lapidge 1983: 281

Æthelthryth (Etheldreda, Audrey) St, abbess, *d.* 679

St Æthelthryth is the most celebrated of the saintly daughters of *Anna, king of East Anglia. She married *Tondberht, ealdorman of the South Gyrwe, and after his death, *Ecgfrith, king of Northumbria. Despite her two marriages, she preserved her virginity, and in 672, she became a nun at Coldingham. Her resolve was strengthened by the support of St *Wilfrid, to whom she gave land at Hexham for the foundation of a monastery. Wilfrid's championship of the queen's religious vocation did not endear him to her husband. In 673, she returned to East Anglia and founded Ely, of which she became abbess. She died, probably of plague, in 679, and was succeeded as abbess by her sister, *Seaxburh.

BIBL. Ridyard 1988

Æthelwalh king of Sussex *d.* before 685

Æthelwalh is the first king of Sussex after *Ælle of whom anything is known. He married Eafa, daughter of *Eanfrith, king of the Hwicce, and was under the overlordship of *Wulfhere of Mercia. It was at Wulfhere's court that he was baptized and a Mercian-led mission was despatched to Sussex. Wulfhere gave to Æthelwalh the Isle of Wight and the province of the *Meonware* (the people of the Meon Valley), recently taken from West Saxon control. It was perhaps this which caused Æthelwalh's downfall, for he was killed by Cædwalla, a West Saxon ætheling making a living by the sword. Cædwalla was driven from Sussex, but when he gained the West Saxon kingship in 685, he overran the kingdom. The conversion of Sussex was completed by St *Wilfrid, who founded the church of Selsey on land given him by Æthelwalh. *Bede recounts how Wilfrid, on his arrival, found Sussex in the grip of a three-year famine, caused by drought, but on the very day of the first mass-baptism a 'gentle but ample rain fell' and a 'happy and fruitful' season followed! It was also Wilfrid who taught the south Saxons the art of fishing; before he arrived, they knew only how to catch eels.

BIBL. *HE* iv, 13-15; Colgrave 1927: 80-5

Æthelweard the Chronicler ealdorman 973–*c*. 998

Æthelweard was a descendant of King *Æthelred I and a kinsman of the West Saxon rulers of the tenth century. His sister *Ælfgifu married King *Eadwig, whom Æthelweard in his *Chronicle* describes as 'All-fair', and it was King *Edgar who appointed him ealdorman of the Western Shires (Cornwall, Devon, Dorset, Somerset and Wiltshire) in 973. In 994 he was one of the negotiators of the treaty with the army of *Olafr Tryggvason, and conducted Olafr to his baptism at Andover. From 992 until his death, *c*. 998, he was the premier ealdorman of King *Æthelred II. His son *Æthelmær succeeded him as ealdorman.

Æthelweard was a cultured and learned man. He was a patron of
*Ælfric the Homilist, who translated *Genesis* and the *Book of Joshua* at
his request and added four homilies to the copy of *Catholic Homilies*
made for his use. Æthelweard himself translated a version of the *Anglo-
Saxon Chronicle* into Latin verse; though incomplete, it is of great importance, since the version of the *Chronicle* upon which it is based is no
longer extant. He dedicated the work to his German cousin, Matilda,
abbess of Essen (*d.* 1011). Her father Liudolf was the son of Otto the
Great of Saxony and Edith, daughter of King *Edward the Elder. The
annal in the existing 'C' text of the *Chronicle* for 982, which records the
death of Matilda's brother Otto, may also reflect Æthelweard's influence.
Otto died in the disastrous battle in South Italy between his uncle, the
Emperor Otto II, and a Muslim army from Sicily. Despite the fact that it
was a complete defeat for the German emperor, from which he only
escaped alive through the speed of his horse, the *Anglo-Saxon Chronicle*
represents it as a German victory.

Æthelweard's *Chronicle* was used by the twelfth-century historian,
William of Malmesbury, who delivered himself of the opinion that 'it is
better to be silent about Æthelweard, a distinguished and outstanding
man, who attempted to explain these Chronicles in Latin, and whose
purpose would have my approval, if his language did not disgust me'. He
further expresses the hope to avoid 'the cliffs of rugged language, against
which Æthelweard miserably dashed, as he hunted resounding and recon-
dite words'. Æthelweard had written in the style of Latin favoured in his
own day, an elaborate and highly decorated language, peppered with
archaic and obscure words. By the twelfth century, a more classical
simplicity was in vogue.

BIBL. Campbell 1962; Whitbread 1959

Æthelweard ealdorman *d.* after 1020

Æthelweard married Æthelflæd, daughter of Ealdorman *Æthelmær,
and succeeded his father-in-law as ealdorman of the Western Provinces.
He was exiled by *Cnut in 1020, and his ealdordom added to that of
*Godwine of Wessex. It was Æthelweard who gave Æthelmær the land at
Eynsham on which to found his monastery 'for the health of my wife's
soul'.

BIBL. Campbell 1962: xvi; *ASC* s.a. 1020

Æthelwine, ealdorman 962−92

Æthelwine, the youngest son of *Athelstan Half-king, succeeded to the
ealdordom of East Anglia on the death of his brother, *Æthelwold, in
962. He was a close friend of King *Edgar, with whom he had been
brought up, and of St *Oswald, bishop of Worcester, on whose advice he
refounded Ramsey as a Benedictine monastery. This friendship brought
him into conflict with *Ælfhere of Mercia, in whose ealdordom Oswald's
episcopal liberty of Oswaldslow threatened the ealdorman's control. Strife
between the two men arose on Edgar's death in 975, when Æthelwine

supported the claims of *Edward the Martyr, the son of Edgar's first wife, *Æthelflæd Eneda, against those of Ælfhere's protégé, *Æthelred II, son of Queen *Ælfthryth. The *Life* of St Oswald, by *Byrhtferth of Ramsey, presents the enmity of the two men in ecclesiastical terms, with Æthelwine as the 'friend of God' (*amicus Dei*) defending the reformed houses against the attacks of Ælfhere. The situation is not so simple, for Ælfhere was benefactor of Glastonbury and Abingdon, while Æthelwine was engaged in a lawsuit with Ely. The true basis of their dispute was political, although the precise circumstances cannot now be reconstructed. After the death of Ælfhere and the exile of his successor *Ælfric *cild*, Æthelwine was the premier ealdorman of Æthelred II until his death in 992.

Æthelwine's activities within his sphere of office are unusually well-documented. He can be seen presiding, as was the function of his office, over shire-courts in the east midlands, and over meetings of individual hundreds and groups of hundreds. In 990/2 he sat with the king's reeve Eadric, at Wandlebury, the Iron Age hill-fort on the Gog Magog Hills, to hear a land-plea concerned with Ramsey Abbey. His own hall and court were at Upwood, near Ramsey. Æthelwine was married three times. His first wife, Æthelflæd, died in 977, the second, Æthelgifu, in 985, the third, Wulfgifu, survived him, dying in 994. His three sons, Leofwine, Edwin and Æthelweard, did not attain their father's eminence; Æthelweard was killed at the battle of Ashingdon in 1016.

BIBL. Hart 1973: 133-8

Æthelwold (Œthelwald), king of Deira *d.* 655

Æthelwold, son of St *Oswald, became king of Deira after the murder of *Oswine by *Oswiu, king of Northumbria. It is possible that Æthelwold aspired to the kingship of Bernicia also, for he made common cause against his uncle, Oswiu, with *Penda of Mercia, and was killed in 655 at the battle of the river *Winwæd*.

BIBL. *HE* iii, 14: 254-5; 23-4: 286-91

Æthelwold bishop 721–40

Æthelwold was a monk of Lindisfarne, and a companion of St *Cuthbert, who cured him of chronic head-pains. He later became prior and then abbot of Melrose until he returned to Lindisfarne as bishop, after the death of *Eadfrith in 721. It was Æthelwold who made the binding for the Lindisfarne Gospels, written and illuminated by his predecessor, probably before his departure for Melrose (between 699 and 705). The binding was later enriched with gold and gems by Billfrith the anchorite; unfortunately it has not survived. Bishop Æthelwold is to be distinguished from his namesake, Æthelwold the anchorite, who succeeded Cuthbert on the Inner Farne.

BIBL. Backhouse 1981: 12-16

Æthelwold (Ethilwald) bishop *fl.* 845/70

One of the more obscure incumbents of the obscure see of *Domnoc* (even its site is disputed, between Dunwich and Felixstowe), Æthelwold is known only from his seal-matrix, found at Eye, Suffolk, and his profession to *Ceolnoth, archbishop of Canterbury from 833 to 870. After his death, the see of *Domnoc* was amalgamated with that of Elmham.

BIBL. O'Donovan 1972: 39; Heslop 1980, fig. 1

Æthelwold ætheling *d*. 903

Æthelwold ætheling was one of the two sons of King *Æthelred I. On the death of his uncle *Alfred, Æthelwold disputed the succession of Alfred's son *Edward the Elder to the West Saxon kingship. He seized the royal manor of Wimborne, where his father was buried, barricaded the gates 'and said that he would live or die there', but when Edward's army encamped at Badbury Rings, he fled, leaving behind his wife, whom he had married illegally without the king's permission. He went to the Viking army in York, by whom he was accepted as king, but within the year he was driven out. It is not clear where he went, but in 902 he arrived in Essex with a fleet, and secured the submission of the East Saxons. He made alliance with the Danes of East Anglia, and began to launch raids into Wessex and Mercia. In 903, Edward retaliated by ravaging the Cambridge area; when his force was ordered to withdraw, the Kentish levies remained behind. Æthelwold's force caught up with them at the Holme, and in the battle, he was killed, along with Eohric, king of East Anglia, and Beorhtsige son of the ætheling Beornoth, who was probably a Mercian. On the Kentish side, Ealdorman Sigehelm was slain. It is clear that Æthelwold's rebellion was a serious threat to Edward the Elder. The line of King Æthelred continued through the tenth century, for *Æthelweard the Chronicler claimed descent from him. It is noticeable that Æthelweard, in his *Chronicle*, makes no mention of Æthelwold's rebellion; perhaps because he was his ancestor.

BIBL. *ASC* s.a. 900, 902-3; Smyth 1975: 49-52

Æthelwold ealdorman 956−62

Æthelwold, son of *Athelstan Half-king and first husband of Queen *Ælfthryth, succeeded his father as ealdorman of East Anglia in 956. Romantic tales of the twelfth century make *Edgar arrange Æthelwold's demise in order to marry his beautiful wife, Ælfthryth, but in fact he seems to have died of natural causes. Ælfthryth bore him two sons; Leofric, who, with his wife Leofflæd, founded St Neots between 979 and 984, and Æthelnoth, of whom nothing more is known. Æthelwold must be distinguished from his paternal uncle of the same name, who was ealdorman of Kent and the south-east between 940 and 946, and whose will, disposing of land in Hampshire, Wiltshire, Berkshire, Surrey and Sussex, is still extant.

BIBL. Hart 1973: 127-31

Æthelwold St, bishop 963−84

Æthelwold, one of the three great reformers of tenth-century England, was born, of unknown parentage, at Winchester. As a young man, he entered the household of King *Athelstan, and then that of *Ælfheah the Bald, bishop of Winchester. He made his monastic profession at Glastonbury. Æthelwold had ambitions to go abroad, to see at first hand the new monasticism fostered at Cluny and its daughters, but King *Eadred offered him the chance to refound the derelict monastery at Abingdon. Here, as abbot, Æthelwold began to introduce the reforms already in being in Frankia, sending one of his monks, Osgar, to Fleury-sur-Loire (a daughter-house of Cluny) to study the reformed Benedictine rule at first-hand. It was at Abingdon, under Æthelwold, that the future king, *Edgar, received his education, and after his accession, he made his old mentor bishop of Winchester, in 963. With the king's support, Æthelwold expelled the secular canons from the Old Minster (the episcopal see of St Swithun's) and replaced them with monks of his own training. Winchester thus became the first cathedral in England to have a monastic chapter. Æthelwold also expelled the clerks from the New Minster, Winchester, and Milton Abbey, Dorset, and reformed Nunnaminster, the house for women in Winchester. He showed particular concern for the decayed churches of the east midlands, refounding Peterborough (966), Ely (970) and Thorney (972).

Under the rule of Æthelwold, Winchester became the centre of a brilliant flowering of art and learning. He rebuilt the shrine of St Swithun in a new cathedral, which was one of the largest churches in tenth-century Europe. The Winchester scriptorium produced a series of splendidly illuminated manuscripts in the so-called 'Winchester style', including a *Benedictional* produced for the use of Æthelwold himself. The use of the elegant and beautiful script known as Carolingian miniscule was introduced into England and used for the writing of Latin, while the older Insular hand was employed for English texts. Nor was music neglected. The earliest piece of European polyphony appears in the *Winchester Tropers*, perhaps the work of Wulfstan the Cantor, one of Æthelwold's monks. Æthelwold himself is said to have been a skilled metalworker; one of his pieces was a candelabrum for his old house at Abingdon. He was also a patron of literature. A school of vernacular English writing flourished under his guidance, seen to its best effect in the work of his pupil, *Ælfric the Homilist. Standard Old English, developed at Winchester, facilitated the translation of Latin texts, in which Æthelwold took a particular interest; he himself translated the *Rule of St Benedict* into English. The Latinity of the period has been much criticized, due to the fact that the fashion at the time was for the 'hermeneutic style' (derived from *Aldhelm) rather than for classical simplicity. Æthelwold's most influential work was the *Regularis Concordia* (*The Agreement of the Rule*), which laid down the norms for the reformed monasteries.

Like most of the great churchmen of his time, Æthelwold was deeply involved in the political life of England. He was one of the few reformers to show sympathy for King *Eadwig, who was unpopular because of his quarrels with *Dunstan and with *Oda. Æthelwold seems to have been a friend of Eadwig's wife, *Ælfgifu, whom Oda forced him to repudiate. Edgar's queen, *Ælfthryth, was closely associated with Æthelwold, who was one of the supporters of her son, *Æthelred II, in the disputed succession which followed Edgar's death. A charter of Æthelred, issued after the death of Æthelwold in 984, laments the passing which 'deprived the country of one whose industry and pastoral care ministered not only to my interest but also to that of all the inhabitants of the country, the common people as well as the leading men'.

BIBL. Yorke 1988a; Gneuss 1972

Æthelwold Moll king of Northumbria 759–65

Æthelwold Moll succeeded to the Northumbrian kingdom after the murder of *Oswulf in 759. He is said to have been 'elected by his own people', which suggests some dispute; Æthelwold was not, it seems, of the royal kindred. He is probably to be identified with Moll, who is mentioned in 757/8 as a *patricius*, which seems to be the highest rank in Northumbria after the king, a position comparable to the mayors of the palace in seventh- and eighth-century Frankia. Since Oswulf was murdered by his own household, some sort of 'palace revolution' may be suspected. Æthelwold was driven out of the kingdom in 765 by Oswulf's kinsman, *Alhred. His son *Æthelred, however, became king in 774. The ealdorman Moll who was murdered at the orders of King *Eardwulf in 799 probably belonged to the same kindred.

BIBL. Thacker 1981: 213-21

Æthelwulf king of Wessex 839–58

Æthelwulf, son of *Ecgberht of Wessex, first appears in the historical record as the conqueror of Kent. He drove out the last king, Baldred, in 825, and the kingdom, with Surrey, Sussex, and (briefly) Essex was taken into Wessex. Henceforth, the south-east became a sub-kingdom of Wessex, held by the acknowledged heir, in the first instance, Æthelwulf himself. When he became king of Wessex in 839, the south-east went to his eldest son, *Athelstan, who predeceased him. During Æthelwulf's time, Berkshire, long contested with Mercia, passed finally into West Saxon control, apparently by mutual consent (see *Æthelwulf, ealdorman). It was probably the Viking threat which brought about the rapprochement between Wessex and Mercia evident in this period. In 843 Æthelwulf fought, unsuccessfully, against 35 ships' crews at Carhampton. The West Saxons were more fortunate in 851, when at *Aclea*, Æthelwulf and his son *Æthelbald 'inflicted the greatest slaughter on a heathen army that we have ever heard of until this present day', as the *Anglo-Saxon Chronicle* of his grandson *Alfred's reign puts it. In the same year, Athelstan won a sea-battle against the Danes off Sandwich. In 853, *Burgred of Mercia asked Æthelwulf's help for a campaign against the Welsh, and in the same year, married his ally's daughter, *Æthelswith. By 855 Æthelwulf was evidently feeling his age. He entrusted the kingdom of Wessex to Æthelbald and that of the south-east to *Æthelberht, and set off on the pilgrimage to Rome. It is possible he intended to remain there, as other kings had done before him, but if so he changed his mind. He returned home via the court of Charles the Bald, king of the Franks, who was experiencing trouble with the same Viking fleets who were ravaging Wessex. It is natural that the two rulers should discuss their common troubles, and they went on to make a formal alliance. Æthelwulf, who was in his fifties, married Charles's daughter, *Judith, a girl of about 14. Charles stipulated that she should be crowned queen, a custom not followed in ninth-century Wessex, and Æthelwulf's agreement is some indication of the importance of the alliance. His return home with a young and fertile wife was not well-received by Æthelbald, who refused to relinquish power to his father, and found some support, particularly in western Wessex, where his adherents included Eanwulf, ealdorman of Somerset, and Ealhstan, bishop of Sherborne. Æthelwulf retired to the south-east, where Æthelberht proved more amenable. He died in 858 and was buried at Steyning, Sussex.

BIBL. Stenton 1971: 231-6; 244-5; Stafford 1981: 137-51; Enright 1979

Æthelwulf monk *fl.* 803/21

Æthelwulf was the author of the little verse history, *De Abbatibus*, which tells the story of his monastery, which, unfortunately, he omitted to name, though it was clearly a cell of Lindisfarne, to whose bishop, Ecgberht (803–21), the tract is addressed. It was founded in the days of King *Osred by a Northumbrian nobleman, Eanmund, its first abbot. Eanmund was one of those nobles forced to retire into the religious life by the enmity of the king. Like *Bede's *Lives of the abbots* of Monkwearmouth and Jarrow, *De Abbatibus* gives a vivid and informative picture of monastic life in the north in the pre-Viking period.

BIBL. Campbell 1967

Æthelwulf ealdorman *d.* 870

The shires of Wessex begin to emerge into the light of history in the eighth century. Dorset and Somerset are recorded from earlier times, but from this period their ealdormen begin to be named, and the former kingdoms of Kent and Sussex became 'shires' of Wessex, as did Devon (Celtic Dumnonia). Berkshire was a region much disputed between Wessex and Mercia. In or before 853, it finally became a part of Wessex, apparently by mutual consent, for Æthelwulf, the ealdorman who had previously served the Mercian kings continued in office under *Æthelwulf of Wessex. In 860, with Ealdorman Osric of Hampshire, he put to flight a Danish force which had sacked Winchester, and during the Viking invasion of 870, defeated a raiding-force at Englefield. He was killed a few days later, at the battle of Ashdown. His body was carried to Derby, deep into Mercia, for burial.

BIBL. Stenton 1971: 234, 239

Agilbert St, bishop 668–90

Agilbert came from an aristocratic Frankish family of the Soissons district. His cousin Audo (Adon) was a friend of St Columbanus and founded the monastery of Jouarre, with his sister Theochilda (Telchilde) as the first abbess. Agilbert spent some time in Ireland before coming to Wessex at the invitation of King *Cenwealh, to become bishop of the West Saxons, in 650. He established his see at Dorchester-on-Thames, following the example of *Birinus. Cenwealh became dissatisfied with his bishop, because he did not speak the West Saxon dialect; he therefore divided the diocese, appointing an Englishman, *Wine, as bishop, with his see at Winchester. Agilbert, not unnaturally, took offence at this, and left Wessex in 660. By 664 he was in Northumbria, and was asked to put the case for Roman observance at the Synod of Whitby. Once again his linguistic difficulties overcame him, and he appointed *Wilfrid, whom he had ordained a priest, to speak in his stead. In 668 Agilbert became bishop of Paris, and it was he who ordained Wilfrid as bishop, at Compiegne. Archbishop *Theodore spent the winter of 668−9 as a guest of Agilbert, on his journey from Rome to Canterbury. Agilbert thus kept in touch with English affairs, though he refused Cenwealh's offer of reinstatement in 670; his nephew *Leuthere (Lothar) took the bishopric of Wessex in his place. Agilbert died about 690, and was buried with his kinsmen in the crypt of Jouarre, where his Roman sarcophagus can still be seen.

BIBL. Farmer 1978: 5; Geary 1988: 172-4

Aidan St, bishop 635−51

Aidan, a monk of the great house of Iona, founded by St *Columba, came to Northumbria at the request of King *Oswald (see Ségéne). He established himself at Lindisfarne, close to the chief royal residence of Bamburgh, as bishop of the Northumbrians. Here he founded the monastery which became one of the most famous in Britain and in Europe. The account of the Irish mission to Northumbria in the pages of *Bede may be romanticized, but has irresistible appeal because of the evident affection in which Bede himself held the memory of Aidan:

'I have written these things about the character and work of Aidan, not by any means commending or praising his lack of knowledge in the matter of the observance of Easter; indeed I heartily detest it, as I have clearly shown in the book which I wrote, called *De Temporibus*; but as a truthful historian, I have described in a straightforward manner those things which were done by him or through him, praising such of his qualities as are worthy of praise, and preserving their memory for the benefit of my readers. Such were his love of peace and charity, temperance and humility; his soul, which triumphed over anger and greed and at the same time despised pride and vainglory; his industry in carrying out and teaching the divine commandments, his diligence in study and in keeping vigil, his authority, such as became a priest, in reproving the proud and mighty, and his tenderness in comforting the weak, in relieving and protecting the poor.'

Aidan died at a village near Bamburgh, whose parish church is dedicated to him, and was buried at Lindisfarne.

BIBL. *HE*, iii, 3-17: 218-67; Farmer 1978: 6-7

Ainbcellach king of Scots Dál Riata 697−8

Ainbcellach was the son of Ferchar Fota who died in 697 and was of the Dál Riata tribe of Cenél Loairn. As such he was well outside the Cenél

Gabhráin dynasty whose kings had ruled Dál Riata for the previous century-and-a-half. Ainbcellach was probably responsible for the slaying of his predecessor, *Eochaid son of Domangart, in 697. His rule was clearly regarded by some as a usurpation which resulted in his expulsion from Dál Riata in 698 when he 'was carried in chains to Ireland'. By 700, the kingship of Dál Riata was in the hands of Fiannamail grandson of Dúnchad who was slain in that year and was succeeded by Ainbcellach's brother, *Selbach. Ainbcellach made a bid to regain his kingship in 719 when he was defeated and slain in a battle at Findglen, perhaps near Loch Avich.

BIBL. Anderson 1973: 179-80

Alban St, protomartyr *fl.* third century

The British martyr Alban is said to have been a soldier converted by a Christian priest, whose life he subsequently saved, at the expense of his own, during one of the persecutions of the third century, either that of Septimius Severus, *c.* 209, or of Decius, in 254, or of Diocletian, *c.* 305. *Bede, who tells his story from the continental *Passio Albani*, says that 'to this day' (731), miracles were occurring at his tomb, and his cult is remarkable in having a continuous history from Romano-British to Anglo-Saxon times.

BIBL. Farmer 1978: 8; *HE* i, 7: 28-35

Alcuin abbot 796−804

Alcuin was the most famous pupil of the school at York, where he studied under *Ælberht; when his teacher became archbishop in 767, Alcuin took over the direction of the scholars. It was in Ælberht's company that he travelled to Rome and Frankia. In 781, at the invitation of Charlemagne, king of the Franks, he joined the Frankish royal court. He remained abroad for the rest of his life, apart from the occasional visit to England. For some years he was at the centre of the group of elite scholars whom Charlemagne had assembled from all over Europe. In 796, his master rewarded his services with the abbacy of Saint-Martin at Tours, and it was here that he spent his last years, dying on 19 May 804. Alcuin's correspondence is of particular value for the study of eighth-century English history, for he retained a close interest in English affairs. He also composed a verse history of York, its bishops, kings and saints. His main importance lies in the contribution he made to Frankish history, especially the beginnings of the 'Carolingian renaissance' of the ninth century.

BIBL. Godman 1982

Aldfrith king of Northumbria 685−705

Aldfrith was the son of *Oswiu of Northumbria and an Irish princess of the Uí Néill. He was brought up in Ireland, spending much time in study, until the unexpected death of his half-brother, *Ecgfrith, brought him to the throne of Northumbria. The chief role in his establishment as king was played by his half-sister, *Ælfflæd, abbess of Whitby, who was advised by

St *Cuthbert to recall Aldfrith from Ireland. He had studied under *Adomnán of Iona and *Aldhelm of Malmesbury, and was remembered as an accomplished poet in the Irish tongue. *Bede praises both his learning and his kingship, saying that 'he ably restored the shattered kingdom, although within narrower bounds'. His Irish connections enabled him to heal the wounds caused by Ecgfrith's expedition of 684. In 686, Adomnán visited him to obtain the release of 60 Irish prisoners captured in that raid; typically their ransom took the form of a book, Adomnán's own work on the Holy Places of Syria (*De Locis Sanctis*). Aldfrith's literary enthusiasm is also shown by his gift of eight hides of land to Jarrow in return for a copy of 'the Cosmographers', a compendium of several classical writers on the topic. Aldhelm sent his royal pupil a copy of his own *Enigmata* (Riddles), and addressed to him the *Epistola ad Adcircium*, a work on poetic metre. *Alcuin remembered Aldfrith as 'a man from the earliest years of his life imbued with the love of sacred learning, a scholar with great powers of eloquence, of piercing intellect, a king and a teacher at the same time'. It was in his time that the great intellectual and artistic flowering of the 'Northumbrian renaissance' came to its height. The Lindisfarne Gospels, written and illuminated by *Eadfrith, the Codex Amiatinus, commissioned by Abbot *Ceolfrith, the Crosses of Ruthwell and Bewcastle, all belong to this period, as does the *Anonymous Life of St Cuthbert*, whose cult Aldfrith promoted. Aldfrith married Cuthburh, sister of *Ine of Wessex, though she later left him to become a nun at Barking, the house for which Aldhelm composed his treatise on virginity; subsequently she founded Wimborne Minster, Dorset. His son *Osred did not live up to his father's example. The great achievements of Northumbrian art and scholarship in the eighth century were fostered by the gifts of this remarkable scholar-king, who deserves to be better-known.

BIBL. Stenton 1971: 88-9; *HE* iv, 26: 430-1; v, 15: 508-9; Godman 1982: 70-1

Aldhelm St, bishop 706−9

Very little is known of the parentage and early life of Aldhelm, the foremost scholar of the seventh century after *Bede. He was a West Saxon, though the suggestion that he was a kinsman of King *Ine (his brother's son) is no more than a guess by his eleventh-century biographer, Faricius. He studied at Canterbury in the time of *Theodore, and about 674 became abbot of Malmesbury. He rebuilt the church there, and founded monasteries on the River Frome in Dorset (perhaps identical with St Martin's, Wareham), and at Bradford-on-Avon, Wiltshire. Pre-Conquest churches are still standing at both sites, and the earliest fabric of St Laurence, Bradford-on-Avon, may be of Aldhelm's time. Among his works is a series of dedicatory poems for churches or altars, the *Carmina Ecclesiastica*, one of which celebrates Withington, Gloucestershire, founded by *Bucge. When in 706 the West Saxon see was divided, Wessex 'west of Selwood' was given to Aldhelm, who made his see at Sherborne, building a cathedral which was much admired by William of Malmesbury, who saw it in the twelfth century. He died in 709 or 710.

Though the known facts of Aldhelm's life are few, his remaining works ensure his survival. Most celebrated was his tract on virginity (*De Virginitate*), written for Abbess Hildelith and the nuns of Barking. Among their number was Cuthburh, formerly the wife of Aldhelm's friend and pupil, King *Aldfrith of Northumbria, and in the treatise, Aldhelm tackled one of the problems faced by English churchmen, the matrimonial customs of the north, so different from those of the Roman world. Northern custom allowed spouses to leave their partners for the monastic life, and even let the abandoned partners re-marry (see *Ecgfrith). This was contrary to the teaching of St Paul (*I Cor* vii 10−11), though allowed in the writing of the eastern father, Basil of Cæsarea (330−79). Aldhelm produced a new *schema* of womanly virtue, comprising not only virginity and marriage, but 'chastity, which, having been assigned to marital contacts, has scorned the commerce of matrimony for the sake of the heavenly kingdom'. This covered cases like that of Cuthburh.

Aldhelm was a skilled poet, both in Latin and in English, though none of his English songs survive. William of Malmesbury tells the story, derived from King *Alfred, of how Aldhelm used to stand on the bridge of Malmesbury, dressed as a gleeman and singing 'profane verses' interspersed with biblical texts, 'to win men's ears and then their souls'. His Latin Riddles, the *Enigmata*, are extant, and represent a very popular genre. That on the whelk indicates the style:

'From twin shells in the blue sea I was born,
And from my hairy body, turn soft wool
A tawny red. Lo, gorgeous robes I give,
And of my flesh provide men food besides;
A double tribute thus I pay to Fate'.

Bede, in his description of Britain, mentions of production of 'whelk-red' among the riches of the island.

Aldhelm's works were very popular in pre-Conquest England, and his style was much imitated. He wrote in what used to be called 'hisperic' Latin, which has come to be called the 'hermeneutic style', characterized by 'the ostentatious parade of unusual, often very arcane and apparently learned vocabulary, in particular words of Greek origin'. The difficulties of translation which this entailed, and changing fashions in Latin style have resulted in the later neglect of Aldhelm's works, now happily rectified.

BIBL. Lapidge and Herren 1979; Pitman 1925; Lapidge 1975a

Aldred priest, *fl.* 968−90

Aldred was a member of the community of Chester-le-Street during the episcopate of Ælfsige (968−90). It was he who composed the colophon to the Lindisfarne Gospels, with the names of the scribe and illuminator, *Eadfrith, the maker of the binding, *Æthelwold, and Billfrith the anchorite, who adorned it with gold and gems. Aldred himself contributed the interlinear translation into Old English.

BIBL. Backhouse 1981: 12-16

Alfred ealdorman 853–88

The name of Ealdorman Alfred is commemorated in the Golden Gospels which he and his wife Wærburh redeemed with 'pure gold' from a 'heathen army' which had looted it, 'because we were not willing that these holy books should remain any longer in heathen hands'. Alfred gave the Gospels to Christchurch, Canterbury. The manuscript, known as the *Codex Aureus*, is a magnificent example of the illuminator's art. Half its pages were dyed purple, and their text written in letters of white, gold and silver. It now belongs to the Royal Library, Stockholm. Alfred's stipulation on presenting the manuscript to Canterbury was that it should be read every month for the souls of himself, his wife and their daughter Ealhthryth. The ealdorman's will also survives, disposing of land in Kent and Surrey. In it a son, Æthelwold, is mentioned in terms which suggest that he was illegitimate, or at least not the child of Wærburh. Alfred is probably the ealdorman of Surrey whose death in 888 is recorded in the *Anglo-Saxon Chronicle*. His predecessor, Huda, was killed in battle against the Danes in 853.

BIBL. Harmer 1914, nos 9 and 10 = Sawyer 1968, no. 1508 = Whitelock 1955, no. 97; Stockholm, Kungliga Bibliothek A 135; Nordenfalk 1977: 99-107, plates 33-38

Alfred the Great king of Wessex 871–99

Alfred was the youngest son of Æthelwulf of Wessex. He succeeded his brother Æthelred I in 871, and the early years of his reign saw a bitter struggle with the armies of *Halfdan and *Guthrum. This conflict culminated in 878, when the Danes surprised the West Saxons at the royal manor of Chippenham, on the morning after Twelfth Night, and Alfred was driven into hiding in the marshes of the Somerset levels. There he fortified the island of Athelney, from which he waged a guerrilla campaign to such effect that by the summer he was able to rally the forces of western Wessex, and bring the Danish force to battle at Edington. Alfred's victory in this battle, and his siege of the Danish base at Chippenham forced a Danish surrender. Peace was made at Aller, near Athelney. The Viking leader, Guthrum, accepted baptism, Alfred standing as his godfather, and a truce was made (the Treaty of Wedmore). In 880, Guthrum's army moved into East Anglia and settled there. Guthrum, who took the baptismal name of Athelstan, ruled as king in East Anglia for ten years, and during that time, kept the peace with Alfred.

The aftermath of the Edington campaign and the Treaty of Wedmore gave Alfred time to reorganize the defence of Wessex. He built a series of fortified strongholds or *burhs*, to defend the borders of Wessex, both land and sea boundaries. The alliance with Mercia, established by the marriage of *Burgred and *Æthelswith, was strengthened. Alfred was already married to the Mercian lady, *Ealhswith, and had been on good terms with *Ceolwulf II (874–9). In or about 884, he gave his eldest daughter *Æthelflæd in marriage to *Æthelred, ealdorman of Mercia, Ceolwulf's successor, who accepted West Saxon overlordship. Indeed after the recapture of London in 886, 'all the English submitted to him (Alfred),

41

except those who were under the power of the Danes'. It seems also to have been Alfred who made overtures to the English rulers of Bernicia, the high-reeves of Bamburgh (see *Eadulf). Alfred's Law-Code, the first to be issued by a West Saxon king since the days of *Ine, drew upon the Kentish code of *Æthelberht and the (lost) code of *Offa of Mercia; a clear attempt to draw the three nations more closely together.

The administration of the kingdom was overhauled in Alfred's time. Its backbone, the king's thegns, were bound more closely to the king; they were expected to serve one month in three at the court, and for this received pay; one-sixth of the king's revenues were used to remunerate the royal thegns and fighting men. Another sixth of his income went to 'foreigners'. These may have included the distinguished continental scholars whom Alfred attracted to his court, but it is clear that some of them were warriors; Frisians are known to have been in Alfred's employ for their qualities of seamanship (see *Wulfheard). It is from Alfred's time that we begin to hear of the high court officials; the seneschal (*discthegn*), the chamberlain (*hræglthegn*), the butler (*birele*) and the marshal (*horsthegn*). The king's endeavours to promote learning and literacy, among the lay aristocracy as well as the clergy, were not entirely due to intellectual interests; he was trying to improve the quality of his administration and record-keeping into the bargain.

Alfred's preparations were tested when Viking raids began again in the 890s. Though his late campaigns have been described as 'inconclusive', it is evident that the free movement of the Viking armies was hampered, both by the *burhs* and their garrisons, and by the efficiency of the royal levies, who were able to follow the Danes over long distances and keep up a constant pressure. In these last years, the English fleet was reorganized. In 896, a new breed of longships was built 'almost twice as long as the others', of 60 or more oars, 'neither on the Frisian nor on the Danish pattern, but as it seemed to [Alfred] himself that they would be most useful'. Frisians not only helped to build the ships but also fought in them, as the casualty-list of a sea battle in the same year shows. The employment of Frisians may be connected with the marriage of Alfred's youngest daughter, *Ælfthryth, to Baldwin II, count of Flanders.

Alfred's model for his own kingship seems to have been Charlemagne and his successors, the kings of the Franks. Alfred as a boy had accompanied his father to Rome, and had visited the court of Charles the Bald, Charlemagne's grandson, whose daughter, indeed, was briefly Alfred's stepmother. The *burhs* of Alfred, in particular, call to mind the fortifications built by Charles the Bald against the Vikings who invaded Neustria. It is in his educational programme, however, that Alfred most closely resembles Charlemagne. He regarded the Viking menace as a punishment for the slackness and ignorance of the English church, and collected about him such men of learning as he could find to remedy the situation. Some came from abroad; the most distinguished were *Grimbald of Saint-Bertin and *John the Old Saxon. Others were from England, especially from Mercia, like *Plegmund, the archbishop of Canterbury, and *Wærferth, bishop of Worcester. According to Asser, it was Wærferth who translated the *Dialogues* of *Gregory the Great into English. This was one of the works 'most needful for men to know' rendered into English at this time; the others were Gregory's *Pastoral Care*, the histories of Orosius, Boethius' *Consolations of Philosophy*, St Augustine's *Soliloquies* and Bede's *Ecclesiastical History*. These works, and others, probably formed the 'curriculum' of the school which Alfred established at his court, and where his own sons and daughters were educated. The aim was to give proficiency in English to laymen, and to train those wishing to enter the church in Latinity.

Most influential among Alfred's scholars was the Welshman *Asser, who wrote the king's biography. We see Alfred largely through Asser's eyes, and those of the anonymous authors of the *Anglo-Saxon Chronicle*, who wrote under the king's sponsorship, if not his actual direction. Both sources are at pains to emphasize Alfred's importance and his success. They see him as a European figure; sending alms (Peter's Pence) to Rome, and even further afield, to the patriarch Elias of Jerusalem, and the shrines of SS Thomas and Bartholomew in India. In the later Old English period, however, Alfred was overshadowed by his son, *Edward the Elder and his grandson, *Athelstan. In the twelfth century, thanks to the efforts of William of Malmesbury, he became one of the best-known of the Old English kings. By the sixteenth century, he had acquired, alone among English kings, the title of 'the Great'. If he was not quite as innovative as his historians would like us to believe, it remains true that his reign is a watershed in English history, marking the beginning of a single nation and a national kingship.

BIBL. Keynes and Lapidge 1983; Nelson 1986

Alfred ætheling *d.* 1036

Alfred, the second son of *Æthelred II and *Emma, was sent to Normandy with his brother, Edward in 1013, when *Swein of Denmark seized the kingdom of England. Edward seems to have returned in the following year with his father, but we hear no more of Alfred until 1036. In that year he arrived in England, ostensibly to visit his mother in Winchester, but was captured by Earl *Godwine of Wessex. His companions were killed, and ætheling taken to Ely, where he was blinded; he subsequently died, and was buried by the monks. Godwine seems to have been acting on the orders of *Harold I, who had seized the treasury at Winchester from Emma, and took the kingdom in the following year. It is possible that Alfred's visit was in fact an attempt to assert his rights as an ætheling, and his murder was undoubtedly political.

BIBL. Stenton 1971: 421; Barlow 1970: 42-6

Alhfrith king of Deira 655−64

Alhfrith was the son of *Oswiu of Northumbria. Since he was old enough to fight at the battle of the *Winwæd* in 655, he cannot have been the son of *Eanflæd, whom Oswiu married after he became king in 642; his mother was probably Rhiainfellt (Riemmelth), grand-daughter of Rhun map *Urien of Rheged. He married Cyneburh, daughter of *Penda of Mercia, and seems to have been a friend of *Peada her brother, for when Peada sought a Northumbrian princess as his wife, it was Alhfrith who persuaded him to become a Christian, and it was Alhfrith's full sister, Alhflæd, whom Peada married. Alhfrith became king of Deira after the death (at the *Winwæd*) of his cousin, *Æthelwold. Alhfrith's relations with his father seem to have deteriorated thereafter. The murder of Peada at the Northumbrian court at Easter 656 (or 657) may have played some part in this, though *Bede reports a story that Alhflæd was involved in her husband's death. Alhfrith's friendship with *Wilfrid may, however, have been the basic problem. He became Wilfrid's patron when the budding saint returned to Northumbria from Lyons in 658, and gave him the monastery of Ripon; a gift which entailed the expulsion of its Celtic-trained community, led by *Eata and *Cuthbert. Wilfrid was very much of the Roman party. He was ordained by *Agilbert, then bishop of Wessex, and under his guidance, Alhfrith (and presumably Deira) adopted Roman customs. At the Synod of Whitby in 664, Wilfrid put the case for the Roman Easter, and when the bishop of Northumbria, *Colmàn, preferred to retire rather than accept the decisions of the Synod, it was Wilfrid who was chosen to replace him. He clearly intended to make his see at York, in Deira, but went to Gaul for his consecration and in his absence, Oswiu chose *Chad in his stead. It was probably this which provoked the split between Alhfrith and his father. Alhfrith is not heard of after 664, and was probably exiled or killed.

BIBL. *HE* iii, 14: 254-5; 21: 278-9; 24: 290-1; 25: 296-7; Farmer 1974

Alhmund (Alkmund) St *d*. 802
   Alhmund, son of *Alhred of Northumbria, was murdered by King *Eardwulf of Northumbria in 802. He was buried at Derby, and his cult became popular in the west midlands; the collegiate church of St Alkmund, Shrewsbury, was dedicated to him. Little is known of his life, and the later legends concerning him are not helpful. He is typical of many murdered royal saints in the pre-Conquest period.

BIBL. Rollason 1983

Alhred king of Northumbria 765—74
   Alhred, a member of the Northumbrian royal dynasty, drove out *Æthelwold Moll, king of Northumbria, in 765. He is now known chiefly as a friend and patron of the continental missionaries. In 773 he and his wife Osgifu were in correspondence with Bishop *Lul, and it was a synod called by Alhred which despatched St *Willehad to preach to the Frisians. In 774, Alhred was deposed 'by the counsel and consent of all his people', in favour of *Æthelred, son of Æthelwold Moll. He fled to the court of *Ciniod, king of the Picts, and is heard of no more. One son, *Osred, became king in 788, and another, *Alhmund, was murdered in 802.

BIBL. Simeon of Durham, *History of the Kings* in Whitelock 1955, no. 3: 242-4; Whitelock 1955, no. 187: 767-8

Alle *fl*. 1012/35
   The Vasby runestone in Uppland, Sweden, commemorates Alle, who 'took *Cnut's geld in England'. He was presumably a Swedish Viking,

possibly one of those to whom Cnut distributed treasure in 1018, when disbanding his fleet.

BIBL. Jansson 1962: 55-6

Alphege St, *see* **Ælfheah**

Alpín king of the Picts and afterwards (?) of Scots Dál Riata 726–33

Alpín first appeared as a contender for the Pictish overlordship when he defeated the Pictish king, *Drest, in 726 and 'reigned in his stead'. His reign over the Picts lasted for two years until he was routed in battle by *Óengus I, son of Fergus, at Moncrieffe Hill in 728, when Alpín's son was slain. It would seem that Alpín lost the overlordship of the Picts at Moin Craibe, while he finally lost his tribal kingdom later that year in another defeat at the hands of *Nechtán son of Derile. Marjorie Anderson believed that Alpín fled to Dál Riata after losing his position in Pictland and that he ruled there jointly with Eochaid, son of *Eochaid son of Domangart, who may have been his stepbrother. It is quite possible that Alpín was of the Dál Riata Gaelic line. Alpín's father is named in the Latin lists and elsewhere as Eochaid, and so he may have been a son of Eochaid son of Domangart of the Cenél Gabhráin. His name appears in the Dál Riata king-list between the reigns of *Dúngal son of Selbach and Muiredach son of Ainbcellach (i.e. between 726 and 733). However, the king-lists put Alpín's reign at only three or four years in Dál Riata. There is reason to suppose that this Alpín was deliberately confused by later compilers and synchronizers with *Alpín the father of *Kenneth mac Alpín who is alleged to have ruled Dál Riata *c.* 839.

BIBL. Anderson 1973: 177-9, 182-3; Smyth 1984: 72-5

Alpín son of Eochaid, king of Dál Riata *c.* 839

The historicity of this king who was the father of *Kenneth mac Alpín is very much in doubt. There is no mention of Alpín in the *Annals of Ulster* which constitutes the major source of contemporary information on Alpín's predecessors and successors in the Scottish kingship. He is said to have seized power in Dál Riata after the defeat and massacre of *Eóganán and the house of Fergus in a battle against the Vikings in 839. Traditions from *c.* 1200 and later, asserted that Alpín was slain while campaigning in Galloway, some sources adding that he was slain by Picts. A thirteenth-century place-name, *Lachtalpin* ('Alpin's Grave'), has been identified with Laight in Wigtonshire. Later Scottish historians believed Alpín's mother to have been of the family of *Óengus II son of Fergus.

BIBL. Anderson 1973: 195-7; Smyth 1984: 180-5

Ambrosius Aurelianus British leader *fl.* late fifth or early sixth century

*Gildas specifically mentions Ambrosius Aurelianus as the leader of a successful British counter-offensive against Anglo-Saxon invaders in the late fifth or early sixth century, of which the British victory at Mount Badon, perhaps under *Arthur, was a part, describing him as 'the last of the Romans'. Gildas' reference to Ambrosius' parents as having 'worn the purple' could suggest descent from one of the British imperial usurpers in 407 – Marcus, Gratian or Constantine – and his grandchildren were ruling somewhere in Britain as Gildas wrote. By the time the *Historia Brittonum* (see under *Nennius) was written in the early ninth century, Ambrosius had been caught up in the legends surrounding *Vortigern in Wales as Vortigern's adversary and credited with the prophecy at Dinas Emrys that the red dragon, representing the Britons, would overcome the white dragon, representing the Anglo-Saxons.

BIBL. Alcock 1971: 26f, 358ff; Wood 1984: 23; Dumville 1984b

Anarawd ap Rhodri king of Gwynedd 878–916

Anarawd appears to have succeeded his father, *Rhodri ap Merfyn, on the latter's death in 878, though Anarawd's brothers may also have ruled territory in Gwynedd. Rhodri was avenged in battle on the Conwy in 880 and Anarawd and his brothers probably then embarked upon the extension of their authority into Powys and Ceredigion which terminated the independent existence of these kingdoms. By *c.* 890 they represented a serious threat to Hyfaidd ap Bleddri, king of Dyfed, and Eliseg ap Tewdwr, king of Brycheiniog, who turned for assistance to *Alfred, king of the West Saxons. Anarawd's response to this was to join forces with the Danes of York, but *Asser records that no good came of it: Gwynedd was ravaged by the Danes in 894, upon which Anarawd also submitted to Alfred who imposed quite oppressive terms upon him, obliging him to accept confirmation with Alfred as his godfather, which was normal procedure when a pagan ruler submitted but not so in the case of fellow Christian princes. In 895, however, with Saxon military aid, received probably from the West Saxon king, Anarawd devastated Ceredigion and Ystrad Tywi, the two parts of the kingdom of Seisyllwg which had been forged by *Seisyll, king of Ceredigion, in the second half of the eighth century, and it may be that Anarawd's brother, Cadell (the father of *Hywel Dda), then began to establish himself here. West Saxon relations with the princes of south Wales collapsed in the course of these events and the subsequent death of Alfred.

BIBL. Kirby, 1971; Dumville 1982

Aneirin British bard *fl.* sixth century

Aneirin was a British bard whom the early ninth-century *Historia Brittonum* (see under *Nennius), dates to the sixth century. The classic poem, the *Gododdin*, attributed to Aneirin, is a series of elegies on heroes of the Celtic world who allegedly fought for Mynyddog the Wealthy, a chieftain of the Votadini who resided at Din Eidyn (Edinburgh), and fell in battle against the men of Deira and Bernicia (the Northumbrians) at *Catræth* (possibly Catterick), possibly but not certainly *c.* 600. The earliest text of the *Gododdin* belongs to the thirteenth century though part of it may depend on a tenth-century exemplar, but how many, if any, of the extant verses were actually composed by Aneirin at the time of the battle is a matter of continuing debate. It must be emphasized that there is no evidence independent of the *Gododdin* for the battle of *Catræth*.

BIBL. Williams 1938; Jackson 1969; Charles-Edwards 1978; Jarman 1988; Dumville 1988; Hehir 1988

Anna king of East Anglia *d. c.* 654

Anna, the son of *Rædwald's brother Eni, is known chiefly as the progenitor of saintly daughters, St *Æthelthryth, St *Seaxburh, St *Æthelburh and St Wihtburh. *Bede describes him as 'an excellent man of royal descent' and says that he became king when *Sigeberht and Ecgric were killed in battle by *Penda of Mercia. The date is not known, but it was to his court that *Cenwealh, king of Wessex, fled, when he was temporarily driven from his kingdom by Penda, in *c.* 644. Indeed it was Anna who persuaded Cenwealh to become a Christian. Anna was a patron of the monastery at Burgh Castle, founded by St *Fursa. Like his predecessors, he was killed by Penda; again, the date is unknown, but Anna's brother and successor, *Æthelhere, was killed at the battle of the *Winwæd* in 655.

BIBL. *HE* iii: 238-9; 18: 268-9; 19: 270-1

Arnór Earls' Poet Orkney poet *c.* 1046–75

Arnór Thórdarson was an Icelander and a skaldic poet who settled in the Orkneys having attached himself first to Earl *Rögnvaldur Brúsason and later to Rögnvaldur's uncle and enemy, Earl *Thorfinn the Mighty. It would seem from Arnór's dirge or *drápa* on Thorfinn that the poet had married a kinswoman of the earl. His earliest surviving works are probably his dirge on Earl Rögnvaldur (*c.* 1046) and two poems on King Magnus the Good of Norway. Part of a poem on Harald Hardrada survives, together with a dirge on that king (1067). According to *Laxdæla Saga*, Arnór composed a dirge on the Icelander, Gellir Thorkelsson, grandfather of Ari the Learned Thorgilsson, the great Icelandic historian. In his poem, according to *Laxdæla Saga*, Arnór praises Gellir for building a church at Helgafell in western Iceland. Since Gellir died in Denmark in 1073 on his way home from a pilgrimage to Rome, Arnór was clearly active up to that time, and it would seem he was still living in the Orkneys, where he is assumed to have died. A remarkable amount of Arnór's verse has survived and both the content of his poetry and his nickname show that his talents were primarily devoted to serving as court poet to the earls of Orkney. His dirge on Earl Thorfinn (*c.* 1064) is one of his finest pieces as well as containing important historical information and reflecting (however dimly) the new Christian ethos of the Norse world in the eleventh century. Arnór's poetry also reflects his crisis of loyalty in the feud between Thorfinn and his nephew Earl Rögnvaldur in the 1040s. Arnór's eventful life as a poet, warrior, and seafarer; his far-flung contacts with Iceland and Scandinavia; his friendship with kings and earls; and above all the language of his poetry, demonstrate how firmly the Scottish Isles formed part of the Norsemen's world in the Middle Ages.

BIBL. Vigfusson and Powell 1883, 1965 reprint ii: 184-98; Pálsson and Edwards 1978: 38-76; Turville-Petre 1967: 147-50

Artgal son of Dumnagual, King of the Strathclyde Britons 872

Artgal was slain in 872 with the connivance of *Constantine I, a son and successor of *Kenneth mac Alpín, king of Scots. In the year prior to Artgal's death, his chief fortress at Dumbarton had been stormed by a Viking army led by Olaf, king of Dublin, and his ally, Ivarr, a Norse faction which was probably allied with Constantine I. The capture of Dumbarton and the slaying of Artgal heralded the end of British rule over the kingdom of Strathclyde which seems to have finally terminated with the reign of *Eochaid son of Rhun, the grandson of Artgal, in *c.* 889. The survivors of the northern British aristocracy in Strathclyde migrated to north Wales in 890.

BIBL. Smyth 1984: 192, 215-16

Arthur British leader *fl.* early sixth century

A British rather than a specifically Welsh figure, Arthur is described as a 'leader of battles' (*dux bellorum*) rather than as a king by the early ninth-century *Historia Brittonum* (see under *Nennius), which, on the evidence possibly of an old battle-catalogue poem, ascribes ten victories to him over unspecified opponents at generally unidentifiable sites, one of which, however, can be located at Chester with another in the Caledonian forest north of the Forth. Arthur's tenth victory is said to have been at Mount Badon, to which *Gildas refers as a defeat of the Anglo-Saxons which helped to halt their advance, though without mentioning Arthur. By the tenth century Arthur's death was associated with a battle at *Camlann* (perhaps *Camboglanna* or Birdoswald, north of Hadrian's Wall) and dated, not necessarily correctly, in the mid-tenth-century Harleian annals to 537. Already by the early ninth century, legendary traditions of Arthur were being located in Wales and Geoffrey of Monmouth, writing his *History of the Kings of Britain* in 1136, represented Cærleon as Arthur's principal residence. At present historians are tending to take a minimal view of the historical value of even the earliest evidence for Arthur, but most probably still see him as an historical figure who successfully established himself as a powerful warlord in early sixth-century Britain. In early Welsh history Arthur was 'the sovereign prince of the island' but he inhabited a largely mythological world. The chivalric Arthur who become so central a figure in the story and romance of the 'Matter of Britain' in the Middle Ages was essentially the creation of Geoffrey of Monmouth in the twelfth century.

BIBL. Alcock 1971; Jackson 1945/6; Jackson 1959; Jones 1964; Dumville 1977; Barber 1979

Arwald king of the Isle of Wight *d.* 687

Arwald is the only known king of the Isle of Wight, apart from *Stuf and Wihtgar. He was killed by *Cædwalla of Wessex, who conquered the island, along with his two younger brothers. Cædwalla gave a quarter of the island to *Wilfrid, who entrusted it to his sister's son, Beornwine, with instructions to effect the conversion of the island.

BIBL. *HE* iv, 16: 382-3

Asaph bishop *fl.* seventh century

Just south of Rhuddlan, Llanelwy became the seat of a bishopric in 1143 and emerged as the centre of the cult of St Asaph, traditionally said to have been a disciple of St *Kentigern, reputed founder of the church of Llanelwy during his alleged sojourn in Wales.

BIBL. Jackson 1958: 313-18

Asser bishop *d.* 908 or 909

A kinsman of Nobis, bishop of St David's (840–73/4), in his *Life of King Alfred*, written 893/4, Asser tells how he was summoned to the court of *Alfred, king of the West Saxons, probably in 885, travelling across 'great expanses of land' to meet him at East Dean or West Dean in Sussex, and agreed to spend six months in any year in his service. It was one of Asser's tasks to read aloud to Alfred when requested to do so and it is known from the Old English preface to the Alfredian translation of Pope Gregory the Great's *Pastoral Care* that he was also involved in the work of translating Latin texts into Anglo-Saxon which the king encouraged, such translations being disseminated throughout Wessex. There were particular reasons for Alfred's approaches to St David's. St David's was one of the major churches in south Wales and a literary centre, the home of the original chronicle which lies behind extant texts of Welsh annals. Moreover, Alfred was anxious to offer protection to Hyfaidd ap Bledri, king of Dyfed, and to other south Welsh rulers who were being attacked both by the Mercians under Ealdorman *Æthelred and by *Anarawd ap Rhodri, king of Gwynedd, and his brothers. It is highly likely, therefore, that Asser's role in the West Saxon court was diplomatic as well as literary, concerned with securing a recognition of Alfred as overlord by the rulers of south Wales which was the cornerstone of Alfredian policy in Wales. Asser was rewarded with a bishopric at Exeter, probably as a suffragan of Sherborne, and then the bishopric of Sherborne in the mid or late 890s, which he held until his death in 908 or 909. Galbraith's view that Asser's *Life* is a mid-eleventh-century composition by Leofric, bishop of Exeter, or a member of his household, has not gained general acceptance.

BIBL. Whitelock 1968; Kirby 1971; Keynes and Lapidge 1983; Campbell 1986; Galbraith 1964: 88-128

Athelstan king of Kent *d. c.* 852

Athelstan was the eldest son of *Æthelwulf, king of Wessex. In 839 he became king of Kent under his father, and in 851, he and his ealdorman, Ealhhere, fought and won a sea-battle against the Vikings off Sandwich: 'the first naval battle in recorded English history'. Athelstan was probably dead by 853, when Ealhhere alone led the men of Kent against the Vikings in Thanet; he himself was killed in the subsequent battle, along with Huda, ealdorman of Surrey.

BIBL. Stenton 1971: 244

Athelstan king of Wessex 924–39

Athelstan, the eldest son of king *Edward the Elder, was born about 895. It is possible that he was illegitimate, or at any rate that his mother, Ecgwynn, was his father's concubine, rather than a legal wife. When Edward became king of Wessex in 899, he married *Ælfflæd, daughter of Æthelhelm, ealdorman of Wiltshire, and it was her eldest son, Ælfweard, who became king of Wessex on Edward's death, but died within 16 days. It seems to have been intended that Athelstan should become king of Mercia; he was fostered by his aunt, *Æthelflæd, Lady of the Mercians, and was accepted as king in Mercia before his eventual succession to Wessex. His candidature was not unopposed; a certain Alfred, whose relationship with the royal dynasty is not known, attempted to seize the crown, and it was not until 4 September 925 that Athelstan was crowned, at Kingston-upon-Thames, at the age of 30. He was and remained unmarried, and it is possible that Edwin, Ælfweard's full brother, was his official heir. He was drowned in 933, while en route to Frankia, and buried at Saint-Bertin's where he was remembered as a king. Perhaps some quarrel with his half-brother lies behind Edwin's flight to Frankia. With the children of Edward's third wife and widow, *Eadgifu, Athelstan seems to have been on better terms. The older son, *Edmund, fought at his side in the battle of *Brunanburh* in 937, and succeeded him in 939.

Athelstan was one of the greatest kings of the West Saxon dynasty, a fact obscured today by the greater fame of his grandfather, *Alfred. It was left to his successors to accomplish the final reconquest of the Danish kingdom of York, but it was Athelstan's campaigns which made this conquest possible. In 927, he expelled *Olafr Sigtryggson from York, a show of force which produced a mutual pact with *Constantine king of Scots and in the same year, the princes of Wales submitted to him. In 934 he launched a joint land and sea attack against the Scots; the land army ravaged as far as Dunottar, and the fleet sailed to Caithness. It was during this campaign that Athelstan presented lavish gifts to the Northumbrian churches, at Beverley, Ripon and above all Chester-le-Street, where he gave to St *Cuthbert the embroideries woven by Ælfflæd for the bishop of Winchester. In 937, Constantine retaliated in kind. In alliance with the Cumbrians and *Olafr Gothfrithson of Dublin, he launched a massive attack on northern England. The result was the battle of *Brunanburh*, the site of which is still a matter of dispute, celebrated in an heroic poem entered in the *Anglo-Saxon Chronicle*: there the royal brothers, Athelstan and Edmund, 'left behind them the dusky-coated one, the black raven with its horned beak, to share the corpses, and the duncoated, white-tailed eagle, the greedy war-hawk, and that grey beast, the wolf of the forest'. The victory at *Brunanburh* was hailed as the greatest feat of arms since the coming of the English to Britain.

Athelstan's standing among his contemporaries is shown by the marriages of his half-sisters. Ælfflæd's daughter, *Eadgifu, had married Charles the Simple, king of the Franks, before her father's death; indeed when Charles was deposed in 923, she fled to England with her son, Louis. In 926, Charles' rival Hugh the Great, despatched an embassy to Athelstan, headed by Adelolf of Boulogne, a grandson of King Alfred. The gifts borne by this embassy included the sword of Constantine the Great, the Holy Lance and numerous other distinguished relics and its purpose was to acquire an English princess for Hugh. He received as his wife Eadhild, sister of Eadgifu. In 928 another embassy arrived, this time from Henry the Fowler, duke of Saxony, who had established himself as king of Germany, seeking a West Saxon princess for his son, Otto. Athelstan sent two; Edith and Ælfgifu. Edith married Otto, the future Emperor, and Ælfgifu became the wife of Conrad of Burgundy. Thus both the dynasties who supplanted the Carolingian rulers of Frankia allied themselves with the rising star of Wessex.

Athelstan's relationship with the rulers of Europe has an importance beyond the merely political. The structure of the Old English state has many similarities with that of the Carolingian empire, and some deliberate borrowing of Carolingian expedients by Athelstan and his successors may be supposed. Athelstan himself was a legislator; five codes in his name have come down to us, as well as the agreement of the London 'peace-guild', which was established to put his commands into practice. Contact with Europe also fostered the monastic reform movement, which reached its height in the reign of his nephew, *Edgar. If Athelstan has not had the reputation which accrued to his grandfather, the fault lies with the surviving sources; Athelstan had no biographer, and the *Chronicle* for his reign is scanty. In his own day he was 'the roof-tree of the honour of the western world'. He died on 27 October 939, and was buried at Malmesbury.

BIBL. Wood 1981: 126-50; Stenton 1971: 339-56

Athelstan 'Half-King' ealdorman 932−56

Athelstan was the son of Æthelfrith, ealdorman of south-east Mercia in the time of Ealdorman *Æthelred and *Æthelflæd, Lady of the Mercians. In 932, he was appointed by his namesake, King *Athelstan, to an ealdordom which covered the newly-reconquered Danish settlements in eastern England, not only East Anglia itself (Norfolk and Suffolk) but also the east midlands and Essex; 'the whole of the eastern Danelaw from the Thames to the Welland, bounded on the south-east by Watling Street and on the north-west by the territory of the Five Boroughs'. The extent of his power earned Athelstan his nickname 'half-king', and explains the key role which he played in the politics of the tenth century. He was a close friend of *Dunstan and a champion of the monastic reform movement; he endowed both Dunstan's abbey of Glastonbury, and Abingdon, refounded by *Æthelwold. One of his brothers, Æthelwold, was ealdorman of eastern Wessex (Kent and Sussex), and another, Eadric, held central Wessex (Hampshire and Wiltshire). His wife, Ælfwynn, was a rich noble-woman from the east midlands, whose lands later formed the nucleus of the endowment of Ramsey Abbey. She was the foster-mother of the future king, *Edgar, who was reared in Athelstan's household with his youngest son, *Æthelwine. Athelstan was the premier ealdorman in the reigns of Athelstan, *Edmund and *Eadred. In 956, he retired from public life to become a monk at Glastonbury; his ealdordom passed first to his son *Æthelwold, and on his death, to the youngest son, *Æthelwine. Athelstan's family was the first of the great comital kindreds which dominated the political scene in the tenth and eleventh centuries and whose offices became, in fact if not in law, hereditary.

BIBL. Hart 1973

Athelstan Rota ealdorman 955—70

Athelstan Rota must be distinguished from his namesakes, *Athelstan Half-king of East Anglia, and the Athelstan who witnessed charters between 940 and 949, and probably preceded Athelstan Rota as ealdorman of south-east Mercia. Athelstan Rota was appointed by *Eadwig, to whose stepmother, *Æthelflæd of Damerham, he was married. His power was based on Oxford and Buckingham, and the territories appurtenant to them.

BIBL. Hart 1975: 299-300

Athelstan ætheling *d*. 1014

The will of Athelstan, eldest son of *Æthelred II, who died in 1014, gives a unique insight into the household of an English ætheling. Among the legatees are the members of his household; Ælfwine the chaplain, Ælfmær the seneschal, Ælfmær and Æthelwine the retainers (*cnihtas*), Ælfnoth the sword-polisher, and an unnamed staghuntsman. It is of some interest that the ætheling's bequests to his chaplain include a sword and a horse with its trappings. Athelstan also remembered three of the leading thegns of the Danelaw, *Sigeferth, his brother *Morcar and *Thurbrand the Hold; one remembers that the ætheling's mother, *Ælfgifu, was the daughter of Earl *Thored of Northumbria. Another legatee is Godwine son of Wulfnoth, who may be identical with *Godwine, Earl of Wessex. As one would expect of a layman of such standing, the will mentions several weapons and items of military equipment; several swords, including one that had belonged to King *Offa, a blade (a sword without the hilts), a shield and a silver-coated trumpet. The ætheling's lands lay in Oxfordshire, Buckinghamshire, Cambridgeshire, Derbyshire, Bedfordshire, Hertfordshire, Hampshire, Wiltshire, and Kent.

BIBL. Sawyer 1968, no. 1503; Whitelock 1955, no. 130: 549-50

Aud the Deep-Minded Norse queen *c*. 855—65

Aud the Deep-Minded (*djúpaudga*) was the daughter of *Ketil Flatnose, Viking ruler of the Hebrides in the middle of the ninth century. She was the queen of Olaf the White, Norse king of Dublin (853—71) and after Olaf divorced her, she returned to her father's household in the Hebrides. Aud bore a son to Olaf, *Thorstein the Red, who established himself as king in northern Scotland. When news of Thorstein's death reached her, she was in Caithness, and fitting out a ship she sailed off with her entire household of slaves, relatives and friends to find a new life in Iceland. Icelandic sources remembered Aud as the founding matriarch of a great family in Laxárdal in western Iceland. Numerous Icelandic sources vouch for Aud's Christian beliefs which were subsequently lost by her immediate descendants. According to the *Longer Olafs Saga* it was Aud's wish to be buried in the sand on the coast of Iceland, with her grave washed by the tide, as she did not wish to lie buried in unconsecrated ground. Such traditions show that Aud's family in the Hebrides belonged to the *Gall-Gaedhil* or mixed Hiberno-Norse cultural milieu.

BIBL. Smyth 1977a: 101-2, 118-25; Smyth 1984: 156, 160-4

Audrey St see **Æthelthryth**

Augustine St, archbishop of Canterbury 597−604/10

Virtually all that is known of St Augustine 'the Less' (so-called to distinguish him from his illustrious namesake, St Augustine of Hippo) comes from *Bede's *Ecclesiastical History*. He was an Italian and a monk of *Gregory the Great's monastery on the Cælian Hill at Rome. It was Augustine whom Gregory chose to lead the mission to the English nation in 596. Armed with letters of introduction to the rulers, lay and ecclesiastical, of Frankish Gaul, they travelled northwards, acquiring Frankish interpreters, and eventually landed in Kent, on the island of Thanet, in 597. Their success was in part due to the Frankish connections of King *Æthelberht of Kent, whose wife, *Bertha, was a Merovingian princess. Æthelberht provided them with accommodation in Canterbury, where the church of St Martin was apparently still functional, and Augustine acquired the site of a former church for the construction of Christchurch, which became his archiepiscopal see. He also found the monastery outside the walls, originally dedicated to SS Peter and Paul, which later became known as St Augustine's. The conversion of the king was the key to the mission's success. Æthelberht was at that time Bretwalda, with overlordship over all the southern English, and it was this which enabled the missionaries to extend their activities outside Kent, particularly into Essex, whose king, *Sæberht, was Æthelberht's nephew. Soon reinforcements had to be sent from Rome; the second party included *Mellitus, *Laurence, *Justus, *Paulinus and Rufianus. In 604, Justus was consecrated bishop of Rochester, and Mellitus bishop of the East Saxons, with his see at London, where a church dedicated to St Paul was built by Æthelberht. London indeed was intended by Gregory to be the archiepiscopal see, but the close connection of Augustine with the king of Kent precluded this and Canterbury took the palm. Before his death, which occurred by 610 at the latest, Augustine consecrated Laurence as his successor.

With the surviving British church, Augustine had no success. A conference at 'Augustine's Oak' on the borders of Somerset and Gloucestershire foundered on the mutual misunderstanding of the Roman and British clergy. Augustine's sense of the dignity of episcopal office (he did not rise to greet the British envoys) ran counter to the ideas of the British churchmen, and the conference broke up with mutual recriminations. The Roman mission after the death of Augustine was less successful. The conversion of East Anglia was begun, but *Rædwald, Æthelberht's successor as Bretwalda, was less amenable to influence. Paulinus had more success in Northumbria, where King *Edwin accepted baptism in 627, but this effort foundered when Edwin was killed in 633. Nevertheless the Roman mission must not be dismissed. The shape of the future church in England was determined by the primacy of Canterbury, and by the acceptance of a direct papal initiative in English affairs.

BIBL. Brooks 1984: 3-14

Aurelius Caninus British king *fl.* early sixth century

One of the British rulers denounced for immorality and murder and accused of starting a civil war by *Gildas who punned his name, 'hound-like', by calling him 'little dog' (or 'puppy'); it is not known of which territory he was king.

BIBL. Jackson 1982: 31

B

Baithene son of Brenainn (Brendan), abbot of Iona 597–600

Baithene (also called Conín) was the second abbot of Iona and the immediate successor of its founder, *Columba. Baithene was Columba's fosterson and first cousin who sailed with Columba from Ireland in 563 and served under him in the monastic life in Scotland. *Adomnán, who mentions Baithene several times in his *Life of Columba*, implies that Columba had chosen him as his successor before he died. Baithene was put in charge of a community of penitents on Hinba while he also served as *praepositus* or prior of a monastic community founded by Columba at Mag Luinge on Tiree in the Inner Hebrides. On another occasion, perhaps early on in his career in Scotland, Adomnán shows us Baithene in the role of proof-reader of psalters in the scriptorium, and yet again as foreman or 'controller of works' supervising the monks at harvest time during Columba's abbacy on Iona. A late *Life* of Baithene survives which is of little use to the historian but it does claim that Baithene died on the same day as Columba (9 June), and it confirms Adomnán's picture of him as a man who divided his time between the scriptorium and the harvest field. Baithene's name appears at the head of the seventh-century list of 12 companions who sailed with Columba from Ireland to northern Britain in 563.

BIBL. Anderson and Anderson 1961: 90, and text; Reeves 1857: 372

Bald physician *fl.* second half of ninth century/first half of tenth century

The *Leechbook* of Bald, 'which he ordered Cild to compile (or, transcribe)', has been described as 'the oldest English medical work to survive in anything like complete form, and... also the oldest to survive in a European language other than Greek or Latin'. The manuscript dates from the mid-tenth century, and the work itself is probably 50 or so years earlier; it may have been compiled in the reign of *Alfred, since it refers to the remedies sent to that king by Elias, patriarch of Jerusalem (*c.* 879–99). It was obviously intended for the use of a practising physician (or leech), presumably Bald himself. The book is arranged in two sections, the first dealing with external disorders and their treatment, the second with internal ailments, and draws upon standard medical texts of the classical period and earlier, now lost, English works. Cild was presumably a scribe.

BIBL. Wright 1955; Cameron 1983; Cameron 1988

Balthild (Bathild, Baldhild) St, queen *d.* 680

Balthild was an English slave, who is first heard of in the household of Erchinoald, mayor of the palace of Neustria. In or about 648, she married King Clovis II and bore him three sons, Clothar III, Theuderic III and Childeric II. When Clovis died in 657, she became regent for her son, Clothar. She was forced out of power in 664 and entered the mon-

55

astery of Chelles, which she herself had founded, with nuns brought from Jouarre. She also founded Corbie. Her *Vita* was composed, soon after her death, by a nun of Chelles.

BIBL. Farmer 1978: 32; Nelson 1978

Bede St, monk and historian *d.* 735

All that we know of the life of Bede, the father of English history and the most eminent scholar of his age, is derived from his own works, notably the *Historia Ecclesiastica gentis Anglorum*, completed in 731. He was born near Jarrow, about 673; both Sunderland and Monkton claim the honour of being his birthplace. In 680, he was given as a child oblate to *Benedict Biscop, founder and first abbot of Monkwearmouth, and it was there that he spent the first year of his vocation. When Monkwearmouth's sister-house at Jarrow was founded in 681, Bede was sent there in the care of *Ceolfrith. The anonymous *Life of Ceolfrith* relates how, when the plague visited Jarrow, all the monks were struck down except the abbot himself, and a small boy, who between them sang the office daily, despite all the difficulties involved. This child must have been Bede himself, for he spent the the rest of his life at Jarrow, apart from a few brief excursions. One of these was to Lindisfarne, whose community commissioned him to write the life of St *Cuthbert, and another to York, where his friend and pupil *Ecgberht was bishop. He lived the life of a scholar-monk, whose delight was 'to learn, or teach, or write'. One of his pupils, *Cuthbert, a later abbot of Monkwearmouth and Jarrow, has left an account of his death, which occurred on the eve of Ascension Day (25 May) 735. Bede was engaged in translating the gospel of St John into English, and was dictating to a pupil, Wilbert:

'Then the boy...said once again: "There is one sentence, dear master, that we have not written down". And he said: "Write it". After a little, the boy said: "There! It is finished". And he replied: "Good! It is finished: you have spoken the truth. Hold my head in your hands, for it is a great delight to me to sit over against my holy place in which I used to pray, that as I sit here I may call upon my Father". And so upon the floor of his cell, singing, "Glory be to the Father and to the Son and to the Holy Ghost", and the rest, he breathed his last'.

After the *Ecclesiastical History* itself, Bede's best-known works are the *Lives of the abbots*, a history of his own monastery, and the two lives of St Cuthbert, one in prose and one in verse. Bede himself would probably have regarded his numerous works of biblical exegesis as more important. His two works on the reckoning of time, *De Temporibus* and *De temporum ratione* had considerable influence in the Middle Ages. They are largely concerned with the computus, the reckoning of ecclesiastical time, and in particular, the establishment of the correct dates for Easter. The *Letter to Ecgberht*, composed in 734, is also important. In this work Bede delivers a fierce critique of the contemporary Northumbrian church and its failings. Today it is as the author of the *Ecclesiastical History* that he is remembered. Had this work never been written, we should know little of the seventh century in England, which we see mainly through Bede's eyes. Bede was a true historian, who knew how to collate and analyse his sources, and took great care to quote his authorities. His book is composed in clear and elegant Latin which would not disgrace the classical stylists and is still capable of inspiring its readers with a love of history and a desire to practise it. It was widely read in the Middle Ages; five eighth-century copies are extant, and it was one of the works 'most useful for men to know' which King *Alfred ordered to be translated into English.

Bede was buried at his beloved Jarrow, which was destroyed in the later Viking raids. In the eleventh century, his remains were translated to Durham by Alfred Westou, and lie now in the Galilee Chapel of the present cathedral. The tomb is now adorned by an epitaph drawn from Bede's own writings, a fitting memorial to the man described by St *Boniface as 'the candle of the Church, lit by the holy Spirit':

'Christ is the morning star, who, when the night of this world is past, brings to his saints the promise of the light of life, and opens everlasting day'.

BIBL. Colgrave and Mynors 1969; Farmer 1983

Benedict Biscop St, abbot 674−89

Benedict Biscop was born into a Northumbrian noble family, the Baducings, about 628. Since he was given the name Biscop (bishop), his parents must have been Christians, and given the assumed date, the bishop for whom he was named must have been *Paulinus. Like most high-born youths, he entered the household of King *Oswiu, and served in his hearthtroop, but at the age of 25, when he had completed his warrior training and was entitled to receive from his lord land sufficient for him to marry and establish his own household, he left secular life for religion. Thus, as *Bede puts it, he abandoned 'earthly warfare with its corruptible rewards so that he might fight for the true king and win his crown in the heavenly city'. He made the pilgrimage to Rome (the first of many visits) and returned full of enthusiasm for the customs of the Roman church. On his return to Northumbria, he gained the support of king *Alhfrith of Deira, Oswiu's son, whose wish to visit Rome in Benedict's company was prevented by his father. In c. 666, Benedict set out for Rome once more. He spent two years at Lerins, where he became a monk. When he returned to the papal court in 668, he met with the archbishop-elect, Wigheard, who had come to be consecrated. Wigheard, however, died at the papal court, and Pope Vitalian therefore chose *Theodore as his successor, with *Hadrian as his assistant. Benedict was charged with conducting the new archbishop back to England. Theodore and Benedict reached England in 669, though Hadrian was delayed, and until his arrival, Benedict was made abbot of St Augustine's, Canterbury. In about 671, he returned once again to Rome, coming back with 'a large number of books on all branches of sacred knowledge'. By this time *Ecgfrith, Oswiu's son, was ruling Northumbria, and it was he who gave Benedict 70 hides at Monkwearmouth, where Benedict established his monastery, in 674. He brought masons from Frankish Gaul to build 'a stone church in the Roman style', the porch of which can still be seen in the fabric of the present building. Frankish glaziers were also imported, who not only made the windows, but also trained English craftsmen in the art. In 679–80, he made his fourth pilgrimage, returning not only with books and relics, but with the archcantor of St Peter's, John, abbot of St Martin's, to teach his monks the Roman liturgy. In 681, Ecgfrith gave him another 40 hides on the Tyne, and here Benedict founded the monastery of Jarrow, staffed with 17 monks (including the young *Bede) under the priest *Ceolfrith, who was appointed abbot. The chancel of Benedict's church at Jarrow still stands, and some of the seventh-century coloured glass, found in the recent excavations, has been replaced in its windows. It was Benedict's intention that the two houses should form one community; thus Monkwearmouth was dedicated to St Peter and Jarrow to St Paul, and his cousin Eosterwine was made abbot of Monkwearmouth. Benedict then made his fifth visit to Rome, in 684. It was at this point that plague struck both houses, and on his return, in 685, Benedict found Eosterwine, and many of the brethren, dead. He therefore appointed the deacon, Sigfrid, abbot of Monkwearmouth. Soon afterwards, he himself fell ill, with a 'creeping paralysis', from which he suffered for three years. Sigfrid also was dying, and at last, Benedict appointed Ceolfrith of Jarrow as abbot of Monkwearmouth as well. On his death-bed, his main concern was that his successor should be chosen by the brethren from among their own number, and not, as happened so often elsewhere, appointed by his own kindred. According to Bede, he declared that he 'would far rather have this whole place...revert for ever, should God so decide, to the wilderness it once was' than that his brother, who was a layman, succeed him as abbot. He died on 12 January 689 and was succeeded by Ceolfrith.

It would be difficult to exaggerate the importance of Benedict's life, and the influence of his double-foundation at Monkwearmouth/Jarrow. It was a centre of Roman influence in the north, as Lindisfarne was of Irish custom. The rule was Benedictine in form; Bede says that Benedict drew upon his experience of 17 continental monasteries in devising it. The architecture and the contents, pictures, icons, altar vessels and furnishing, were all derived from continental models, though not untouched by English taste. It was Benedict who laid the foundations of the library of which Bede himself made such good use; one of his latest concerns was that these books, 'so necessary for improving the standard of education in this church', should be preserved together and intact. Bede said of him that 'he refused to bring forth children of the flesh, being predestined by Christ to raise up for Him sons nurtured in spiritual doctrine who would live forever in the world to come'.

BIBL. Farmer 1983; Fletcher 1981

Beorhtfrith ealdorman d. after 711

Beorhtfrith, a Northumbrian ealdorman apparently associated with Bamburgh, was described by *Eddius Stephanus as 'second in rank only to the king'. After the death of King *Aldfrith in 705, he took the part of the king's young son, *Osred, against *Eadwulf. The young man's supporters were besieged in Bamburgh, but were miraculously relieved when they swore to restore St *Wilfrid to his property. At the Synod of the River Nidd in 706, Beorhtfrith testified in Wilfrid's favour. He is next heard of fighting against the Picts in 711, and thereafter disappears from the historical record. He was probably a kinsman (perhaps the son) of Ealdorman Beorht, or Beorhtred, whom King *Ecgfrith sent to ravage Ireland in 684 and Beorht, who was killed fighting the Picts in 698, was the son of Beornhæth, the *subregulus* (underking) who, with Ecgfrith, routed a Pictish army in the early 670s. The titles applied to these men (*subregulus, dux regius*) suggests that they belonged to the highest stratum of Northumbrian society; it has been suggested that, like the men described in later sources as *patricii* (patricians), they were court dignitaries, resembling the Frankish mayors of the palace.

BIBL. Thacker 1981

Beorhtric king of Wessex 786—802

Beorhtric, who claimed descent from *Cerdic, succeeded *Cynewulf as king of the West Saxons in 786. He had the support of *Offa of Mercia, whose daughter *Eadburh he married, against *Ecgberht, who fled into exile in Frankia. It was in Beorhtric's time that the first Viking raid on Wessex occurred; three ships' crews landed at Portland, Dorset, and killed Beaduheard, the reeve of Dorchester, who had ridden out to meet them under the impression that they were peaceful traders.

BIBL. *ASC* s.a. 789

Beorhtwald archbishop of Canterbury 692—731

After the death of *Theodore, the archbishopric of Canterbury was vacant for two years until the election of Beorhtwald on 1 July 692. A Kentishman and former abbot of Reculver, he was consecrated in Frankia by Godin, bishop of Lyons, and received from Pope Sergius not only the pallium but also two papal letters of privilege; an unusual step, probably taken because not all the English kings were favourable to him. The main problem was the position of St *Wilfrid, who in 690 had fallen out with *Aldfrith of Northumbria, and was in exile in Mercia. A synod at Austerfield in 702, under Beorhtwald's presidency, attempted to resolve the conflict but was unsuccessful, and it was only after Aldfrith's death that the matter was resolved. Beorhtwald continued his predecessor's policy of dividing the huge dioceses into more manageable units. In 706, on the death of *Hædde of Wessex, his see was split in two, Daniel succeeding to Winchester, and *Aldhelm to Sherborne. About the same time, Selsey became a bishopric for the South Saxons, under Eadberht, its abbot. The division of the West Saxon diocese led to a dispute between Beorhtwald and King *Ine, and the temporary breaking-off of relations, but the matter was swiftly resolved. Beorhtwald seems to have been an energetic and successful archbishop.

BIBL. Brooks 1984: 76-80

Beorhtwulf king of Mercia, 840—52

Beorhtwulf succeeded Wigmund, son of *Wiglaf, as king of the Mercians in 840. It is not certain whether or not he was connected with the Mercian royal kindred; he may have been a descendant of *Beornred, who was deposed by *Offa in 757, or of *Beornwulf who ruled from 823—5. His son Beorhtfrith attempted to marry Wigmund's widow, *Ælfflæd, daughter of *Ceolwulf I, but the plan was frustrated by Ælfflæd's son, St *Wigstan, whom Beorhtfrith murdered in pique. In 852, Beorhtwulf was succeeded by *Burgred, who was perhaps a kinsman.

BIBL. Hart 1977

Beornwulf king of Mercia 823–6

Beornwulf succeeded the deposed *Ceolwulf I as king of the Mercians in 823. In 825, he was defeated by *Ecgberht of Wessex at the battle of *Ellendun* (Wroughton), in which the Mercian supremacy came to an end. Early in the next year Beornwulf was killed attempting to stem a revolt in East Anglia. One of his ealdormen, Ludeca, became king, but was killed, also in East Anglia, in 827, with five Mercian ealdormen. Beornwulf's antecedents are unknown. He may be identical with the ealdorman of the same name who witnessed charters of *Cœnwulf in 812 and Ceolwulf in 823, in a low position which suggested to Stenton that he had been 'one of the less distinguished ealdormen of the Mercian kingdom'. On the other hand, he may have been a descendant of the Beornred who ruled Mercia in 757. It has also been suggested that the later kings, *Beorhtwulf and *Burgred, belonged to Beornwulf's kindred.

BIBL. Stenton 1971: 231; Hart 1977

Beowulf *fl.* sixth century

The Old English epic poem known as *Beowulf*, after the name of its hero, survives only in a single manuscript, written in Standard Old English about 1000. It is almost certainly much older than this, though no date can be established with certainty. The story is set in Scandinavia, in the fifth and sixth centuries, among the Geats (of Gotarike in South Sweden) and the Danes. Beowulf, a nobleman in the service of Hygelac, king of the Geats, travelled to the court of Hrothgar, king of the Danes, who was having trouble with the monster, Grendel, which was infesting his great hall, called Heorot. Beowulf killed the monster, but its even more dangerous mother returned to the hall, seeking vengeance. Beowulf followed Grendel's mother to her lair, beneath the waters of an icy lake, in the midst of the wilderness, and slew her with a magic sword. He returned, laden with treasure to the land of the Geats, where he received from his king 7000 hides of land and princely authority over the region. Eventually he became king of the Geats, but in his old age, a dragon was disturbed in its mound by the theft of a cup. Beowulf and his hearthtroop set out to destroy it, but when it came to the point, all the warriors fled, except the young Wiglaf. Together Beowulf and Wiglaf slew the dragon, but Beowulf was mortally wounded. The poem ends with his burial in the mound at Hrossness. This account of the plot does not do justice, either to the literary merits of the poem, or to its invaluable insight into the ethos of the warrior-aristocracy for whom it was written.

BIBL. Klaeber 1951; Alexander 1973; Wormald 1978

Berchán Scottish bishop, poet and prophet *c*. 770

According to the Book of Leinster, Berchán son of Muiredach was the great-grandson of *Ainbcellach, a Scots king of Cenél Loairn who seized the Dál Riata kingship in 697−8 and who died in 719. Berchán became a cleric and settled in Ireland at Clonsast (Cluain Sosta), Co. Offaly, where he founded a monastery. He was remembered in Gaelic tradition as a prophetic writer and he is best known as the apocryphal author of the *Prophecy of Berchán* — a twelfth-century Middle Irish poem of some 204 stanzas alleging to predict the quality and length of reigns of Scottish and Irish kings, beginning with the time of *Columba and *Áedán mac Gabhráin, and ending with Donald Bán (1093−7) son of *Duncan I. Although the prophecies in the Scottish section are attributed to a fifth-century author, it seems clear that Berchán of Clonsast was the person to whom the poem was originally attributed. Berchán is supposed to have uttered the first half of the work in *c*. 718 and to have died *c*. 778 which is not impossible if he were the great-grandson of Ainbcellach of Dál Riata. Although the earliest manuscript of the *Prophecy* dates to the eighteenth century, fragments of the work are preserved in the Book of Leinster, *c*. 1170, and the poem is seen as an eleventh-century compilation. Berchán's festival was kept on 4 August. His name may be commemorated in the Scottish placename of *Kilbarchan* in Renfrew, while *St Braghan's Well* survived at Clonsast into modern times. Berchán's nickname of *Fer-dá-leithe* ('Man of Two Portions') was explained in medieval tradition as referring to his two careers — one in Ireland and the other in his Scottish homeland.

BIBL. Anderson 1922, i: xxxiv-vi; O'Curry 1861: 412-18

Bertha queen *d*. after 601

Bertha was the daughter of Charibert, king of Paris, and his first wife, Ingoberg (*d*. 589). She was born after 561 (when Charibert and Ingoberg were married) and married *Æthelberht, king of Kent, perhaps in the late 570s. The marriage-agreement stipulated that Bertha, a Christian, should be allowed to practise her faith, and bring with her her chaplain, *Liudhard. Æthelberht gave his queen the church of St Martin, just outside the walls of Canterbury, for her use. It is quite possible that some kind of Christian community still survived in Kent, under the rule of the still-pagan English. The marriage of Æthelberht and Bertha is one of many indications of the close relationship between Kent and Frankia in this period; the Merovingian kings of Frankia seem to have claimed some sort of hegemony over south-east England. It was to Kent, with its Christian queen, that Pope *Gregory the Great despatched the mission of St *Augustine in 596, and he sent letters to Bertha, as well as to her husband, urging her to assist the evangelization of the English. The last such letter is dated 601. She must have died soon afterwards, for Æthelberht took another wife; the step-mother whom King *Eadbald married to the scandal of his churchmen.

BIBL. Brooks 1984: 6; Mayr-Harting 1972: 253-6

Bertha (Bertana) abbess 675—81

Bertha was the first abbess of Bath, a double-monastery for men and women founded by *Osric, king of the Hwicce, in 675. She was dead by 681, when her successor, Beorngyth, appears. Both Bertha, and Folcburg, her successor's prioress, have Frankish names. Bath lay in the land of the Hwicce in the seventh century, but on the borders of Wessex, a kingdom with strong Frankish connections (see *Agilbert, *Leuthere) and may have been influenced from this quarter.

BIBL. Sims-Williams 1975: 1-10

Beuno St, abbot *fl.* first half of the seventh century

The cult of St Beuno, traditionally an abbot, was widespread in both Powys, Beuno's reputed homeland, and Gwynedd, with a principal focus at Clynnog Fawr in Gwynedd and others at Berriew and Meifod in Powys. The fourteenth-century *Life* of Beuno, although probably based on an older composition, is of no historical value but it places Beuno in the first half of the seventh century. He is commemorated in the early ninth-century Irish *Martyrology of Tallaght* (under 21 April).

BIBL. Bowen 1954: 81ff.; Miller 1979b: 79ff.; Henken 1987: 74-88

Birinus (Birin, Berin) St, bishop *d.* 650

The origins of St Birinus, 'apostle' and first bishop of the West Saxons, are unknown. He was sent to England by Pope Honorius I (625—38) and consecrated in Genoa by Archbishop Asterius. His name suggests that he was Frankish, and it was a Frank, *Agilbert, who succeeded him as bishop of the West Saxons. His see was at Dorchester-on-Thames. A nearby village, Berinsfield, preserves his name.

BIBL. Farmer 1978: 43; *HE* iii, 7

Bjor son of Arnsteinn *d. c.* 1016

A commemorative runestone at Galteland, in south Norway, was erected by Arnsteinn for his son Bjor, who died as a member of *Cnut's army in England; probably during the final campaigns of the Danish conquest in 1015—16. Bjor's presence shows that Norwegians as well as Danes and Swedes were in Cnut's employ.

BIBL. Lund 1986: 118

Blathmac monk of Iona 825

The violent death or martyrdom of Blathmac mac Flainn at the hands of Viking 'gentiles' is recorded in the *Annals of Ulster* at 825. Walafrid Strabo, abbot of Reichenau (838—49), wrote a Latin poem in hexameters on the martyrdom of Blathmac, in which it is implied that this monk exercised the authority of an abbot over a token community which remained on Iona after the main body of monks retreated to Kells under the abbacy of *Cellach in 814. It is clear from Walafrid's account that Blathmac had belonged to a royal dynasty in Ireland (most likely the Northern Uí Néill) and that he may have begun his career as a warrior. He deliberately chose to live on Iona knowing that he could be slain by Viking raiders, and he seems to have been an ordained priest at this time. Blathmac refused to reveal the whereabouts of the shrine of Columba to the Vikings and was 'torn limb from limb' by his tormentors. His festival was kept in Ireland on 24 July and on the continent on 19 January.

BIBL. Anderson 1922, i: 263-5; Reeves 1857: 388-9; Smyth 1984: 147-8

Boniface St, *see* **Curetan** bishop of Rosemarkie

Boniface St, archbishop of Mainz *d*. 754

The 'apostle of Germany', Boniface, was born about 675, perhaps at Crediton, certainly in Wessex and given the name Wynfrith; he adopted 'Boniface' when he entered religion. He was given as a child to the monastery at Exeter but soon moved to Nursling, where he grew to manhood. He conceived the desire to work as a missionary in Frisia, following in the footsteps of St *Wilfrid and St *Willibrord, but his first visit there coincided with an outbreak of hostilities between Radbod, king of the Frisians, and the Frankish ruler, Charles Martel, mayor of the palace. In 718, he went to Rome, and received a commission to preach from Pope Gregory II. He spent some years in Frisia, working with Willibrord. In 722, he returned to Rome to be ordained bishop, and began his mission in Hesse and Thuringia with the felling of the sacred oak at Geismar. As his mission proceeded, a series of monasteries were founded, staffed largely by monks and nuns from England. By 732, Boniface's work had progressed enough for him to be raised to archbishop. In 735 he went to Bavaria, to organize the church in that region; in 739 bishoprics were established at Salzburg, Freising, Regensburg and Passau. In 741 or 742, the sees of Wurzburg, Buraburg and Erfurt followed, but only Wurzburg survived; the two others were incorporated into Boniface's own see at Mainz. It was in 741 that Charles Martel died, leaving his two sons, Carloman and Pepin III, as rulers of Frankia. Carloman was deeply involved in the reforming ideals of the time, and a series of synods was held with the purpose of reorganizing the Frankish church. Boniface wished to establish a hierarchical structure of archbishoprics and bishoprics on the lines already laid down in England, but the Frankish bishops were unwilling to countenance this. Carloman, his main supporter, retired to Rome and the monastic life in 747, and left Pepin as sole ruler. In 750, with papal approval, the last Merovingian king, Childeric III, was deposed, and Pepin became the first Carolingian monarch of Frankia; it was possibly Boniface who consecrated him king in 751. This was almost Boniface's last public act. In 753 he resigned his see of Mainz to his friend and supporter, *Lul, and returned to the mission-field in Frisia. On 5 June 754, he and his companions were attacked and killed. Though the murders seem to have been the work of brigands rather than pagans, Boniface was regarded as a martyr. Within a few years his *Life* had been written by his disciple Willibald. His cult centred on the great monastery of Fulda, where he was buried. The extensive correspondence of Boniface is one of our chief sources for the history of England, and indeed of Frankia, in the eighth century.

BIBL. Talbot 1954; Reuter 1980; Levison 1946

Botulf (Botolph) St, abbot *d*. 680

Botulf, who was presumably an East Anglian, is said to have studied in Frankia, possibly at Chelles, a house much frequented by English men and women. In 654, he established his own monastery at *Icanho*, whose actual site is still problematic; both Boston, which preserves Botulf's name (*Botulfes stan*) and Iken, Suffolk, have been proposed. It was an important house in its day. *Ceolfrith, later abbot of Monkwearmouth and Jarrow, went there in 669, to study the monastic customs, and the house had some part in the foundation of Much Wenlock, Shropshire, established by St *Mildburh. *Icanho* was completely destroyed during the Viking conquest and settlement of East Anglia.

BIBL. Whitelock 1972

Bresal abbot of Iona 772—801

Bresal son of Ségéne succeeded *Suibhne as seventeenth abbot in succession to *Columba. During Bresal's abbacy, the prestige of Iona as a holy place for the Irish reached new heights with the retirement of two Irish kings to that monastery before they died. The first was the highking, Niall Frossach, who died on Iona in 778, and the second was Artgal king of Connacht, who died on Iona in 791 having spent eight years there in retirement. Bresal's rule over Iona witnessed the most devastating event in the history of the monastery — the outbreak of Viking barbarity which began with 'the devastation of all the islands of Britain' in 794. Iona was sacked in the following year. Bresal is said in the *Annals of Ulster* to have held the *principatus* of Iona for 31 years when he died in 801. He may therefore have acted as co-adjutor during the last two years of Suibhne's rule. If we can equate this abbot with a cleric of the same name from Durrow, then his festival was kept in the calendar at 18 May. He was succeeded by *Connachtach.

BIBL. Anderson and Anderson 1961: 100; Reeves 1857: 386-8

Brihtheah bishop 1033—9

Brihtheah, son of an anonymous Berkshire thegn and Wulfgifu, sister of Archbishop *Wulfstan, became abbot of Pershore in the 1020s. In 1033 he was raised to the bishopric of Worcester by *Cnut. His office was a boon to his family, several of whom were enriched out of the bishopric's estates. They included his half-brother, Æthelric, son of Wulfgifu by a (second) marriage to the Worcestershire thegn, Wulfric; Æthelric's son, Godric; an unnamed sister and her husband; and another kinsman, Azur, who was also Brihtheah's chamberlain. It was Brihtheah who escorted Cnut's daughter *Gunnhildr to Germany for her marriage to the future Emperor, Henry III, son of Conrad II.

BIBL. Cooper 1970: 2-3; Williams 1988: 24-6

Brihtric thegn *d.* after 1009

Brihtric was one of the many brothers of *Eadric Streona, ealdorman of Mercia (1007–17). In 1009, when the great fleet mustered at Sandwich to oppose the invading Danes, Brihtric accused the South Saxon thegn, Wulfnoth, of treason. Wulfnoth persuaded 20 ships' crews to join him, and began to ravage the south coast. Brihtric pursued him with 80 ships, 'intending to make a reputation for himself'. He did; but not the one he wanted. His fleet was caught in a great storm and wrecked, except for a small remnant which was burnt by Wulfnoth. The ship-levy dispersed in disorder, which was particularly unfortunate, since at the same moment, *Thorkell the Tall arrived with his 'great raiding-army'. Brihtric's eventual fate is unknown. One of the brothers of Eadric Streona was murdered in Kent, and it is said that when Eadric demanded the due vengeance from his lord, *Æthelred II, the king replied that the man had got his just desserts. Unfortunately the brother is unnamed, and since several others are recorded, we cannot know if it was Brihtric.

BIBL. *ASC* s.a. 1009; Wharton 1691, ii: 132

Bruide mac Bili king of Pictish Fortriu *c.* 672–93

Bruide succeeded to the Pictish overlordship after the expulsion of *Drest in 672. The Northumbrian king, *Oswiu, had died in 670 after a long reign during which he had forced the Picts into submission and forced them to accept kings such as *Talorgen son of Enfret and later Drest, as puppets of his own appointing. The expulsion of Drest is seen as a Pictish reaction to the tyranny of Oswiu, and Bruide is consequently seen as a king chosen or accepted by the Picts to lead the opposition to Northumbrian influence. Those who accept this interpretation also see Bruide as the invader of Northumbria in 672 — an invasion described by *Eddius Stephanus in his *Life of Wilfrid* — when a Pictish army was massacred by the Northumbrians.

Bruide is called, in a very early poem attributed to *Adomnán, 'the son of the king of Dumbarton', identifying him as the son of the Strathclyde king, Bili son of Neithon. His rule over Fortriu and southern Pictland is often explained by the phenomenon of matrilinear succession believed to have been practised by the Picts. Genealogies attached to the *Historia Brittonum* refer to Bruide as the cousin of *Ecgfrith of Northumbria, a relationship which is taken to mean that Bruide and Ecgfrith were related through the Pictish mother of Talorgen son of Enfret. But Bruide, as the son of a Strathclyde king, might just as easily have been related to the Northumbrian royal house through his father's family. Bruide's brother, *Owen (Eugein) map Bili, had ruled as king of Strathclyde, and through his great victory over the Scots in 642 had made the Strathclyde Britons the strongest force in what is now Scotland. This paved the way for Bruide's taking of the Pictish kingship in 672. Irish annals record a series of sieges in the period 680–3 which have been ascribed by Skene and other historians to Bruide's energetic rule. He may well have led the attack on Dunnottar in 681 in a campaign to conquer the Pictish kingdom of Círchenn. In 682 Bruide is specifically named as the leader who

65

'destroyed' the Orkneys, clearly establishing his overlordship of those islands in the tradition of his predecessor *Bruide mac Maelchon, a century before. Bruide's most memorable achievement was the defeat of the Northumbrian army led by Ecgfrith at Dunnichen Moss or *Nechtanesmere*, south of Forfar in Angus, in 685. Ecgfrith lost his life in this battle and his warriors were massacred. Bruide drove the English invaders south and re-established the Pictish hold over Stirlingshire and West Lothian. The Northumbrians were henceforth confined to territory south of the Forth. An Irish poem refers to Bruide as fighting at Dunnichen Moss 'for the heritage of his grandfather' which could suggest that Bruide's grandfather, *Neithon of Strathclyde, had previously claimed the kingship of Fortriu and so was the same ruler as the otherwise Pictish king, *Nectu grandson of Verb, who died c. 621. Bruide son of Bili died in 693. He was one of the greatest of Pictish overlords and one of the strongest rulers in late seventh-century Britain. He was a contemporary and perhaps a close friend of *Adomnán, abbot of Iona, who may be the author of an elegy in Old Irish which survives on Bruide. Bruide is the earliest king to be styled 'king of Fortriu' in the *Annals of Ulster*. That title may refer both to the Pictish kingdom centred on Strathearn and to the overlordship of the Picts in general.

BIBL. Anderson and Anderson 1961: 96-7; Anderson 1973: 170-5; Duncan 1975: 53-4; Smyth 1984: 62-7, 135-6

Bruide mac Maelchon Pictish king c. 556–84

Bruide is the earliest historical Pictish king. He was a contemporary of *Áedán mac Gabhráin and of *Columba. Bruide is described by *Bede as 'a most powerful king' who ruled over the Picts and who granted the island of Iona to Columba. Bede may have obtained this information from his superior, *Ceolfrith, abbot of Monkwearmouth and Jarrow, who had contact with Pictish envoys in the early eighth century. On the other hand, a much earlier and therefore more reliable Dál Riata tradition, preserved in the *Annals of Ulster* held that Iona was given to Columba by *Conall son of Comgall, king of Dál Riata. *Adomnán mentions Bruide mac Maelchon several times in his *Life of Columba* and shows Columba visiting the court of the Pictish king. In spite of several miracles which Columba is said to have wrought in the presence of Bruide, Adomnán does not say that Bruide accepted Christianity and we may assume that the Pictish kingdoms remained largely pagan for a century after Columba's time. It is clear from Adomnán that Bruide's kingdom was centred on the Moray Firth and that Columba travelled to the king's fortress from Iona via the Firth of Lorn, the Great Glen and Loch Ness. Bruide most probably ruled from the hill-fort at Craig Phádraig near where the River Ness flows into the Moray Firth. Bruide exercised an overlordship over the king of Orkney, and Columba along with other Christian ascetics negotiated with Bruide for the safe conduct of monks travelling through those northern isles. Relations between Bruide and the Scots kingdom of Áedán mac Gabhráin cannot always have been good. Áedán led an expedition against Orkney in 580, while in 558 the *Annals of Ulster* record 'a flight before the son of Máelchu [ie Bruide]' in the same year as Gabhrán, the father of Áedán mac Gabhráin, died. Bruide was again actively campaigning in *c*. 561 although the circumstances of that expedition are unknown. His death is recorded in the *Annals of Ulster* at 584.

BIBL. Anderson and Anderson 1961: 43-6, 81-6 and text; Anderson 1973: 89-92, 130; Anderson 1922, i: 56-62, 89-91; Smyth 1984: 103-7

Bruide son of Derile Pictish king 697−706

Bruide was presumably responsible for the expulsion of his predecessor, *Taran son of Entifidich, from the kingship of the Picts in 697. Bruide and his brother *Nechtán ruled in succession as kings of the Picts from 697 until 724. Together with a third brother, Ciniod (Cináed), who was slain in 713, these sons of Derile formed a close-knit family group which dominated Pictland in the first quarter of the eighth century. Their parent, Derile, may have been a female and if so her name may have meant 'Daughter of Islay'. Bruide was one of the kings who ratified the Law of *Adomnán at the Synod of Birr in the Irish midlands in the first year of his reign (697).

Bruide's reign saw a conflict (698) between the Picts and the 'Saxons', i.e. the Bernician Angles, in which the Bernicians seem to have been defeated since one of their leaders, Beorhtred (see Beorhtfrith), is named among the slain. In 699, Taran, Bruide's predecessor and presumed rival, left the kingdom for Ireland. Bruide died in 706 and was succeeded by his brother, *Nechtán.

BIBL. Anderson 1973: 175-6; Smyth 1984: 134-7

Bruide son of Fergus (*Bredei* son of *Uuirguist*) Pictish king 761−3

Bruide was the brother and immediate successor of the powerful *Óengus son of Fergus, who ruled the Picts for over 30 years. Talorgen, yet another brother within this dynasty, helped Óengus conquer Dál Riata back in 736 and was slain by the Strathclyde Britons in 750. Bruide is described as king of Fortriu in the *Annals of Ulster* in 763. He was succeeded among the Picts after a brief reign by *Ciniod son of Feredach.

BIBL. Anderson 1973: 86-7, 187

Brúsi Sigurdarson earl of Orkney *c*. 1014−36 *see* **Rögnvaldur Brúsason** and **Thorfinn the Mighty**

Bucge (Bugga) abbess *d. c*. 723−7

Bucge, daughter of *Centwine, king of Wessex, was abbess of a monastery, whose church, dedicated to St Mary, was celebrated in verse by *Aldhelm. She may have been related to Aldhelm, who is said to have been the son of *Kenten* (?Centwine) and of the royal stock of Wessex. A Latin epitaph of Bucge says that she ruled for 34 years as abbess, but, like Aldhelm's poem, does not name her monastery. It was once thought to be Withington, Gloucestershire, a house associated with Aldhelm, but this was founded by *Æthelred of Mercia and *Oshere of the Hwicce for Dunna and her daughter, also called Bucge. Since Withington continued to descend in the line of the Hwiccian kings (see *Æthelburh, abbess) this Bucge cannot be Centwine's daughter.

BIBL. Lapidge and Rosier 1985: 40-1; Lapidge 1975b; Whitelock 1955, nos. 68, 75: 454-5, 464

Bucge (Bugga) abbess *d. c.* 760

Bucge, whose full name was Heahburh (Hæaburg), was related to the Kentish royal house. Her mother, Eangyth, was abbess of an unidentified but probably Kentish monastery. Both ladies are known from the correspondence of St *Boniface. About 719 or 720 they asked his advice about a pilgrimage to Rome, though it is not known whether they actually went. Bucge herself did make the pilgrimage in 738—9, against the advice of Boniface who warned her of the dangers of Arab raiders in Italy. She and Boniface met in Rome, when she asked for his prayers on behalf of her kinsman, King *Æthelberht II of Kent. Bucge and her mother are typical of the many English men and women who supported the missionaries in Germany; their own personal gifts included money and an altar frontal. Bucge has been confused with another of Boniface's correspondents, *Eadburh of Minster-in-Thanet, but must be distinguished from her, and also from her own older namesakes, *Bucge, daughter of *Centwine of Wessex, and Bucge, abbess of Withington, Gloucestershire.

BIBL. Greenaway 1980: 42-5; Lapidge and Rosier 1985: 40, n.32

Burgred king of Mercia 852—74

Burgred succeeded *Beorhtwulf, who may have been a kinsman, as king of Mercia in 852, when Viking raids on Britain were becoming more and more threatening. In 851, the Mercian host had been put to flight by a Viking force which stormed London, although it is noticeable that they did not follow up their victory by attacking Mercia, but moved off to Surrey. However, the Viking threat persuaded Burgred to seek a closer alliance with Wessex. In 853 he and *Æthelwulf launched a joint assault against the Welsh, and in the same year, Burgred married Æthelwulf's daughter, *Æthelswith; Berkshire changed hands at about this time, moving from Mercian to West Saxon control, and this arrangement may have been part of the marriage-settlement. In 855, Vikings were campaigning in the Wrekin area, and since Anglesey was attacked at the same time, it is likely that these raiders came from the Irish-Norse settlements. The next recorded assault is that of the 'Great Army' of *Ivarr the Boneless and *Halfdan, which wintered at Nottingham in 868, either with Burgred's connivance or because he could not oust them. The West Saxon alliance was further cemented in this year by the marriage of *Alfred and *Ealhswith, and a joint Mercian and West Saxon siege of Nottingham (unsuccessful) ensued. The 'Great Army' returned to the attack in 874, occupying Repton, a house patronized by Burgred's rivals, the line of *Wiglaf. It is likely that *Ceolwulf II was supporting the Danes; at all events, the occupation of Repton resulted in the expulsion of Burgred, and the accession of Ceolwulf. Burgred went to Rome and died there; a journey undertaken by other kings in happier times. It is likely that Beorhtsige, son of the ætheling

Beornoth, who was killed in 904, fighting in the entourage of the rebellious West Saxon ætheling, *Æthelwold, was one of Burgred's kinsmen.

BIBL. Stenton 1971: 245-52

Byrhtferth of Ramsey monk *d. c.* 1012

Byrhtferth of Ramsey, a pupil of *Abbo of Fleury, is chiefly famous for his *Enchiridion* (*Manual*), concerning the computus (the reckoning of time). His characteristic style has been identified in a number of other works, notably the earliest life of St *Oswald, bishop of Worcester, archbishop of York, and founder of Ramsey; and the early sections of the *Historia Regum* (History of the kings), attributed to the twelfth-century writer, Simeon of Durham, and including the *Passio* of the Kentish royal martyrs, *Æthelred and Æthelberht, whose relics were translated to Ramsey by Ealdorman *Æthelwine. Byrhtferth has also been identified as the author of the *Life* of St *Ecgwine, bishop of Worcester, whose relics were venerated at Evesham, another monastery connected with St Oswald. Byrhtferth's range and output are much greater than was once thought and 'it seems likely that he will come to be regarded as a major figure in late Anglo-Saxon literary culture'.

BIBL. Crawford 1966; Lapidge 1982; Hart 1982

Byrhtnoth ealdorman 956—91

Byrhtnoth, son of Byrhthelm, succeeded Byrhtferth (who may have been a kinsman) as ealdorman of Essex in 956. He married *Ælfflæd, daughter of Ælfgar, ealdorman of the same region (946—51). Byrhtnoth seems to have been closely associated with the ealdorman of East Anglia, *Athelstan Half-king, and with Athelstan's son and eventual successor, *Æthelwine. Indeed in 990—1, when Æthelwine was ill, he was probably his deputy. In 991 he was certainly responsible for the defence of the eastern shires, and it was in this capacity that he faced the Viking host of *Olafr Tryggvason at Maldon. The battle of Maldon, in which Byrhtnoth was killed, has been dismissed as a mere skirmish, but it was far from this; it marks the beginning of a new and dangerous phase in the warfare of the late tenth and early eleventh centuries. The Viking force which encamped on Northey Island, in the Blackwater, numbered 93 or 94 ships' crews, and *Swein of Denmark, as well as Olafr Tryggvason, was probably among the leaders. The defeat of the eastern levies, and the loss of one of the most experienced ealdormen was a severe blow, and it is significant that the first Danegeld of *Æthelred II's reign was paid in the aftermath of the battle. The importance of the battle is also shown by its commemoration in the Old English epic poem, *The Battle of Maldon*. This is a notable piece of heroic propaganda, laying stress on the obligations of loyalty and fidelity, and praising the exploits of Byrhtnoth's men, who fell to a man around the body of their slain lord. One of the finest pieces of English verse is put into the mouth of the 'old *geneat*', Byrhtwold:

'Heart shall be higher, courage keener,
Mind more steadfast, as strength decays.
Here lies our lord, hacked and hewn,

The good man on the ground. May grief follow
Whoever flees from the fighting now.
I am an old man, I go not hence,
But here by the side of my dear lord,
The man I loved, I mean to lie'.

BIBL. Scragg 1981; Hart 1987

C

Cadafael ap Cynfedw king of Gwynedd *fl.* mid-seventh century

Of unknown descent but denigrated in the medieval Welsh Triads as one of 'Three kings who were sprung from villeins', Cadafael ap Cynfedw, king of Gwynedd, was, according to the *Historia Brittonum* (see under *Nennius), present with the army of *Penda, king of the Mercians, in the campaign against *Oswiu, king of the Bernicians, which Bede dates to 655. At the *Winwæd*, possibly the river Went near Leeds, where Penda was defeated and slain, Cadafael, whose name means 'Battle Chief' or 'Battle Seizer', withdrew on the eve of the battle and thereby gained the epithet 'Battle Shirker'. His regnal dates are unknown.

BIBL. Lloyd 1911, vol. I: 190-1; Bromwich 1961, 289-90

Cadell founding-figure of a Powys dynasty *fl.* fifth century

A legendary figure in the hagiographical literature in the early ninth-century *Historia Brittonum* (see under *Nennius) written 829/30, concerning St *Germanus, Cadell 'bright hilt' is represented as a slave-boy, blessed by the saint, who effectively took the kingship of Powys from *Vortigern and transmitted it to his own descendants. It appears that some at least of the early kings of Powys were called Cadelling (of the lineage of Cadell) and the name Cadell was preserved in the later genealogies, but by the early ninth century the inscription on the pillar of *Eliseg, erected by *Cyngen, king of Powys, shows that the kings of Powys were also claiming descent from Vortigern, whom Cadell was said to have supplanted, and Vortigern's name was similarly preserved in the royal genealogies of Powys along with Cadell's. It may be that the hagiographical legend symbolises a protracted struggle between two rival dynasties, one claiming descent from Cadell and the other from Vortigern, which later court pedigrees obscured.

BIBL. Bartrum 1966: 128-9; Kirby 1976a: 101ff.; Dumville 1977

Cadfan ab Iago king of Gwynedd, *fl.* early seventh century

A mid-seventh-century inscribed stone from Llangadwaladr, Anglesey, commemorates 'Cadfan King, wisest and most renowned of all kings', the father of *Cadwallon, who probably died as king of Gwynedd *c.* 625.

BIBL. Alcock 1971: 244

Cadoc St, abbot *fl.* sixth century

The two *Lives* of St Cadoc, traditionally remembered as an abbot, by Lifris and Caradoc of Llancarfan in the Vale of Glamorgan belong to the late eleventh century and early twelfth and are too far removed from the historical Cadoc to supply details of his actual career. His cult was widespread in southeast Wales, with its principal centre at Llancarfan, which

Cadoc is said to have founded; it was also established at Llanspyddid in Brycheiniog, and Llangadog Fawr in Dyfed.

BIBL. Bowen 1954: 38; Savory 1984: 365ff.; Henken 1987: 89-98; Goetinck 1988

Cadwaladr ap Cadwallon king of Gwynedd *fl.* second half of the seventh century

To the author of *Armes Prydein* in the tenth century, Cadwaladr was a promised deliverer who would one day return to lead his people in a victorious campaign against the English. However, nothing of substance is known of this seventh-century king of Gwynedd, who died, according to the *Historia Brittonum* (see under *Nennius), in the great plague of 664 but, according to the Harleian annals, in a lesser plague in 682. He was remembered as the founder of the church of Llangadwaladr, near Aberffraw on Anglesey.

BIBL. Bromwich 1961: 292-3; Williams 1955; Bromwich 1972

Cadwallon ap Cadfan king of Gwynedd, *d.* 634

Cadwallon ap *Cadfan was attacked and driven out of his kingdom of Gwynedd by *Edwin, king of the Northumbrians, but returned to invade Northumbrian territory in alliance with *Penda, king of the Mercians, and to slay Edwin in battle at Hatfield in a year *Bede gives as 633. So savagely, according to Bede, did Cadwallon ravage that the Northumbrians thought he meant to exterminate them. He was defeated and slain within the year, however, at the battle of Heavenfield, near Hexham, by *Oswald, son of Æthelfrith, who succeeded as king of Northumbria. A battle-catalogue poem recalls his military exploits, and what is generally regarded as an early bardic poem in praise of Cadwallon, 'a man like *Mælgwn', celebrates the far-flung campaign of 'the most brilliant lord king' who burnt York.

BIBL. Lloyd, vol. I: 1911: 182-8; Bromwich 1961: 293-6; Foster 1965: 231; Gruffydd 1978: 29-43

Cædmon poet *d.* 680

The story of Cædmon, the Whitby cowherd turned poet, is told by *Bede. Cædmon was a monastic servant, who was unable to sing and therefore found himself at a disadvantage at festivities when the harp was passed from hand to hand, and the revellers took turns to entertain the company. It was therefore his custom to leave before being called upon, and sleep in the cattle-byre. One night as he was settling down to sleep, he saw a stranger, who commanded him to sing 'about the beginning of created things'. Cædmon found that he was miraculously able to sing and to compose. He told the reeve what had occurred and the reeve brought him before Abbess *Hild. She discovered that if biblical stories were read to Cædmon, he could render them into English verse. At her command, Cædmon left the secular life and entered the Whitby community to use his gift in the service of the church. He died in 680.

BIBL. *HE* iv, 24: 414-21

Cædwalla king of Wessex 685–9

Cædwalla was a member of the royal West Saxon kindred, and like many young æthelings (see *Guthlac), spent some years in exile before he came to power. During this time, he ravaged Sussex, killing its king, *Æthelwalh. He succeeded *Centwine as king of Wessex in 685, and continued his aggressive expansion into the south-east. He brought Kent temporarily under West Saxon control, and conquered the Isle of Wight, whose native royal line he exterminated. It was during the harrying of the isle that he was seriously injured, and in 688, he made the pilgrimage to Rome. Here he was baptized on Easter Day, 689, with Pope Sergius I as his godfather. Ten days later he died, and was buried at Rome; the archbishop of Milan composed his epitaph. His late baptism was not unusual in the seventh century, and it is unfair to describe him, as some have done, as a 'bloodthirsty young heathen'. He was a supporter of *Wilfrid, to whom he gave one quarter of the Isle of Wight for religious purposes, and he founded the monastery of Farnham, Sussex. His conquest of Kent was not permanent, for in 687, his brother Mul was burnt by the Kentishmen. It was left to Cædwalla's successor, *Ine, to exact the wergeld.

BIBL. *HE* iv, 12: 368-9; 15-16: 380-5; v, 7: 468-73

Caintigern *see* **Kentigerna** St

Canute *see* **Cnut**

Catroe (Cadroe) Scottish monk and pilgrim *c.* 900–71

The *Life* of Catroe was written by a contemporary Continental monk (Reimann or Ousmann) who had access to detailed information on the saint's earlier life in Scotland. He was born into an aristocratic family, given to foster-parents at an early age and prepared (by a tutor named Béoán) for a life in the Church, in a Scottish monastery which had close ties with Iona. Catroe was educated at Armagh in Ireland, probably at the time when *Máelbrigte (died 927) ruled jointly as abbot of Armagh and Iona. Catroe eventually set out on a long pilgrimage assisted by *Constantine II, king of Scots, and by *Donald son of Áed, king of the Cumbrians (Strathclyde Britons) who was Catroe's kinsman. Catroe is said to have journeyed south through York and Leeds, and in the south of England he was befriended by King *Edmund and by Archbishop *Oda of Canterbury (wrongly described as Otto, 'archbishop' of Winchester). Catroe sailed from Port Lympne on the Kentish coast and arrived at Boulogne. In his continental career, this Scottish cleric continued to consort with the powerful, numbering among his new friends Otto the Great and the Empress Adelaide. He became a monk of Fleury, a prior of Wassor and abbot of St Felix and St Clement near Metz. He died in his 71st year and in the thirtieth year of the pilgrimage, probably in 971.

BIBL. Anderson 1922, vol. I: 431-43; Smyth 1984: 209

Ceadda St, bishop *d.* 672 *see* **Chad**

Cearl king of Mercia before *c*. 626

Cearl preceded *Penda as king of the Mercians. His daughter, Cwenburh, married *Edwin of Northumbria, and bore him two sons, Osfrith and Eanfrith, both born during his exile from Northumbria in 604–16. Penda's enmity to Edwin suggests that he was a political rival of Cearl. Cwenburh's sons both met their deaths by Penda's agency; Osfrith was killed with his father at the battle of Hatfield Chase in 633, and Eanfrith was murdered by Penda when he sought refuge in Mercia.

BIBL. *HE* i, 186-9; Davies 1977: 17-29

Ceawlin king of Wessex *d*. 593

Ceawlin, son of Cynric and grandson of *Cerdic, is said to have been overlord (Bretwalda) of the southern English before *Æthelberht of Kent. In his time the English advance against the British kings of the west was resumed, after the period of peace which followed the battle of Badon Hill, *c*. 500 (see *Arthur). In 577, Ceawlin and Cuthwine (who was apparently his co-king) won a battle at Dyrham, Somerset, against three British leaders, Coinmail, Farinmail and Condidan, and captured the 'cities' of Gloucester, Cirencester and Bath. This victory brought the valley of the lower Severn into English hands, and opened the way to settlement in the west. Ceawlin's other attempts to extend West Saxon control north of the Thames did not meet with the same success, for the battle of *Fethanleag* (possibly Stoke Lyne, Oxfordshire) in 584 seems to have been a West Saxon defeat. In 592 Ceawlin was driven from his kingdom by a rival, and 'perished' in unspecified circumstances the following year.

BIBL. Stenton 1971: 28-30

Cedd St, bishop *d*. 664

Cedd was one of four brothers described by *Bede as 'famous priests of the Lord' (see *Chad). He was a disciple of *Aidan, and therefore trained in the traditions of Irish Christianity. In 653, he was sent to the Middle Angles at the request of their king, *Peada, with three other priests, the Englishmen Adda and Betti and the Irishman Diuma. Diuma became the first bishop of the Mercians in 655, but Cedd moved on to the East Saxons, whose king, *Sigeberht Sanctus, had been converted to Christianity by his friend *Oswiu of Northumbria. As bishop of the East Saxons, Cedd founded communities at Tilbury, and at Bradwell-on-Sea, whose church, St Peters-on-the-Wall, built inside the Roman fort of Othona, is still to be seen. Cedd's episcopal style is vividly illustrated by a story of Bede; one of Sigeberht's nobles was excommunicated by Cedd for an irregular marriage, and the bishop forbade the faithful to enter the man's house or to take food with him. The king, however, disregarded this command and accepted an invitation to dine with the noble, who was a friend of his. As he was leaving the man's house, Sigeberht came face to face with Cedd. The king fell trembling at the bishop's feet, begging his pardon. Cedd prodded the prostrate king with his episcopal staff and prophesied that Sigeberht would meet his death in the same house, which, of course, he did. Cedd himself died during a visit to his native Northumbria, at Lastingham, where he had founded a monastery on land given him by *Æthelwold, king of Deira.

BIBL. *HE* iii, 22: 280-5

Cellach abbot of Iona 802—14

Cellach son of Congal was the nineteenth abbot of Iona and the last in a continuous line from *Columba who occupied the monastic island. Cellach's rule over Iona witnessed the ever-deepening crisis of Viking attack. The monastery was burned by heathens in 802 and four years later 68 members of the community were slain in yet another atrocity. A marginal note in the *Annals of Ulster* states that Kells was handed over 'without battle' to the monks of Columba in 804 while the new building for the enlarged community of exiles began there in 807. Cellach must have been personally responsible for the decision to evacuate the majority of monks at least from the island off Mull and for the new building programme at Kells in Co. Meath. The Kells building was completed in 814, when Cellach resigned his office of *principatus*, handing over to his successor, Diarmait. Cellach died in the following year.

BIBL. Anderson and Anderson 1961: 100; Reeves 1857: 388

Centwine king of Wessex 676—85

Centwine, perhaps the son of *Cynegils and brother of *Cenwealh of Wessex, did not come to power immediately upon his brother's death in 672, for both Cenwealh's widow, *Seaxburh, and his kinsman Æscwine ruled Wessex after him. Centwine continued the expansion against the Britons of Dumnonia; in 682 he 'drove the Britons to the sea', which probably indicates the conquest of at least part of Devon. This compensated for Mercian gains in the Thames Valley, for in Centwine's reign the see of Dorchester-on-Thames, established by Cynegils, was in Mercian control. Centwine is said to have married a sister of *Iurminburg, queen of Northumbria and had at least one child, his daughter *Bucge (died *c.* 723—7). He was remembered as a benefactor of Glastonbury Abbey, and is said to have resigned his kingdom to take vows as a monk.

BIBL. Finberg 1964b: 99; Hoskins 1970: 17-18; Lapidge and Rosier 1985: 48

Cenwealh king of Wessex 643—72

Cenwealh was the son of *Cynegils, in whose reign the West Saxons first became Christian. Cenwealh at first refused conversion, and consequently (in *Bede's view) lost his earthly kingdom also; soon after his accession, he was driven from Wessex. The immediate cause of his downfall was his repudiation of his Mercian wife, a sister of *Penda, who took exception to her treatment. Cenwealh spent the next three years in exile, among the East Angles, whose king, *Anna, persuaded him to accept the faith. When in 648 he returned in triumph to his kingdom, he took up the Christian cause. In 650, on the death of *Birinus, he gave the West Saxon see, at Dorchester-on-Thames, to *Agilbert. Later, however, Cenwealh, 'who knew only the Saxon language', grew tired of the Frankish Agilbert's 'barbarous speech' and divided the West Saxon diocese, establishing the Englishman, *Wine, at Winchester, about 660; though he subsequently fell out with Wine also, and tried to secure Agilbert's return. Cenwealh's problems with his bishops did not prevent him having close relations with king *Alhfrith of Deira, the champion of Roman Christianity, and with *Benedict Biscop, the founder of Monkwearmouth and Jarrow. He also campaigned extensively against the British of Dumnonia; his victory at Posbury in 661 brought Somerset under West Saxon control. He was a benefactor of Glastonbury and Sherborne. He was succeeded by his wife *Seaxburh.

BIBL. Finberg 1964b: 98-9; Hoskins 1970: 13-17; Stenton 1971: 66-9, 122, 132

Ceolfrith St, abbot 688–716

Ceolfrith, who was born in 642, began his monastic career at Gilling in 659 or 660, a house ruled by his kinsman, Tunberht. He became dissatisfied with the Celtic customs observed there and moved, first to Ripon, and then to St *Botulf's monastery of *Icanho*. When in 674 *Benedict Biscop founded Monkwearmouth, Ceolfrith became a member of that most Roman of communities; in 681 he was made abbot of the sister-house at Jarrow, and in 689 succeeded Benedict as abbot of the two communities. It was Ceolfrith who reared Monkwearmouth-Jarrow's most famous son, *Bede. Bede left a very loving portrait of his father in God as 'a man of acute mind, conscientious in everything he did, energetic, of mature judgement, fervent and zealous for his faith'. Ceolfrith greatly enlarged the library at Jarrow and commissioned three complete bibles, only one of which survives. This, the *Codex Amiatinus* now in the Bibliotheca Laurenziana, Florence, was intended as a gift for the pope. It is now the oldest surviving complete text of the Latin bible. Seven scribes have been identified among its writers and decorators; it runs to 1 030 folios, each double-skin measuring 27½" by 20½", and weighs over 75lb. About 1 550 calves were required to provide the vellum. The *Amiatinus* and its lost sisters (a few leaves from one of them are preserved in the British Museum) give some indication of the learning, skill and wealth of Monkwearmouth-Jarrow in the seventh century. In 716, Ceolfrith set off for Rome, taking the *Amiatinus* with him, but he never reached his goal. He died at Langres, Burgundy, on 25 September 716. His remains were eventually returned to Jarrow, where they lay until the Vikings came. Two lives of Ceolfrith were composed soon after his death; the Anonymous *Life*, and that in Bede's *Lives of the Abbots*. It is the Anonymous which relates how the plague ravaged Jarrow, killing all the monks except the abbot himself and one small boy, who between them sang the daily office, including the antiphons, until helpers arrived. The child must, of course, have been Bede.

BIBL. Bede's *Lives of the Abbots of Wearmouth and Jarrow* in Farmer 1983; Farmer 1978: 73-4

Ceolnoth archbishop of Canterbury 833–70

The long archiepiscopate of Ceolnoth, which suggests he must have been a young man at his election, saw the growing rapprochement of the church of Canterbury with the rising power of the West Saxon kings. Though Ceolnoth attended the synod at Croft in 836, held under the auspices of the Mercian king, *Wiglaf, this is the last occasion when a full synod of the southern province was presided over by a Mercian ruler. In 838, *Ecgberht of Wessex and his son *Æthelwulf made a number of gifts to Canterbury, acknowledged the spiritual authority of the archbishop over the Kentish minsters (see *Wulfred) and guaranteed free elections. The grants of 838–9 were the last acts of royal munificence for some time. In 850–1 the Vikings over-wintered on Thanet for the first time and Canterbury was sacked. Since the West Saxon rulers were the most effective in protecting their people against the Danes, the archbishop had even greater cause to support them.

BIBL. Brooks 1984: 143-9

Ceolred king of Mercia 709–16

Ceolred, son of *Æthelred, succeeded his cousin *Cœnred as king of Mercia, when the latter retired to Rome to enter religion in 709. He was the last king of *Penda's line; his successor, *Æthelbald, came from a collateral branch of the Mercian royal kindred. Ceolred and his contemporary, *Osred of Northumbria, were used as dire warnings by St *Boniface in a letter of admonition to King Æthelbald: the two kings, said Boniface, 'by the prompting of the devil showed by their wicked example an open display of these two greatest of sins (fornication and robbing churches) in the provinces of the English' as a result of which they were 'thrown down from the regal summit of this life and overtaken by an early and terrible death'. Ceolred indeed 'feasting in splendour amid his companions, was — as those who were present have testified — suddenly in his sin sent mad by a malign spirit' and died.

BIBL. Stenton 1971: 203; Whitelock 1955, no 177: 751-6

Ceolwulf St, king of Northumbria 729–37; *d.* 764

Ceolwulf, the king to whom *Bede dedicated the *Historia Ecclesiastica*, was the brother of King *Cœnred (716–18); he succeeded *Osric in 729. His piety was not, apparently, matched with political acumen; in 731 he was deprived of his kingdom, and though he was restored to power, he retired as a monk to Lindisfarne in 737. He was subsequently venerated as a saint, which may or may not be connected with his benefactions to the monastery, which enabled the monks to drink beer and wine, whereas before they had been able to afford only milk.

BIBL. Farmer 1978: 74

Ceolwulf I king of Mercia 821–3

Ceolwulf, brother and successor of *Cœnwulf of Mercia, was consecrated on 17 September 822 by Archbishop *Wulfred; the record of the event, which occurs in an early Mercian charter, is one of the earliest references to the consecration of an English king (see also *Ecgfrith). Despite this auspicious beginning, Ceolwulf's reign ended in disaster, for he was 'deprived of his kingdom' in 823, for reasons which are still obscure. His heir was his daughter, *Ælfflæd, who married Wigmund, son of King *Wiglaf, and became the mother of St *Wigstan, and, quite possibly, of *Ceolwulf II.

BIBL. Sawyer 1968, no. 186; Whitelock 1955, no. 83: 474-5; Stenton 1971: 230-1

Ceolwulf II king of Mercia 874—9

Ceolwulf II, the last king of independent Mercia, succeeded *Burgred in 874. He is described in the West Saxon *Anglo-Saxon Chronicle* as 'a foolish king's thegn', and presented as a puppet of the Danes, to whom he promised that 'the kingdom should be at their disposal whenever they might require it'. In 877, the Danes did indeed partition Mercia, keeping the eastern regions for themselves, while they 'gave some to Ceolwulf'. This account of Ceolwulf's reign is, however, partial and distorted. He bears the same name as the last king of Mercia who can be shown to have been a member of the ancient ruling dynasty, and, if he was not a member of that dynasty himself, he did at least persuade some of the Mercians that his claims to be an Iceling were true. It is likely that Ceolwulf was a political opponent of King Burgred, who was the brother-in-law of the West Saxon king, *Alfred. The immediate cause of Burgred's abandonment of his kingdom in 874 was the Danish occupation of Repton in the winter of 873—4. Repton, the burial place of *Æthelbald, was a house closely associated with Mercian royalty and the cult-centre of St *Wigstan, whose mother, *Ælfflæd, was a daughter of *Ceolwulf I. The occupation of Repton and the alliance of the Danish host with Ceolwulf II look like a successful coup against a rival, who had West Saxon backing; hence the hostility of the *Anglo-Saxon Chronicle*. Ceolwulf was certainly regarded as a true king in Mercia; indeed his claims were implicitly accepted even by Alfred of Wessex, to judge from the coinage which the two kings issued jointly. After Ceolwulf's death in 879, however, Mercia began to fall under West Saxon overlordship.

BIBL. Stenton 1971: 254, 259; Nelson 1986: 59-60

Cerdic king of Wessex d. 534

Cerdic, the founder of Wessex, was claimed as the ancestor of the West Saxon royal line, the *Cerdicingas*. He landed with his son Cynric at *Cerdicesora*, in 495. The annals which record this and subsequent exploits are no more reliable than those for Kent and Sussex (see *Ælle, *Hengest), and the course of West Saxon settlement is more involved and more obscure than later legend allows. Cerdic's own origins are complicated by the fact that he, like some of his successors (see *Cædwalla, *Ceawlin) bears a Celtic name, the British Ceretic (Caradoc). A British strain in the West Saxon royal house is not unlikely.

BIBL. Stenton 1971: 19-25; Yorke 1989

Ceretic (Coroticus) king of the Strathclyde Britons c. 450 or 480

Ceretic's name appears in the Harleian genealogies as an ancestor of the later kings of Strathclyde. His grandfather, Cinhil, and great-grandfather, Cluim, may have borne the Roman names Quintillius and Clemens respectively, and so perhaps ruled as *fœderati* or allies of Rome on the frontiers of Britain. Ceretic's kingdom on the Clyde evolved in the fourth and fifth centuries from the half-Romanized tribe of British Damnonii. He may be accepted as the first historical king of Strathclyde, being the Coroticus, *regem Aloo* (or 'king of Alcluith', Dumbarton Rock on the Clyde) whose soldiers received a letter from St *Patrick. The followers of Coroticus were addressed by the saint as Christians and as Roman citizens, and Patrick writing from his Irish mission (*c.* 450 or 480 depending on how one dates Patrick's career) accused the Strathclyde king of carrying off some of his newly converted Irish flock (men and women) and of selling them into slavery to the pagan Picts. Ceretic was an ancestor of *Riderch Hen.

BIBL. Kirby 1962: 77-9; Hood 1978: 35-8, 55-9

Chad (Ceadda) St, bishop *d.* 672

Chad and his brothers, *Cedd, Cælin and Cynebill, were described by *Bede as 'famous priests of the lord'. Like his brother Cedd, Chad was a disciple of *Aidan and received his education in Ireland. He became abbot of Lastingham after Cedd's death in 664, and was appointed as bishop of the Northumbrians by King *Oswiu after the Synod of Whitby. This led to considerable confusion over the limits of his jurisdiction and that of *Wilfrid, who had also been appointed bishop in, or of, Northumbria. In 669, Wilfrid's claims to the whole see were confirmed by Archbishop *Theodore, and Chad's orders were found wanting; however, his qualities were recognized by Theodore, who completed his consecration and sent him as bishop to the Mercians, whose bishop, Jaruman, had died in 667. Chad's Irish training brought him into some conflict with Theodore, vividly described by Bede: 'because it was the custom of the reverend bishop Chad to carry out his evangelistic work on foot rather than on horseback, Theodore ordered him to ride whenever he was faced with too long a journey; but Chad showed much hesitation, for he was deeply devoted to this religious exercise, so the archbishop lifted him onto the horse with his own hand'. The contrast between Irish austerity and humility and Roman pomp and dignity could not be better pointed. Chad is credited with establishing the see of the Mercians at Lichfield, close to the royal residence of Tamworth. He founded a monastery close by, and another at Barrow, Lincolnshire, on land given by King *Wulfhere. He died on 2 March 672, being summoned to heaven by the soul of his brother, Cedd.

BIBL. *HE* iv, 3: 336-47; Mayr-Harting 1972: 88-9; Farmer 1978: 75

Cillene Droichtech abbot of Iona 726-52

Cillene Droichtech succeeded his namesake, *Cillene Fota, as fourteenth abbot in succession to *Columba. Cillene's long rule over Iona coincided with the turbulent reign of the Pictish king *Óengus I who from 736 seems to have ruled as overlord of Scots Dál Riata. Although a member of the

Irish Uí Néill dynasty (as were most of Columba's successors) Cillene hailed from the Southern Uí Néill in the Irish midlands. According to the seventeenth-century *Martyrology of Donegal*, it was Cillene who took the shrine of Adomnán to Ireland to establish peace between the Cenél Conaill and Cenél nEógain in the north of that country. Contemporary annals do record a battle between those two tribes in 727 and record that in the same year 'the relics of Adomnán are brought over to Ireland and [his] *Law* is promulgated anew'. Cillene is described as an anchorite at his death in 752 which suggests that he lived as a recluse for at least some of his time as abbot of Iona. In that case, the Columban community may have been ruled by the veteran, Fedlimid, who had become co-adjutor to *Fáelchú back in 722, and who lived to the great age of 87, dying in 759. Cillene's nickname *droichtech* is thought to mean 'the Bridge Builder'. He was succeeded by *Sléibíne and his festival was kept on 3 July.

BIBL. Anderson and Anderson 1961: 99; Reeves 1857: 382-5

Cillene Fota ('the Tall') abbot of Iona 724−6
    Cillene succeeded *Fáelchú as thirteenth abbot in succession to *Columba. Although Fáelchú (who was 82 at his death in 724) had a certain Fedlimid as his co-adjutor during the last two years of his rule, we are specifically told in the *Annals of Ulster* that it was Cillene who succeeded to the *principatus* of Iona when Fáelchú died. Cillene's genealogy is unknown − which is unusual for an Iona abbot − and his festival day is uncertain.

BIBL. Anderson and Anderson 1961: 99; Reeves 1857: 382

Cináed mac Alpín *see* **Kenneth I mac Alpín**

Ciniod son of Feredach, Pictish king 763−75
    Ciniod or Cináed (Kenneth) succeeded *Bruide son of Fergus as king of the Picts in 763. As the son of *Uuredech* in the Pictish king-lists, his father was very probably the same person as Feredach, the brother of *Dúngal son of Selbach of Cenél Loairn, both of whom were captured and put in chains by *Óengus I, son of Fergus, when he attacked Dál Riata in 736. Bruide, the immediate predecessor of Ciniod, was the brother of Óengus and so presumably belonged to a rival faction of contenders for the Pictish overlordship. Ciniod fought a battle against *Áed Find, king of Dál Riata in 768. Since the battle was fought within Fortriu, Áed would seem to have been the invader, and this engagement (whose outcome is uncertain) is seen to mark a stage in the recovery of Dál Riata which had been conquered by the Picts under Óengus son of Fergus in 736. Ciniod's name is given in the unusual form of *Cinadhon* at the notice of his death in the *Annals of Ulster*, so he is clearly the father of Eithni 'daughter of Cinadhon' whose death is noted in the same source under 778.

BIBL. Anderson 1973: 86-7; Anderson 1922, vol. 1: 245-7

Cnut (Canute, Knútr) king of the English 1016−35
    Cnut, son of *Swein Forkbeard, king of Denmark, accompanied his father on the invasion of England in 1013. Swein's landing in the Humber

was followed by the submission of the northern magnates, and when he crossed Watling Street to repeat his success in the south, Cnut was left in control of the Danish fleet in Northumbria. It was probably at this point that he married *Ælfgifu of Northampton, whose connections would have made her a very desirable catch. Swein was accepted as king of the English by Christmas, 1013, and *Æthelred II was forced to flee to Normandy. When Swein died on 2 February 1014, the Danish host chose Cnut as his successor, but the English magnates negotiated the return of Æthelred, who drove Cnut from the north. In 1015, he returned to attack Wessex. *Eadric Streona, ealdorman of Mercia, deserted to Cnut, and the two launched an attack on *Leofwine, ealdorman of the Hwicce. They were opposed by *Edmund Ironside and his brother-in-law, *Uhtred of Bamburgh, ealdorman of Northumbria. Early in 1016, Cnut led his army north to York, thus threatening Uhtred's position, and forcing him to seek terms. Under cover of the negotiations, Cnut had Uhtred murdered, and installed his own brother-in-law, *Eirikr of Hlathir, as earl of Northumbria. The death of Æthelred on 23 April left Edmund Ironside as king of the English. Five general engagements were fought between Cnut and Edmund, culminating in the Danish victory of Ashingdon. Edmund was fatally wounded in this battle, and by the agreement of Alney (near Deerhurst, Gloucestershire), divided the kingdom, Cnut taking the north, and Edmund Wessex. Edmund's death on 30 November left Cnut as the main candidate for the kingship. It was nevertheless some time before his claims were established. In 1017, he made *Thorkell the Tall, Æthelred's old commander, earl of East Anglia, and by Christmas was ready to rid himself of his untrustworthy ally, Eadric Streona, whom he had murdered. *Eadwig, the last surviving son of Æthelred's first marriage, was exiled, and the interests of Æthelred's sons by his second marriage, *Edward and *Alfred, were neutralized when Cnut took their mother, *Emma, as his queen; without, apparently, repudiating Ælfgifu. In 1018, at Oxford, Cnut was acknowledged as king of the English.

Cnut's reign is not as well documented as that of Æthelred, and the Scandinavian impact on England is not easy to assess. England became part of a North Sea empire when Cnut became king of Denmark, following the death of his brother, Haraldr, in 1018/19. By 1028, he had added Norway to his possessions, ousting *Olafr Helgi, who was killed at the battle of Stiklastadir in 1030. Cnut appointed first his nephew *Hakon, and then his son Swein, under Ælfgifu's guardianship, as regents of Norway. Among the Danish earls whom he appointed to England were his brother-in-law, *Eilaf, who received Gloucestershire, and his nephew Hakon, who became earl of Worcestershire. Cnut's military followers, his housecarls, also received land in England (see *Urk), as did the household retainers of his earls. It would not, however, be correct to describe eleventh-century England as Anglo-Scandinavian rather than Anglo-Saxon. By the 1030s, the two most powerful earls in England, *Godwine of Wessex and *Leofric of Mercia, were English (though Godwine had a Danish wife, Gytha). Cnut's chief advisor in his early years, Archbishop *Wulfstan of York, was also English. He inspired Cnut's law-codes (I and II Cnut), which are essentially compendia of English custom. The Danish kingdom was a more recent creation than the kingdom of England, and it is more likely that the latter should influence the former than vice-versa. Despite the fact that the Danish title of earl (*jarl*) replaced the English ealdorman, the earldoms of the eleventh century were essentially the tenth-century ealdordoms, with some modifications. Cnut's lordship of the North Sea made him a force in European affairs. His visit to Rome in 1027, to attend the coronation of the Emperor Conrad II, brought him into contact with the rulers of Europe, and in his letter to the English people describing his journey, he emphasizes the benefits, especially the commercial benefits, which this has brought to the English. One of his last acts was to arrange the marriage of his daughter, *Gunnhildr, to Conrad's son, Henry (the future Emperor Henry III). But even before Cnut's death, his empire was crumbling. The return of Olafr Helgi's son, Magnus, to Norway led to the expulsion of Ælfgifu and Swein, and when Cnut died in 1035, Magnus attacked Denmark itself. In the wars between Denmark and Norway, the union of Denmark and England was lost.

BIBL. *ASC* s.a. 1016; Whitelock 1955, no. 49: 416-8 (Cnut's letter of 1027); no. 50: 419-30 (Cnut's Secular Code, II Cnut); Stenton 1971: 384-414; Williams 1986

Cœnred ætheling *fl.* 670/94

Cœnred, an ætheling of the West Saxon royal kindred, was the father of King *Ine, and of Ingeld, ancestor of *Alfred the Great. Two daughters are also recorded, Cwœnburh, and Cuthburh, who married *Aldfrith of Northumbria and founded Winborne Minster, Dorset. In the early 670s, Cœnred gave land in Dorset for the foundation of a monastery at Fontmell Magna. He was living in 688/94, for his son Ine refers to the instruction of his father Cœnred in the preamble to his law-code, issued between those dates. As Stenton pointed out, Cœnred's association with Dorset, 'west of Selwood', carries the link between Alfred's family and western Wessex back to the seventh century; it was from Wessex 'west of Selwood' that Alfred gathered forces for his great battle against *Guthrum's Danes in 878.

BIBL. *ASC* s.c. 718; Stenton 1971: 65-6; Whitelock 1955, no. 55: 441-3 = Sawyer 1968, no. 1164

Cœnred king of Mercia 704–9

Cœnred, son of *Wulfhere, succeeded his uncle *Æthelred as king of Mercia when the latter became a monk at Bardney. Like Æthelred, Cœnred also renounced his earthly kingdom for the kingdom of Heaven; in 709 he went to Rome to become a monk. He was succeeded by his cousin *Ceolred.

BIBL. Stenton 1971: 203

Cœnred king of Northumbria 716–18

Cœnred, son of Cuthwine, claimed descent from *Ida, the founder of the royal dynasty of Bernicia. He became king of Northumbria after the murder of *Osred in 716. Cœnred's brother *Ceolwulf was the dedicatee of *Bede's *Ecclesiastical History*.

BIBL. Kirby 1974b: 20-1

Cœnwald (Cenwald) bishop 929–57/8

Cœnwald, who became bishop of Worcester in 929, was King *Athelstan's ambassador to Germany; he conveyed the king's gifts to the monasteries of Saint-Gall, Reichenau and Pfäfers. He is said to have been a monk, and must therefore have been a member of the nascent reform party among English ecclesiastics, but little more is known of his career.

BIBL. Stenton 1971: 444

Cœnwulf (Cenwulf) king of Mercia 796–821

Cœnwulf, who succeeded *Ecgfrith as king of Mercia, claimed descent from a younger brother of *Penda and *Eowa, called Cenwealh. He was able to maintain the supremacy of Mercia in southern England, with authority in Sussex, Essex, East Anglia and Kent. In Kent, Cœnwulf was faced with a revolt led by *Eadberht Præn, who had driven out the pro-Mercian archbishop of Canterbury, *Æthelheard. In 798, Eadberht was captured and mutilated, and Cœnwulf's own brother, *Cuthred, became king of Kent. After an attempt to get the southern metropolitan see removed to London, Cœnwulf agreed, in 803, to demote Lichfield from archiepiscopal status, and restore the unity of the province of Canterbury. His hold on Kent was weakened with the appointment of *Wulfred as archbishop in 805, and the subsequent legal wrangle over control of the Kentish minsters. In 802 also, *Ecgberht made good his claim to the kingship of Wessex, and though he made no attempt to challenge Mercian dominance during Cœnwulf's lifetime, he was certainly never Cœnwulf's man. In the west, Cœnwulf had greater success. In 816, Mercian armies penetrated into Snowdonia, and in 818 Dyfed was harried; this campaign against the Welsh was continued under Cœnwulf's brother and successor, *Ceolwulf I. Cœnwulf died in 821, and was buried at Winchcombe, which he had founded, or at least extensively endowed. He left no living sons (see *Cynehelm) and his heir was his daughter *Cwœnthryth. Cœnwulf may have been related to the kings of the Hwicce.

BIBL. Stenton 1971: 225-32; Brooks 1984: 120-34; Bassett 1989b: 6-17

Coifi heathen priest *fl.* 616–33

Like most early writers, *Bede is extremely reluctant to disclose any information on heathen beliefs and customs, but does include some details concerning the heathen priest Coifi in his (semi-legendary) account of the conversion of Northumbria. Coifi is represented as advocating the acceptance of Christianity, on the grounds that the pagan deities had been insufficiently conscious of his merits. After the decision to convert was taken, Coifi was the first to violate the heathen cult centre, at Goodmanham, near York. Mounting a stallion, a beast which hitherto he had been forbidden to ride, he took a spear and cast it into the shrine, which was then fired, with all its enclosures. Coifi's action suggests that he was a priest of Woden (Odin), to whom sacrifices in this form were made.

BIBL. *HE* ii, 13: 252-3; Davidson 1964: 50-1

Colmán St, bishop *d*. 676

Colmán, an Irishman and a monk of Iona (see Cummēne), succeeded *Finan as bishop of Northumbria. It was in his time that the Easter controversy came to a head, and the Synod of Whitby was held to determine the matter. Colmán spoke for the Celtic system of reckoning the date of Easter, and when the decision went against him, he chose to leave Northumbria. He led the monks of Lindisfarne, those who were of like mind, both Irish and English, to the island of Inishbofin, off the west coast of County Mayo, and there established a monastery. Even here, however, dissension arose. As *Bede tells us, 'they could not agree together, because the Irish, in summer time when the harvest had to be gathered in, left the monastery and wandered about, scattering into various places with which they were familiar; then, when winter came, they returned and expected to have a share in the things which the English had provided'. Since these problems could not be resolved, the English monks were removed from the monastery and settled in Mayo 'of the Saxons', while the Irish remained at Inishbofin ('the white cow's island'). Mayo 'of the Saxons' became a centre of Roman influence in Ireland, and it may have been here that *Ecgberht the Englishman settled. At Lindisfarne itself, Colmán was succeeded by another Irishman, Tuda, who had been trained in southern Ireland, and followed the Roman custom. He died in the plague of 664, and was succeeded, at Colmán's request, by *Eata of Melrose.

BIBL. *HE* iii, 25-6: 294-311; iv, 4; 346-9; Farmer 1978: 86-7

Columba (Columcille) founder and first abbot of Iona 521−97

Columba or Columcille ('Dove of the Church') was born in 521, probably at Gartan in Donegal in north-west Ireland. He was a member of the Irish dynasty of Northern Uí Néill who ruled as kings of Tír Conaill. His great-grandfather was Niall of the Nine Hostages, the half-legendary founder of the Uí Néill dynasty of highkings.

We know little of the first 42 years of his life spent in Ireland, there being few early miracle stories relating to this period. He seems to have been committed to a life in the Church from an early age and he studied as a deacon in Leinster, one of his mentors very probably being St Finian of Clonard. Columba experienced a major spiritual and political crisis in 561 when he was excommunicated by a church synod for his involvement, directly or indirectly, in the battle of Cul Drébene in which Columba's uncle and his cousins of the Northern Uí Néill were the victors. He was later pardoned by a synod held at Teltown in Co. Meath, but an immediate consequence of this affair was his exile, voluntary or imposed, to the Scots kingdom of Dál Riata in 563.

Columba is said to have set out for Scotland initially with 12 companions. He may have founded his first monastery in Scotland on *Hinba*, but he eventually settled on Iona which became the headquarters of the Columban monastic *paruchia* not only in Dál Riata but also throughout northern Britain and Ireland. Columba can be said to have given cohesion and organization to Christianity in Dál Riata and his association, first with the Scots kings *Conall son of Comgall, and later with *Áedhán mac Gabhráin, set a pattern for future co-operation between the Columban church and the ruling dynasty of the Scots. Columba was said by his biographer, *Adomnán, to have chosen Áedhán mac Gabhráin as the successful candidate for the Scottish kingship and to have 'ordained' him at his inauguration in 574. In the following year, at the Convention of Drumceat (Druim Cett) in Ulster, Columba negotiated between the Scots king and the Irish highking Áed mac Ainmerech. Journeys to Skye and elsewhere in western Pictland, and to the fortress of *Bruide mac Maelchon, the Pictish king, near the Moray Firth, may not be sufficient evidence to allow claims that Columba was responsible for the conversion of the Picts, but his courageous missionary and diplomatic overtures to that pagan people clearly paved the way for the subsequent rapid evangelization of Pictland by the church of Iona.

Any appraisal of Columba's achievement must take into the account the extraordinary influence which he wielded far outside his immediate location in south-western Scotland. Columba's activities concentrated on the shores of Ardnamurchan, the Sound of Mull, the Firth of Lorn and the waters between Tiree and Iona. But his monasteries at Derry and at Durrow (founded from Iona 585−9) gave him enormous influence in Irish politics. He was the friend and relative of Irish highkings, and he was on friendly terms with *Riderch Hen, king of the Strathclyde Britons. Subsequently, with the foundation of Lindisfarne by *Aidan in 635, Columba's spiritual influence passed to the Northumbrian Church and to Anglo-Saxon Christianity generally. In his life as a monk, Columba was remembered in his own community as a pastor and a scholar and as a man of rigorous self-discipline and strength of character. He was also gentle and loving while devoted to a life filled with monastic duties and with prayer. He died in the chapel of Iona soon after midnight on Sunday morning, 9 June 597. Columba's spiritual biography which was written by Adomnán, constitutes one of the most celebrated documents of its kind to survive from the early Middle Ages.

BIBL. Anderson and Anderson 1961: 66-90 and text; Herbert 1988: 9-35; Reeves 1857 text and notes; Smyth 1984: 84-115

Comgán (Congan) St *c*. 700−30

According to the Breviary of Aberdeen, Comgán was an abbot associated with Turriff in the diocese of Aberdeen. He is also associated with Lochalsh near Skye. He was regarded as the brother of *Kentigerna, the daughter of the Leinster king, Cellach Cualann, who settled on Loch Lomond and whose death is recorded in contemporary annals in 734. The deaths of three of Kentigerna's sisters and two of her brothers are recorded in the *Annals of Ulster* in the first half of the eighth century, but that of Comgán is not among them. The name appears only once in early Irish genealogical collections while its variant Congan is equally rare and is applied to a woman. Comgán's nephew, *Fáelán, who also settled in Scotland has marginally better claims to historicity. Comgán's festival was kept on 13 October.

BIBL. Anderson 1922, vol. 1: 231

Conall son of Comgall, king of Scots Dál Riata 558—74

Conall succeeded his uncle, *Gabhrán, as fifth king of Dál Riata. In 568 he led an expedition against the islands of Seil and Islay in the Inner Hebrides in alliance with Colmán Bec ('the Little'), a Southern Uí Néill king from the Irish midlands. Conall is credited in the *Annals of Ulster* with granting Iona as a place for a monastic settlement to *Columba, while *Adomnán in his *Life of Columba* shows that saint staying with Conall in Dál Riata soon after his arrival from Ireland in 563.

BIBL. Anderson and Anderson 1961: 225-7; Bannerman 1974: 78-9

Conall son of Tadg (*Canaul* son of *Tarl'a*), Pictish king and later king of Scots Dál Riata *c*. 785—807

One of the few firm historical facts relating to Conall is the record of his defeat in battle at the hands of Constantine in 789, the statement that he escaped from that encounter with his life and that the battle was fought between the Picts themselves. The victor was clearly *Constantine son of Fergus who later went on to assume the kingship of Dál Riata in 811. Conall is identified with *Canaul* son of *Tarl'a* whose name appears immediately before that of Constantine in the Pictish lists where he is accorded a five-year reign. After his loss of power in Pictland, Conall son of Tadg retreated westward to Dál Riata where it appears from the Dál Riata king-lists he succeeded Domnall as king of Dál Riata in 805, and he was slain two years later by his Scottish successor in the Dál Riata kingship, Conall mac Aedháin. Conall's death took place in Kintyre, according to the *Annals of Ulster*, in 807. His reign in Pictland and Argyll witnessed the opening of the Viking onslaught against Scotland and the Isles. Conall's separate rule over Pictland and Dál Riata points to a merging of Pictish and Scottish dynasties at this time, a process which was intensified during the early years of the Viking wars.

BIBL. Anderson 1973: 191-2

Conall Crandomna king of Scots Dál Riata 650—60

Conall was a son of *Eochaid Buide and a brother of *Domnall Brecc whose reign (629—42) saw Dál Riata enter a marked decline. In the aftermath of Domnall Brecc's military defeats at the hands of Irish, Pictish, and Strathclyde neighbours, the kingship of Dál Riata was seriously weakened and shared between candidates. Conall's partner in the kingship was *Dúnchad son of Conaing.

BIBL. Anderson 1973: 154-7; Bannerman 1974: 103-4

Conamail son of Failbe, abbot of Iona 704—10

Conamail succeeded *Adomnán as tenth abbot of Iona at a time when a virtual schism existed within the Columban community. Adomnán had succeeded in winning over only a section of the Columban *paruchia* to

Roman practices in relation to the dating of Easter and other liturgical uses. It would seem that Conamail presided as abbot over the recalcitrant Iona monks who clung to Celtic liturgical practices, and that he may have been opposed to Adomnán's leadership. Conamail's descent, not from Columba's kindred — as was usual for Iona abbots — but from the Irish tribe of Colla Uais, lends some support to the idea that he led a conservative party on Iona. Marjorie Anderson suggested that Conamail may have owed his promotion to the Scottish tribe of Cenél Loairn who at this time had seized the kingship of Dál Riata from the traditional ruling dynasty of Cenél Gabhráin. The reign of *Selbach of the Cenél Loairn dynasty (700–23) must have had a marked effect on the Iona community which lay within his territory. Conamail died as abbot of Iona in 710, but three years previously *Dúnchad son of Cennfaelad received the *principatus* of Iona. It may be that by 707, Conamail had become too infirm to rule, or otherwise that Dúnchad had been promoted by the rival Roman party in the Columban community. Conamail's festival was kept on 11 September.

BIBL. Anderson and Anderson 1961: 98; Reeves 1857; 378-9

Connachtach abbot of Iona 801–2
Connachtach's brief rule on Iona as its eighteenth abbot coincided with the burning of that monastery by Viking raiders in 802. He is described as a distinguished scribe by the *Annals of the Four Masters* which may suggest he was responsible for some of the magnificent illumination carried out in the *Book of Kells* which was completed in the Columban community about this time. He was succeeded by *Cellach, and his festival is ascribed with little certainty to 10 May.

BIBL. Anderson 1922, vol. 1: 258; Reeves 1857: 388

Connad Cerr king of Scots Dál Riata 629
Connad was the son of *Eochaid Buide according to the *Senchus Fer nAlban*. He is described as a son of *Conall (son of Comgall) in a later Latin king-list. His reign only lasted three months when he was slain in battle at Fid Eoin in Ulster. In this engagement Connad Cerr tried unsuccessfully to interfere in some internal feud among the Dál nAraide, traditional allies of the Scots kings. The battle was a major confrontation in which Connad Cerr was supported by two grandsons of *Áedán mac Gabhráin and by a contingent of Northumbrian Angles led by *Oisiric mac Albruit*, identified as Osric son of Ælfric (see *Edwin). But Osric, who is said to have been slain at Fid Eoin, did not die until 634.

BIBL. Bannerman 1974: 96-9

Constantine king of Dumnonia *fl.* early sixth century
*Gildas denounced Constantine, ruler of Dumnonia (Devon and Cornwall) — the 'whelp' of the lioness of Dumnonia, as Gildas called him — for immorality, perjury and sacrilege, and for the murder, while in a church disguised as an abbot, of two royal princes.

BIBL. Jackson 1982: 30-1

Constantine I king of Scots 862—77

During Constantine's reign, northern Britain was attacked on several fronts by formidable Viking armies. Olaf, the Norwegian king of Dublin, led an expedition against the Picts in 866 in which he took their hostages, while in 870—1, the same Olaf along with *Ivarr 'king of all the Northmen of Britain and Ireland' sacked Dumbarton and carried its people into slavery. Constantine's sister may have been married to Olaf of Dublin and his Scottish dynasty profited from these Viking attacks against his Pictish and Strathclyde British neighbours. In 872, Constantine connived at the killing of *Artgal, king of the Strathclyde Britons. He was defeated by a Danish army at Dollar in 875 — a war-band probably led by *Halfdan on his way from York to claim the kingdom of his brother Ivarr at Dublin. Irish sources claim that Constantine I was eventually slain by the remnants of this same war-band on its return through Lowland Scotland two years later in 877. Constantine was buried in Iona.

BIBL. Smyth 1977a: 106-8, 146-9; Smyth 1984: 191-5, 215, 220

Constantine II king of Scots 900—43

Constantine II was a grandson of *Kenneth mac Alpín and his long and successful reign witnessed a period of crucial consolidation and development within the medieval Scottish kingdom. His earliest military ventures show him acting as the ally, if not the overlord, of the Bernician Angles who sought his help in their struggle with the Danes of York. Constantine twice came to the support of the Bernicians in two battles fought at Corbridge on the Tyne against the Danish king, *Ragnall of York. The Scots were defeated in both battles (in 914 and 918), but in the second encounter the Danes suffered heavy losses and may have been enforced to come to terms with Constantine. For the remainder of his reign, Constantine proved a consistent ally of the York Danes who were themselves threatened by the rising power of Wessex under *Edward the Elder and his son *Athelstan. Constantine was among those northern leaders who made peace with Edward in 920, and seven years later he renewed that peace with Athelstan at Eamont near Penrith. Athelstan stood sponsor to Constantine's son at baptism and the Scottish king promised not to support the claims of *Gothfrith, king of Dublin, to the kingship of Scandinavian York. Constantine broke this peace with Wessex in 934 when he renewed his alliance with *Olafr Gothfrithson, the newly elected king of Norse Dublin, and Athelstan retaliated by invading the Scots kingdom as far as Dunnottar or perhaps Edinburgh. Constantine may have been forced to give his son as a hostage to Athelstan in 934, but by 937, the Scottish king was again on the offensive against Wessex fighting as the chief ally of his son-in-law, Olafr Gothfrithson, in the battle of *Brunanburh*. While *Brunanburh* proved to be a crushing defeat for Olafr Gothfrithson and Constantine, Olafr eventually swept back to York in 939 and Constantine's influence in northern England increased accordingly. Constantine abdicated in 943 and retired as a monk to St Andrews. He is said to have incited his successor, *Malcolm I, to undertake an invasion of England as far as the Tees in 948—9, some sources even claiming that Constantine led the expedition himself, having come out of retirement for a week 'to visit the English'. In spite of his longstanding alliance with pagan Northmen, Constantine was a supporter of the Church and its rulers. He was remembered as a friend of St *Catroe, and he reached an agreement with Bishop Cellach of St Andrews pledging himself to uphold the rights of the Scottish church in 906. During his reign, St Andrews emerged as the most important centre of Scottish Christianity, and Constantine died there, in religion, in 952.

BIBL. Smyth 1975: 63, 96-9, 107, 110; 1979: 40-4, 48-9, 63-6, 78, 171-2; Smyth 1984: 197-8, 201-8, 233-5

Constantine III (the Bald) king of Scots 995−7

Constantine was the son of *Culen Ring and he was the last of the descendants of Áed son of *Kenneth mac Alpín to hold the Scottish kingship. He was one of the conspirators who had been plotting against *Kenneth II, Constantine's father and uncle having fallen previously in the feud with Kenneth's dynasty. Constantine was slain, probably by Kenneth III, at *Rathinveramon*, and was buried on Iona.

BIBL. Anderson 1922, vol. 1: 517-19

Constantine St, king of the Strathclyde Britons c. 600

In Joceline's late twelfth-century *Life* of *Kentigern, Constantine is given as the son of *Riderch Hen, a late sixth-century king of the Strathclyde Britons, and his queen, *Languoreth*. This source also claims that this boy, who was of saintly disposition, succeeded his father in the kingdom and excelled all his predecessors as a powerful king of Strathclyde. Serious problems arise from trying to identify this Constantine in earlier sources. The *Annals of Ulster* record 'the conversion of Constantine to the Lord' in 588. While this Constantine might well be a son of Riderch Hen, the year would seem too early for such a son (and also a successor, if we are to accept the narrative in Kentigern's *Life*) to have retired to a monastery. Early Irish martyrologies record the festival of a certain Constantine on 11 March and identify him as a Briton or as a son of Fergus, king of the Picts. This may be a confused reference to *Constantine son of Fergus, king of Picts and Scots who died in 820. Such a Constantine would be too recent to find a mention in the *Martyrology of Óengus* (composed c. 800), and besides, the Constantine of Irish calendars was supposed to have been the contemporary or successor of Mochuta of Rahan in Mide in central Ireland, which monastery he was supposed to have retired to, after his abdication in Britain. Mochuta died in 637, and it would have been possible for a son of Riderch Hen to have retired to Rahan about that time, but if so, we are still left to explain the entry in the *Annals of Ulster* under 588. Finally, the Breviary of Aberdeen adds to the complexity of the problem by claiming that Constantine was the son of Paternus, king of Cornwall, who first retired to an Irish monastery and from there journeyed to Scotland, first to *Columba and later to Kentigern who sent him to preach in Galloway. Eventually, he was alleged to have suffered martyrdom in Kintyre in 576 — a date which cannot be reconciled with the career of the son of Riderch Hen as outlined above. Clearly, the careers of at least three Constantines have been confused in the medieval records.

BIBL. Anderson 1922, vol. 1: 91-4, 135

Constantine son of Fergus, king of Scots and Picts 789−820

Constantine was one of three Kings of the Cenél Gabhráin to hold the kingship of the Scots and Picts prior to the reign of *Kenneth mac Alpín. Constantine assumed the Pictish kingship in 789 having defeated his rival *Conall son of Tadg in battle, and his name appears in Pictish king-lists under the form of *Castantin* son of *Uurguist.* He may not have succeeded to the kingship of Dál Riata until 811. His reign over both Picts and Scots represents an important stage in the unification of medieval Scotland although historians are not agreed on whether the Scottish or Pictish element dominated at this time. Constantine's reign witnessed the opening of the Viking Age in Scotland and he founded (or refounded) an important church at Dunkeld to compensate for the loss of Iona, by then engulfed in Norse territory. The Gaelic abbot of Dunkeld was soon (865) to be described by a contemporary chronicler as 'chief bishop of Fortriu'. Constantine was described as 'king of Fortriu' at his death in 820.

BIBL. Anderson 1973: 191-4; Smyth 1984; 177-80

Cormac Ua Liatháin explorer and monk *c.* 560−90

Cormac son of Dimma was of the Irish tribe of Uí Liathaín whose territories lay in coastal Cork. *Adomnán's detailed accounts of Cormac's voyages of exploration in the Scottish Isles and in the North Atlantic are important, because they pre-date the more elaborate and less well authenticated tales of Brendan's voyages. The first expedition set out from Irrus Domnann on the coast of north-west Mayo and failed to find land, or a 'desert in the ocean' − the real object of these monastic journeys. The second involved a voyage lasting for several months through the Northern Isles of Scotland when *Columba negotiated a safe passage for Cormac and his companions through the Pictish kingdom on Orkney. This voyage may be dated before the death of Brendan of Birr (565 or 573) and while Columba was not yet long in Scotland. Cormac returned safely from his second expedition to visit Columba on Iona. The third and longest voyage lasted for 14 days' sail on the outward journey, due north into the Atlantic, in a skin-covered boat propelled by oars and sail and crewed by several companions. Cormac and his mariners also returned via Iona from this voyage which clearly involved a route through the Scottish Isles towards the Faroes using Iona as a base camp. It is evident from Adomnán's *Life of Columba* that while Cormac was a monastic founder in his own right, he was also regarded as a monk of Columba's *familia.* Other Irish sources associate Cormac with Durrow which he probably ruled as its first abbot, and where he was a contemporary of *Laisran who was later an abbot of Iona. Yet another tradition in the Calendar of Óengus (*c.* 800) asserts that Cormac was slain by wolves. His festival was kept at 21 June. He enjoyed the appropriate nickname of *Cormac Leir* ('Cormac of the Sea').

BIBL. Anderson and Anderson 1961: 222-5, 440-7, 500-1; Reeves 1857: 116 n.*a*, 222 n.*e*, 264-77

Coroticus *see* **Ceretic**

Crinan abbot of Dunkeld *c*. 1020–45

Crinan (or Crónán) was abbot of Dunkeld, one of the chief churches of Scotland, but he was also, through his marriage with Bethoc, the father of *Duncan I of Scotland. Since *Malcolm II had not left a male heir on his death in 1034, the succession passed to his grandson, Duncan, the son of Malcolm's daughter Bethoc and of Crinan of Dunkeld. Duncan's authority was challenged by *Macbeth who slew Duncan in 1040 and drove his infant sons into exile. Crinan of Dunkeld seems to have raised a rebellion against Macbeth in 1045 with a view to placing Malcolm Canmore on the throne. According to the *Annals of Tigernach* he was slain in an internal feud in Scotland along with 180 of his supporters. Crinan may have attacked Macbeth with help from *Siward, earl of Northumbria, who was sheltering Crinan's grandson, Malcolm Canmore at this time. Crinan most likely ruled as a lay-abbot of Dunkeld, a church which had become firmly identified with the political fortunes of the dynasty of *Kenneth mac Alpín from the middle of the tenth century. Crinan may have been the son of Duncan, an earlier abbot of Dunkeld who was slain in a feud between the rival kings *Dub and *Culen in 965. Crinan had a great-grandson, Æthelred, Earl of Fife, who was also abbot of Dunkeld (and the son of Margaret and Malcolm III Canmore).

BIBL. Anderson 1922, vol. I: 583-4; Duncan 1975: 99-100, 165; Skene 1886-90, vol. 1: 390-2, 407

Cú-Chuimne the Wise monk and canonist of Iona *c*. 700–47

Cú-Chuimne was the author of one of the finest extant Hiberno-Latin poems which testifies to devotion to the Virgin Mary in the eighth-century Irish church. He is also associated along with Rubin of Dair Inis in Munster (*d*. 725) with a compilation of Irish Canons known as the *Collectio Canonum Hibernensis* — a miscellany of church law, pastoral advice and practical matters on administration. The collection became an important work of reference, not only for the insular Celtic church but for Gaulish and Breton churches as well. Two verses associated with Cú-Chuimne are found in a marginal note beside the contemporary notice of his death in the *Annals of Ulster*. This information suggests that Cú-Chuimne turned his back on a life of fornication (perhaps with nuns) in preference for a career of scholarship. In the *Annals of Ulster* the verses are ascribed to Cú-Chuimne's foster-mother, while in the *Liber Hymnorum* the first verse is ascribed to *Adomnán and the second, by the way of reply, to Cú-Chuimne himself. The association with Adomnán may well be historical. Cú-Chuimne died in 747 as a monk of Iona during the abbacy there of *Cillene Droichtech. But he could have served as a younger man under Adomnán who died on Iona in 704. Perhaps as the verses imply, he was Adomnán's pupil. Adomnán is one of the latest authorities cited in the *Collectio Canonum* ascribed to Cú-Chuimne.

BIBL. Kenney 1929: 247-50, 269-70

Culen Ring king of Scots 966–71

Culen was the son of *Indulf, king of Scots, and his Scandinavian byname (Old Norse *Hringr*) betrays the Viking influence on the tenth-century Scottish court. Culen seized the Scottish kingship from his predecessor, *Dub, whom he drove into exile in Moray in 966. It is possible that Culen, unlike his father, Indulf, had not held the sub-kingdom of Strathclyde before he took power in Scotland, and that it was his exclusion from Strathclyde by *Donald son of Owen which drove him to revolt against Dub in the first instance. Culen was slain by Riderch son of Donald of Strathclyde, perhaps in Lothian, in 971.

BIBL. Anderson 1922, vol. 1: 475-7; Smyth 1984: 210-11, 223-4

Cumméne Find abbot of Iona 657−69

Cumméne succeeded *Suibhne as seventh abbot of Iona in 657. His father's name is given variously as Ernán, Dinertach, or Fiachna. He was a kinsman of *Columba, being the nephew of Abbot *Ségéne (623−52) and a grand-nephew of *Laisran the third abbot, who had served under Columba. It was during Cumméne's abbacy that the dispute in Northumbria between those who followed the Celtic liturgy of Iona (and Lindisfarne) and those, led by *Wilfrid, who preferred Roman ways, developed into a confrontation at Whitby in 664. Bishop *Finán of Lindisfarne had died in 661, and Cumméne of Iona despatched *Colmán, one of his community, to succeed him. Opposition to Colmán's Celtic liturgical usage developed to the point of convening a synod at Whitby where *Oswiu, king of Northumbria, sided with Wilfrid's party in adopting Roman ways. The long-term results of this decision were catastrophic for Iona whose vast influence over the northern and midland churches of England was reduced at a stroke. Cumméne may have been prompted by these disasters to defend the reputation of Iona's saintly founder, which the decision handed out at Whitby could be seen to have ignored if not slighted. Cumméne's book on *The miraculous powers of Saint Columba* survives in only one passage quoted by *Adomnán, but the work clearly formed a basis for Adomnán's own *Life* of Columba. Cumméne speaks of Columba's special relationship with *Áedán mac Gabhráin and his Scottish successors, and he refers to recent disasters in Dál Riata in the reign of *Domnall Brecc. Cumméne is reported to have visited Ireland in 661, when he may have spent a lengthy time in the Columban monastery on Rathlin Island. He died in 669 (perhaps having fallen victim to the Great Plague which raged from 664 to 668) and was succeeded by *Failbe in the abbacy of Iona. An alternative form of his nickname *find* ('the Fair'), is given by Adomnán and other writers as *Albus* ('the White'). His festival was celebrated on 24 February.

BIBL. Anderson and Anderson 1961: 91 and text; Herbert 1988: 43-5; Reeves 1857: 375-6; Smyth 1984: 86-7, 95-6, 117-18

Cunedda founding figure of the First Dynasty of Gwynedd *fl*. fifth century

The early ninth-century *Historia Brittonum* (see under *Nennius) claims that 146 years before *Maelgwn, Cunedda, with his eight sons, came to Gwynedd in north Wales from Manaw of the Gododdin in north Britain (in the vicinity of Stirling). By the mid-tenth century the name of a grandson had been added, and all of them were identified as the princes who gave their names to territories adjacent to Gwynedd — including, for example, Ceredig (the eponym of Ceredigion) and Meirion, the alleged grandson (the eponym of Meirionydd). Cunedda and his sons are said on their arrival in Gwynedd to have driven out the Irish (or Scots) invaders from their territories. The period of 146 years may represent a calculation based on the assumption that Cunedda belonged to the time of the usurping Roman emperor, Magnus Maximus, who died in 388 and who was believed in Welsh legend to have established in power a number of British ruling families; an addition of 146 to 388 gives 534, the year in which Maelgwn's father, Cadwallon 'Long hand', king of Gwynedd, is said to have died and in which Maelgwn could have become king. The later genealogy of the First Dynasty of the kings of Gwynedd traces their descent back to Cunedda.

The picture this 'foundation-legend' or 'origin-story' presents, therefore, is of Cunedda moving from north Britain with a numerous progeny to combat the Irish and to establish his political dominance in north Wales in the late fourth century, almost as an act of late Roman frontier policy. How historical is it? There appears to have been no significant Irish settlement in west Wales before the early fifth century, and it may not have been until the mid-tenth century that the eponyms of the kingdoms bordering on Gwynedd — at least one of whom (Ceredig) may date to the mid-sixth century — were identified as Cunedda's sons. In the genealogies Cunedda appears as the great-grandfather of Maelgwn but in the earlier *Historia Brittonum* as the *atavus* of Maelgwn, which signifies grandfather's great-grandfather. This raises the possibility that it was Cunedda's reputed grandfather, Padarn of the Red Robe, who was responsible for the migration to Gwynedd. There seems no reason to suppose that such a migration could not have taken place. At a time of far-reaching movements of people around Britain — Irish, Picts, Anglo-Saxons — some degree of internal displacement is to be expected. Furthermore, if the traditional ancestor of the First Dynasty of Gwynedd came from Votadini territory, this might help to explain its subsequent military involvement against the Northumbrians at a time when the survival of the Votadini was threatened by the Northumbrian advance to the Forth. But whether from north Britain or not, Cunedda may be seen as one of a number of British leaders who created new British kingdoms in north Wales in the context of British-Irish warfare in the course of the fifth century and early sixth.

BIBL. Alcock 1971; Miller 1976/8; Davies 1982: 89 ff.

Cuneglasus British king *fl.* early sixth century

Calling him 'the bear', *Gildas parodied the name of Cuneglasus (Cynlas), which means 'Tawny hound' as 'Tawny Butcher' and included him among the British kings whom he condemned for the immorality and violence of their lives. Gildas locates him in the 'Bear's fortress', *Dineirth*, which was in the cantref of Rhos east of the Conwy, part of the kingdom of Gwynedd in north Wales, and a Cynlas ab Owain appears as the grandson of Einion, son of *Cunedda, in the genealogies of the kings of Gwynedd, the cousin, therefore, on this evidence of Maelgwn.

BIBL. Jackson 1982: 33-4

Cunomor (Mark) British ruler in Dumnonia *fl.* sixth century

Cunomor (Cynfawr) was a sixth-century ruler of territory in Dumnonia (Devon and Cornwall) and possibly also in Armorica (Brittany) and even south Wales, who is mentioned by Gregory of Tours at the end of the sixth century and who appears as a tyrannical usurper in ninth-century Breton saints' *Lives*. The *Life* of Paul Aurelian, founding saint of Saint-Pol-de-Leon in Brittany, represents Paul as visiting Cunomor, otherwise called Mark, as he journeyed from south Wales to Brittany. An inscribed stone from Castle Dore on the Fowey estuary bears the inscription 'Drustaus filius Cunomori' — 'Drustan son of Cunomor' — who perhaps came to be identified as Tristan, tragic hero of medieval poetry and romance, a nephew of King Mark, who courted and loved Isolde.

BIBL. Bromwich 1961: 329-33, 443-8; Chadwick 1969: 212-14, 221-23; Alcock 1971: 161, 212; Chédeville and Guillotel 1984: 71 ff.; Padel 1981: 53-81

Curetan (Kiritinus, Boniface) St, bishop of Rosemarkie *c.* 690–710

Curetan was one of the witnesses at the Synod of Birr in 697 which promulgated *Adomnán's *Law of Innocents* protecting women and non-combatants in time of war. He is commemorated in the Martyrologies of *Tallaght* (tenth-century) and of *O'Gorman* (twelfth-century) on 16 March, where he is associated with Rosemarkie on the Black Isle (Ross). This was the area where Christianity first came to northern Pictland from Iona up the Great Glen. The region is rich in Pictish sculpture and Christian cross-slabs which may well have originated in the Moray area under Columban influence in the seventh century. Eastern Mediterranean influence on the iconography of the Pictish Class II monuments at Nigg and Hilton of Cadboll (both close to Rosemarkie) is of interest in view of the claims made for Curetan's Eastern origins in his *Life*. The legend or *vita* of Curetan is found under the name of *Boniface* in the early sixteenth-century Breviary of Aberdeen. But since his festival in that source is given as 16 March (the same day as for Curetan in earlier Martyrologies) and since in the *vita* Boniface is portrayed as the contemporary of *Nechtán son of Derile, king of the Picts and contemporary of Adomnán, the identification of Boniface with Curetan seems secure. The legend of Boniface resembles that of *Serf and was clearly invented to support the Roman party in Pictland (originally led by Adomnán and later by Nechtán son of Derile) by showing how some early Scottish saints had impeccably orthodox Roman and Mediterranean credentials. Boniface is said to have been of Hebrew origin, descended from the sister of SS Peter and Andrew and to have been ordained priest by the Patriarch of Jerusalem. As in the case of his older contemporary, Serf, he went to Rome and got himself elected to the Papacy. He then personally led a mission to Pictland (Pictavia) arriving at Restenneth in Angus. Nechtán encountered the pilgrims at Restenneth and he and his warriors and ministers accepted baptism at their hands. The Pictish king also handed over the place of his baptism to the Holy Trinity, granting it to Boniface. The saint is said to have founded 150 churches before his death at 84. Other traditions associate Boniface-Kiritinus with the church at Invergowrie, and it is notable that all three churches at Rosemarkie, Invergowrie and Restenneth have dedications to St Peter — tying in well with historical associations with Nechtán son of Derile and his Romanizing party. We may dismiss Curetan's Near Eastern origins as fiction, but the invention came into being in order to underline the support this ally of Adomnán gave to King Nechtán during the Easter Controversy in Pictland in the early eighth century.

BIBL. Anderson 1922, vol. 1: 205, 211; Skene 1886-90, vol. 1: 277-8; vol. 2: 229-32; Smyth 1984: 127-8, 134

Cuthbald abbot 673/4−c. 690

Cuthbald is said to have been abbot of Medeshamstede (Peterborough) between *Seaxwulf (who became bishop of the Mercians in 675) and Ecgbald (c. 687/90). A number of daughter-houses of Medeshamstede are said to have been founded in Cuthbald's time, including Breedon (see *Hædda), Bermondsey and Woking, Repton, Thorney and Brixworth. Brixworth is particularly noteworthy in view of the survival there of an early church, described as 'the greatest English building of the pre-Danish period' and 'perhaps the most imposing architectural memorial of the seventh century yet surviving north of the Alps'.

BIBL. Stenton 1933; Whitelock 1972: 12-14; Clapham 1930: 33

Cuthbert St, bishop 685−7

Cuthbert, though indissolubly connected with the community of Lindisfarne, began his monastic career at Melrose, under Abbot *Eata, in 651, when he was about 18 years of age. The house was decidedly Irish in tone (its prior, Boisil, was an Irishman), and Cuthbert was trained in the traditions of Celtic Christianity. He moved with Eata to Ripon, where land for a monastery had been provided by *Alhfrith of Deira, but the king's insistence that Roman customs should be followed led to their withdrawal and return to Melrose, where Cuthbert succeeded Boisil as prior. Ripon was given to *Wilfrid, who championed the Roman cause at the Synod of Whitby, in 664; when the Northumbrian church agreed to accept Roman customs, Melrose obeyed the edict. Eata himself was made abbot of Lindisfarne after *Colmán withdrew to Ireland, and Cuthbert accompanied him as prior. In 676, he withdrew from the communal life to become a hermit on the Inner Farne, but in 685 he was prevailed upon to accept the bishopric of Hexham, after the deposition of Tunberht. Cuthbert's extreme unwillingness to leave Lindisfarne was only overcome when Eata, who was by this time its bishop, exchanged the see of Lindisfarne for that of Hexham. Two years later, Cuthbert resigned his bishopric and returned to the Inner Farne, where he died on 20 February 687.

Cuthbert's posthumous influence surpassed his earthly authority. In 698 his body was discovered incorrupt, and was enshrined in the church of Lindisfarne. A cult rapidly developed; the anonymous *Life of Cuthbert* was composed before 705, and subsequent Lives, one in verse and one in prose, were commissioned from *Bede himself. The popularity of Cuthbert's cult must in part have been due to the patronage of the Northumbrian kings, whose chief residence, Bamburgh, was Lindisfarne's close neighbour. The shock which ran through northern Europe when Lindisfarne was sacked by the Vikings in 793 is vividly expressed by *Alcuin, in a letter to the Northumbrian king, *Æthelred (see *Higbald).

The shrine itself, however, remained intact, and it was not for another century that the community moved away from its exposed island to Chester-le-Street (see *Eardwulf). The coffin of Cuthbert, which contained relics of St *Oswald and others as well as Cuthbert himself, was enshrined in the new church. Here it was enriched by subsequent kings; the remnants of the splendid silk vestments presented by *Athelstan are displayed in the treasury of Durham Cathedral (where the community finally settled), along with other treasures, including Cuthbert's own pectoral cross.

BIBL. Colgrave 1940; Rollason 1987a

Cuthbert archbishop of Canterbury 740−60

Cuthbert, who succeeded *Nothhelm as archbishop of Canterbury, was the first to be buried in Christchurch, instead of St Augustine's. It was to him that *Boniface sent a copy of the reforming decrees of the Frankish synod held in 747. Within the year, Cuthbert had held an English council at *Clofesho* to deal with abuses in the English church, notably lay control of monasteries and minsters. Cuthbert also built a church to the east of Christchurch Cathedral, dedicated to St John the Baptist, for use as a baptistry.

BIBL. Brooks 1984: 51, 80-5

Cuthbert abbot, *d*. after 764

Cuthbert, a pupil of *Bede, composed a first-hand account of his master's death, which was widely circulated in England and on the continent in the Middle Ages. He subsequently became abbot of Monkwearmouth and corresponded with *Lul, whom he supplied with copies of the prose and verse lives of St *Cuthbert, composed by Bede.

BIBL. Colgrave and Mynors 1969: 580-7

Cuthred king of Kent 798−807

Cuthred, brother of *Cœnwulf of Mercia, was established as king in Kent, after the suppression of *Eadberht Præn in 798. In his time, Viking raids on the south-east became sufficiently severe for the community at Lyminge to be granted a church and land in Canterbury as a refuge against pagan attack. Cuthred died in 807.

BIBL. Brooks 1984: 131-2; Sawyer 1968: no. 804

Cwœnthryth abbess *d*. after 827

Cwœnthryth, daughter of *Cœnwulf of Mercia, was abbess of the family monastery at Winchcombe, Gloucestershire, and also had charge of the religious houses at Minster-in-Thanet and Reculver, which Cœnwulf apparently claimed as the heir of the Kentish kings, who had founded them. Cœnwulf, and Cwœnthryth as his heir, were involved in a long dispute over the ownership of the Kentish minsters with Archbishop *Wulfred, which was settled at the Synod of *Clofesho* in 825, in Wulfred's favour. Cwœnthryth appears in later legend as the murderer of her brother St Kenelm (see *Cynehelm), but there is no historical basis for this story which has all the appearance of a folk-tale.

BIBL. Brooks 1984: 182-5, 190-7

Cynan ap Brochfæl king of Powys *fl.* early seventh century
Cynan ap Brochfæl appears to have been a king of Powys *c.* 600. His son, Selyf 'Serpent in battles', was slain at the battle of Chester *c.* 615 by the northern Angles under the leadership of *Æthelfrith. An early battle-catalogue poem ascribed to *Taliesin celebrates Cynan's victories from Anglesey to the River Wye, describing him as Cadelling (of the lineage of *Cadell).

BIBL. Bromwich 1961: 318-19; Foster 1965: 228-30; Davies 1982: 94

Cynddylan ap Cyndrwyn ruler in Powys *fl.* mid-seventh century
Cynddylan, possibly a king in Powys, figures in the unhistorical cycle of poems ascribed to *Llywarch Hen as an heroic warrior of the borders whose sister, Heledd, in the deserted hall of Cynddylan laments her brother's death in battle against the Saxons, the destruction of his residence of *Pengwern* (located perhaps either on the Wrekin or at nearby Wrock-wardine) and his burial at Baschurch. A reference to Cynddylan as present at the battle of *Maserfeld* (probably Old Oswestry), which *Bede dates to 642 and where the northern king, *Oswald, was slain, seems to locate him in the first half of the seventh century. A quite separate, possibly contemporary, elegy attributed to the bard Meigant alludes to a campaign in the vicinity of Lichfield (in the heart of the Mercian kingdom) where not even 'book-holding monks were afforded protection'.

BIBL. Kirby 1977: 36-8; Davies 1982: 99-100; Gruffydd 1982: 10-28; Jarman 1981: 99-102; Rowland 1989

Cynegils king of Wessex 611–43
Cynegils, king of Wessex, seems to have ruled in conjunction with his son, Cwichhelm. In 628, the two kings were defeated by *Penda of Mercia at the battle of Cirencester, which probably resulted in the loss to Wessex of the lands around the lower Severn conquered by *Ceawlin and Cuthwine from the British in 577. Northumbrian hostility was provoked by the attempt of Cwichhelm to have King *Edwin assassinated, *c.* 625; relations were only restored in the time of *Oswald, who married Cynegils's daughter Cyneburh. It was Oswald who persuaded Cynegils to accept Christianity; he founded the see of Dorchester-on-Thames for *Birinus the 'apostle' of Wessex, *c.* 635. Cwichhelm seems to have predeceased his father, for when Cynegils died in 643, he was succeeded by another son, *Cenwealh.

BIBL. Stenton 1971: 66-7; 118

Cynehelm (Kenelm) St, ætheling *d*. 812

Cynehelm, son of *Cœnwulf of Mercia, probably predeceased his father, for he is not heard of after 812. He was buried in the family monastery of Winchcombe, Gloucestershire, ruled by his sister *Cwœnthryth. By the tenth century, if not earlier, he was venerated as a saint. The account of his passion, the earliest version of which appears to date from the eleventh century, cannot be reconciled with the known facts of his life. He is said to have become king on the death of his father (in 821), while still a child. He was then murdered by his tutor at the instigation of his jealous sister, at Clent, Worcestershire, and his body was concealed. However, a letter deposited by a dove on the altar of St Peter's at Rome, and interpreted by a passing English pilgrim, revealed the whereabouts of the royal corpse. It was duly translated to Winchcombe, and Cwœnthryth's eyes fell out as she was reciting a psalm backwards (presumably to prevent its arrival). The obvious legendary and folk motifs in this farrago do not nullify the fact of Cynehelm's existence; he was a real Mercian ætheling, though little is known of him. Even the most apparently nonsensical tales may contain a stratum of truth.

BIBL. Rollason 1983: 9-10

Cynewulf king of Wessex 757–86

The history of Wessex is very obscure between the retirement of *Ine in 726 and the accession of Cynewulf in 757, which coincided with the murder of *Æthelbald of Mercia. The subsequent civil war in Mercia enabled Cynewulf to regain the shires of Berkshire and Wiltshire seized by Æthelbald. In 779, however, Cynewulf was defeated by *Offa at Bensington, and though he seems never to have submitted to Mercian overlordship, he was very much in the shadow of his great contemporary. In 786, when Cynewulf died, *Beorhtric, who was more sympathetic to Offa, became the king of Wessex. Cynewulf was killed by his kinsman, the ætheling Cyneheard, in the course of a dynastic quarrel, related at length in the *Anglo-Saxon Chronicle*. At the beginning of his reign, Cynewulf had expelled Cyneheard's brother, Sigeberht, from the kingdom. In 786, Cyneheard learnt that the king was visiting his mistress at the *burh* (the fortified manor-house) of *Merantun* (unidentified). The king and his lady were in the bower, that is, a separate building within the main enclosure-wall, while the royal bodyguard was in the hall; Cyneheard was able to kill the king before his men were aware of the attack. He then besieged the hall and killed the men of the bodyguard. When the rest of the royal army came up on the following day, Cyneheard closed the gates in the enclosure-wall and held it against the host, but eventually the gates were forced and the ætheling and his men were killed. The annal, besides its general interest, reveals clearly the lay-out of an English fortified manor-house of the period.

BIBL. *ASC* s.a. 757; White 1989

Cynewulf poet *fl*. ninth century

Most surviving Old English poetry is anonymous, but Cynewulf's work is identified by the runic 'signatures' which he incorporated into his poems.

He lived apparently in the ninth century, probably in Mercia, or possibly Northumbria, but no biographical details are available. His themes were religious; *Christ* is a meditation on the Ascension; *Elene* tells the story of the discovery of the Holy Cross by St Helena, mother of Constantine the Great; *Juliana* is about one of the Diocletian martyrs; and *The Fates of the Apostles* concerns the missionary journeys of Jesus' disciples.

BIBL. Sisam 1932

Cyngen ap Cadell king of Powys *d. c.* 855

When Cyngen, king of Powys, set up the pillar of *Eliseg at Llantysilio-yn-Ial near Llangollen to honour his grandfather's military exploits against the Saxons, he also celebrated his own, and though the words of the inscription on the pillar are now largely illegible he appears to be claiming to have restored the monarchy and kingdom of Powys, presumably in the aftermath of Saxon conquest in 822/3. His sister, Esyllt, was given in marriage to *Merfyn ap Gwriad, who established himself as king of Gwynedd in 825 and thereby founded a new dynasty. Cyngen died in Rome in (probably) 855. He was not necessarily the last native king of Powys but before *c.* 890 Powys had fallen under the control of the grandsons of Merfyn and Esyllt.

BIBL. Lloyd, vol. I 1911: 324-5; Bartrum 1966: 1ff.

Cynlas British king *fl.* early sixth century *see* **Cuneglasus**

D

David (Dewi) St, abbot and bishop *fl.* sixth century

The earliest reference to St David or Dewi Sant, traditionally a bishop and abbot, occurs on a mid-seventh-century inscription (now fragmented) at Llandewi-Brefi: he is also referred to in the early ninth-century Irish *Martyrology of Óengus* and *Martyrology of Tallaght* (under 1 March). In the ninth-century *Life* of Paul Aurelian, founder of Saint Pol-de-Leon, David is referred to as 'aquaticus', signifying that he lived on bread and water, but the earliest extant *Life of David* by Rhigyfarch, the son of Sulien, bishop of St David's, was not written until *c*. 1080–90. The cult of David was evidently well-established in south Wales with its principal focus at Menevia (St David's), and other important centres at Henfynyw (Old Menevia), near Aberaeron, and Llandewi-Brefi, but few if any details of the historical David are known. Rhigyfarch portrays him as having introduced a strict order of life into his foundation at St David's, involving manual work, silence and a vegetarian diet, but to some extent this picture may have been coloured by the ascetic movement which characterized Celtic monasticism in the eighth and ninth centuries. The Irish annals place the death of David in 589, the mid-tenth-century Harleian annals in 601, neither necessarily correctly.

BIBL. Bowen 1961: 50ff.; Chadwick 1958c: 131ff.; James 1967; Evans 1988; Henken 1987: 31-73

Deiniol St, abbot and bishop *fl.* sixth century

Nothing is known of St Deiniol, the focus of whose cult was Bangor in Arfon, with another important centre at Bangor-is-Coed (Bangor-on-Dee) in Powys, the latter described by *Bede as a monastery of over 2,000 men; but the mid-tenth-century Harleian annals record Deiniol's death in 584, not, of course, necessarily correctly. He is commemorated in the early ninth-century Irish *Martyrology of Tallaght* (under 11 September).

BIBL. Bowen 1961: 78; Miller 1979b: 62ff.; Henken 1987: 187-9

Deusdedit archbishop of Canterbury 655–64

Deusdedit, a West Saxon, was the first Englishman to become archbishop of Canterbury. His given name seems to have been Frithuwine ('peace-friend'). He was consecrated on 12 March 655 by Ithamar, bishop of Rochester. He died of the plague in 664.

BIBL. Brooks 1984: 67-9

Diarmait monk of Iona 563–*c*. 607

Diarmait is named in the late seventh-century list of 12 companions who sailed with *Columba from Ireland to northern Britain in 563. Diarmait is placed fourth in the list after *Baithine (Columba's successor), Baithine's brother, and Columba's uncle, Ernán. Diarmait, if not a close relative of Columba must have sprung from a kin which was connected with Columba's royal household in northern Ireland. *Adomnán makes frequent mention of Diarmait in his *Life* of Columba, referring to him as a 'devoted servant' (*pius minister*). He acted as Columba's personal messenger; attended on his master in his writing office; organized preparations for Mass; he is seen as bell-ringer summoning the monks to assembly, and generally acted as an ecclesiastical batman. Diarmait accompanied Columba on an expedition up the Great Glen into the land of the northern Picts, and at another time Adomnán shows the attendant travelling in Columba's party through Ardnamurchan and chatting on the way with *Laisran, a future abbot of Iona. Diarmait attended on his master in the closing hours of Columba's life, and the remarkable detail offered by Adomnán on that episode may have survived as a written record from Diarmait himself. Adomnán tells us that Diarmait survived Columba by 'many years'.

BIBL. Anderson and Anderson 1961: (text); Smyth 1984: 86, 88, 98, 115

Domangart son of Domnall Brecc, king of Scots Dál Riata 660–73

Domangart probably succeeded in expanding and re-uniting the kingdom of Dál Riata under his single rule, the kingship having been divided since his father's defeat at Mag Rath in 637. He is one of the few kings designated 'king of Dál Riata' in contemporary annals at this time, and the emphasis on his title may point to his re-unification of the kingdom. During his reign, the Scots made successful inroads into Pictish-held territory on the Isle of Skye. In 668 we read of a migration of 'the sons of Gartnait' along with the people of Skye to Ireland, while in 670 the 'family' or dynasty (*genus*) of Gartnait returned from Ireland. The detailed record of this long-standing feud points to Dál Riata expansion northwards along the western coast of Scotland at the expense of the Picts. It is significant that the Irish missionary, *Màelrubai, founded his monastery at Applecross in 673 in the last year of Domangart's reign. Applecross looks out on Skye, that very area of western Pictland which for 30 years previously had been bitterly contested by Scots Dál Riata and the Picts. It would seem that the Scots had finally achieved their goal, and that the foundation of Applecross marks the beginning of permanent Gaelic (i.e. Scottish) ecclesiastical influence in that region.

BIBL. Bannerman 1974: 92-3; Anderson 1973: 105, 154-7

Domangart son of Fergus Mór, king of Dál Riata *c*. 501–7

Domangart was the second king of Dál Riata in succession to his father, *Fergus Mór, the founder of the Scots dynasty. An apocryphal Irish tradition claims that Domangart (together with numerous other Irish royal contemporaries) was present at Patrick's deathbed. Domangart may have become a cleric before his death, which is recorded in the *Annals of Ulster* in 507. His two sons are mentioned in *Adomnán's *Life of Columba*.

BIBL. Bannerman 1974: 75-6

Domnall Brecc king of Scots Dál Riata 629–42

Domnall was the son of *Eochaid Buide who succeeded to the Dál Riata kingship on the death of his brother *Connad Cerr in the battle of Fid Eoin in Ulster. Domnall's reign marks a disastrous turning point in the early history of the Scots dynasty when it lost ground not only in its Irish homeland but also among all of its northern British neighbours. It was also a time when the Scottish church, ruled from Iona, suffered serious setbacks from which it never recovered in northern England. Domnall's fighting career began in 622, when his father Eochaid Buide ruled Dál Riata. In that year Domnall was the victorious ally of the Irish Uí Néill king in distant Meath. *Adomnán, following *Cumméne Find (an earlier biographer of *Columba), believed that Domnall Brecc had incurred the wrath of Columba who had prophesied success for the dynasty of *Áedán mac Gabhráin only if it respected the community of Iona and the dynasty of Columba's kindred in Ireland. So while Columba was believed to have blessed Domnall, his own kinsman and son of the Irish highking Áed mac Ainmerech, equally he was believed to have (posthumously) cursed Domnall Brecc for attacking that same Domnall son of Aed in the battle of Mag Rath in Co. Down, in 637. In that battle the Scots king was fighting as the ally of the Ulster king of Dál nAraide against the Uí Néill kindred of Columba. The outcome for Domnall was disastrous. He was heavily defeated and the Scots in Argyll probably lost all control of their Ulster lands from this time onwards. Cumméne believed this defeat also resulted in the collapse of Dál Riata power in Scotland and that for the next 30 years Dál Riata fell under the domination of 'strangers'. These 'strangers' may have been Picts and Strathclyde Britons – the latter becoming especially powerful in the reign of *Owen map Bili. *Oswiu of Northumbria (642–70) also brought the Scots into a tributary position, while at the Synod of Whitby in 664, Oswiu backed the Roman party to the exclusion of the administrative and liturgical influence of Iona on the Northumbrian church which Iona had previously ruled from Lindisfarne.

Domnall Brecc may have been compelled to share the kingship of Dál Riata with Ferchar son of Connad Cerr who died in *c*. 650. Domnall suffered two defeats perhaps at the hands of the Picts, the first in 635 at Calathros (perhaps in Islay) and the second in Glenn Mureson in 638. He fell fighting against the Strathclyde Britons in Strathcarron, Stirlingshire, in 642. The victor was Owen map Bili, king of Strathclyde.

BIBL. Bannerman 1974: 99-103; Anderson 1973: 152-4

Domneva St, queen and abbess, *d*. 6954 *see* **Eafa**

Donald I (Domnall) king of Scots 858–62

Donald I was the son of *Alpín and the brother and successor of *Kenneth mac Alpín. He may have been the son of a Norse woman, his dynasty having come to power in Scotland partly profiting from alliances with the Norsemen. During his reign, the laws of Dál Riata as defined in the era of *Áed Find were imposed on Scot and Pict alike at Forteviot in Fortriu. Donald may have been assassinated in 862 and sources locate the scene of his death alternatively at Raith-inber-amon, Belachoir, or at

Scone. He was buried on Iona. Although a Scottish king, Donald is described as 'king of the Picts' in the contemporary record of the *Annals of Ulster* at his death in 862 — a reference to the recent conquest of that people by Donald's brother, Kenneth.

BIBL. Anderson 1922, vol. 1: 290-2; Smyth 1984: 190-1

Donald II king of Scots 889—900

Donald was the son of *Constantine I and the grandson of *Kenneth mac Alpín. Unlike his predecessors of the house of Kenneth who had recently come to rule over the Picts *and* Scots, Donald II is the first king to be described as 'King of Scotland' (Rí Alban) in the contemporary *Annals of Ulster*. Earlier members of his dynasty are styled 'king of the Picts' in that source. Donald's reign saw a temporary respite from the Viking wars, but during his time the Orkney earldom came into being and the Norsemen made territorial gains in Caithness and neighbouring areas. The attack on Dunnottar by Norsemen in *c*. 895 may have been led by the Norwegian king, Harald Finehair, who was active in the Northern Isles in this reign. Donald's rule restored the house of Kenneth to the Scottish kingship and excluded the influence of the Strathclyde party in the person of *Eochaid son of Rhun. Donald is likely to have banished the survivors of the Northern British aristocracy in Strathclyde who, in 890, fled for refuge to the court of *Anarawd ap Rhodri in north Wales. At any rate, Donald became the progenitor of a dynasty of sub-kings who ruled in Strathclyde until the eleventh century and who held that territory as tributaries of the kings of the Scots. Donald died in Forres in 900 and was buried in Iona.

BIBL. Anderson 1922, vol. 1: 395-6; Smyth 1984: 216-17

Donald son of Áed, king of the Strathclyde Britons *c*. 940—3

Donald was a grandson of *Kenneth mac Alpín and a brother of *Constantine II, king of Scots. Donald is said in the contemporary *Life* of *Catroe to have been a kinsman of that saint and to have befriended him on his pilgrimage from Scotland through England to the Continent. Donald is the same person as *Dunmail* whose two sons, according to Roger of Wendover, were blinded by King *Edmund of Wessex in 946 when he handed over their kingdom of Strathclyde-Cumbria to *Malcolm I of Scotland. According to the *Life* of Catroe, Donald's kingdom extended as far as Leeds. That cannot have been the case, but his kingdom probably extended southwards to Stainmore in the Pennines.

BIBL. Anderson 1922, vol. 1: 441, 445-6

Donald son of Owen, king of the Strathclyde Britons *c*. 962—75

Donald's father, *Owen son of Donald II, had been king of Strathclyde and fought in the battle of *Brunanburh* against King *Athelstan. Donald probably succeeded to the Strathclyde kingdom in 962 when *Dub vacated Strathclyde in that year to become king of the Scots. Donald strove to establish his immediate family as a dynasty of Scottish sub-kings in Strathclyde with the help of his ally and overlord, *Kenneth II of Scotland.

He seems to have succeeded in excluding the Scots ruler, *Culen Ring, from the kingship of Strathclyde in the years while Culen was waiting to succeed to the kingship of the Scots, and eventually, in 971, Culen was slain by Donald's son, Riderch, in Lothian. Two years later, Donald appears as *Dufnal* among the list of kings who rowed *Edgar on the Dee in 973 soon after the English king's coronation at Bath. Donald's son, Malcolm, also appears on the list of kings who submitted to Edgar where he is described as 'King of the Cumbrians'. It seems that by 973, Donald had abdicated in favour of his son and had joined a monastic community. He died while on pilgrimage in Rome in 975. Donald's son, Malcolm, continued to rule the Strathclyde Britons until his death in 997. *Owen the Bald, yet another son of Donald, also succeeded his father in the kingdom.

BIBL. Anderson 1922, vol. 1: 478, 480; Smyth 1984: 224, 226-7

Donnán abbot of Eigg *d*. 617

Donnán probably hailed from Ireland. A few dedications to this saint in Kintyre, Arran, Wigtownshire and Ayrshire may point to an earlier phase in his career before he finally settled on the island of Eigg in the Inner Hebrides to the south of Skye. It is clear from *Adomnán's *Life* of *Columba and other evidence that this region was still in the hands of the northern Picts who were still pagan at the beginning of the seventh century. Donnán had established missionary outposts among the Picts of the west and north of Scotland as place-names and ecclesiastical dedications indicate. These include *Kildonnan* on Eigg, together with place-names on South Uist, Little Loch Broom in Wester Ross, Skye, and Lewis. The distribution is mutually exclusive to early church sites associated with Columba and it would seem that Donnán's mission was carried out independently of the church of Iona to the south. It is notable that Donnán and his monks met their violent deaths on Eigg during the abbacy of *Fergna on Iona who, through his nephew, passed on tales of Columba to Adomnán. Yet Adomnán makes no mention of Donnán whose martyrdom must have made a dramatic impact on the early seventh-century monastic world. The record of the burning of Donnán along with 150 of his community on Eigg on Sunday 17 April 617, is the only contemporary notice we have of his career. The number of his slaughtered followers is put elsewhere at 52 and later medieval Irish traditions assert that Donnán had excited the anger of a local queen whose sheep had been disturbed on Eigg by Donnán's community. The northern Picts were clearly not ready for Christianity in Donnán's time and they may have feared incursions from the Christian kingdom of Dál Riata.

BIBL. Anderson 1922, vol. 1: 142-4; Smyth 1984: 107-12

Dorbene bishop of Iona 713

According to the *Annals of Ulster*, Dorbene 'obtained the Chair of Iona and having spent five months in the primacy died on Saturday 28 October'. The detail offered concerning the exact date of Dorbene's death (Saturday, fifth of the Kalends of November) is unusual in this source and suggests that Dorbene's appointment was a very special one. His office of *primatus* must have been that of a bishop, since *Dúnchad son of Cennfaelad was then abbot of Iona. He is very likely to have been the same Dorbene who wrote the colophon to the earliest surviving (Schaffhausen) manuscript of *Adomnán's *Life* of *Columba. This manuscript written in an early eighth-century Irish hand, probably on Iona, ends with the request to the reader to 'pray to God for me, Dorbene, that I may possess eternal life after death'. See *Fáelchú son of Dorbene.

BIBL. Anderson and Anderson 1961: 102-5

Drest son of Donuel (Drust son of Domnall) Pictish king *c*. 663—72
    Drest succeeded his brother Gartnait (657—63) in the Pictish kingship *c*. 663. The name of the father of these brothers is given as *Donuel* in the Pictish king-lists and as *Domnall* in contemporary Irish annals. Marjorie Anderson has suggested that Gartnait and Drest might well have been sons of the Dál Riata king, *Domnall Brecc, who was slain in 642. What does seem clear is that Drest and his brother Gartnait, together with *Talorgen son of Enfret (*d*. 657) all ruled as puppet kings of *Oswiu of Northumbria to whom the Picts may have been forced to pay tribute from *c*. 655. After Oswiu's death, the Picts rebelled against his son, *Ecgfrith, and were routed by the Northumbrians in *c*. 672. Drest had been expelled from his kingdom in that very year (*Annals of Tigernach*), possibly as part of the Pictish rebellion against Northumbrian overlordship. Drest is accorded a six or seven-year reign in the Pictish king-lists, but he ruled for eight or nine years if we are to accept the contemporary annals.

BIBL. Anderson 1973: 172; Smyth 1984: 62, 70

Drest (Drust) Pictish king 724—9
    Drest, who is accorded a five-year reign in Pictish king-lists, ruled the Picts intermittently from 724 until 729. He was probably responsible for driving his predecessor, *Nechtán son of Derile, into a monastery in 724, because Drest succeeded Nechtán in that year and when Nechtán re-emerged to regain his kingship in 726, Drest had him taken captive. But Drest was himself driven out of the kingdom by a third claimant, *Alpín, also in 726. Drest was back in the contest in 727 when he was defeated in three battles by the fourth and ultimately successful candidate, *Óengus I son of Fergus. Drest was finally slain by Óengus on 12 August 729 in the battle of Druim Derg Blathuug.

BIBL. Anderson 1973: 177-8; Smyth 1984: 73-4

Dub king of Scots 962—6
    Dub was the son of *Malcolm I and he first ruled as sub-king of Strathclyde while *Indulf held the kingship of the Scots. Towards the end of his short reign, Dub was challenged by his rival for the kingship — *Culen Ring the son of Indulf. Dub was at first victorious in a battle in Perthshire, but shortly afterwards he was driven from his kingdom and slain by the men of Moray in Forres, in 966. His body was carried from the bridge of Kinloss near the Moray Firth back for burial in Iona.

BIBL. Anderson 1922, vol. 1: 472-4; Smyth 1984: 223-5

Dumnagual map Teudebur king of the Strathclyde Britons 752—60

Dumnagual succeeded his father, *Teudebur, in 752, the Northern Britons at this time losing the region of Kyle in south-west Scotland to *Eadberht of Northumbria. The *Historia Regum* attributed to Symeon of Durham records that Eadberht of Northumbria combined forces with *Óengus son of Fergus, king of the Picts, to attack Dumbarton on 1 August 756. Although the Britons were forced to accept terms, Eadberht lost most of his army ten days later while withdrawing from Strathclyde, and it was probably as a result of this catastrophe that he retired to a monastery in 758. It may be indicative of Northern British strength that it took the combined resources of the Picts and Northumbrians to overcome Dumbarton. Dumnagual died in 760 and there is no mention of any of his successors until the reign of his great-grandson, *Artgal son of Dumnagual.

BIBL. Kirby 1962: 83-4

Duncan I king of Scotland 1034—40

Duncan succeeded his grandfather, *Malcolm II, to the kingship of Scotland in November 1034. The circumstances were highly unusual, Malcolm having left no male heir, and Duncan being the son of Malcolm's daughter, Bethoc and *Crinan, abbot of Dunkeld. Duncan had served his grandfather as king of the Strathclyde Britons in succession to *Owen the Bald and he is the last recorded king of Strathclyde-Cumbria. He is not however named with the two kings, *Maelbaethe* (?Macbeth) and *Iehmarc*, who along with Malcolm II submitted to *Cnut in 1031—2. Duncan may have been at the receiving end of an attack by *Eadulf, earl of Northumbria (1038—41), on the Britons of Cumbria in 1038, mentioned in the *Historia Regum* attributed to Symeon of Durham. Duncan retaliated in the following year by leading an abortive raid on Durham. Eadulf was eventually slain and succeeded in his earldom by *Siward, who was in turn a kinsman of Duncan's wife. In the last year of his reign (1033) Malcolm II slew 'the son of the son of Boite son of Kenneth'. The form of identification of Malcolm's victim highlights his descent from Boite son of *Kenneth III, and reminds us that *Macbeth's stepson and successor, *Lulach, was described as the 'nephew (or grandson?) of the son of Boite'. To the enemies of Malcolm II, Boite represented a rival and legitimate claimant to the Scottish kingship, his father, Kenneth III, having been slain by Malcolm II in 1005. By slaying Boite's grandson in 1033, Malcolm II was trying to stamp out all opposition to the succession of his own grandson Duncan. But succession through the female line was bound to be challenged, and Duncan was defeated and slain at Pitgaveny near Elgin on 15 August 1040, by *Macbeth, earl (*mórmaer*) or king of Moray. Duncan's sons fled the kingdom after their father's death. His son, Malcolm III Canmore finally found refuge with his kinsman, Siward earl of Northumbria. Duncan's other sons were Donald III (Bán) and Máelmuire, ancestor of the earls of Atholl. Duncan was a first cousin of *Thorfinn the Mighty, Norse earl of Orkney, Malcolm II's daughter having married *Sigurd the Stout of Orkney. During Duncan's reign, *Orkneyinga Saga* describes a great conflict between Earl Thorfinn and a certain Scottish king *Karl Hundason. The saga acknowledges that while Malcolm II had been a staunch ally of Thorfinn, his successor, Karl Hundason, was his great enemy. It is much more likely that these Norse traditions relating to Karl Hundason refer to Macbeth rather than to Duncan, since Duncan and the Orkney earls had a mutual enemy in Macbeth. *Berchán's Prophecy* describes Duncan as a man 'of many diseases' — an idea which developed from an earlier textual corruption. The same source claims that Duncan lived to be an old man which is a nonsense when set against the contemporary statement in the *Annals of Tigernach* that Duncan was young when he was slain. He was buried in Iona.

BIBL. Anderson 1922, vol. 1: 571-82; Barrow 1978: 98; Duncan 1975: 99-100, 113, Skene 1886–90, vol. 1: 399-405

Dúnchad son of Cennfáelad, abbot of Iona 710–17

Dúnchad succeeded *Conamail as eleventh abbot in succession to *Columba in 710, but he already held the *principatus* of Iona from 707. It is not clear whether Dúnchad was brought to power at Iona by a pro-Roman faction who sought to outlaw older Celtic practices in relation to Easter and other usages, or whether he simply assisted the ageing Conamail who had become too infirm to rule. *Bede records in his *Ecclesiastical History* that Iona eventually celebrated the Roman Easter for the first time during the abbacy of Dúnchad in 716 — a date confirmed by Irish annals. According to Bede, the Iona community was finally persuaded to adopt Roman usage by the Northumbrian bishop, *Ecgberht, who had spent several years in Ireland. Dúnchad died soon after this dramatic change in Iona's customs in 717, but prior to his death and perhaps connected with the change to Roman practices, in 716 we learn that a certain *Fáelchú son of Dorbene assumed the 'Chair' or *Kathedra* of Columba. The same or another *Dorbene had earlier been appointed to this Chair also in Dúnchad's time as abbot, back in 713, but he died after five months and his successor if any in that office is not named. Dúnchad was of a particularly distinguished line of Columba's royal kin. His grandfather, Máelcobha (*d.* 615), his great-uncle Domnall (*d.* 642) and his great-grandfather Áed mac Ainmerech had all been highkings of the ruling Uí Néill dynasty in Ireland. His festival was kept on 25 May.

BIBL. Anderson and Anderson 1961: 98-9; Reeves 1857: 379-81

Dúnchad son of Conaing, king of Dál Riata *c.* 650–4

Dúnchad's father is given as Conaing in contemporary annals and in the *Senchus Fer nAlban*. As such, Dúnchad was almost certainly a grandson of *Áedán mac Gabhráin. In Scottish king-lists on the other hand, his father's name is given as *Dubhán* ('Little Black One') — perhaps a nickname for Conaing. Dúnchad shared the Dál Riata kingship with *Conall Crandomna and he was slain in 654 by the Picts who were led by their king, *Talorgen son of Enfret (Eanfrith) in a battle at Srath Ethairt.

BIBL. Anderson 1973: 155-6, 164; Bannerman 1974: 103

Dúngal son of Selbach, king of Scots Dál Riata 723–6

Dúngal succeeded to the kingship of Dál Riata when his father,

*Selbach, retired to a monastery in 723. He was of the line of Cenél Loairn who had only recently seized the kingship at the expense of the traditional Cenél Gabhráin kings. Dúngal was expelled from the kingship in 726 and while there is no evidence to suggest that either he or his father held the overlordship of Dál Riata after this time, Dúngal remained a prominent dynast within his own Cenél Loairn group. He may have been drawn into hostilities against the powerful Pictish ruler, *Óengus I son of Fergus, through his support for the Pictish king, *Drest, who was expelled from his kingdom in the same year as Dúngal lost his Dál Riata overlordship. If Drest had rallied his Pictish followers against Óengus with Dúngal's support, that would also tie in with a feud between Dúngal and Óengus regarding Bruide the son of Óengus. In 733, Dúngal pursued Bruide to the island monastery of Tory, off the Donegal coast, and profaned its sanctuary by dragging Bruide from it. In the following year, Óengus invaded Dál Riata and wounded Dúngal who fled across to Ireland 'to be out of the power of Óengus'. Meanwhile, Eochaid, the king of Dál Riata who had ousted Dúngal back in 726 died in 733 but Dúngal failed to re-established himself. The tribal kingship of Cenél Loairn was also lost by Dúngal in 733 when we are told it passed to his first cousin, Muiredach son of *Ainbcellach. The complete conquest of Dál Riata seems to have been accomplished by Óengus in 736 when he and his brother, Talorgen, led a concerted attack on that kingdom. Óengus wasted the lands of Dál Riata, captured Dunadd and put Dúngal son of Selbach and his brother Feradach in chains. Talorgen the brother of Óengus, meanwhile, routed Muiredach the king of Cenél Loairn. Nothing more is known of the fate of Dúngal after his capture by Óengus in 736.

BIBL. Anderson 1973; 181-2, 184-5

Dunstan St, archbishop of Canterbury 959—88

Dunstan was born near Glastonbury, in Somerset, of a noble family, about 909. His uncle, Athelm, was archbishop of Canterbury from 923—6; *Ælfheah the Bald, bishop of Winchester, and Cynesige, bishop of Lichfield, were also kinsmen. In the 930s, Dunstan was a member of the household of King *Athelstan (to whom he may have been related) but at the urging of his kinsman Ælfheah, he became a monk, soon after Ælfheah's appointment to Winchester in 933/4. Athelstan's brother and successor, *Edmund, made Dunstan abbot of Glastonbury in 942/3. Among those who came to Glastonbury to study was *Æthelwold, who, like Dunstan, had begun his career in the entourage of Ælfheah the Bald. The reform movement in the English church, with which Dunstan was so closely associated, gained strength when, on Edmund's death in 946, his brother *Eadred succeeded. He and his mother *Eadgifu were close friends of Dunstan; Eadgifu was instrumental in the refoundation of Abingdon, of which Æthelwold became abbot in 955. A setback occurred in the reign of Eadred's nephew, *Eadwig, who banished Dunstan from England. He went abroad, to the court of Arnulf, count of Flanders, a grandson of King *Alfred, and a patron of the continental reform movement. In Flanders Dunstan came into contact with the ideas of Gerard of Brogne and John of Gorze; John indeed was still alive at the time of Dunstan's exile, and though there is no indication that they ever met, the comital monastery of Blandinium, at Ghent, to which Dunstan repaired, had been reformed under John's direct influence. Blandinium had been endowed by Arnulf's father, Count Baldwin, and his wife *Ælfthryth, King Alfred's daughter; Arnulf himself had increased the endowment and supervised the translation there of the relics of Saint-Wandrille in 944. In the same year, he requested Gerard of Brogne to reform the monastery of Saint-Bertin, of which his son Adelolf, a frequent visitor to the English royal court, had been lay abbot. The aggrieved monks, disliking their new rule, sought refuge in England, and were given sanctuary at the abbey of Bath, by King Edmund.

Flanders, under its reforming count, was thus advantageous to a man like Dunstan, who had ambitions for the renewal of monastic life in his own country. His contacts with Blandinium continued after his return to England after Eadwig's death; indeed Womar, the abbot of the house during Dunstan's exile, retired to the New Minster at Winchester, and died there in 981.

In 957, *Edgar, the younger brother of King Eadwig, became king of the Mercians and Northumbrians, though Eadwig continued to hold Wessex. He recalled Dunstan to England, and made him bishop of Worcester, adding the see of London in 958 or 959. When in 959 Eadwig died, Edgar succeeded to the whole kingdom, and lost no time in appointing Dunstan as archbishop of Canterbury. It was the energetic patronage of Edgar which secured the success of the reform movement in tenth-century England. Dunstan's influence was widely felt in Edgar's time, and he played a crucial role in the succession-dispute which ensued on the king's death in 975; it was his support which ensured the succession of *Edward the Martyr over *Æthelred II. Edward was murdered in 978, and it was Dunstan who crowned the young Æthelred on 4 May 979. He continued in office under Æthelred until his own death on 19 May 988.

As the founding-founder of the English reform movement Dunstan is of prime importance. He established Benedictine monasticism at Glastonbury and fostered the talents of the younger men who continued and extended his work. As the friend and advisor of successive kings, he looks forward to the great ecclesiastical politicians of the eleventh and twelfth centuries. His patronage of art helped the flowering of painting, sculpture and metalwork which accompanied the tenth-century reform. His earliest biographer, writing within twenty years of his death, describes him as 'filled with all spiritual gifts...Not only did he minister the comforts of the true faith to others but he also demonstrated the right path to heaven by his salutary preaching'. His aims were 'to renew that which was cast down, to vindicate that which was neglected, to enrich holy places, to love the just, to recall the erring to the way, to build the churches of God and so to live up to the name of a true pastor among all men'.

BIBL. Brooks 1984: 243-53; Dales 1988

E

Eadbald king of Kent 616/8−40

Eadbald, son of *Æthelberht of Kent, succeeded his father in 616/8. He was still a pagan at the time of his accession and in accordance with pre-Christian custom, married his father's widow, which implies that he was either the son of an earlier wife of Æthelberht than *Bertha, or that Æthelberht had remarried after Bertha's death; given the length of Eadbald's reign, the latter is probably the case. The Roman mission, deprived of royal support, almost foundered, but *Laurence managed to win over the king, who accepted conversion. His sister *Æthelburh married *Edwin of Northumbria and was instrumental in the conversion of the north. Kent seems to have preserved its independence under Eadbald, but was losing ground to the larger kingdoms; Eadbald was unable to restore *Mellitus to the bishopric of London against the will of the pagan successors of King *Sæberht of Essex, and the Bretwaldaship of the southern English passed first to *Rædwald to East Anglia, and, after his death c. 625, to the Northumbrian kings. Edwin of Northumbria seems not to have exercised power over Kent, but his death in 633 changed relations. His eventual successor, *Oswald, came from the rival Northumbrian dynasty of Bernicia, and was hostile to the Deiran æthelings; Æthelburh had to send Edwin's son, Uscfrea, and his grandson, Yffi son of Osfrith, to her friend Dagobert, king of the Franks, for fear of King Eadbald and King Oswald. Clearly she believed her brother might sacrifice his young kinsmen to gain favour with his new overlord. Both children died in Gaul. This Northumbrian influence is shown also in the marriage of Eadbald's son Eormenred to Oslafa, a Northumbrian princess. Eadbald's own wife, the Frankish Ymme, who was possibly a Merovingian princess, was the mother both of Eormenred and of Eadbald's successor *Eorcenberht.

BIBL. Stenton 1971: 112-13

Eadberht king of Northumbria 737−58

Eadberht, son of Eata, succeeded his cousin *Ceolwulf as king of Northumbria in 737. He proved an able and effective ruler, though he was faced with a minor crisis in 750, when Offa, son of King *Aldfrith, appears to have made a bid for the kingship. Offa took sanctuary at St Cuthbert's shrine on Lindisfarne, but despite the holiness of the site, was dragged out by Eadberht's men. The irate king went so far as to arrest the bishop of Lindisfarne, Cynewulf, in revenge for this limited support of his rival. In 758, Eadberht resigned his kingship to his son, *Oswulf, and became canon at York, where his brother, *Ecgberht, was archbishop. He died in 768.

BIBL. Godman 1982: xlv-xlvi, 101, 109; Kirby 1974b: 21, 25

Eadberht Præn king of Kent 796−8

The career of Eadberht Præn epitomizes the vicissitudes of minor royalty during the Mercian supremacy of the eighth century. A scion of the Kentish royal kindred, he was forced into exile in Frankia by the enmity of *Offa of Mercia. He is said to have been a priest, but this also may have been imposed upon him, rather than accepted voluntarily; it was not uncommon at the time for rival kings to be forcibly tonsured in order to render them unfit for secular office. When Offa died in 796, Eadberht renounced his orders and seized the Kentish kingdom, expelling the pro-Mercian archbishop of Canterbury, *Æthelheard. These actions led to his excommunication in 798 by Pope Leo III. *Cœnwulf of Mercia invaded Kent, and defeated the armies of Eadberht, who was blinded, mutilated and imprisoned in Cœnwulf's family monastery at Winchcombe. He was eventually released in 811, and his subsequent fate is unknown.

BIBL. Brooks 1984: 114, 121-5

Eadburh St, abbess *d*. 751

Eadburh, abbess of Minster-in-Thanet in succession to St *Mildrith, translated the relics of her predecessor into a new church, consecrated by *Cuthbert, archbishop of Canterbury (740−60). Minster-in-Thanet had a high reputation for learning and the arts in the eighth century. One of Eadburh's pupils was St *Lioba, who refers to her as 'mistress' in a letter to St *Boniface, and claims that Eadburh taught her the art of writing Latin verse. Eadburh herself seems to have been a skilled illuminator; it was from her that Boniface commissioned a copy of the *Epistles of Peter* 'in letters of gold', and a fine copy of the *Acts of the Apostles*, still extant and inscribed with the name 'EADB', may be her work. She is sometimes identified with *Bucge, daughter of Eangyth, another correspondent of Boniface, but in fact the two ladies appear to be distinct.

BIBL. Greenaway 1980: 41, 42-3; Brooks 1984: 201; Ridyard 1988: 16-17

Eadburh queen *d*. after 814

Eadburh, daughter of *Offa of Mercia, married *Beorhtric of Wessex in 789. Their union symbolized Mercian control of Wessex, which ended when Beorhtric's rival *Ecgberht seized power in 802. It is not surprising, therefore, that Eadburh's reputation suffered at the hands at those concerned to glorify Ecgberht's line. *Asser, in his *Life* of *Alfred, calls her 'a tyrant after the manner of her father' and describes with approval how, after Beorhtric's death, she was first exiled to Frankia, and then expelled thence for immorality, dying 'a miserable death' in Pavia. Since Pavia was on the pilgrim route to Rome, the widowed queen was presumably en route to the Holy City. The pilgrimage was not without its dangers; in a letter to Archbishop *Cuthbert, St *Boniface informed him that 'it would be well and favourable for the honour and purity of your Church and a sure protection against vice if your synod and your princes would forbid matrons and nuns to make their frequent journeys back and forth to Rome. A great part of them perish and few keep their virtue. There are many towns in Lombardy and Gaul where there is not a courtesan or a harlot but is of English stock'.

BIBL. Keynes and Lapidge 1983a: 71-2, 235-6; Talbot 1954: 133

Eadfrith bishop 698–721

The tenth-century colophon of the Lindisfarne Gospels, written by *Aldred, states that the book was written by Eadfrith, usually identified as the bishop of Lindisfarne who succeeded Eadberht in 698. Whether he was the actual scribe of the manuscript or merely commissioned it is unclear. In keeping with the mixed Celtic and Roman usages of Lindisfarne, the decoration of the Gospels is an amalgam of Germanic, Roman and Celtic themes, usually described as 'Hiberno-Saxon', and regarded as one of the great masterpieces of that genre. As well as the Gospels, Eadfrith was also responsible for promoting the cult of St *Cuthbert. He commissioned the prose *Life* of Cuthbert from *Bede, and the earlier, anonymous life is also dedicated to him. Eadfrith also restored Cuthbert's hermitage on the Inner Farne for the anchorite Felgild. He was buried near to St Cuthbert, and his remains accompanied those of the saint on their subsequent wanderings, until they eventually came to rest at Durham.

BIBL. Backhouse 1981: 12-16

Eadgifu queen of the Franks 918–51

Eadgifu, daughter of *Edward the Elder and *Ælfflæd, married Charles the Simple, king of the Franks, after the death of his second wife, Frederun (917). When Charles was deposed in 923, Eadgifu fled to England with their son Louis, known as Louis d'Outremer ('from over the sea') because of his upbringing at the court of Eadgifu's half-brother, *Athelstan. When Ralph of Burgundy, king of the Franks, died in 936, Hugh the Great, who had married Eadgifu's sister, Eadhild, organized the return of Louis as king of the Franks. He was crowned on 19 June 936, and in gratitude bestowed on Hugh the title 'duke of the Franks'. Eadgifu accompanied her son but her influence waned after 939, when he married Gerberga, sister of the German emperor, Otto the Great. She retired, willingly or not, into a nunnery in Laon, but in 951 renounced the cloister to marry Herbert, count of Vermandois, a man some years her junior.

BIBL. Stenton 1971: 345-7; McKitterick 1983: 313-18

Eadgifu queen *d*. after 966

Eadgifu, daughter of Sigehelm, ealdorman of Kent, was the third wife, and widow, of *Edward the Elder. Her father was killed at the battle of the Holme in 903, opposing the king's cousin *Æthelwold. Eadgifu married the king at some date after 919, and bore him two sons, *Edmund and *Eadred, and a daughter, Eadgifu, who married Louis of Aquitaine. Another daughter, St Eadburh, became a nun at Winchester. Eadgifu was a strong influence on her younger, unmarried son, and a promoter of the aims of the monastic reform movement. In the reign of Edmund's son *Eadwig she suffered eclipse and her estates were confiscated, but Eadwig's brother and successor *Edgar, who shared her ecclesiastical aims, restored her property. She made a substantial grant of land to Christchurch Canterbury in 960, possibly as a thank-offering. Her last appearance was as a signatory to her grandson's charters in 966 and she probably died soon afterwards.

BIBL. Hart 1975: 315

Eadred king of the English 946–55

Eadred, the younger of the two sons borne by *Eadgifu to *Edward the Elder, succeeded to the kingdom after the murder of his brother *Edmund in 946. The political apogee of his reign was the final submission of Northumbria to West Saxon control on the death of *Eirikr Bloodaxe in 954. Eadred was a wholehearted supporter of the monastic reform movement and it was he who promoted *Æthelwold to the abbacy of Abingdon in 955. He died the same year after a long illness, leaving the kingdom to his nephews, *Eadwig and *Edgar. His will, which survives, reveals the constitution of a king's household, with its seneschals (*discthegnas*), chamberlains (*hræglthegnas*), butlers (*birele*) and chaplains. Among his bequests was the sum of 1600 pounds in silver to his former subjects 'that they may be able to purchase themselves relief from want and from the heathen army'.

BIBL. Hart 1975: 317; Sawyer 1968, no. 1515

Eadric Streona ealdorman 1007–17

Eadric Streona ('the Grasping'), a Shropshire magnate, rose to prominence at the court of *Æthelred II. In 1006, *Ælfhelm, ealdorman of Northumbria, was killed; later sources name Eadric as his murderer, and describe how he invited the ealdorman to his home in Shrewsbury, and killed him on a hunting expedition. Since Æthelred II spent Christmas 1006 at Shrewsbury (an unusual venue for royal visitations), the story is likely to be true. Certainly in 1007 Eadric was made ealdorman of Mercia, an office which had been vacant since 985. By 1012 he was the premier ealdorman in England, and Hemming, the monk of Worcester, who wrote towards the end of the eleventh century, says that he 'presided over the whole kingdom of the English and had dominion as if he was a sub-king'. He achieved the signal honour of marrying one of the king's daughters (Edith) as did his contemporary, Ealdorman *Uhtred of Bamburgh, another man whom Æthelred had special reason to honour. Eadric had a reputation, both in his own time and afterwards, for duplicity and greed. In 1015, he was accused of murdering the northern thegns *Sigeferth and *Morcar, and by the twelfth century it was believed that he had even despatched *Edmund Ironside, though this is almost certainly untrue. The mainspring of Eadric's actions seems to have been his loyalty to Æthelred; the crimes which he committed were almost certainly done with the king's connivance and probably at his orders. As a result, he made powerful enemies, including his brother-in-law, the ætheling *Edmund, and *Ælfgifu of Northampton, daughter of Ælfhelm, and first wife of *Cnut. When, after the death of Æthelred in 1016, Edmund and Cnut were contending for the kingship, Eadric was in a cleft stick. His vacillation in the years 1015–16, when he supported first Edmund, then Cnut, then Edmund, then Cnut again, were a vain attempt to play his enemies off against each other. When Edmund's death in 1016 left Cnut with no rivals to the English kingship, Eadric's fate was sealed. At the Christmas feast in 1017, he came to claim his due from the new king. '"Shall you", said Cnut, "Who have betrayed your lord with guile, be capable of being true to me?" And summoning *Eirikr, his commander, he said, "Pay this man what we owe him." He raised his axe without delay and cut off his head.'

BIBL. Williams 1986; Campbell 1949: 30-3

Eadulf of Bamburgh *d*. 913

The *Annals of Ulster* describe Eadulf as 'king of the northern Saxons', and his rule probably extended over the old kingdom of Bernicia, which was never conquered or settled by the Vikings of York. He is said to have been on intimate terms with King *Alfred of Wessex, though details are lacking. However, it is reasonable that the West Saxons should seek an alliance with the independent English rulers of the north against the Scandinavian settlers (see also *Ealdred, *Uhtred).

BIBL. Whitelock 1955: 262 (History of Saint Cuthbert); Simpson 1989

Eadulf Cudel ealdorman 1016−*c*. 1019

Eadulf *Cudel* ('cuttlefish') succeeded to Bamburgh and the ealdordom of Bernicia when his brother *Uhtred was murdered in 1016. Two years later he suffered a disastrous defeat at the hands of King *Malcolm II of Scotland at the battle of Carham. By the following year, his nephew *Ealdred was holding Bamburgh.

BIBL. Kapelle 1979: 21-6

Eadulf Evilcild ealdorman 963−*c*. 994

Eadulf *Evilcild* was ealdorman of Bamburgh in succession to *Oswulf, to whom he was probably related. Very little is known about him, and his curious nickname is difficult to explain. The appellation *cild* (child in Modern English) is applied to several noblemen in the tenth and eleventh centuries. The primary meaning of *cild* was 'boy, young man' and like many related words (*beorn*, thegn, knight) acquired the secondary meaning 'warrior'. By the tenth century it seems to have denoted high rank; all those who bore it seem to have been ealdormen or king's thegns. The nickname *Evilcild* seems to imply that Eadulf was unworthy of his rank, or perhaps of his warrior status. Why this should be so is unknown. His successor in Bamburgh, Waltheof, appears in 994.

BIBL. Whitelock 1959: 77-8, 81

Eadulf ealdorman *c*. 1038−41

Eadulf, son of *Uhtred of Bamburgh and Sige, daughter of Styr Ulfsson of York, succeeded to the ealdordom of Bamburgh when his half-brother *Ealdred was murdered. In 1040 he successfully defended his ealdordom against King *Duncan of Scotland, but in the following year he was murdered by Earl *Siward of Northumbria at the instigation of King

*Harthacnut. His brother, Gospatric, was driven out of Northumbria and fled to Scotland; he died in 1064. Eadulf's son, Osulf of Bamburgh, was killed in 1067.

BIBL. Kapelle 1979: 24-6

Eadwig king of the English 955–9

Eadwig 'All-Fair', the elder son of *Edmund and St *Ælfgifu, succeeded to the kingdom of England in 955, on the death of his uncle *Eadred, when he was about 15 years old. His short reign was fraught with crisis. He earned the enmity of some ecclesiastics by his exile of *Dunstan in 956; at the same time he deprived his grandmother *Eadgifu, one of Dunstan's most powerful supporters, of all her property. It is tempting to see a palace revolution in the background, for in 956, *Athelstan Half-king, ealdorman of East Anglia, retired, and his family lost ground to Eadwig's kinsmen, *Ælfheah the seneschal, and his brother *Ælfhere, whom Eadwig made ealdorman of Mercia. Much of the blame for Eadwig's actions was laid at the door of his wife *Ælfgifu and her mother, Æthelgifu. She was a kinswoman of the young king, a descendant of *Æthelred I, and it is noteworthy that her brother, *Æthelweard the Chronicler, praises the king, saying that he 'deserved to be loved'. In 957, the kingdom was divided, Eadwig remaining king of Wessex, while his younger brother, *Edgar, became 'king of the Mercians and Northumbrians'. This division has been seen as a northern revolt against the unpopular rule of Eadwig, and was so presented by the enemies of the young king; but it is equally possible that the division had been agreed upon earlier. In 957, Edgar was about 14 and therefore of age, and was perhaps assuming power as sub-king and designated heir. This version of events is suggested by the *Anglo-Saxon Chronicle* (D) which records the accession of both æthelings in 955. The brief and scanty sources for the period make it difficult of interpretation.

BIBL. Yorke 1988b: 74-80

Eadwig ætheling *d.* after 1017

Eadwig was one of the sons of *Æthelred II by his first wife, *Ælfgifu. In 1017, he was exiled from England by the victorious *Cnut and opinions differ as to his ultimate fate. The *Anglo-Saxon Chronicle* claims that Cnut had him murdered, but according to William of Malmesbury, he returned to England, and died at Tavistock Abbey. The abbey's tradition claims him as the benefactor who endowed the house with Plymstock, Devon.

BIBL. Finberg 1951: 3

Eadwig ceorlacyng, *d.* after 1017

Eadwig *ceorlacyng* was one of the English nobles exiled by *Cnut in 1017. Nothing further is known about him and his curious nickname, 'king of the ceorls (peasants)' is unexplained.

BIBL. *ASC*, s.a. 1017.

Eadwulf king of Northumbria 705

When *Aldfrith of Northumbria died in 705, his heir was his son *Osred, a child of eight. His succession was opposed by Eadwulf, whose support seems to have been in Deira; his son was being fostered by *Wilfrid at Ripon. Wilfrid, however, seems to have gone over to Osred's party, an act which led to his expulsion from Northumbria by Eadwulf. His forces besieged the young Osred and his supporters in Bamburgh, but were defeated by *Beorhtfrith, Osred's ealdorman, and Eadwulf was expelled. His origins are unknown, but it is possible that he was a son of *Æthelwold, king of Deira (c. 652−5).

BIBL. Kirby 1974b: 10, 18-20

Eafa (Æbbe, Domneva) St, queen and abbess d. 694

Eafa, daughter of *Eormenred, married *Merewalh, king of the Magonsæte. She bore him four children, St *Mildryth, St *Mildburh, another daughter, Mildgyth and a son, Merefin. In 673 she left her husband to become abbess of Minster-in-Thanet, a house founded on land given to her by her cousin *Ecgberht of Kent as the blood-price for her murdered brothers, SS *Æthelred and Æthelberht.

BIBL. Rollason 1982

Ealdhun bishop 990−1018

Ealdhun succeeded Ælfsige as bishop of Chester-le-Street in 990. Five years later the community moved, first to Ripon and then to a more secure position at Durham, to avoid the Viking raiders. At Durham Ealdhun built a new cathedral, the White Church. His move was assisted by *Uhtred of Bamburgh, who married the bishop's daughter, Ecgfrida. In 998, the relics of St *Cuthbert were translated into the new church, and the Lindisfarne community settled into its final home.

BIBL. Rollason 1987b: 52-4

Ealdred of Bamburgh 913−c. 930

Ealdred succeeded to the lordship of Bamburgh on the death of his father *Eadulf, but was almost immediately driven out by the Viking *Ragnall of York. He fled to Scotland and enlisted the help of *Constantine II, but a Scots army was defeated at the first battle of Corbridge in 914. A second battle in the same area in 918 resulted in another Viking victory, but at considerable cost and Ealdred may have been restored to at least a part of his lands. In 920 he and his brother *Uhtred were among the northern leaders who submitted to *Edward the Elder. Ealdred's relations with the West Saxon rulers are ambiguous. In the first decade of the tenth century he seems to have co-operated with Edward and *Æthelred of Mercia (see *Uhtred) and the *History of St *Cuthbert* says that he 'was loved by King Edward as his father Eadulf had been loved by King *Alfred'. In 926 King *Athelstan confirmed to him an estate at Chalgrave, Bedfordshire, and when in the following year Athelstan claimed the kingdom of York, after the death of *Sigtrygg Caech, Ealdred made formal submission to him. But despite these courtesies, it is more probable that Ealdred acknowledged Constantine of Scotland, rather than Athelstan of Wessex, as his lord. No contemporary source records his title, but his son *Osulf was styled 'high-reeve'; a translation of the Gaelic *mórmær*, 'great steward'. This, according to some commentators 'is precisely what the ruler of Bamburgh had become in relation to his Scottish overlord'.

BIBL. Wainwight 1975a; Smyth 1984: 196-7, 199, 235; Sawyer 1968: no. 396

Ealdred ealdorman c. 1019−c. 1038
Ealdred, the son of *Uhtred of Bamburgh and Ecgfrida, daughter of Bishop *Ealdhun of Durham, succeeded to the ealdordom of Bamburgh about 1019, after the death of his uncle *Eadulf Cudel. He avenged the murder of his father by killing *Thurbrand the Hold, thus bringing upon himself the enmity of Thurbrand's son Karl. A long period of warfare between Bamburgh and York ensued, and in about 1038, Karl succeeded in killing Ealdred. His brother, *Eadulf, succeeded to the lordship of Bamburgh.

BIBL. Hart 1975: 143-50 (The tract *De obsessione Dunelmi*); Kapelle 1979: 17-26

Ealhhelm ealdorman 940−51
Ealhhelm was appointed to an ealdordom in central Mercia, probably centred on Worcester, by *Edmund in 940. His antecedents are unknown, but he may have been connected with *Æthelflæd of Mercia, and his sons were addressed as kinsmen by subsequent West Saxon kings. The most prominent were *Ælfheah, seneschal of King *Eadwig and later ealdorman of central Wessex and *Ælfhere, ealdorman of Mercia (956−83). Two other sons, Eadric and Ælfwine, were prominent among the king's thegns. His daughter Æthelflæd received a bequest under the will of Wynflaed (died 950) and was perhaps the wife of *Ælfric cild, ealdorman of Mercia. The identity of Ealhhelm's wife is unknown.

BIBL. Williams 1982

Ealhswith wife of King Alfred, d. 902
Ealhswith was the wife of King *Alfred and mother of all his recorded children. Her father was Æthelred *Mucil*, ealdorman of the *Gaini* (a Mercian people otherwise unknown) and her mother Eadburh was a Mercian princess of the royal kindred; she has the same name as *Offa's daughter. The marriage took place in 868, and is probably connected with the Mercian alliance with Wessex in that year, against the Danes who had occupied Nottingham. There is no evidence that Ealhswith was ever queen; *Asser explains that the West Saxons (unlike the Mercians) did not have queens, and this seems to have been the case throughout the ninth century, though the situation seems to have been otherwise in earlier years (see *Æthelburh, *Seaxburh) and by the tenth century queens were being consecrated again (see *Ælfthryth).

BIBL. Keynes and Lapidge 1983: 77, 240-1

Eanflæd St, queen and abbess *d. c.* 704

Eanflæd, daughter of King *Edwin and his Kentish wife *Æthelburh, was the first Northumbrian to be baptized by *Paulinus, soon after her birth in 626. On her father's death in 633, she was taken back to Kent by her mother and brought up there. In 642, she was married to the Northumbrian king *Oswiu, in an attempt to reconcile the Deiran and Bernician dynasties. One of her kinsmen, *Oswine, Edwin's nephew, was at this time ruling Deira, but in 651, Oswiu had him murdered. Eanflæd prevailed upon her husband to found a monastery at Gilling in recompense for this act; a form of wergeld, like that exacted by another Kentish princess, *Eafa, for the murder of her brothers. Eanflæd's insistence on keeping the Roman Easter, after the manner of her Kentish upbringing, was also something of a problem for 'it sometimes happened that Easter was celebrated twice in the same year, so that the king had finished the fast and was keeping Easter Sunday, while the queen and her people were still in Lent and observing Palm Sunday' (*HE* iii 25). It was not, however, for 20 years that this discrepancy was regarded as sufficiently serious for a Northumbrian synod to be called to resolve it. This was the Synod of Whitby of 664, which resolved the problem in favour of the Roman usage. Eanflæd had connections with Whitby, whose abbess, *Hild, was her kinswoman, a great-niece of Edwin. It was to Hild that Eanflæd entrusted her daughter *Ælfflæd, and it was to Whitby that she herself retired after her husband's death in 670. She translated her father's relics to the monastery and had them enshrined in St Peter's church, near to the altar of St Gregory. The Whitby *Life of *Gregory the Great* was written during the joint abbacy of Eanflæd and Ælfflæd.

BIBL. Colgrave 1968: 39-44, Farmer 1978: 132

Eanfrith king of the Hwicce *d. c.* 674

Eanfrith and his brother Eanhere are the first known rulers of the Hwicce, a sub-kingdom of Mercia established, in all likelihood, by *Penda after the battle of Cirencester in 628. The origins of its ruling dynasty are obscure; they may have been the leaders of an exiled Bernician war-band which had taken service with Penda, or perhaps native nobility of the area which they came to rule. They can be traced down to the end of the eighth century, and then vanish; unless *Cœnwulf of Mercia was indeed a member of the Hwiccian royal line.

BIBL. Finberg 1961b; Bassett 1989b: 6-17

Eanred king of Northumbria ?810−?41

Eanred son of *Eardwulf succeeded his father as king of Northumbria and ruled for more than 30 years. Considering the chaotic political conditions in Northumbria for the 50 years preceding his accession, this was no mean feat, but little is known of him beyond his submission to the overlordship of *Ecgberht of Wessex in 829.

BIBL. Stenton 1971: 95

Eardwulf (Hardulph) St, king of Northumbria ?796—?810

In 791, Eardwulf, a Northumbrian nobleman, fell foul of King *Æthelred, who had him arrested and taken to Ripon, where he was 'killed' outside the gates of the monastery. The monks carried him into the precinct and 'after midnight, he was found alive in the church'. This miraculous escape is alluded to in an almost contemporary source, a letter of *Alcuin to Eardwulf himself, in 796, after he had become king of Northumbria. Following his deliverance, Eardwulf fled into exile, but returned after the murder of Æthelred, to be elected as king. His consecration and enthrone-ment is the second recorded consecration of an English king (see *Ecgfrith); four bishops officiated, Eanbald of York, Æthelberht of Hexham, *Higbald of Lindisfarne, and Badwulf of Whithorn. In 798 the same conspirators who had murdered Æthelred attacked Eardwulf, but were defeated, and in 799, Moll, who was probably a kinsman of Æthelred, was killed 'by the urgent order of King Eardwulf'. Eardwulf was also responsible for the death of St *Alhmund, who was killed 'with his fellow fugitives' in 800. It seems that some Northumbrian dissidents took refuge in Mercia, for in 801, Eardwulf attacked *Cœnwulf of Mercia, and peace was only made by the intervention of the bishops of both nations. These enemies whom Cœnwulf harboured were presumably connections of Æthelred, who had married the Mercian princess Ælfflæd, Cœnwulf's kinswoman. Later Eardwulf himself was driven out of his kingdom. Like many other English exiles of the time, he found refuge at the court of Charlemagne, Emperor and king of the Franks, and with Frankish help recovered his kingdom. He died in ?810 and was succeeded by his son, *Eanred. His remains were eventually buried in the Mercian monastery of Breedon-on-the-Hill, Leicestershire, whose church is dedicated to him and where his cult developed.

BIBL. Stenton 1971: 94-5; Rollason 1983: 3-4

Eardwulf bishop 854—99

It was Eardwulf, bishop of Lindisfarne, who, after the second Viking sack in 875, moved the community from the exposed site on Lindisfarne to Chester-le-Street, where it remained until 995 (see *Ealdhun). The move suggests a political rapprochement between the Northumbrian church and the kingdom of York, then ruled by *Guthfrith, who seems to have been well-disposed towards Lindisfarne.

BIBL. Rollason 1987b: 45-61

Eata St, bishop 678—86

Eata was one of the Northumbrian monks trained by *Aidan at Lindis-farne. He subsequently became abbot of Melrose, and then of Ripon, before it was given to *Wilfrid. When after the Synod of Whitby in 664, Bishop *Colmán left England, Eata was appointed abbot of Lindisfarne. In 678, after the expulsion of Wilfrid from the Northumbrian see, Eata was made a bishop; his see was originally Hexham, but was moved to Lindisfarne when Tunberht was made bishop of Hexham in 681. In 685, however, Tunberht was deposed, for unknown reasons, in favour of

119

*Cuthbert. Cuthbert was unwilling to leave Lindisfarne, so Eata removed back to Hexham leaving Lindisfarne to Cuthbert. He died in 686.

BIBL. Farmer 1978: 116

Ecgberht king of Kent 664–73

Ecgberht, son of *Eorcenberht of Kent, is chiefly remembered for the murder of his cousins, SS *Æthelred and Æthelberht. The motive was obviously political, to remove potential rivals, but the young princes quickly became the object of veneration, fostered by their sister *Eafa, abbess of Minster-in-Thanet. This house was founded on land given to her in reparation by King Ecgberht. Ecgberht also founded Reculver for his priest, Bassa; the remains of the seventh-century church, built within the ruins of a Roman fort, were still standing up to the beginning of the nineteenth century. Chertsey Abbey also owes its origin to Ecgberht, a fact which implies that he controlled Surrey, if only briefly. He was succeeded by his brother *Hlothhere.

BIBL. *ASC* s.a. 669; Sawyer 1968, no. 1165; Stenton 1971: 61, 130, 132

Ecgberht the Englishman St, bishop *d.* 729

The career of Ecgberht is related by *Bede, who greatly admired him. He was one of those noblemen who, in the days of Bishop *Finán (651–61) and Bishop *Colmán (661–4), left for Ireland 'either for the sake of religious studies or to live a more ascetic life'. Ecgberht found a home at *Rathmelsigi* (unidentified), along with another young English-man, Æthelhun. Æthelhun indeed came from an ecclesiastical family; one brother, Æthelwine, became bishop of Lindsey (680–92), another, Ealdwine, was abbot of Partney, and a sister, Æthelhild, was abbess of an unidentified monastery nearby and a friend of Queen *Osthryth. In the plague of 664, many of the monks of *Rathmelsigi* died, including Æthelhun, but Ecgberht made a vow that, if he was spared, he would live as an exile, never returning to his native island of Britain (the 'pilgrimage for Christ', undertaken by many Christians, especially among the Irish, at this time). He lived to a great age, being in his nineties when he died. His main ambitions were to preach the Word to the peoples of Germany from among whom the English had come (Bede lists them as 'Frisians, Rugians, Danes, Huns, Old Saxons and *Boruhtwaru*') and to persuade the northern Irish to adopt the Roman Easter (the southern Irish had followed the Roman reckoning since *c.* 636). The first ambition Ecgberht realized only by proxy; it was he who despatched *Willibrord to Frisia in 690. The second ambition he achieved in person. In *c.* 712, he went to Iona, and persuaded the community there to accept the Roman Easter (see *Dúnchad). He spent the rest of his life on Iona, dying in 729. It is not certain where his previous ministry had been based, but Mayo 'of the Saxons' was a centre of Roman influence in Ireland, and it may have been here that Ecgberht had worked.

BIBL. *HE* iii, 27: 312-15; v, 9-10; 474-85; 22; 552-5; Farmer 1978: 127; Chadwick 1963c: 186-205; Duncan 1981

Ecgberht archbishop of York 732–66

Ecgberht came from the royal line of Bernicia, being the brother of *Eadberht, king of Northumbria. A pupil of *Bede, he succeeded *Wilfrid II as bishop of York in 732. It was during his reign, in 735, that York was raised to archiepiscopal status, and Ecgberht received his pallium from Pope Gregory III. The school of York, under its master *Ælberht, became famous throughout Europe from this period. Ecgberht's brother, King Eadberht, eventually became a canon of York Minster under him.

BIBL. Godman 1982: 98-101

Ecgberht king of Wessex 802–39

Ecgberht, who is said to have been a descendant of Ingeld, brother of King *Ine, was the son of a West Saxon ætheling, Ealhmund, probably the same who made himself king of Kent for a brief moment in 784. When *Cynewulf of Wessex was killed in 786, Ecgberht attempted to take power, but was driven out by *Beorhtric, protégé of *Offa of Mercia. Ecgberht spent at least three years, perhaps more, as an exile in Frankia, at the court of Charlemagne. In 802 he returned to Wessex after the death of Beorhtric and this time was accepted as lawful king. He has been described as 'the real creator of the kingdom' (Stenton). In the south-west, he accomplished the final conquest of the Cornish Britons, whose kingdom was permanently incorporated into Wessex. His greatest triumph was the victory at *Ellendun* (Wroughton) in 825, when he defeated *Beornwulf of Mercia and brought the long Mercian supremacy to an end. Soon afterwards Ecgberht sent his son *Æthelwulf into Kent; the king, Baldred (*c.* 823–6) was expelled, and the entire south-east, Sussex and Essex as well as Kent, submitted to West Saxon rule. In 829, Mercia itself was overrun and Ecgberht became Bretwalda. His supremacy, however, did not outlast the Mercian revival in 830, when *Wiglaf became king. Ecgberht's later years were dominated by the increasing Danish raids. In 835 Sheppey was attacked and in the following year 35 ships' crews defeated Ecgberht's army at the battle of Carhampton. In 838, the British of Dumnonia made common cause with a Viking fleet and were defeated by Ecgberht at the battle of Hingston Down. In 839, Ecgberht finally died and was succeeded by his son Æthelwulf.

BIBL. Stenton 1971: 231-5

Ecgfrith king of Northumbria 670–85

Ecgfrith was the son of *Oswiu of Northumbria and of *Eanflæd daughter of *Edwin. In 655, he was a hostage in Mercia, when *Penda invaded the north, but survived to succeed to his father's throne in 670. His younger brother, *Ælfwine, became under-king of Deira. Ecgfrith successfully defended his kingdom against *Wulfhere of Mercia in 674, and may have been briefly acknowledged as Bretwalda, but in 679 he experienced a disastrous defeat at the hands of Wulfhere's brother, *Æthelred, at the battle of the Trent, in which Ælfwine was killed. This catastrophe spelt the end of the Northumbrian supremacy, and Ecgfrith turned his attention to the north. His attacks on Rheged are suggested by the list of lands with which he endowed the church of Ripon between 671 and 678, including estates in Ribble, Dent and Catlow, 'which the British clergy deserted when fleeing from the hostile sword wielded by the warriors of our own nation' (*Eddius). The warriors of Rheged seem to have found refuge in Ireland, for an assault against Ireland was launched in 684, and was bitterly condemned by *Bede. Ecgfrith was also pushing northwards into Lothian; in about 681, an Anglian bishop, Trumwine, was established at Abercorn. The Picts also were attacked about 672 and a massacre, 'filling two rivers with corpses, so that, marvellous to relate, the slayers, passing over the rivers dry-shod, pursued and slew the crowd of fugitives', was recorded by Eddius. Here, however, Ecgfrith had over-reached himself. In 685, leading a great army north into the land of the Picts, he was defeated and killed, with most of his army, at the battle of Nechtanesmere (see *Bruide mac Bili). Bede, recounting this disaster, regards it as a judgement for Ecgfrith's attacks on the Irish, 'a harmless race that had always been most friendly to the English'. Ecgberht was twice married, first to the virginal St *Æthelthryth, who left him to found the abbey of Ely, and secondly to *Iurminburg, who won fame, or rather infamy, for her hostility to *Wilfrid. He was succeeded by his half-brother, *Aldfrith, to whom he bequeathed a much straitened kingdom.

BIBL. *HE* iii, 24: 290-1; iv, 21: 400-1; 26: 426-31; Colgrave 1927: caps 17, 19-22, 24; Stenton 1971; 85-8, 134-8

Ecgfrith king of Mercia July–December 796
Ecgfrith, son of *Offa and his queen, Cynethryth, was consecrated king in his father's lifetime, in 787; the first recorded consecration of an English king. When Offa died in 796, Ecgfrith succeeded him, but died soon afterwards; an eventuality regarded as a judgement on his father's policies by *Alcuin, who, in a letter to the Mercian nobleman Osberht, wrote as follows:

'That most noble young man has not died for his sins, but the vengeance for the blood shed by the father has reached the son. For you know how much blood his father shed to secure the kingdom upon the son.'

Alcuin's words imply that Offa had embarked on a systematic purge of his near kindred to remove rival claimants to Ecgfrith; the consecration of the heir in his predecessor's lifetime also seems to be a stratagem directed to this end. The next successor on Ecgfrith's untimely death was a distant kinsman, *Cœnwulf. Offa's attempts to establish his own line as hereditary kings of Mercia were ultimately unsuccessful, and in the ninth century the kingdom fell prey to dynastic rivalry as well as Viking attacks.

BIBL. Whitelock 1955, no. 202; Stenton 1971: 217-20, 225

Ecglaf *geneat*, *fl.* 896
Since the *geneatas* were of free but non-noble status, few are known by name, but in a document of 896 we have not only a named *geneat* but also some indication of his function. At a meeting of the Mercian witenagemot, *Wærferth, bishop of Worcester, complained that his church had been robbed of nearly all the woodland at Woodchester, Gloucestershire, by

the nobleman Æthelwold. Æthelwold agreed to restore the church's losses, and commanded his *geneat* Ecglaf to ride the bounds of the disputed territory with the bishop's priest, Wulfhun, who was to read out the boundary-marks from the charter relating to the estate, in the bishop's possession. Finally, a compromise was agreed; the disputed land was leased to Æthelwold and his son Ealhmund, with eventual reversion to Worcester.

BIBL. Harmer 1914: 24-5, 56-7, 107-9

Ecgwine St, bishop 693−711 *d*. 717
Very little is known of the life of Ecgwine, bishop of Worcester. He was buried at Evesham, which he founded, and it was there that his cult developed; a *Vita*, which contains little historical material, was composed after the translation of his relics in 1039, by *Ælfweard, bishop of London.

BIBL. Farmer 1978: 127

Ecgwynn wife of King Edward the Elder *d*. *c*. 899
Ecgwynn was the first wife of *Edward the Elder, and mother of *Athelstan. Her origins are unknown, and there is some question about the legality of her marriage; later writers describe her as a concubine. Her son Athelstan was born about 894, and was brought up in Mercia, apparently with the intention that he should eventually become its ruler. The only other child of the marriage was a daughter, Eadgyth, who married *Sigtrygg Caech, king of York.

BIBL. Yorke 1988b: 66-7, 68-70

Eddius Stephanus monk *d*. *c*. 720
Eddius Stephanus, the biographer of St *Wilfrid, is usually identified with the Kentish Eddi, an expert in ecclesiastical music, who accompanied Wilfrid to Northumbria in 669 and became a monk at Ripon. The *Life* of Wilfrid, 'the first commemorative biography in Anglo-Saxon England', was composed between 709 (the year of Wilfrid's death) and 720.

BIBL. Colgrave 1927: ix-xi; Farmer 1974: 38; Kirby 1983

Edgar king of the English 959−75
Edgar was the younger of the two sons of King *Edmund and St *Ælfgifu. He was fostered by Ælfwynn, wife of *Athelstan Half-king, ealdorman of East Anglia, and reared with her youngest child, the future ealdorman *Æthelwine. The family was closely associated with the monastic reform movement, and Edgar's education was entrusted to St *Æthelwold, abbot of Abingdon. When his uncle *Eadred died in 955, his brother *Eadwig became king, but in 957, Edgar was made king of the Mercians and Northumbrians, Eadwig retaining Wessex. One of Edgar's first actions was to recall St *Dunstan, whom Eadwig had exiled, and promote him first to the bishopric of Worcester, and then to London. After Edgar became king of all England on Eadwig's death, Dunstan became archbishop of Canterbury. Edgar's reign is closely associated with the success of the

monastic reform movement, of which he was an enthusiastic patron; 'from his earliest years (he) began to fear, love and worship God with all his heart'. The reform and re-endowment of the English Benedictine monasteries proceeded apace. The immense transference of land from lay to ecclesiastical control which this entailed, and the arbitrary nature of this transference provoked considerable resentment, which surfaced after the king's death in 975. Edgar, though conventionally pious, was not notably religious. His marital affairs were regarded as scandalous by later commentators, and may have provoked comment at the time. His first wife, *Æthelflæd Eneda, may have been associated with his foster-father's kindred; the marriage seems to have been over by 960 or thereabouts, by which time Edgar was associated wih Wulfthryth, who bore him a daughter, St *Edith. It is not quite clear that Edgar was married to Wulfthryth, though the later belief that she was a nun whom he had seduced is almost certainly untrue. In 964, he married *Ælfthryth, daughter of the Devonshire nobleman *Ordgar, and widow of Edgar's foster-brother, *Æthelwold of East Anglia. Later sources accuse Edgar of encompassing her husband's death (as Solomon did with Uriah, husband of Bathsheba), but this seems no more than a romantic tale. Nevertheless the king's devotion to the Benedictine cause should not lead us to overrate his personal ethics.

Edgar's reign was remembered as a Golden Age. His coronation at Bath in 973 does indeed mark a watershed, for he was the first king to be crowned as king of the English, though others before him had used the title on occasion. The 973 ceremony was almost certainly a second coronation, and intended to mark a new stage in the development of West Saxon kingship. The choice of Bath, a Roman site, on the borders of Wessex and Mercia, is probably significant; previous West Saxon king-makings had been conducted at Kingston-on-Thames. The ceremony was followed by a show of force; Edgar's army was marched to Chester along the frontier with Wales, while his fleet sailed to the same destination through the Irish sea. At Chester the kings of the north assembled to make their submission; eight names are recorded, those of *Kenneth king of Scots, Malcolm king of the Cumbrians (see *Donald son of Owen), Magnus king of the Isles, and five others, Dufnal (*Donald son of Owen), Siferth, *Hywel, Jacob (*Iago) and Juchil. *Ælfric says only that they 'submitted to Edgar's direction' but the twelfth-century writer, 'Florence' of Worcester, gives a more ambitious version of events: they

'swore that they would be faithful to him and be his allies by land and sea. And on a certain day he went on board a boat with them, and, with them at the oars and himself seizing the helm, he steered it skilfully on the course of the River Dee, proceeding from the palace to the monastery of St John the Baptist, attended by all the crowd of ealdormen and nobles also by boat. And when he had completed his prayers he returned with the same pomp to the palace. As he entered he is reported to have said to his nobles that any of his successors might indeed pride himself in being king of the English, when he might have the glory of such honours, with so many kings subservient to him.'

The significance of such a ceremony (even supposing it took place as described) is debatable; Kenneth of Scotland might have interpreted the meeting in a different light from the twelfth-century writers. It is clear, however, that Edgar's military powers were both extensive and effective. His methods were not, even at the time, universally commended. The panegyric on his succession (composed somewhat later by Archbishop *Wulfstan of York) records that 'one grave fault, however, was all too characteristic of him, namely that he was far too fond of foreign, vicious customs, and introduced heathen practices far too eagerly into the land: he invited foreigners hither, and encouraged harmful elements to enter this country'. The implication seems to be that, like *Alfred before him, Edgar hired contingents of Viking warriors to swell his troops. The sources for Edgar's reign are too scanty (even the *Anglo-Saxon Chronicle* is not a contemporary source for his time) for any detailed description of his policies and methods. The general effect of his efforts is, however, admirably summed up in the laudatory poem on his death:

'No fleet however proud,
No host however strong,
Got itself prey in England,
While this noble king held the throne.'

BIBL. *ASC* s.a. 973; Stenton 1971: 364-72; Nelson 1977: 63-71

Edith (Eadgyth) St of Wilton, 961–84
Edith was the daughter of King *Edgar by Wulfthryth, who is sometimes described as a concubine, though she may well have been the king's second wife. Twelfth-century writers assert that she was a consecrated nun seduced by Edgar, but this seems to be romantic embroidery, based on the fact that both Wulfthryth and her daughter became nuns of Wilton, of which Wulfthryth was abbess by *c.* 965. The standards of learning at the house seem to have been high; Edith's tutors included the continental scholars Radbod of Rheims and Benno of Treves. She was an accomplished young woman, skilled in embroidery and manuscript illumination, and also very conscious of her royal blood; when reproached by Bishop *Æthelwold for her fine clothes, she replied that as true a heart beat beneath her gold embroidery as beneath his tattered furs. She died young, before her mother, and her cult was established by 997. The medieval seal of Wilton Abbey, which has a portrait of Edith, may originally have been her own personal seal.

BIBL. Ridyard 1988: 37-44, 140-75; Fell 1984: 125-6, pl. 49

Edmund St, king of East Anglia 841–69
Edmund, the patron saint of Bury St Edmunds, was the last known English king of East Anglia, killed by the host of *Ivarr the Boneless in 869, after the battle of Hoxne. He was buried first at Hellesdon, Norfolk, and thence translated to Bury, where his cult quickly developed; it was already widespread by 903, and in the 930s, the story of his death was related by his armour-bearer to King *Athelstan. St *Dunstan, who was present on this occasion, related it to *Abbo of Fleury, who composed the first *Life* of St Edmund. In his introductory letter to Dunstan, Abbo describes the armour-bearer and the effects of his tale:

'He had been, he said, with King Edmund as his armour-bearer on the day he suffered as a martyr. You were much struck by the old man's description, so that you remembered every detail. He had given it very simply, you said, and in a way that carried conviction: it brought tears to your eyes.'

Abbo's *Life* was composed between 985 and 987, at the request of the monks of Ramsey, and a little later an English version was written by *Ælfric. The story of the finding of the king's head, severed from his body, runs as follows, in Ælfric's version:

'Then they went searching, and continually calling out, as is usual among those who frequent the woods, 'Where are you now, comrade?' And the head answered them: 'Here, here, here!'. . .until they all came to it by means of the calling. There lay the grey wolf who watched over the head, and had embraced the head with his two feet, ravenous and hungry, and because of God dare not eat the head, but kept it safe from the beasts.'

When Edmund's companions took up the head to carry it back to the town, the wolf accompanied them, 'as if he were tame', to see them safely on their way. The passage has symbolic interest; the wolf, like the eagle and the raven, was a creature of the battlefield, an eater of the slain, and all three were associated with the god of battle, death, poetry, kings and warriors, Odin himself. Odin, offered the corpse of the murdered Edmund, refused the sacrifice, and protected it for the true God in whose service the king had died.

BIBL. Swanton 1975: 97-103 (The passion of St Edmund, king and martyr); Stubbs 1874: 378ff.; Smyth 1977c

Edmund king of Wessex 940–6

Edmund was the eldest son of *Edward the Elder and his third wife, *Eadgifu. He was born about 921, and was presumably brought up by his half-brother, *Athelstan, who became king, first of Mercia and then of Wessex, in 924. Edmund is associated with his brother in the poem commemorating the great English victory at *Brunanburh* in 937, where 'the sons of Edward, with their well-forged swords, slashed at the linden-shields'. The prominence given to Edmund in the poem suggests that he was his brother's designated heir; at all events he succeeded in 940. The earlier part of his reign was occupied in a struggle with *Olafr Gothfrithson, king of Dublin, and his cousin and namesake, *Olafr Sigtryggson, over the territory of the Five Boroughs. This dispute was eventually resolved in Edmund's favour. He was killed at the royal manor-house at Pucklechurch, Gloucestershire, when he intervened to break up a brawl and was stabbed by a thegn called Leofa. His younger brother *Eadred succeeded as king.

BIBL. Stenton 1971: 356-60

Edmund Ironside king of the English 24 April–30 November 1016

Edmund was the second son of *Æthelred II by his first wife, *Ælfgifu, daughter of *Thored of Northumbria. After the death of his brother *Athelstan in 1014, Edmund was the senior ætheling, but his position was compromised by his father's second marriage to *Emma of Normandy, who had been crowned queen, and the issue of that match. The use of Emma's eldest son *Edward, as his father's emissary in 1014, must have been a particularly worrying development. In 1015, Æthelred engineered the deaths of the two leading thegns of the north, *Sigeferth and *Morcar, both of whom had been connected with Edmund's brother, and probably Edmund himself. The widow of Sigeferth was imprisoned at Malmesbury. Though the background to this incident is obscure, it is probable that the marriage of *Cnut to *Ælfgifu of Northampton, a relative by marriage of Morcar, lay at the root of the king's hostility. Edmund took a different view; he rescued Sigeferth's widow, married her, seized the property of her husband and his brother, and as a result, obtained the submission of the Danish north to his own rule. Edmund's motive was probably to force his father to recognize his position as heir, over his half-brother, Edward; perhaps he also had some idea of neutralizing Cnut's influence in the north, gained by his marriage with Ælfgifu of Northampton. When Cnut invaded England in the winter of 1015–16, it was Edmund, supported by his brother-in-law *Uhtred of Bamburgh, who took the initiative in opposing him. The campaigns were not, however, decisive. When Æthelred died on 23 April 1016, Edmund was acknowledged king and 'defended his kingdom valiantly during his lifetime'. Five general engagements were fought between Danes and English in the summer of 1016; Edmund won the battle of Sherston, but the fight at Ashingdon was the decisive victory for Cnut. At Alney Island, near Deerhurst, Gloucestershire, the two contenders met to divide England, Edmund taking Wessex, and Cnut, Mercia and the north. On 30 November Edmund died, apparently of wounds received at Ashingdon. His two young sons were smuggled abroad to save them from the fate which befell many Englishmen, of being murdered by Cnut. One, Edward ætheling, eventually returned to England in 1057; his daughter Margaret married Malcolm Canmore, king of Scots, and their daughter Edith/Matilda became the wife of Henry I and ancestress of the kings of England.

BIBL. Stenton 1971: 388-97; Stafford 1978: 36-7; Williams 1986: 3-6

Edward the Elder king of Wessex 899–924

Edward, the eldest son and second child of *Alfred and *Ealhswith, succeeded his father as king of Wessex in 899. His major achievement was the conquest of the Danish settlements in East Anglia and the east midlands, and the incorporation of these, formerly independent, areas into the kingdom of Wessex. His immediate problem on becoming king was the revolt of his cousin *Æthelwold, settled only when the latter was killed at the battle of the Holme in 903. The assault on the Danish colonies was launched at the battle of Tettenhall, 910, which crippled the Danish kingdom of York, and enabled Edward, with the help and support of his sister, *Æthelflæd of Mercia, to roll up the southern territories. A prominent role in the success of these campaigns was played by the burhs, fortified and garrisoned strongpoints which served both to protect English-held territory and to launch assaults against the Danes. As the English advance continued, more and more *burhs* were built in the conquered lands. The larger of these were to form administrative centres around which the midland shires were created in the course of the tenth century, and after which most of these shires were named. The rationale of the system is explained in the *Burghal Hidage*, a unique administrative document from Edward's reign; it dates from *c*. 914. It is a list of the *burhs* of Wessex (to which, in one version, the Mercian *burhs* of Worcester and Warwick are added) and explains how the fortifications were built and maintained:

'For the maintenance and defence of an acre's breadth of wall, sixteen hides are required: if every hide is represented by one man, then every pole of wall can be manned by four men.'

Thus, for instance, the 1 600 hides assigned to the Dorset *burh* of Wareham, implies, at 16 hides for every four poles (22 yards), a wall 2 200 yards long to enclose the *burh*. The accuracy of the assessment is shown by the fact that the ninth-century walls of Wareham, still standing, measure 2 180 yards.

Edward also presided over the incorporation into Wessex of what remained of Mercia, after the partition under *Ceolwulf II. When Æthelred of Mercia died in 911, the areas dependent upon Buckingham, Oxford and probably London were taken into West Saxon control; and after the death of Æthelflæd in 918 the same fate befell the rest of the kingdom. *Ælfwynn, its last independent ruler, was deprived of all power in 919 and Edward's last campaign, in the course of which he died, was conducted against the men of Chester who had allied with the Welsh to resist West Saxon absorption. It is possible that Edward did not intend to amalgamate the two kingdoms. On his death in 924, he was succeeded as king of Wessex by his son Ælfweard, the eldest of his children by his second wife, *Ælfflæd. In Mercia, however, Æthelstan, his son by his first wife, *Ecgwynn, was accepted as king. Athelstan, who may have been illegitimate, was reared in Mercia, apparently with this end in mind. Only the death of Ælfweard, 16 days after his father, brought Athelstan to the kingship of Wessex as well as Mercia. Edward and his son Ælfweard were buried in the New Minster, Winchester, which he had founded. He was survived by his third wife, Eadgifu.

BIBL. Stenton 1971: 266, 319-39

Edward the Martyr king of the English 975−8

Edward was the son of *Edgar and his first wife, *Æthelflæd Eneda. He was brought up and educated by Sideman, bishop of Crediton, and is said to have been 'learned in divine law'. He succeeded his father as king in 975, not without difficulty. Though he had the support of *Dunstan and *Æthelwine of East Anglia, a strong party favoured the accession of his half-brother, *Æthelred II. The most prominent among the young ætheling's supporters were his mother, *Ælfthryth, who had been a crowned queen (unlike Æthelflæd Eneda), *Ælfhere of Mercia, and probably Bishop *Æthelwold of Winchester. Edward's short reign was shadowed with dissension, both the rivalry between Æthelwine of East Anglia and Ælfhere of Mercia, and a reaction against the newly-founded and reformed monasteries which had proliferated under his father. It was not monasticism as such which was opposed (though the reformers presented their enemies as foes of God and the Church). What disturbed many Englishmen was the shift in the political status and economic enrichment of the new monasteries; in particular, Ælfhere of Mercia resented the ecclesiastical liberty of Oswaldslow, created in the midst of his territory for the bishop of Worcester.

Edward was remembered as an ill-tempered and violent youth, given to outbursts of ungovernable rage; it may have been in part his personality which provoked his murder, on 18 March 978, at Corfe in Dorset. He was visiting his stepmother and half-brother at the time, and the crime was carried out by their adherents. No names are named in contemporary sources; the association of Ælfthryth herself in the murder comes from twelfth-century commentators. The corpse was hastily interred at Wareham 'with no royal honours'. But even unpopular kings cannot just be done away with. It was over a year later that his successor Æthelred II was consecrated at Kingston, on 4 May 979. In the following year, Æthelred's champion, Ælfhere, fetched the murdered king's body from Wareham, and conveyed it 'with great ceremony' to Shaftesbury, a house closely connected with the royal West Saxon line (its first abbess was the daughter of King *Alfred). At the formal translation of Edward's relics in 1001, Æthelred refers to his brother, in a charter to Shaftesbury, as 'the saint, my brother Edward, whom, drenched with his own blood, the Lord has seen fit to magnify in our time through many miracles'. In 1008, the observance of St Edward's feast, on 18 March, was ordered throughout England.

BIBL. Fell 1971; Ridyard 1988

Edwin St, king of Northumbria 617–33

Edwin, son of *Ælle of Deira, was driven into exile when *Æthelfrith of Bernicia made himself king of the whole of Northumbria. Edwin's wanderings in exile took him to Mercia, where he married the daughter of King *Cearl, Cwenburh, who bore him two sons, Osfrith and Eadfrith. Later tradition maintains that he was fostered by *Cadfan, king of Gwynedd, and baptized by Rhun map *Urien of Rheged. It was in East Anglia that he found the means to destroy his enemies, for he secured the support of King *Rædwald, who defeated and killed Æthelfrith at the battle of the River Idle in 617. In 625 Edwin re-married, taking as his wife *Æthelburh, daughter of King *Æthelberht of Kent. She brought with her the Roman missionary *Paulinus, and it was he, according to *Bede, who converted Edwin to Christianity and accomplished the evangelization of Northumbria. It was Edwin who built the first church at York, where Paulinus established his see. The royal residence of Yeavering, where Paulinus baptized in the River Glen, has been excavated and shows something of the state kept by Edwin, who was Bretwalda as well as king of all Northumbria; the buildings included a hall over 80 ft long and a stepped amphitheatre, perhaps for meetings of the Northumbrian witenagemot. Edwin was a warlord of note; he conquered the British kingdom of Elmet (the Leeds region) and imposed tribute on the 'Mevanian Islands' (Man and Anglesey), a feat which involved the use of a fleet. His success brought him many enemies. In 626, a West Saxon assassin sent by King Cwichhelm (son of *Cynegils) almost succeeded in killing Edwin, who was saved only by the heroism of his thegn, Lilla; he threw himself between his lord and the assassin's dagger, and was killed in his place. In 633, an even more dangerous enemy succeeded where Cwichhelm had failed. *Cadwallon, king of Gwynedd, allied with *Penda of Mercia to invade Northumbria, and Edwin was defeated and killed at the battle of Hatfield Chase on 12 October. His death threw Northumbria into confusion. His widow, Æthelburh, fled to Kent, taking with her Bishop Paulinus, *Eanflæd and Uscfrea, her children by Edwin, and Yffi, son of Osfrith, who had been killed with his father. Only *James the deacon remained in York to keep alive the work of the Roman mission. Eadfrith deserted to Penda's following, and was later murdered. The kingdom of Deira passed to Osric, son of Edwin's uncle, Ælfric, but Bernicia went to Eanfrith, son of Æthelfrith, who returned from exile on Edwin's death. Both kings renounced the Christian faith, and both were killed within the year by Cadwallon. It was *Oswald, Eanfrith's brother, who restored the kingdom, killing Cadwallon at the battle of *Denisesburn* or Heavenfield, near Hexham.

Edwin's memory was preserved at Whitby, founded by his great-niece, St *Hild. His daughter Eanflæd, when she became abbess of Whitby, translated her father's remains to the church of St Gregory, and there Edwin was venerated as a saint. As the first Northumbrian king to hold the overlordship of the English, he was a hero to Bede, who portrayed his reign as a Golden Age, and Bede's tribute may stand as Edwin's memorial:
'The king cared so much for the good of the people that, in various places where he had noticed clear springs near the highway, he caused stakes to be set up and bronze drinking-cups to be hung on them for the refreshment of travellers. No one dared to lay hands upon them except for their proper purpose because they feared the king greatly, nor did they wish to, because they loved him dearly.'

BIBL. *HE* ii, 9-20: 162-207; iii, 1: 212-15; Stenton 1971: 78-81; 113-16; Chadwick 1963b: 138-66

Edwin ealdorman *d*. 982
Edwin was appointed ealdorman by *Edward the Martyr, probably in 976. His sphere of authority included Kent as well as Sussex. The community at Rochester accused him of abetting the theft of some of their estates, largely, it seems, because he gave judgement against them in a lawsuit. He died in 982 and was buried at Abingdon, which seems to indicate that he was a West Saxon, but little is known of him.

BIBL. *ASC* s.a. 982; Robertson 1956: 366; Campbell 1973: no. 36, xx—xxii

Edwin thegn *d*. 1039
Edwin was one of the sons of *Leofwine, ealdorman of Mercia. In the reign of *Cnut, he held office in Herefordshire, probably as sheriff, and in 1039 was killed fighting against the Welsh at the battle of Rhyd y Grœs.

BIBL. *ASC* s.a. 1039, 1052

Eilaf (Elaf, Eilifr) earl 1018–*c.* 1035

Eilaf's first appearance in England was as a member of the 'immense raiding-army', of *Thorkell the Tall in 1009. This host dispersed after the murder in 1012 of Archbishop *Ælfheah, and Eilaf is next found as one of *Cnut's earls: he was given a command which included Gloucestershire, probably in 1018. In 1022 he led an expedition into Wales, ravaging Dyfed and sacking St David's. He fought against Cnut at the battle of Holy River in 1027, but was later reconciled with the king, and seems to have remained in England (though perhaps no longer in office) until Cnut's death in 1035, when he returned to Scandinavia. The date of his death is unknown. His brother *Ulf was Cnut's brother-in-law, the husband of Estrith, and his sister, Gytha, married *Godwine, earl of Wessex, in 1020.

BIBL. Williams 1986: 6-11; Campbell 1949: 82-7

Einar I earl of Orkney *see* **Torf Einar**

Einar II Falsemouth (*Rangmunnr*) earl of Orkney 1014–20

Einar was the son of Earl *Sigurd the Stout of Orkney who was slain in the battle of Clontarf in Ireland in 1014. On the death of his father, Einar shared the earldom with his brothers Sumarlidi and Brúsi. On Sumarlidi's death Einar was challenged for a third of the inheritance by his youngest brother, *Thorfinn the Mighty, who had been reared on the Scottish mainland, perhaps under the protection of *Malcolm II of Scotland. The ensuing conflict between Thorfinn and Einar was resolved with the slaying of Einar by Thorkel, the fosterer of Thorfinn, in Thorkel's hall at Sandwick in *c.* 1020. Einar was remembered in Norse tradition as a harsh bully who extorted excessive taxes from the farmers and who made himself unpopular by forcing his men to follow him on unprofitable Viking raids about the British Isles. On his death, the earldom of Orkney was shared by his brothers Brúsi and Thorfinn the Mighty.

BIBL. Pálsson and Edwards 1978: 38-43

Einion ab Owain prince of Deheubarth *d.* 984

Einion was a grandson of *Hywel Dda. The Welsh annals record that his lands were attacked by the English under *Ælfhere, ealdorman of Mercia, in alliance with *Hywel ap Ieuaf, king of Gwynedd, in 983. He himself ravaged in Gower in 970 and 977, territory controlled perhaps even at this date by his brother, *Maredudd, and he was killed in 984 by the men of Gwent.

BIBL. Lloyd 1911, vol. I: 345

Eirikr Bloodaxe king of York 947–8; 952–4

Eirikr Bloodaxe was one of the sons of Harald Finehair, king of Norway. He was already established as lord of the Norse earldom of Orkney when in 947 he was invited by the York Vikings to become their king. His rule was opposed not only by *Eadred of Wessex, who invaded Northumbria in force in 948, but also by *Olafr Sigtryggson, king of Dublin. It was

Olafr who became king of York when Eirikr was forced to withdraw by West Saxon pressure in that year. By 952, however, opinion was veering away from Olafr and towards Eirikr, and he was able to return. By the end of the year he had lost his chief supporter, Archbishop *Wulfstan I of York, who was captured and imprisoned by King Eadred, and two years later, he was driven from York. As Eirikr travelled towards Carlisle, he was betrayed by *Osulf of Bamburgh, and was ambushed and killed by Earl Maccus whose identity is uncertain; he may have been a son or nephew of Olafr Sigtryggson. The final battle took place at 'a certain lonely place which is called Stainmore'. The survivors of Eirikr's party, led by his widow, Gunnhildr, fled to Orkney, and Earl Osulf, who had engineered his demise, was made Earl of Northumbria by King Eadred.

Eirikr was long remembered by the saga writers of the north, who embroidered his tale with many legendary exploits. His funeral lay, the *Eiriksmal*, which is nearly contemporary with his death, still survives; it describes his triumphal entry into Valhalla, where 'the benches tremble as though Baldur were coming back to Odin's hall'. His most celebrated posthumous role is as the implacable enemy of Egill Skallagrimson, the Icelandic skald (poet). It was for Eirikr that Egill composed the *Head-Ransom*, presented to the enraged king in return for his life; the following extract gives the flavour:

'King reddened sword, Came ravens a horde, Bright lifeblood outpoured, as shafts flew abroad. Scot's scourge bade feed Trollwife's wolfsteed, Hel trod with her feet the eagle's nightmeat.'

After all this it is something of a surprise to find the name of this terrible Viking king and warrior in the list of those for whom prayer was to be offered in the Durham *Liber Vitæ*. One wonders whether he would have been pleased or not.

BIBL. Smyth 1979: 155-90; Jones 1968: 94-5, 349-50; Auden and Taylor 1981: 60-1

Eirikr of Hlathir earl 1016–23

Eirikr was the son of Hakon, earl of Hlathir (Trondheim), who supported the Danish kings, Harold Bluetooth and *Swein Forkbeard, and whose rule came to an end when *Olafr Tryggvason seized power in Norway in 995. When Olafr was killed at the battle of Svold in 1000, Eirikr returned to Hlathir as earl. He married Gytha, Swein Forkbeard's daughter, who bore him a son, *Hakon. In 1013, after Swein's death, he joined his brother-in-law, *Cnut in England, and was made earl of Northumbria after the murder of *Uhtred of Bamburgh in 1016. He probably died in or soon after 1023, when his last signature appears on a charter of Cnut. Later tradition maintained that he died from loss of blood after surgery.

BIBL. Campbell 1949: 66-73

Elfoddw bishop d. 809

Styled 'archbishop of Gwynedd' in the mid-tenth century Harleian annals in the notice of his death in 809, Elfoddw was responsible for persuading the Welsh churches to accept the Roman Easter in 768, thereby bringing the Church in Wales into belated conformity with that in the rest of the British Isles.

BIBL. Lloyd 1911, vol. 1: 203; Chadwick 1958b: 43-4, 91-2

Eliseg ap Gwylog king of Powys *fl.* eighth century

Eliseg, king of Powys in the mid-eighth century, is commemorated on a monument known as Eliseg's Pillar, erected at Llantysilio-yn-Ial near Llangollen by his great-grandson, *Cyngen, king of Powys, who died in Rome in (probably) 855. The pillar extols the praises of Eliseg who 'annexed the inheritance of Powys...from the power of the English' and traces his ancestry back through *Vortigern to the usurping Roman emperor, Magnus Maximus.

BIBL. Lloyd 1911, vol. 1: 244-5; Bartrum 1966: 1

Emma queen 1002−52

Emma, the youngest daughter of Richard I, duke of Normandy, and his wife, Duchess Gunnor, was married to *Æthelred II, as his second wife, in 1002. Æthelred was the first English king since his ancestor, *Æthelwulf (in 855) to take a foreign bride. The occasion was presumably to enlist the aid of Duke Richard II against the Scandinavian raiders who had been using the ports of Normandy as a base to attack England but the stratagem was not a noticeable success. Emma, whom the English re-christened Ælfgifu, bore Æthelred three children, *Edward (the Confessor), *Alfred and *Goda (Godgifu). Her marriage-settlement included the city of Exeter, and when the town was sacked by Vikings in 1003, the blame was laid on Emma's reeve, the 'French ceorl', Hugh. In 1013, Emma and her children fled to Normandy to escape the advance of *Swein Forkbeard's armies. There she remained until 1018, when she returned to marry *Cnut, Swein's son, who had conquered her first husband's kingdom. By Cnut she had two more children, *Harthacnut and *Gunnhildr. After Cnut's death, the kingdom was seized by *Harold I, and Emma was forced once again into exile; she fled to Bruges, where she commissioned a eulogy of her second husband, the *Encomium of Queen Emma* (*Encomium Emmæ Reginæ*), a work remarkable in many respects, not least in completely concealing the fact of Emma's marriage to Æthelred II. She returned to England in 1040, when, on Harold's death, her son Harthacnut became king, but ill-luck still followed her. Harthacnut died unexpectedly in 1042, and was succeeded by his half-brother, Edward the Confessor. He, apparently dissatisfied with his mother's lukewarm support, deprived her of her property in 1043. She continued to live in England until her death, in 1052.

BIBL. Campbell, A 1949; Campbell, M 1971: 66-79

Eochaid Buide king of Scots Dál Riata 608−29

Eochaid succeeded to the kingship of his father, the powerful *Áedán mac Gabhráin, on the latter's death or abdication in 608. *Adomnán in his *Life of Columba* implies that in spite of the large number of sons of Áedán, Eochaid succeeded to the whole kingdom. Adomnán tells how *Columba persuaded Áedán to settle the succession on Eochaid Buide, one of Áedán's younger sons. Áedán preferred his older sons for the office, but Columba dissuaded him from this by prophesying the deaths of Artuir and Eochaid Find in battle (against the Miathi) and that of Domangart in battle against the English. The implication is that Eochaid, who received Columba's special blessing, was still only a small boy before the battle against the Miathi in *c*. 590. Eochaid is styled 'king of the Picts' in the record of his death in the *Annals of Ulster* (quoting from the Book of Cuanu), which suggests he had conquered some Pictish territory, and is in keeping with his father's hostility towards the Picts and with the possibility that *Gartnait, king of the Picts, was his brother. The eleventh-century Irish saga, *Fleadh Dúin na nGédh*, claims that Congal Caech king of Dál nAraide in Ulster, was the grandson of Eochaid Buide.

BIBL. Anderson 1973: 149-52; Bannerman 1974: 95-6

Eochaid son of Domangart king of Scots Dál Riata 697
This grandson of *Domnall Brecc had a very brief reign in Dál Riata. His killers, in 697, were most likely of the dynasty of Cenél Loairn led by Eochaid's successor, *Ainbcellach son of Ferchar Fota. Eochaid's name appears as one of the ratifiers of *Adomnán's *Law of Innocents* in 697.

BIBL. Anderson 1973: 157, 183; Anderson 1922, vol. 1: 205

Eochaid son of Rhun, king (?) of Scots 878−89
The name of Eochaid's father, Rhun, appears at the end of the genealogy of British kings of Strathclyde in a pedigree appended to the *Annales Cambriae*. Eochaid's grandfather, *Artgal, who was slain in 872 was the last king of Strathclyde whom we can be certain belonged to a Northern British house. Eochaid son of Rhun appears to have made a final attempt to preserve Strathclyde as a separate British kingdom by allying himself with *Giric, a nephew of *Kenneth mac Alpín who seized the Scottish throne in 878. Although Eochaid was himself a grandson of Kenneth mac Alpín through his mother, he had every reason to join Giric in the struggle against the sons of Kenneth who had helped to destroy his grandfather. Some sources claim that Eochaid ruled jointly over the Scots kingdom along with Giric who was his foster-father. Both rulers were probably deposed in 889 and from then on, Strathclyde became a sub-kingdom of the Scottish realm, ruled over by a member of the Scottish (Dál Riata) royal house.

BIBL. Anderson 1922, vol. 1: 363-8; Smyth 1984: 215-18

Eóganán son of Óengus, king of Scots and Picts 837−9
Eóganán appears in Pictish king-lists as *Uuen* son of *Unuist*, but as the grandson of Fergus he was in the main Cenél Gabhráin line of Dál Riata kings. Eóganán features in the St Andrew legend along with his brothers Nechtán and Finguine as residing at Forteviot in Perthshire during the reign of their father, *Óengus II. This along with other evidence suggests that the Scottish kings of Dál Riata had already taken over the southern Pictish heartland sometime before 834. Eóganán fell in a disastrous battle against the Norsemen in 839 in which he and his brother Bran and many

of the Pictish aristocracy were annihilated. Partly as a result of this battle *Kenneth mac Alpín seized the kingship of the Scots in 840.

BIBL. Anderson 1973: 193, 195; Smyth 1984: 179-80

Eorcenberht king of Kent 640−64

Eorcenberht, son of *Eadbald and grandson of *Æthelberht, became king of Kent in 640. He was, according to *Bede, 'the first king to order idols to be destroyed throughout the whole kingdom'. He married *Seaxburh, one of the saintly daughters of *Anna of East Anglia, who bore him two daughters and a son. One daughter, Eorcengota, became abbess of Faremoutiers-en-Brie; another, Eormenhild, married *Wulfhere of Mercia, before becoming abbess of Minster-in-Sheppey, founded by her mother. The son, *Ecgberht, succeeded to the kingdom when Eorcenberht died, probably of plague, on 14 July 664; the same day as Archbishop *Deusdedit.

BIBL. *HE* iii, 7: 236-8; iv, 1: 328-9

Eorcenwald (Erkenwald) St, bishop 675−93

Eorcenwald, who may have been related to the Kentish royal house, founded the monasteries of Chertsey, of which he was abbot, and Barking, presided over by his sister *Æthelburh. In 675 he was consecrated bishop of London by Archbishop *Theodore. His diocese extended over Essex and Middlesex, and seems to have been under West Saxon control, for *Ine of Wessex, in the preamble to his law-code, called Eorcenwald 'my bishop'. He died at Barking, on 30 April 693, and was buried in St Paul's. His cult was popular throughout the Middle Ages.

BIBL. *HE* iv, 6: 354-5; Farmer 1978: 134

Eormenric *see* **Iurmenric**

Etheldreda *see* **Æthelthryth**

Ethilwald bishop, *fl.* 845/70 *see* **Æthelwold**

Eugein map Beli *see* **Owen map Bili**

F

Fáelán (Fillan) Scottish saint *c.* 730–40

Fáelán's festival is noted in the *Martyrology of Óengus* (*c.* 800) under 20 June, associated in the later notes in that source with Strathearn in Scotland. The Breviary of Aberdeen (9 January) identifies him as the son of *Kentigerna, the daughter of the Leinster king, Cellach Cualann, who migrated with her brother, *Comgán, and with her son, Fáelán, to Strathfillan in Scotland and later (on her own account) to Loch Lomond. The same source claims that Fáelán, by Divine inspiration, left his mother and uncle and settled at *Glendeochquhy* (perhaps Glen Dochart in Perthshire) where he built a church. The churches at Aberdour and at Pittenweem on the northern shores of the Forth, at Forgan in north-east Fife, and at St Fillans on the eastern end of Loch Earn are associated with Fáelán. Skene believed that this Scottish Fáelán had been a disciple of the early sixth-century Irish saint, Ailbe of Emly. But Fáelán's name is found among the Leinster aristocracy of his supposed mother, Kentigerna, and Kentigerna's own historical existence is in no doubt. It is very possible that confusion has arisen between two separate Fáeláns one of whom had a festival on 9 January and the other on 20 June.

BIBL. Anderson 1922, vol. 1: 231; Skene 1886-90, vol. ii: 33, 175, 407

Fáelchú son of Dorbene, abbot of Iona 717–24

Fáelchu succeeded *Dúnchad son of Cennfaelad as twelfth abbot in succession to *Columba in 717, but in the previous year he had assumed the *Kathedra* or 'Chair' of Columba on Saturday 29 August. Presumably Dúnchad had become too infirm to rule by that time, although Fáelchú was 74 at his appointment and must therefore have been 82 at his death in 724. During Fáelchú's last two years of office, a certain Fedlimid held the government or *principatus* of Iona. Because of Fáelchú's own great age in 716, it is highly unlikely that his father Dorbene was the same person as the bishop of that *name who obtained the 'Chair of Iona' as recently as 713 or the Dorbene who had his name inscribed on the colophon of the earliest manuscript of *Adomnán's *Life* of Columba. The colophon is written in the steady hand of a younger man. On the other hand, the name *Dorbene* is extremely rare. Fáelchú was clearly of the Romanizing party on Iona since he came to power at the time of transition from Celtic to Roman usage. He was already 62 when Adomnán, the champion of Roman usage in the Columban world, died, so it is likely that he had served as a monk under Adomnán on Iona. Fáelchú was succeeded by *Cillene Fota. His festival day is uncertain.

BIBL. Anderson and Anderson 1961: 99; Reeves 1857: 381-2

Failbe abbot of Iona 669–79

Failbe, son of Pipan, succeeded *Cumméne Find as eighth abbot of

Iona in 669. A member of *Columba's aristocratic Irish kin, Failbe was Cumméne Find's third cousin. *Adomnán, who came to Iona from Ireland during Failbe's abbacy, informs us in his *Life of Columba* that Failbe had served on Iona during abbot *Ségéne's rule there (623–52). Failbe was present when a prominent Irish ecclesiastic, Ernéne son of Crasen, visited Iona very probably in 633–4 and Failbe is also reported as having met *Oswald of Northumbria sometime after that king had won his victory over Cadwallon in 634. Failbe had therefore served some 45 years or more as a monk on Iona. As abbot he visited his Irish *paruchia* in 673, returning to Iona three years later. It is suggested, but by no means proven, that Adomnán may have ruled Iona in his absence. Failbe was an invaluable source of information for Adomnán in compiling his *Life of Columba*. As a man who had served under three abbots, the first of whom — Ségéne — had access to people and relatives who had known Columba, he was able to provide Adomnán with information which was independent of *Cumméne's work on St Columba. Failbe died in 679 and was succeeded by *Adomnán. His festival was kept on 22 March. He is commemorated in the *Martyrology of Óengus* as a 'strong light over the rampart of the sea, Failbe, the warrior of Iona'.

BIBL. Anderson and Anderson 1961: 91-2; Reeves 1857: 376

Feader and **Thorstein**, housecarls *d*. 1041

In 1040, a 'severe tax' for the support of the royal fleet was levied on England, assessed at 'eight marks to the rowlock', for a total of 62 ships. The tax, collected in 1040–1, amounted to 21,099 pounds of silver. This move on the part of the new king, *Harthacnut, was extremely unpopular, and the men of Worcester refused to pay. Moreover they killed the two royal housecarls who had been sent to collect the tax, in the church of St Mary, Worcester; the names of the unfortunate men were Feader and Thorstein. In revenge, Harthacnut called up his men and those of earls *Leofric, *Ranig and *Thuri (of Mercia, Hereford and the east midlands respectively) and had all Worcestershire ravaged. The whole area was notably hostile to Harthacnut; *Lyfing, bishop of Worcester, was deposed in 1041.

BIBL. *ASC* s.a. 1041

Felix St, bishop *d*. 647

Felix was a Burgundian priest, perhaps from one of the houses founded by the Irish missionary, St Columbanus. He arrived in England in the time of Archbishop *Honorius (627–53), who sent him to *Sigeberht of East Anglia. Sigeberht established Felix as bishop of the East Angles, with his see at *Domnoc*, a site as yet unidentified; it has been variously located at Dunwich and Felixstowe, the last of which preserves the bishop's name. Felix founded a monastery at Soham, where he died. His successor was his deacon, Thomas. Like *Birinus in Wessex, Felix exemplifies the Frankish strain in the English church.

BIBL. Whitelock 1972: 3-7

Felix monk and hagiographer *fl.* 713/49

Little is known of Felix, biographer of St *Guthlac, except that he was a monk, and an East Angle, for the *Life of Guthlac* was composed for *Ælfwald, king of East Anglia (713–49).

BIBL. Colgrave 1956: 15-9

Fergna Brit (Virgno) abbot of Iona 605–23

Fergna was the fourth abbot in succession to *Laisran and he was the last abbot of Iona who had served the community as a monk during *Columba's lifetime. He was, according to *Adomnán in his *Life of Columba*, 'a young man of good ability' when he witnessed a vision of a heavenly light which enveloped Columba while praying in the chapel on Iona. Fergna's nickname, *Brit* ('the Briton') implies that he spent some time among that people, possibly as a novice in a monastery. He was a member of Columba's kindred but unlike his predecessors in the abbacy, he was not so closely related to Columba. Comman, Fergna's nephew (a sister's son), became a priest, and related to Adomnán the details of the vision which Fergna had witnessed on Iona as a young man. During Fergna's rule, *Donnán and his monastic community were butchered on Eigg to the north of Iona. Fergna is the first abbot of Iona to be described as a bishop in the later martyrologies. His festival was kept by the Irish Church on 2 March. He was succeeded in 623 by Abbot *Ségéne.

BIBL. Anderson and Anderson 1961: 90 and text; Reeves 1857: 372-3

Fergus Mór son of Erc, king of Dál Riata *c.* 500

Fergus Mór ('the Great') is accepted as the first historical king of Dál Riata and the founder of the dynastic colony in Argyll *c.* 500. Fergus is said to have migrated from the Dál Riata homeland in north-east Ireland where he and his brothers were regarded as contemporaries of St Patrick. His death is recorded in the *Annals of Tigernach* at 501.

BIBL. Bannerman 1974: 73-5

Fillan *see* **Fáelán St**

Finán St, bishop 651–61

Finán, an Irish monk of Iona, succeeded *Aidan as bishop of Northumbria in 651. He built a new church at Lindisfarne 'after the Irish method, not of stone but of hewn oak, thatching it with reeds'. It was Finán who baptized King *Peada at Wallbottle in 653, and despatched *Cedd and his companions to convert the Middle Angles. When a little later *Sigeberht Sanctus of Essex accepted the Faith at the urging of King *Oswiu, Finán baptized him, and recalled Cedd from Middle Anglia to become bishop of Essex. It was in Finán's time that dissension first arose in Northumbria over the reckoning of Easter. The monk Ronan, 'who, though Irish by race, had learned the true rules of the church in Gaul or Italy', urged acceptance of the Roman method of calculation, but Finán, 'a man of fierce temper', would not accept his arguments. He died in 661 and was succeeded by *Colmán.

BIBL. *HE* iii, 21-2: 278-83; 25: 294-7; Farmer 1978: 150

Findlaech son of Ruaidhri, king of Moray *c*. 1000—20

Findlaech (Finlay) was the father of *Macbeth. He is described as a *mórmaer* or chieftain of Moray in the *Annals of Tigernach*, while the *Annals of Ulster* describe him as king of Scotland at the record of his death in 1020. His nephew, Malcolm, is also styled 'king of Scotland' — this time by Tigernach — at his death in 1029. There is little doubt that Findlaech's ancestors were regarded as kings in their own right in Moray, and were perhaps descended from a branch of the Cenél Loairn who migrated from Argyll up the Great Glen at the onset of Viking raids in the early ninth century. The ruling Scottish dynasty in Perth and Fife (descended from *Kenneth mac Alpín) no doubt preferred to view their rivals in Moray as sub-kings or earls — hence the title *mórmaer* accorded to Findlaech and his cousins in some sources. Findlaech is almost certainly the same person as *Finnleikr* the Scottish earl who in *Orkneyinga Saga* challenged Earl *Sigurd the Stout of Orkney for control of Caithness. According to the saga, *Finnleikr* was defeated by Sigurd in a battle at Skitten Myre near Duncansby in Caithness sometime prior to 1014. Findlaech's son, Macbeth, may be the same person as *Karl Hundason, a Scottish king who is assigned a prominent role in *Orkneyinga Saga*. Findlaech was slain in 1020 by the sons of his brother, Máelbrigte. These were clearly Malcolm (died 1029) and Gillacomgain who was married to Gruoch as her first husband — her second husband being Macbeth.

BIBL. Anderson 1922, vol. 1: 551, 571, 580; Pálsson and Edwards 1978: 36-7

Frane (Frani) thegn *fl*. 983/93

Frane is named, with *Godwine and Frithugist, as a leader of the English host which was routed by a Viking army in Lindsey in 993. Frane and his companions were accused of starting the flight 'because they were Danes on the father's side'; Frane and Frithugist (though not Godwine) certainly have Danish names. Frane can be identified as a Northampton-shire landowner, Frane of Rockingham, who was a benefactor of Peter-borough Abbey. Frithugist, whose father bore the Danish name *Cate*, was also a benefactor of Peterborough; his lands lay in Lincolnshire.

BIBL. *ASC* s.a. 993; Hart 1975: 335-7; Hart 1966: 172, 174, 244

Frideswide (Frithuswith) **St** d. 727

Very little is known of St Frideswide, patroness of the University of Oxford. She is said to have been buried at Oxford in 727, but the earliest life dates only from the twelfth century, and is clearly legendary. However, Frideswide's name occurs in the early eleventh-century list of resting-places of the saints, beside that of Cuthburh of Wimborne, King *Ine's sister. The church in Oxford dedicated in her honour was already in existence at that date. During the massacre of St Brice's Day, ordered by *Æthelred II in 1002, the Danes of Oxford took refuge in St Fridewide's, but the enraged populace of Oxford burnt it over their heads. In 1004, King Æthelred issued a charter confirming the possessions and rights of the church and replacing those documents which had been destroyed in the fire. Frideswide may have been related to *Frithuwold of Surrey, and to Queen Frithugyth, wife of Æthelheard, king of Wessex (726–40).

BIBL. Stenton 1936; Blair 1989: 106

Frithegod monk *fl.* 948/55

Frithegod was a protégé of *Oda, archbishop of Canterbury, who commissioned him to write a life of St *Wilfrid on the occasion of that saint's translation from Ripon to Canterbury in 948. Despite a later tradition that Frithegod was the most learned man of his age, his identity and career are obscure in the extreme. It is possible that he was a Frankish monk and scholar, for his name is unusual in England but commoner on the continent (in the form *Fredegaud*). If so, his presence in Oda's entourage is another example of the close relationship between England and Frankia in the tenth century.

BIBL. Lapidge 1988

Frithugist *see under* Frane and Godwin

Frithuwold sub-king *fl.* 672/4

One of the earliest authentic English charters is a grant to Chertsey Abbey in the name of Frithuwold 'sub-king of the province of the men of Surrey', issued in the years 672–4. The gift is confirmed by his lord, *Wulfhere of Mercia, whose sister, Wilburh, he had married. Frithuwold was probably a kinsman of the Middle Anglian magnate, Frithuric, who gave the site of Breedon-on-the-Hill to Abbot *Hædde, and who witnessed the Chertsey grant. Frithuwold's sub-kingdom probably included not only Surrey but much of the Chilterns and at least part of Buckinghamshire, for his daughter, St *Osyth, was born in his palace of Quarrendon, near Aylesbury.

BIBL. Blair 1989; Sawyer 1968: no. 1165

Fursa (Fursey) St *d.* 649/50

Fursa, an Irish missionary-monk, arrived in East Anglia in the time of King *Sigeberht, who gave him the Roman fort of *Cnobheresburh* (Burgh Castle, Suffolk) in which to found a monastery. He left this house in the charge of his brother, Foillan, to go to Gaul, where he died in 649 or 650. Almost immediately after his departure, the kingdom of East Anglia was attacked by the heathen — presumably the Mercians under *Penda — and the monastery was despoiled. The inhabitants were saved by King *Anna, Sigeberht's successor, but decided to leave England for Gaul, where Foillan was eventually murdered by brigands.

BIBL. Whitelock 1972: 5-6

G

Gabhrán son of Domangart, king of Scots Dál Riata 538–58

Gabhrán was the fourth king of Dál Riata in succession to his brother Comgall. He is mentioned in *Adomnán's *Life of Columba* and tradition at least as old as the eleventh century claims his wife was Luan, daughter of Brychan, a Celtic ruler now thought to have been located in Lothian or Southern Pictland. Alternatively, his queen was from the southern Welsh kingdom of Brycheiniog (Brecknock). Gabhrán's son, *Áedán mac Gabhráin, was one of the more remarkable early Scottish rulers.

BIBL. Bannerman 1974: 77-8

Gartnait king of the Picts *c*. 584–602

Gartnait succeeded *Bruide mac Maelchon as king of the Picts in *c*. 584. He is accorded an 11- or 20-year reign in the Pictish king-lists, the latter number tallying better with the record of his death in the *Annals of Tigernach* in 599. Gartnait's father is given as *Áedán mac Gabhráin in the *Senchus fer nAlban* and other sources, but in the king-lists, his parent's name is given as *Domelch*, which is taken by some scholars to be the name of Gartnait's mother and indicative of the Pictish system of matri-linear succession. His successor was *Nechtán or Nectu grandson of Verb. This Nectu of the Pictish king-lists may have been a grandson of Gartnait, if we accept him as being the same person as Nechtán son of Cano who died according to the *Annals of Ulster* in 621. Since Gartnait son of Áedán mac Gabhráin is said in the *Senchus fer nAlban* to have had a son called Cano, then Nectu grandson of Verb and Nechtán son of Cano son of Gartnait would seem to be the same person. A later Irish saga (*Scéla Cano meic Gartnáin*) compiled in the eleventh century confused this Cano grandson of Áedán mac Gabhráin with a son of a Pictish ruler, Garnait, who led a migration of fugitives from Skye across to Ireland in 688.

BIBL. Anderson 1973: 116, 154; Bannerman 1974: 92-4

Gere *fl*. first half of the eleventh century

Gere was a Swedish landowner, commemorated on the runestone at Kalsta in the parish of Haggeloy (Uppland):
'Starkar and Hjorvard had this stone raised in memory of their father, Gere, who in the west had his place in the *thingalith*.'
If 'the west' here refers to England, Gere may have been one of the *lithsmen* who appear in English sources in the period 1012–51; they were probably the crews who manned and fought the royal fleet maintained by the English kings in this period.

BIBL. Jansson 1962: 50; Hooper 1989: 204-6

Germanus St, bishop *d*. (?)437

Germanus, a Gallo-Roman of noble birth, became bishop of Auxerre in

141

418, after a life spent in government and the army. In 429 he was sent to Britain by Pope Celestine at the urging of the deacon, *Palladius, to root out the Pelagian heresy. At this date some remnants of Roman administration and social organization still lingered, at least in southern Britain, but attacks from Caledonia (Scotland) and Ireland were common. Germanus assisted a British force to rout an army of Picts, Scots and Saxons — the 'Alleluia' victory, so-called after the Christian battle-cry. He made a second visit in c.436–7 to combat a Pelagian revival. (Pelagianism was effectively suppressed in the course of the fifth century.) His *Life*, written by his follower Constantius of Lyons, is one of the few sources for the history of Britain in the fifth century. The cult of a Radnorshire saint, Garmon, may lie behind the Welsh traditions in the *Historia Brittonum* (see under *Nennius) about a Germanus who confronted *Vortigern for his immoral acts and hounded him to death on the Teifi, but this does not imply a historical basis for such traditions.

BIBL. Thompson 1984; Kirby 1968

Germanus abbot 970–5

Germanus, a monk of Fleury-sur-Loire, was invited by St *Oswald to assist in the reform of the chapter at Worcester. He was made presbyter of the house at Westbury-on-Trym, where monks were trained for their duties in the new monastic church of St Mary at Worcester, built by St Oswald. Subsequently the Westbury community was transferred to Ramsey (also founded by Oswald) and Germanus was made abbot of Winchcombe. He was expelled, with his monks, after the death of Edgar in 975, and returned to Fleury. Later accounts of his career are confused. He may have been abbot at Ramsey in the years 992–3, and it is possible that he is the Germanus who became abbot of Cholsey in 993; if so, he died in 1013.

BIBL. Hart 1975: 337-8

Gildas author *fl.* mid-sixth century

A product of the late Latin tradition of rhetoric and probably a leading figure in the British Church of his day, if not a reformer, Gildas vigorously condemned contemporary early sixth-century secular and religious society in his *De Excidio Britanniæ* (*The Ruin of Britain*). This work has attracted most attention for its review of the progress of the Anglo-Saxon conquest down to the battle of Mount Badon and its aftermath and for its letter of denunciation of five British kings (see under *Aurelius Caninus, *Constantine, *Cuneglasus, *Maelgwn and *Vortepor), but for a proper appreciation of Gildas' intentions in writing and his methods of exposition it must be studied in its entirety. Unfortunately, though the death of Maelgwn, one of the kings denounced by Gildas, is dated to 547 (to be corrected to 549) in the mid-tenth-century Harleian annals, no certainty attaches to it, and, though Gildas appears to have been writing in the forty-fourth year after the battle of Badon, the date of the *De Excidio* remains imprecise. The annals place the death of Gildas *sapientissimus* ('most wise') in 570, but not necessarily correctly. Later *Lives* are unhistorical.

BIBL. Chadwick 1969: 261-2; Lapidge and Dumville 1984; Savory 1984: 389ff.; Henken 1987: 135-40

Giric I king of Scots 878–89

Giric was a nephew of *Kenneth mac Alpín and as the son of *Donald I he sought to prevent the Scottish kingship becoming the exclusive property of Kenneth's sons and their descendants. He came to power after slaying *Áed son of Kenneth in Strathallan in 878. He was assisted in usurping the kingship by his kinsman and foster-son, *Eochaid son of Rhun, king of the Strathclyde Britons, who may have shared the Scottish kingship with Giric. Both rulers may have been deposed by *Donald II in 889. During his reign, Giric is credited with liberating the Scottish church from Pictish laws and customs — an act which would have been in keeping with earlier records of his father *Donald I having imposed the laws of Dál Riata upon the Picts. Giric is also believed to have extended Scots rule over Bernicia — the first Scottish king to have interfered in territories south of the Forth since the time of *Áedán mac Gabhráin.

BIBL. Anderson 1922, vol. 1: 397-8; Smyth 1984: 188, 215-18, 235-6

Giric II king of Scots 997–1005 *see* **Kenneth III**

Goda (Godgifu) countess *d. c.* 1049

Goda was the daughter of *Æthelred II by his second wife, *Emma of Normandy. In 1013, when *Swein Forkbeard's armies were rolling up the shires of England, Emma and her children took refuge in Normandy. In the 1020s (probably in 1024) Goda's kinsman Duke Robert the Magnificent arranged her marriage to his close friend, Drogo, count of Amiens and the Vexin. She bore him two sons, Walter and Ralph, of whom the younger became earl of Hereford in the reign of his uncle, Edward the Confessor. Drogo accompanied Duke Robert on his pilgrimage to Jerusalem in 1035, from which neither of them returned, and Goda married Eustace, heir to the county of Boulogne. She was probably dead by 1049.

BIBL. Bates 1987: 34-48; Williams 1989

Godwine ealdorman *d.* 1016

Ealdorman Godwine was one of the Englishmen slain at the battle of Ashingdon in 1016. His sphere of authority was probably Lindsey, for in 993, a certain Godwine, in company with *Frane of Rockingham (Northamptonshire) and the Lincolnshire thegn Frithugist, was leading the English levies of Lindsey against the invading Danes. Though Godwine's name is common, it is likely that he was the son of *Ælfheah, ealdorman of Hampshire. He held land in Oxfordshire and Warwickshire, and gave Towcester, Northamptonshire, to Frithugar, abbot of Evesham, in exchange for the lands on which the abbey stood.

BIBL. Williams 1982

Godwine earl 1018–53

Godwine, Earl of Wessex, was the son of a South Saxon thegn, Wulf-noth. The family seems to have been of no more than local importance in the early eleventh century, and were perhaps connected with the ætheling *Athelstan, eldest son of *Æthelred II. In 1008, Wulfnoth was accused of treason by *Brihtric, brother of *Eadric Streona, ealdorman of Mercia; the circumstances are obscure, but Wulfnoth was able to persuade 20 ships' crews of the fleet to defect to him, and engage in pirate activity along the south coast. The outcome is unknown. Godwine's eventual advancement was due to *Cnut, who made him earl, probably of Hampshire and central Wessex, in 1018. He accompanied the king to Denmark in the same year, and impressed Cnut sufficiently to be promoted to the command of the whole of Wessex in 1020. It was probably at this time that he was married to Gytha, a Danish lady of high rank; one of her brothers, *Eilaf, was earl of Gloucestershire, and the other *Ulfr, was the husband of Cnut's sister, Estrith. By 1035, Godwine was one of the most powerful men in England. After the death of Cnut, he supported the claims of *Harthacnut and his mother *Emma against *Harold Harefoot, but in 1036 changed sides. He was implicated in the murder of the ætheling *Alfred, on Harold's orders. Godwine's treachery was not forgotten when Harthacnut came to power in 1040. He and *Lyfing, bishop of Worcester, were accused of Alfred's murder by *Ælfric Puttoc, archbishop of York. Godwine bought the king's favour by the gift of a ship 'having a gilded prow, and furnished with the best tackle, handsomely equipped with suitable weapons and eighty hand-picked soldiers, each of whom had on his arms two gold armlets weighing sixteen ounces, wore a triple mail-shirt, a partly-gilded helmet on his head, and had a sword with a gilded hilt fastened round his loins, and a Danish battle-axe rimmed with gold and silver hanging from his left shoulder, and in his left hand a shield, whose boss and studs were gilded, in his right hand a spear'. Godwine's position was secure enough for him to survive even the return of Alfred's full brother, Edward the Confessor, in 1042. His daughter, Edith, became Edward's wife, and his sons, Swein and Harold, and nephew, Beorn Estrithson, received earldoms. Godwine fell briefly from power in 1051, when Edward had him exiled, but returned the following year. He died, still in enjoyment of all his honours, in 1053.

BIBL. Raraty 1989

Gothfrith king of Dublin 921–34

Gothfrith was the brother of *Sigtrygg Caech, whom he succeeded in Dublin when Sigtrygg became king of York in 921. In 927, Gothfrith invaded Northumbria after his brother's death, but was repulsed by King *Athelstan. His son, *Olafr Gothfrithson, was the Viking leader at the battle of *Brunanburh*.

BIBL. Smyth 1979: 18–30

Gregory the Great St, pope 590–604

Pope Gregory I, known as Gregory the Great, was born in Rome, about 540. After having held the prefecture of the city of Rome, he became a monk in a house which he himself founded on the Caelian Hill, converting his family home for the purpose; the date was 574 or 575. From 578, he was a member of the household of Pope Benedict I, charged with the duty of distributing papal charity in the city. After Benedict's death in 579, Gregory was sent by his successor, Pelagius II, to Constantinople, as papal ambassador (*apocrisiarios*), and remained there for seven years. He was recalled in 586, and when Pelagius died in 590, Gregory was chosen as his successor. Gregory was a man of action, a skilled administrator, but also a theologian. His mission to the English, conceived before his elevation to the papacy, was a striking innovation in its time. Earlier attempts to convert the barbarians had been undertaken by individuals as the opportunity presented itself, but a papal initiative was something new. In 596 he despatched a group of his own monks, under St *Augustine, to *Æthelberht of Kent, to convert the English. The numerous letters which he wrote are the chief source of our knowledge of this mission, and were used extensively by *Bede when he came to write the *Ecclesiastical History of the English nation*. Bede describes Gregory as 'our apostle', and he remained a popular figure in England, where his cult was well-established from an early date. Indeed the earliest *Life* of Gregory was composed at Whitby, by an anonymous writer.

BIBL. Colgrave 1968; Richards 1980

Grimbald St, dean *d*. 901

Grimbald was a Frank, born at Thérouanne, who became a member of the community of Saint-Bertin (in Saint-Omer) between 834 and 844. He was recommended to the attention of King *Alfred by his former abbot, Archbishop Fulk of Rheims (883–900), and became one of the group of scholars, English and continental, whom Alfred established at Winchester in pursuit of his educational reforms. He refused the archbishopric of Canterbury and became dean of the college of secular canons established at the New Minster of Winchester. It was there that he died and was buried.

BIBL. Farmer 1978: 182-3; Grierson 1940

Gruffudd ap Llywelyn king of Gwynedd 1039–63

The son of *Llywelyn ap Seisyll by Angharad, daughter of *Maredudd ab Owain, Gruffudd succeeded in Gwynedd on the assassination of Iago ab Idwal, great-grandson of *Idwal ab Anarawd, king of Gwynedd, in 1039, and immediately defeated and slew the brother of *Leofric, earl of Mercia, on the Welsh border near Welshpool. He devoted his early years as king to a sustained attack on Hywel ab Edwin in Deheubarth whom he finally slew in battle at the mouth of the River Tywi in 1044, thereby securing the southern kingdom for himself, but only for a short while until he was driven out by *Gruffudd ap Rhydderch in 1045. It was not until 1055 that Gruffudd was able to slay Gruffudd ap Rhydderch and re-take possession of Deheubarth. Morgannwg was probably also secured *c*. 1055–60. In his last years, therefore, Gruffudd was king over the whole of Wales, the first ruler and the last to achieve such a position.

In the 1050s successive raids across the border into England, directed particularly at Hereford and the surrounding area, and campaigns in 1055 and again in 1058 (with Norse aid) in support of Ælfgar, son and heir of Earl *Leofric, gained Gruffudd additional territory east of Offa's Dyke and revealed him as a formidable opponent. He married Ælfgar's daughter, Ealdgyth, later to become the queen of Harold II in 1066. The response of Harold, earl of Wessex, at first was to seek to come to terms by which in 1056 Gruffudd swore oaths that he would be a loyal sub-king of Edward the Confessor; but when Gruffudd's hostile actions were resumed Harold attacked his residence at Rhuddlan immediately after Christmas 1062 and burned his ships, Gruffudd escaping only with difficulty, and he followed this up in 1063 with an invasion by land and sea with the help of his brother Tostig. The Welsh had now to submit, give hostages and promise to pay tribute. They were also compelled to renounce Gruffudd who was slain on 5 August by a certain Cynan, not certainly the father of Gruffudd ap Cynan who was later to reign as king of Gwynedd. Edward gave north Wales to Gruffudd's half-brothers, Bleddyn and Rhiwallon, sons of Cynfyn ap Gwerystan, but only on condition that they would serve him by land and sea and pay great tribute. Deheubarth passed back under the control of its native dynasty in the person of Maredudd ab Owain ab Edwin.

BIBL. Lloyd 1911, vol. II: 358-71; Davies 1982: 106, 108; Davies 1990: 36-7, 77-8, 80-1, Barlow 1970: 204-12; Smith 1971; Maund 1985; Davies 1987: 24-6

Gruffudd ap Rhydderch king of Deheubarth 1045−55

A son of *Rhydderch ab Iestyn and already established in Gwent, Gruffudd came to power in Deheubarth in 1045 in the aftermath of the overthrow of Hywel ab Edwin, king of Deheubarth, by *Gruffudd ap Llywelyn, king of Gwynedd, in 1044, and rapidly emerged as a significant threat not only to Gruffudd ap Llywelyn's aspirations in southern Wales (inflicting a serious defeat on him in Ystrad Tywi, by now traditionally a dependent territory of Dyfed, in 1047) but also to the security of the earldom of Hereford in England; in retaliation, Edward the Confessor had Gruffudd's brother, Rhys, put to death early in 1053, and Gruffudd himself was slain by Gruffudd ap Llywelyn in 1055.

BIBL. Lloyd 1911, vol. II: 361-4; Davies 1982: 108; Davies 1990: 36-7; Barlow 1970: 99, 126; Smith 1971

Gruoch Scottish queen *c*. 1025−55

Gruoch was the wife of *Macbeth whom she married as a second husband some time after 1032. She was the daughter of Boite and the grand-daughter of *Kenneth III who was slain by *Malcolm II in 1005. Gruoch's family therefore had inherited an on-going feud with the house of Malcolm II. Her first husband was Gillacomgain the *mórmaer* or chieftain of Moray, whose brother, Malcolm, and whose uncle, *Findlaech, are styled kings of Scotland in contemporary annals. Although Gruoch's husband and his brother, Malcolm, had slain Findlaech (Macbeth's father) in 1020, it would seem that her subsequent marriage to Macbeth healed this dynastic war within Moray and united the houses of Moray and Kenneth

III in their mutual hostility to Malcolm II and his grandson *Duncan. After Macbeth had slain Duncan in 1040, he ruled over all of Gaelic Scotland. The king and his wife were jointly involved in a grant of land at Kirkness to the Culdees of Lochleven which may suggest that Gruoch's ancestral territory lay in Kinross and Fife. Shakespeare's portrayal of Lady Macbeth as a ruthlessly ambitious woman who goaded her husband into slaying the innocent Duncan while he slept in Macbeth's castle, has no historical foundation.

BIBL. Anderson 1922, vol. 1: 571-2, 580-1, 603-4; Skene 1886-90, vol. 1: 406

Gunnar Rode's son *fl.* first half of the eleventh century
Gunnar, son of Rode, was a Swedish Viking, buried at Bath, as we learn from the runestone erected in his memory by his son, Gunnkel:
'Gunnkell set this stone in memory of Gunnar his father, Rode's son.
Helge laid him, his brother, in a stone coffin, in England, in Bath.'
The stone stands at Navelsjo (Smaland).

BIBL. Janssen 1962: 52-3

Gunnhildr *d.* 1038
Gunnhildr, daughter of King *Cnut and *Emma of Normandy, married Henry (later the Emperor Henry III) at Nijmegen in June 1036. She died two years later, in 1038. Her only child was Beatrice, abbess of Quedling-burg, who died childless in 1061.

BIBL. Campbell 1949: xlvii, xlix

Gunnhildr *d.* after 1044
Gunnhildr was the niece of *Cnut, the daughter of one of his sisters and Wyrtgeorn, king of the Wends. She married, first, her cousin *Hakon, earl of Worcestershire, and after his death in 1030, Haraldr, son of *Thorkell the Tall. It is possible that Haraldr succeeded to Hakon's earldom, but the only certain fact of his career is that he was murdered in 1042, while returning from a pilgrimage to Rome. He was killed by Ordulf, Duke of Saxony, at the behest of Magnus, king of Norway, whose sister was Ordulf's wife. Magnus was presumably clearing the ground of Cnut's kinsman in pursuit of his claim to the kingship of Denmark. Gunnhildr was still living in England, but in 1044, she and her sons by Haraldr, Thorkell and Hemming, were expelled by Edward the Confessor. She fled to Bruges and thence to Denmark; her ultimate fate is unknown.

BIBL. Williams 1986: 9-11

Guthfrith king of York *c.* 883—95
The brief reign of Guthfrith, king of York, is recorded in the *History of Saint Cuthbert*, composed before 995. It seems that St *Cuthbert appeared to Eadred, abbot of Carlisle, and commanded him to go to the Danish army across the Tyne, and find Guthfrith son of Harthacnut, the slave of a certain widow. Eadred was to redeem him, and the army was to elect him

king, on the hill called *Oswigesdune*, by placing a gold ring on his arm. In return, Guthfrith was to give to St Cuthbert (that is, to the community of Chester-le-Street) all the land between Tyne and Wear, with rights of sanctuary. This was duly done and the new king and his people swore 'peace and fidelity' on the body of the saint, which was brought from Chester-le-Street for the ceremony. Stripped of its legendary accretions, this story shows the rapprochement between the newly-established Danish kingdom of York, and the Christian communities of Northumbria, symbolized in Danish recognition and confirmation of the rights and possessions of Chester-le-Street, where the Lindisfarne community had found refuge (see *Eardwulf). Guthfrith himself was certainly a Christian, for he was buried in York Minster, but the description of the king-making ceremony (if it can be trusted) is purely pagan.

BIBL. Rollason 1987b: 45-59

Guthlac St, hermit *d*. 714

Guthlac, son of Penwealh, was an ætheling of the Mercian royal house. He began his career at the age of 15 in the manner usual for one of his rank, as the leader of a war-band, though (according to his biographer, *Felix) he always restored to those he conquered one third of the booty which he had taken from them. At the age of 24, he decided to abandon the warrior-life, and became a monk at Repton. Two years later he decided to live the life of a hermit, choosing for his retreat the island of Crowland in the midst of the Fens. As was the fate of most medieval hermits, the remoteness of the spot did not prevent those with spiritual and medical problems beating a path to his door. Among numerous visitors was his kinsman *Æthelbald, then exiled from Mercia due to the enmity of King *Ceolred. Guthlac prophesied the future greatness of Æthelbald, who, when he became king, showed his gratitude by promoting Guthlac's cult.

BIBL. Colgrave 1956

Guthrum king of East Anglia 879–90

Guthrum first made his mark upon England as leader of the 'great summer-army', which joined forces with the army of *Ivarr in 871. When in 875 this force split up, Guthrum moved in on Wessex. In 878 he was defeated by *Alfred at the battle of Edington and forced to come to terms. He accepted baptism, with Alfred standing as his godfather. The Treaty of Wedmore established a lasting peace between the two parties, and Guthrum and his men settled East Anglia, of which he became king, under his baptismal name of Athelstan.

BIBL. Smyth 1977d: 240-54

Gwallawg ruler of Elmet *fl*. sixth century

The early ninth-century *Historia Brittonum* (see under *Nennius) includes Gwallawg among the allies of *Urien of Rheged who besieged the Northumbrian Angles on Lindisfarne. Two of the early bardic poems ascribed to *Taliesin celebrated Gwallawg's martial qualities, one poem describing him as 'a judge over Elmet', the British kingdom in the former West Riding of Yorkshire which was conquered by *Edwin, king of Northumbria, in the early seventh century.

BIBL. Williams, I 1960; Williams, JEC 1968; Bromwich 1961: 375-7

Gwenddolau ap Ceidiaw *fl.* sixth century
   A north British chieftain who perished at the battle of Arfderydd (Arthuret), dated in the Welsh annals — though not necessarily correctly — to 573, Gwenddolau appears in bardic tradition as the lord of Myrddin (*Merlin), whose death Myrddin grievously lamented.

BIBL. Bromwich 1961: 379-80; Clarke 1973

Gwrthefyr king of Dyfed *fl.* first half of sixth century *see* **Vortepor**

H

Hadrian (Adrian) St, abbot *d*. 709/10

A monk of North African origin, and abbot of *Hiridanum* (near Naples), Hadrian was offered the archbishopric of Canterbury in 665, but refused it in favour of the Greek monk, *Theodore. He was sent with Theodore to Kent but was detained for some time by Ebroin, mayor of the palace of Neustria under Theodoric III, king of the Franks. Hadrian spent the winter of 668 at Meaux, until Ebroin, who suspected that he might be an imperial ambassador, finally allowed him to proceed to England. Once arrived, he became abbot of St Augustine's in Canterbury, where he and Theodore presided over a flourishing school. He died at St Augustine's on 9 January, in either 709 or 710 and was buried in his monastery.

BIBL. *HE* iv, 1-2: 328-32; Farmer 1982: 3

Hædde St, bishop 676–706

Hædde succeeded *Leuthere as bishop of Winchester in 676. On his death in 706, the West Saxon see was divided; Daniel was appointed to Winchester, and a new see was established at Sherborne for *Aldhelm. Hædde's only known religious foundation was Farnham, Surrey.

BIBL. *HE* iv, 12: 368-9; v, 18: 572-7; Farmer 1978: 187

Hædde (Hedde, Headda) bishop 691–716/27

Hædde, a monk of Peterborough (*Medeshamstede*), was the first abbot of Breedon-on-the-Hill, Leicestershire, founded by the ealdorman Frithuric between 675 and 691. In 691, Hædde became bishop of Lichfield in succession to *Seaxwulf, and the see was amalgamated with that of Leicester in 709. He is said to have dedicated St *Guthlac's church at Crowland. He died at some time between 716 and 727. Hædde is to be distinguished from his namesake, Hædde, abbot of Peterborough, who was killed, with his monks, by the Viking 'great army' in 870. Breedon-on-the-Hill was in its time a famous and flourishing monastery. Nothing survives of the original church, but a quantity of high-quality sculpture of eighth-century date was incorporated into the later fabric, and still exists. One of the eighth-century archbishops of Canterbury, Tatwine (731–4), had been a monk of Breedon.

BIBL. Dornier 1977b; Cramp 1977

Hakon earl 1018–30

Hakon was the son of Eirikr, earl of Hlathir, and a sister of *Cnut. The earls of Hlathir ruled Norway as vassals of the kings of Denmark, but in 1014 were driven out by *Olafr Helgi. Hakon's father Eirikr was already in England, and Hakon joined him there, as one of Cnut's most trusted followers. Eirikr was made earl of Northumbria in 1016 and two years later, Hakon became earl of Worcestershire. In 1028, Cnut made him regent of Norway, but he died in 1030. The *Anglo-Saxon Chronicle*, which calls him 'the brave earl (*se dohtiga eorl*)', says that he died at sea, and later sources place his death in the Pentland Firth, when his ship went down on a voyage to Norway. His wife, *Gunnhildr, who was also his cousin (another niece of Cnut's), survived him.

BIBL. Campbell 1949: 71-73; Williams 1986

Halfdan king of York 875−7
Halfdan was the brother of *Ivarr the Boneless, and co-leader with him of the 'great army' which arrived in Britain in 865. In 871, they were joined by the 'great summer-army' of *Guthrum, and during these years struck terror into the English kingdoms of Wessex, Mercia, East Anglia and Northumbria. Halfdan became the commander of the host when Ivarr returned to Dublin in 870/1. He presided over the settlement of Deira, which became the Viking kingdom of York, in 876, when he shared out the land to his men, who 'began to plough and support themselves'. In 877 he departed for Dublin, in an attempt to recover the kingdom of his brother Ivarr and was killed at the battle of Strangford Lough.

BIBL. Smyth 1977e

Halfdan king of York *d.* 910
Halfdan of York was killed at the battle of Tettenhall, 910, with his co-king, Eowils, and 12 other leaders of the York Danes. Nothing further is known of him.

BIBL. Smyth 1975: 75, 101

Hardulph St, king of Northumbria 796−810 *see* **Eardwulf**

Harold I Harefoot king of the English 1035−40
Harold was the younger son of *Cnut and his English wife, *Ælfgifu of Northampton. On his father's death in 1035, he was made regent of England 'for himself and his brother *Harthacnut', by a council at Oxford, and with the support of Earl *Leofric of Mercia, the leading men of Mercia and Northumbria, and the *lithsmen* of London (the crews of the royal fleet). It is evident that Harold meant to seize the kingship, and was taking advantage of the fact that his half-brother, Harthacnut, was occupied in Denmark. A compromise was reached, by which Queen *Emma, Cnut's widow, was to hold Winchester and Wessex for her son, with the help of the royal housecarls and Earl *Godwine of Wessex. Within the year, however, Godwine had switched sides, and Harold was able to seize the Treasury at Winchester. Emma's attempts to enlist the aid of her older sons failed disastrously when *Alfred the ætheling was murdered, on Harold's orders, in 1036. Emma fled abroad, and Harold was acknowledged as king throughout England. The only known incident of his reign was his seizure of Sandwich from Christchurch, Canterbury, though in his charter of restoration, Harold threw the blame on his counsellor, Steorra. He

died at London in 1040 and was buried at Westminster, but his half-brother, Harthacnut, had his body dug up and thrown into the Thames marshes. The corpse was rescued by the Danish garrison and buried in their own cemetery.

BIBL. *ASC* s.a. 1035-40; Barlow 1970: 42-8

Harthacnut king of the English 1040−2

Harthacnut was the son of *Cnut and *Emma of Normandy, born *c.* 1020. When his father died in 1035, it was clearly intended that he should succeed both to the kingdom of Denmark and to that of the English, but in neither case was he unopposed. Just before Cnut's death, the Norwegians had thrown off Danish suzerainty and taken as their king Magnus, son of *Olafr Helgi. Magnus promptly attacked Denmark, with the aim of adding it to his hegemony. Harthacnut attempted to establish his mother as regent in England while he dealt with Magnus, but his half-brother, *Harold, seized power, because, as the *Chronicle* says, Harthacnut 'remained too long in Denmark'. It was not until Harold's death in 1040 that Harthacnut was able to take the kingship of the English. The English magnates were at first willing to accept him, but almost immediately matters began to go awry. The occasion was the tax levied for the support of the royal fleet, the heregeld. In the time of Cnut, the fleet had numbered 16 ships, paid for at eight marks to the rowlock (the usual number of oars was 60 to 80). Harthacnut, presumably with an eye to Magnus of Norway, raised the number of ships to 62, paid for at the same rate. Assuming the ships to be 60-oarers, this would mean a sum of 480 marks (£320) per ship; the total for the whole fleet would amount to £19,840 and in fact, £21,099 was raised in 1041. This vast imposition was bitterly resented, and the men of Worcester even refused to pay and murdered the royal housecarls sent to collect the geld (see *Feader). Even the version of the *Chronicle* most favourable to Harthacnut ('C') remarks that 'all who had been zealous on his behalf now became disloyal to him'. Harthacnut lost further support when he had *Eadulf of Bamburgh murdered while under a safe-conduct, after which, as the same source says, 'he was then a pledge-breaker'; a dangerous thing to be in a society held together by mutual oaths. It was presumably this rising tide of dissatisfaction that prompted Harthacnut's half-brother, Edward, to return to England in 1041. It seems that he was able to force the king to acknowledge him as his heir, and indeed the 'C' *Chronicle* maintains that Edward 'was sworn in as king'. In 1042, Harthacnut was a guest at the wedding-feast of his staller, *Tovi the Proud and Gytha, daughter of *Osgod Clapa, at Lambeth. Suddenly, 'as he stood at his drink', the king collapsed, falling to the ground 'with horrible convulsions, and those who were near there took hold of him, but he never spoke again, and passed away on 8 June'. He was buried beside his father in the Old Minster, Winchester. The 'C' Chronicler's harsh judgement was that 'he never did anything worthy of a king'.

BIBL. *ASC* s.a. 1040-2; Barlow 1970: 47-50

Helmstan a thief *fl.* 900

The unedifying story of Helmstan is preserved in a letter to *Edward the Elder, whose author does not identify himself, but is probably Ordlaf, ealdorman of Wiltshire. Helmstan, Ordlaf's godson, was accused of theft, and sought his godfather's support. Ordlaf petitioned King *Alfred on Helmstan's behalf, as 'the king stood in the chamber at Wardour, washing his hands'. In return, Helmstan made over to Ordlaf his land at Fonthill, Wiltshire, continuing to live there as Ordlaf's tenant. A few years later, 'he stole the untended oxen at Fonthill, by which he was completely ruined, and drove them to Cricklade, and there he was discovered and the man who had tracked him rescued the tracked cattle. Then he fled and a bramble scratched his face; and when he wished to deny it, that was brought as evidence against him'. This escapade led to Helmstan's outlawry and the forfeiture of his land, but once again, Ordlaf (who as ealdorman presided over the shire court) intervened, and the sentence was lifted; King Edward revoked the outlawry and Helmstan was allowed to withdraw to one of his estates.

BIBL. Whitelock 1955, no. 102: 501-3

Hengest *fl.* 449−88

Hengest is the traditional founder of the kingdom of Kent. He and his brother Horsa are said to have entered the service of *Vortigern as mercenaries. They landed at Ebbsfleet, with three shiploads of men, in 449. Soon they rebelled against their employer, summoned reinforcements from the continent, and overran Kent. Horsa was killed in the process, and Hengest took his own son, Œric, surnamed Oisc, as co-ruler. There seems to be very little historical foundation for any part of this widespread legend.

BIBL. Sims-Williams 1983; Brooks 1989a

Higbald bishop 781−802

It was while Higbald was bishop at Lindisfarne that the Viking sack of 793 took place, an event which sent waves of shock running throughout the world of northern Christendom. *Alcuin addressed to Higbald a letter of sympathy and encouragement in his ordeal, and his description (in a letter to King *Æthelred) of the Viking assault is perhaps the most famous piece to come from his pen:

'Lo it is nearly three hundred and fifty years that we and our fathers have inhabited this most lovely land, and never before has such terror appeared in Britain as we have now suffered from a pagan race, nor was it thought that such an inroad from the sea could be made. Behold, the church of St Cuthbert spattered with the blood of the priests of God, despoiled of all its ornaments; a place more venerable than all in Britain is given as a prey to pagan peoples.'

It was not, however, this raid which drove the community from Lindisfarne. The monks continued to live on their island for another century, in some comfort. Alcuin, in a later letter, reproaches Higbald for allowing secular

153

poems celebrating the deeds of pagan heroes sung during meals, rather than readings from the Fathers:

'For what has Ingeld to do with Christ? The house is narrow: it cannot contain them both: the King of Heaven will have no part with so-called kings who are heathen and damned.'

BIBL. Whitelock 1955, no. 194; Wormald 1978: 42-9

Hild St, abbess 657–80

Hild, abbess of Whitby, was born about 614. Her mother's name was Breguswith, and her father, Hereri, was a nephew of *Edwin of Deira, who followed his uncle into exile in the days of *Æthelfrith of Bernicia. He met his death by poison at the court of Ceredig, king of Elmet (*d.* 616), a circumstance which may have prompted Edwin's subsequent conquest of Elmet. Hild was brought up, with her sister Hereswith, at the court of her great-uncle, and was baptized by *Paulinus. Hereswith married Æthelric, brother of *Anna, king of the East Angles, to whom she bore a son, the future king Ealdwulf, but by 647 she had entered the Frankish monastery of Chelles. Hild intended to join her, but was persuaded by *Aidan to become abbess of Hartlepool instead. In 657 she moved to Whitby (*Streoneshalh*), as abbess, and there she spent the rest of her life. She was a notable teacher and many of the ecclesiastical lights of seventh-century Britain received their early education at Whitby; it was there also that the Synod of the Northumbrian church met in 664. Hild accepted the decision of the synod to follow Roman ecclesiastical custom, though her own sympathies tended to the Irish usage. She was the patroness of the herdsman-poet *Cædmon, a former servant of the abbey. She died, after a long illness, on 17 November 680.

BIBL. *HE* iv, 22-3: 404-14

Hlothhere king of Kent 673–85

Hlothhere, the younger son of *Eorcenberht, succeeded his brother *Ecgberht as king of Kent in 673. Less ruthless (or less efficient) than his brother, he neglected to dispose of his nephew Eadric, who in 684 invaded Kent with South Saxon aid, and forced Hlothhere to share the kingship with him. The second Kentish law-code is issued in both their names. Hlothhere was severely injured in the fighting and died the following year, followed rapidly by Eadric in 686. A prolonged period of crisis followed, until Eadric's son, *Wihtred, succeeded in making himself king in 690.

BIBL. *HE* iv, 5: 352-3; 26: 430-1; Whitelock 1955, no. 30: 360-1

Honorius St, archbishop of Canterbury 627–53

Honorius arrived in Britain in 601, accompanied by *Justus, *Paulinus and Rufianus, to join their fellow-Italians in the conversion of the English. In 627, Honorius succeeded Justus as archbishop of Canterbury, being consecrated at Lincoln by Paulinus. He was the last of the Roman missionaries sent by *Gregory the Great to be archbishop; his successor, *Deusdedit, was an Englishman.

BIBL. *HE* ii, 18: 196-7

Horsa see **Hengest**

Hrani see **Ranig**

Huneberc nun *fl.* eighth century

Huneberc was one of the many Englishwomen who went to the continent to assist in the conversion of Germany in the eighth century. She became a nun of Heidenheim, the house founded by St *Willibald, and it was she who wrote the account of Willibald's life and travels, the *Hodoeporicon*, from his own words, and also the *Life* of his brother Winnebald, abbot of Heidenheim.

BIBL. Talbot 1954: 152-77

Hygeberht archbishop of Lichfield 787−803

Hygeberht was the first and only archbishop of Lichfield, which was raised to archiepiscopal status at the Synod of Chelsea in 787, with the approval of Pope Hadrian I. Its province was carved out of that of Canterbury, and included the sees of Hereford, Worcester, Leicester, Lindsey and East Anglia. The purpose behind this action was political and resulted from the enmity between *Offa, king of Mercia, and *Jænberht, archbishop of Canterbury, who upheld the claims of Kent to independence from Mercian suzerainty. The establishment of Lichfield as an archbishopric weakened the power of Canterbury, but was in fact an admission of defeat on Offa's part, an acknowledgement that he was unable to subdue Kentish independence. It was Hygeberht who consecrated Offa's son, *Ecgfrith, as king of the Mercians in 787; he also consecrated Jænberht's successor, *Æthelheard, in 792. After the death of Offa in 796, the situation changed. Æthelheard was more amenable to Mercian aspirations, and the anomalous see at Lichfield proved an embarrassment. After an attempt to get the archiepiscopal see transferred from Canterbury to London, *Cœnwulf of Mercia obtained papal consent to abolish the archiepiscopate of Lichfield, which was demoted to a mere bishopric at the Synod of *Clofesho* in 803.

BIBL. Brooks 1984: 111-27

Hywel (Dda) ap Cadell king of Deheubarth *d.* 950

It is not known when Hywel ap Cadell, grandson of *Rhodri Mawr, became king in Dyfed but the record in the Welsh annals of the beheading of Rhodri ap Hyfaidd, the last known native prince of Dyfed in Arwystli, Powys, in 904 or 905, suggests a violent struggle for royal power in Dyfed by Hywel's father, Cadell, and possibly by Hywel himself. Cadell died as king (though not specifically of Dyfed) *c.* 910 and Hywel appears as king (again, however, not specifically of Dyfed) when he submitted to *Edward the Elder, king of Wessex, in 918 in the company of his brother Clydog, and *Idwal ab Anarawd. At some stage during these years, Hywel − he is described as king of the West Welsh in the annal for 927 in the *Anglo-Saxon Chronicle* at the time of his submission to Edward's son and successor, *Athelstan (924−39) − married Elen, Rhodri ap Hyfaidd's niece, and brought together Seisyllwg and Dyfed to form the enlarged kingdom of Deheubarth which he ruled until his death in 950. He was never free for much of his reign from the political and military necessity to submit to the powerful kings of Wessex and acknowledged Athelstan as overlord in 927 when the Wye was demarcated as the frontier between English and Welsh, subsequently attending Athelstan's court as a sub-king on a number of occasions, and present also in 949 at the court of Athelstan's brother, *Eadred (946–54). Together with Idwal, king of Gwynedd, and *Morgan ab Owain, king of Morgannwg, he was compelled to accompany Athelstan on his campaign against *Constantine, king of the Scots, in 934. Not surprisingly the *Armes Prydein (Prophecy of Britain)*, which seems to have been composed in Dyfed, either in the 930s or the 940s, called for a war with the West Saxons which would drive them out of Britain. Hywel devoted his energies, however, when Idwal was slain in battle against the Saxons in 942, to the annexation of Gwynedd and Powys and the expulsion of Idwal's sons.

In 928 or 929 Hywel went on a pilgrimage to Rome, and his epithet Dda ('the Good') implies a ruler of some distinction. His most substantial achievement would seem to have been the beginning he made — it can have been barely more than that — to the codification of Welsh customary law. Welsh law survives in Welsh in three great thirteenth-century collections or Codes, the Dimetian or Book of Blegywyrd (representing Deheubarth), the Venedotian or Book of Iorwerth (representing Gwynedd) and the Gwentian or Book of Cynferth (representing Gwent in Morgannwg), together with other Latin versions. The genesis of these collections is said to have been a great assembly convened by Hywel Dda at Whitland in Dyfed, but how much of the Law of Hywel (Cyfraith Hywel) goes back to Hywel's time may never be resolved.

It is possible that Hywel was influenced by the legislative activities of contemporary Anglo-Saxon rulers — in particular *Alfred and Athelstan — but he should not be seen as a fervent admirer of all things English. The close proximity of a powerful Wessex gave him no scope to defy the English with impunity and Hywel's annexation of Gwynedd and Powys suggests a ruler unhappy with the status of sub-king and eager for personal and dynastic aggrandizement.

A coin inscribed HOWÆL REX from the mint at Chester is possibly to be interpreted as a penny of Hywel Dda.

BIBL. Lloyd 1911, vol. I: 222ff.; Kirby 1976b; Dumville 1983; Pryce 1986; Jenkins 1986; Harding 1986; Dykes 1976: 12-14; Blunt *et al* 1989: 8, 138, 271

Hywel ab Ieuaf king of Gwynedd *d*. 985

Hywel, a grandson of *Idwal the Bald, was one of the kings and princes who are said to have submitted to *Edgar, king of the West Saxons, at Chester in 973. He expelled his uncle, *Iago ab Idwal, king of Gwynedd, in 974, perhaps with English aid, for the Welsh annals show that he certainly deployed Saxon troops in Llŷn in 978 at a time when Iago was seeking, possibly with the help of Irish Vikings, to re-establish himself. Hywel secured the kingship in 979 and in 980 slew Custennin ab Iago who had been ravaging Llŷn and Anglesey with the help of Vikings from Man and the Isles led by Godfrey, son of Harald. With the assistance of *Ælfhere, ealdorman of Mercia, he also attacked the lands of *Einion ab Owain in Deheubarth in 983, but two years later he was slain, by the English, reputedly through treachery.

A coin inscribed HOWÆL REX from the mint at Chester is possibly to be interpreted as a penny of Hywel ab Ieuaf (but see also under *Hywel (Dda) ap Cadell).

BIBL. Lloyd 1911, vol. I: 344

Hywel ap Rhys king of Glywysing *fl.* second half of ninth century

A representative of the obscure dynasty of kings of Glywysing, who submitted to *Alfred, king of the West Saxons, *c.* 885, Hywel is probably to be identified with the 'Hoelt' who erected a monument at Llantwit Major to commemorate his father, Rhys, and with the Hywel who died in Rome in 885 or 886. He was the grandfather of *Morgan ab Owain.

BIBL. Kirby 1971: 18; Pugh 1971: 3; Victory 1977: 69

I

Iago ab Idwal king of Gwynedd expelled 979

On the death in battle against the English of *Idwal the Bald, king of Gwynedd in 942, his sons, Iago and Ieuaf, were expelled from their kingdom by *Hywel Dda who then controlled Gwynedd until his death in 950. When Hywel died, Iago and Ieuaf re-emerged to fight the sons of Hywel at Nant Carno, on the borders of their territories, and in 952 they ravaged Dyfed twice and in 954 Ceredigion, in which year they also fought the sons of Hywel again. These campaigns appear to have effectively prevented any aspirations on the part of Hywel's sons to re-establish their father's hegemony over north Wales.

Iago attended the court of *Eadred, king of the West Saxons, in 955, together with *Morgan ab Owain, king of Morgannwg, and *Owain ap Hywel, king of Deheubarth. He was also present among the British kings who acknowledged the overlordship of *Edgar, king of the West Saxons, at Chester in 973.

In 969 Iago seized and imprisoned his brother, Ieuaf, and though Ieuaf lived until 988 he plays no further part in the annalistic record. Ieuaf's son, *Hywel, however, was also in attendance on Edgar at Chester in 973 and in 974 Hywel expelled Iago from the kingdom. Though he fought back, Iago was driven out a second time in 979 and made prisoner by a force of Irish Vikings. The date of his death is not known.

BIBL. Lloyd 1911, vol. I: 337, 343ff.; Bromwich 1961: 411-12; Stenton 1971: 369

Ida king of Bernicia 547–59

The origins of Bernicia go back to the occupation of the fortress of Bamburgh by Ida, traditionally dated to 547. Of Ida himself, and the six kings who succeeded him until the accession of his grandson *Æthelfrith in 592, very little is known; even the sequence of the kings is unclear. What is obvious is that before the time of Æthelfrith, the Bernician kings had little more than a foothold on the coast of Northumbria, and were under constant attacks from the British of the North, especially *Urien of Rheged. Urien indeed is said to have besieged the English on Holy Island (Lindisfarne) for three days and only his assassination by a rival British chieftain saved the Bernicians from disaster. Only the British defeat at *Catræth* (Catterick), lamented in the *Gododdin*, turned the tide in favour of the English.

BIBL. Kirby 1967: 22-5; Jackson 1969; Miller 1979a

Idwal ab Anarawd king of Gwynedd 916–42

Idwal Foel ('the Bald') submitted, with *Hywel (Dda) ap Cadell and his brother, Clydog, in 918 to *Edward the Elder, king of the West Saxons. He was present at the court of Edward's son and successor, *Athelstan, on a number of occasions between 928 and 937, after which he may have distanced himself from the West Saxons, and it was against the English that he perished in battle in 942. His sons were expelled and his territories annexed by Hywel Dda.

BIBL. Lloyd 1911, vol. I: 337; Dumville 1983, 149-50

Illtud St, abbot *fl.* early sixth century

The early twelfth-century *Life* of St Illtud is quite unhistorical, but his cult was widespread in south-east Wales with its centre at Llanilltud Fawr, otherwise Llantwit Major, said to have been founded by Illtud. The *Life* of St *Samson, probably of ninth-century date though possibly earlier, represents Samson as a pupil at Illtud's school at Llanilltud Fawr and describes Illtud as the most learned of the Britons, and the ninth-century *Life* of Paul Aurelian claims that Paul, *David and *Gildas also studied under Illtud. This at least suggests that by the ninth century, possibly earlier, Llanilltud was regarded as a learned centre and Illtud remembered as a great teacher.

BIBL. Bowen 1961: 41ff.; Evans 1971: 88ff.; Savory 1984: 391ff.; Henken 1987: 108-14

Imma thegn *fl.* 679

The story of the young warrior, Imma, is not strictly historical, but is nevertheless of considerable interest. His tale is recounted by *Bede, as an illustration of the efficacy of prayers for the dead. Imma was a warrior (thegn) in the hearthtroop of *Ælfwine, king of Deira, who was killed in the battle of the River Trent, 679, when *Ecgfrith of Northumbria, his brother, was defeated by *Æthelred of Mercia. Imma was left for dead on the battlefield, and was taken prisoner by the men of an unnamed Mercian noble (*gesith*). In order to evade the blood-feud which would have claimed his life if it were known that he had fought in the opposing army, Imma pretended to be a poor peasant, a married man, who had merely been supplying the Northumbrian army with food and provisions. He was imprisoned in chains, but his fetters kept falling off, because his brother, Tunna, a priest and abbot of *Tunnacestir* (unidentified), was saying masses for his soul. The Mercian nobleman eventually persuaded Imma to reveal his true status, promising not to prosecute the feud against him, despite the fact that many of his kinsmen had been killed at the Trent. Eventually, Imma was sold to a Frisian merchant, who took him to London, and allowed him to ransom himself. Imma made his way home to his brother, Tunna, where the story of the loosened fetters and the funerary masses was told. The story gives a vivid picture of the vicissitudes of seventh-century life, and of the social conditions of the day.

BIBL. *HE* iv, 22: 400-5

Indulf king of Scots 954-62

Indulf was the son of *Constantine II and his Norse name (*Hildulfr*) reflects the strong Scandinavian influence on the Scottish court in the tenth century. Indulf ruled as sub-king of Strathclyde during the reign of *Malcolm I and, on Malcolm's death in 954, Indulf moved up to the

Scottish kingship while Malcolm's son *Dub succeeded to the kingdom of Strathclyde. Indulf pursued his father's policy of interfering in the affairs of Northumbria south of the Forth, and it was during his reign that Edinburgh was captured and occupied by the Scots, and Lothian was annexed to the Scottish kingdom. Indulf's successes south of the Forth coincided with the collapse of the Scandinavian kingdom of York in 954 when Bernician territory fell an easy prey to its Scottish neighbours. Indulf fell in battle against the Danes in 962 and was buried on Iona.

BIBL. Anderson 1922, vol. 1: 468-71; Smyth 1984: 221, 223, 225, 232

Ine king of Wessex 688−726

Ine, son of *Cœnred, succeeded Cædwalla as king of Wessex in 688. He continued the expansion against the British of Dumnonia begun under *Cenwealh. In 710, he was fighting against Geraint of Dumnonia and is said to have built a fortress at Taunton, later destroyed (for unknown reasons) by his wife, *Æthelburh. He was the dominating influence in south-east England. In 694 he exacted from Kent the wergeld for Cædwalla's brother, Mul, killed in 687; he referred to *Eorcenwold, bishop of London, as 'my bishop'; and *Nothhelm (Nunna), king of Sussex, was his kinsman. Ine was a benefactor of Glastonbury, and founded the see of Sherborne for *Aldhelm, who may have been his kinsman. This act was not entirely voluntary for Ine seems to have resisted the division of the West Saxon see (see *Wealdhere). Ine is best remembered for his law-code, the first West Saxon code, and the only one known before the time of *Alfred. Its detailed provisions shed much-needed light on early West Saxon society. In 726, Ine resigned his office to retire to Rome, where he died. His brother, Ingeld, was the ancestor of King *Alfred, but his successor was another kinsman, Æthelheard (726−40).

BIBL. Stenton 1971: 71-3; Whitelock 1955, no. 32: 364-72 (Ine's Code)

Ingimund (Hingamund) *fl.* 902/5

When in 902 the Norsemen were expelled from Dublin, one group, led by Ingimund, fled to north Wales. Driven off by Clydog ap Cadell (*d.* 917), they moved into north-western England. Some kind of bargain was struck with *Æthelflæd, Lady of the Mercians, who gave Ingimund land near Chester, in the Wirral, to settle on, but about 905 he attempted to seize the town, and had to be driven off. Æthelflæd restored and refortified Chester in 907. This settlement in the Wirral was part of a much larger influx of Norwegians from Ireland, Scotland and the Hebrides, as well as Scandinavia, who were colonizing the north-west in the first decade of the tenth century. It was against them that the *burhs* of Eddisbury (914), Runcorn (915) Thelwall (919) and Manchester (923) were built.

BIBL. Wainwright 1975b; Smyth 1975: 61-2, 78-9

Iurminburg queen *d*. after 685

Iurminburg, the second wife of *Ecgfrith of Northumbria, was castigated by *Eddius for her hostility to his patron, St *Wilfrid, though he
also recorded her change of heart: 'after the death of the king, from
being a she-wolf she was changed into a lamb of God, a perfect
abbess'. He neglects, unfortunately, to give the name of the abbey to
which she retired. Iurminburg's background is unknown, but her name
suggests that she belonged to the Kentish royal house (see *Iurminric).
Her sister was married to *Centwine of Wessex.

BIBL. Colgrave 1927: 48-9

Iurminric (Eormenric, Irminric) king of Kent *d*. *c*. 580

*Bede has preserved a genealogy of King *Æthelberht of Kent,
which names Iurminric as his father: 'the son of Octa, the son of Œric
whose surname was Oisc, whence the kings of Kent were known as
Oiscingas'. He adds that Oisc was the son of *Hengest, and came to
Britain with his father. The historicity of Hengest and Oisc is dubious
in the extreme, and Iurminric's name suggests Frankish connections;
the element 'Iurmin-' is common in Frankish names, but very rare in
England outside the Kentish dynasty. There was a strong Frankish
element in the settlement of Kent.

BIBL. Brooks 1989a

Ivarr the Boneless king of Dublin *d*. 873

Ivarr the Boneless, one of the many sons of *Ragnarr Lothbrok,
appeared in Ireland in 857, in the employ of the Norwegian king of
Dublin. Between 864 and 871, he was campaigning in Britain, for he
and his brother *Halfdan were the main leaders of the 'great army'
which over-wintered on Sheppey in 865. It was this force which overran
East Anglia, killing the last king, St *Edmund, in 869, and destroyed
the English kingdom of Deira. In 870, Ivarr left the 'great army' to
return to Dublin, where he died, as 'king of all the Scandinavians of
Ireland and Britain' in 873.

BIBL. Smyth 1975: 16-18

J

Jænberht archbishop of Canterbury 765–92

Jænberht was a Kentishman, closely associated with King Ecgberht II (c. 765/79). He was abbot of St Augustine's, Canterbury, and on 25 February 765, was consecrated as archbishop at the court of *Offa, king of Mercia. Offa's overlordship was bitterly resented in Kent, and was temporarily overthrown by a Kentish rising of 776, culminating in a Mercian defeat at the battle of Otford. It was not until 785 that Offa was able to re-establish control. Jænberht proved a staunch upholder of Kentish independence, and in 787, Offa's envoys persuaded Pope Hadrian I to elevate the Mercian bishopric of Lichfield to archiepiscopal status. The Mercian *Hygeberht became archbishop and the see of Lichfield was carved out of that of Canterbury. The situation was reversed only after Offa's death, in 803.

BIBL. Brooks 1984: 113-20

James the deacon d. after 664

James was a member of the mission which accompanied *Paulinus to Northumbria in 625. When Paulinus left the kingdom after the death of *Edwin in 633, James remained in the north, preaching and baptizing from a centre in the vicinity of Catterick. His efforts seem to have been a success, for York remained a centre of Roman influence, even after the establishment of Irish monks at Lindisfarne. James is last heard of as one of the participants at the Synod of Whitby in 664. *Bede says that he died 'old and full of days', but omits to give the date, though he says that James lived 'right up to our days'.

BIBL. *HE* ii, 16: 192-3; ii, 20: 206-7

John of Beverley St, bishop 688–717, d. 721

John was born at Harpham, in the East Riding of Yorkshire, and educated at Canterbury and at Whitby, under St *Hild. In 688 he was made bishop of Hexham, but removed to York in 705, when Hexham was restored to St *Wilfrid. It was during his time at York that he founded Beverley Minster, whose abbot, Berhthun, recounted to *Bede the various miracles performed by John, included in the *Ecclesiastical History*. These stories give a vivid picture of the household and activities of a seventh-century bishop. One of the most attractive concerns a young clerk, Herebald. He was travelling with the bishop when the young laymen of John's bodyguard asked their lord's permission to race their horses on a suitable piece of level ground. Herebald had received from John a particularly magnificent mount, and, wishing to show off its paces, asked to join in, but John, who had only reluctantly agreed to the race, absolutely forbade him. The young clerk could not resist the temptation to disobey and to join the race, whereupon his horse threw him, and he fell on the only

stone in the whole area, cracking his skull. He was carried home uncon-
scious and his life was despaired of, but John sat all night by his bed,
praying for him, and in the morning he recovered. On the next day, he
was able to ride again, this time more soberly.

BIBL. *HE* v 2-6: 456-9

John the Old Saxon abbot *d*. after 904
John was one of the continental scholars invited to England by King
*Alfred; he came from Saxony. He helped in the translation of the *Cura
Pastoralis* (Pastoral Care) of *Gregory the Great. When Alfred founded a
monastery at Athelney, it was staffed with Frankish monks, and John was
made abbot, but the foundation was not a success. John and his monks
fell out and they attempted to assassinate him. By 904 he had relinquished
the abbey and may have retired to Malmesbury, if he is the 'John the
wise' whose burial is recorded at that place.

BIBL. Lapidge 1981

Judith queen 856−60, *d*. after 870
Judith, daughter of Charles the Bald, king of the Franks, married
*Æthelwulf, king of Wessex, at Verberie on 1 October 856. She was at
the time about 14 years of age; her husband was around 50. The match
was a political move. Æthelwulf and Charles the Bald had both suffered
from the Viking fleets which infested the coasts of England and Frankia,
and were making common cause against them. Judith was Æthelwulf's
second wife, and to secure her position, Charles insisted that his daughter
should be crowned as Æthelwulf's queen, though this was not customary
in ninth-century Wessex. In the event, Æthelwulf's marriage provoked
something of a crisis in Wessex, and his eldest son, *Æthelbald, refused to
surrender authority to his father. Æthelwulf died in 858, and Æthelbald's
first act was to marry his stepmother, which caused considerable scandal.
However he also died in 860, and Judith returned to Frankia. Her adven-
tures were not at an end. In 863, she was abducted by Baldwin 'Iron-
Arm', a Flemish adventurer, much to the disgust of her father, who
attempted to have him excommunicated. Baldwin and Judith journeyed to
Rome to intercede with the pope, Nicholas I, who took their part, and
persuaded the king to recognize the match. Charles made Baldwin count
of Ghent, and later added the counties of Ternois and Flanders. These
grants were the foundation of the county of Flanders, of which Baldwin
II, son of Iron-Arm and Judith, was the first count. He married *Ælfthryth,
daughter of *Alfred the Great.

BIBL. Stafford 1981; Dunbabin 1985: 69

Justus archbishop of Canterbury 624−7
Justus was one of the monks sent to England by *Gregory the Great in
601, to join the previous mission which arrived in 597. He was the first
bishop of Rochester, consecrated in 604, and attended a council at Paris
in 614, in company with Peter, abbot of St Augustine's. During the pagan

reaction which followed the death of *Æthelberht of Kent in 616, he fled to Gaul, but was subsequently restored to his see. In 624, he was elevated to be archbishop of Canterbury, and died in 627.

BIBL. Brooks 1984: 11-14

K

Karl Hundason Scottish ruler *c.* 1034—7

Karl Hundason is a mysterious Scottish ruler whose career is recorded in *Orkneyinga Saga* where he is portrayed as an enemy of the Orkney earl, *Thorfinn the Mighty. Thorfinn is claimed in the saga to have been the grandson (on his mother's side) of *Malcolm II of Scotland who appointed the young Thorfinn at the age of five to be earl over Caithness. Thorfinn relied on help from Malcolm in his struggles with his brother for control of the Orkney earldom, but on Malcolm's death (1034) *Orkneyinga Saga* claims that the new Scots king, Karl Hundason, became Thorfinn's enemy. Thorfinn (who was then based at Duncansby) is said to have withheld tribute from Karl for Caithness and this led to war between the Scots and the Norsemen. Karl Hundason appointed his nephew, Mutatan or Muddan (Old Irish *Matudán*), as rival chieftain over Caithness, and Mutatan having been routed by Thorfinn in battle retreated to consult Karl Hundason who was then in Berwick in the south. The Scots next attempted a pincer movement against the Norsemen, with Mutatan attacking Caithness for the second time, while Karl's fleet sailed north into the Pentland Firth. Thorfinn won a great naval victory over Karl off Deerness on Orkney (celebrated in the verses of *Arnór Earls' Poet), whereupon Karl retreated south to the Moray Firth to recruit more troops. Meanwhile, Karl's nephew, Mutatan, was ambushed and slain in his house at Thurso in Caithness by Thorkel the Fosterer, chief ally of Earl Thorfinn in his war against the Scots. Finally, Thorfinn won a second and decisive naval battle over Karl Hundason at Tarbat Ness in Easter Ross *c.* 1035. Thorfinn crushed Karl and his combined armies of Scots and Irish, and afterwards the Norsemen are said to have pillaged as far south as Fife, ruthlessly stamping out all resistance. No more is told of Karl Hundason who is variously identified by modern historians. He is sometimes equated with *Duncan I, grandson of Malcolm II, or with some otherwise unknown Scottish mórmaer or chieftain in Moray, Caithness or Argyll. He is also identified (with greater probability) with *Macbeth. This is supported by Karl's interest in Caithness and by his apparent strength in Moray. According to *Njáls Saga*, Earl Thorfinn's father, *Sigurd the Stout, fought against a certain Hundi in a battle at *Dungalsgnípa* (near Duncansby) for control of Caithness. If this was the same battle which in *Orkneyinga Saga* was fought at Skitten Myre in Caithness between Sigurd and Finnleikr, and *if* Finnleikr and Hundi were the same person, then Karl Hundason would also be Karl son of Finnleikr and therefore even more likely to be Macbeth son of *Findlaech. There is nothing improbable in the fact that a Scottish king such as Macbeth would be known to his Norse neighbours under a Scandinavian name.

BIBL. Crawford 1987: 71-4; Duncan 1975: 100; Pálsson and Edwards 1978: 50-6; Skene 1886—90, vol. 1: 400-4; Taylor 1936-7: 334-41

Kenelm St *see* **Cynehelm**

Kenneth I mac Alpín (Cináed mac Alpín) king of Scots and Picts 840–58

Kenneth was not the first king to rule over the Scots and Picts, but he was the founder of a dynasty which suppressed the Pictish kingdom, imposed Gaelic language and culture on Pictish territories and gave to the kingdom of Scotland its line of medieval kings. Kenneth's family origins are obscure and the historicity of his father, *Alpín, is in doubt. He may have belonged to an obscure branch of Dál Riata which gained in military experience and power as a result of constant border warfare with Norsemen in Argyll. The fragmentary evidence which survives suggests that Kenneth rose to power with the help of Norse allies in the Hebrides in 836, that he later gave his daughter in marriage to Olaf the White, the Norse king of Dublin, and that he availed of the Viking massacre of the Dál Riata house of Fergus in 839 to usurp the kingship of both Scots and Picts. While Kenneth became king of Dál Riata in 840, he did not thereby automatically become king of the Picts. *Eóganán, the Pictish ruler who was slain by Vikings in 839, was succeeded by either two or even by five Pictish kings, the last of whom died sometime between 843 and 848. Kenneth had to overcome the last of his Pictish rivals by treachery and bloodshed and it was not until the slaying of Drust, at Forteviot, that he became the sole ruler of the Picts and Scots in *c*. 847. At about this time also (847), the relics of St *Columba were divided up, one portion taken by the abbot of Iona back to Ireland and the other secured by Kenneth mac Alpín for the Scottish church, which he housed most likely at Dunkeld. Kenneth died at Forteviot in Perthshire in February 858 and was buried on Iona.

BIBL. Anderson 1973: 196-200; Duncan 1975: 56-9; Skene 1886–90, vol. 1: 308-24; Smyth 1984: 176-85

Kenneth II king of Scots 971–95

Kenneth II was the son of *Malcolm I. He began his reign by plundering northern England as far as Stainmore, and at a meeting with King *Edgar at Chester in 973 he very likely obtained recognition of his overlordship in Strathclyde-Cumbria and in Lothian. In addition to consolidating a Scottish hold over the Southern Uplands, Kenneth's reign marked a turning point in the Scottish system of royal succession. Kenneth strove successfully to exclude the descendants of Áed son of *Kenneth mac Alpín from the kingship and he began a process whereby the Scottish kingship was to be confined within much narrower limits of succession within his own dynasty. Kenneth's immediate aim was to settle the kingship on his son *Malcolm II. In this he was opposed not only by the descendants of *Indulf but by the descendants of his own brother, *Dub. In 977 Kenneth slew his rival, *Olaf son of *Indulf, but according to Fordun, Kenneth was eventually brought down by a conspiracy involving the future *Constantine III (the grandson of Indulf) and by Giric the grandson of Dub. He was assassinated in Fettercairn, Kincardineshire, and was buried on Iona. One of Kenneth's wives — a princess from Leinster and the Liffey Plain — was the mother of Malcolm II.

BIBL. Anderson 1922, vol. 1: 511-16; Smyth 1984: 224-8, 232-3

Kenneth III king of Scots 997—1005

Kenneth was the son of *Dub. It is not clear from the sources whether it was Kenneth who succeeded *Constantine III in 997 or Kenneth's son Giric II, or whether father and son ruled jointly. Both Kenneth and Giric are ascribed an eight-year reign and were said to have been slain by *Malcolm II in 1005 at Monzievaird near the Earn. The slaying of Kenneth by Malcolm contributed to the feud which resulted in the slaying of Malcolm's grandson, *Duncan I, by *Macbeth in 1040. Macbeth's wife, *Gruoch, was a granddaughter of Kenneth III.

BIBL. Anderson 1922, vol. 1: 518-24; Smyth 1984: 225

Kentigern (Mungo) first bishop of Glasgow and patron of the Strathclyde Britons c. 550—612

Kentigern is said to have been the illegitimate son of *Teneu or Thaney, a Northern British princess from territory south of the Forth. She was punished and cast adrift by her father in a coracle in the Firth of Forth, because of her illicit pregnancy. Teneu was conveniently washed ashore at Culross in Fife, where her son, Kentigern (who was born there), was cared for by St *Serf. It was Serf who was alleged to have given Kentigern his more endearing name of Munghu. Having grown up under Serf's supervision, Kentigern left him secretly and headed west for Glasgow, where he found a Christian cemetery already in existence from the time of St *Ninian. He founded his episcopal see at Glasgow (having been consecrated by an Irish bishop) and his diocese was co-extensive with the kingdom of Strathclyde-Cumbria. He lived as an ascetic, his bed having the appearance of a stone sarcophagus, and he fasted and prayed standing naked in the river. He fell foul of a tyrannical Cumbrian ruler, called Morken, and, persecuted by Morken's relatives, Kentigern fled to Wales, going first to St *David and later being associated with the young St *Asaph. After seven apocryphal journeys to Rome, he was eventually recalled from his Welsh exile by the new Strathclyde ruler, *Riderch Hen, who re-established Kentigern as chief bishop of the kingdom, with status higher even than that of the king himself. He based himself once more at Glasgow, built a church at Hoddam in Dumfriesshire, and erected crosses all over his diocese as far afield as Borthwick in Midlothian. He is said to have had a friendly meeting with *Columba which is plausible in view of the friendship which *Adomnán describes between Columba and Riderch Hen. Kentigern is alleged to have survived to the preposterous old age of 160 or 185. He died on entering a warm bath, on 13 January, the year, according to Annales Cambriae, being 612.

BIBL. Anderson 1922, vol. 1: 126-39; Jackson 1958: 273-357

Kentigerna (Caintigern) St, anchoress c. 700—34

Although we cannot account for many of the details of Kentigerna's life, there are few Scottish saints with better historical credentials. Her death is recorded in the contemporary Annals of Ulster in 734 where she is identified as the daughter of Cellach Cualann, king of the Uí Mail, based at Kilranelagh in Wicklow, and overlord of the Leinstermen in south-east

Ireland who died in 715. Unusually for this early period in any part of the British Isles, three of Kentigerna's sisters and their marriages are known, while two of her brothers ruled as kings of Uí Mail. The Breviary of Aberdeen confirms that Kentigerna was the daughter of the king of Leinster and that she herself was first married to a king called Feriacus. She later migrated to Scotland with her brother, *Comgán, and her son, *Fáelán, to Strathfillan. Later she retreated as a solitary to Inchcailloch ('Nun's Island') in Loch Lomond. Her festival was kept on 7 January.

BIBL. Anderson 1922, vol. 1: 230-1; Smyth 1982: 57 (chart), 82

Ketil Flatnose Viking ruler of the Hebrides *fl.* 855

Ketil was the son of a Norwegian chieftain, Björn Rough Foot, and he is associated in Scandinavian sagas with the expedition of Harald Finehair of Norway to the Scottish Isles in the middle of the ninth century. The king who led this expedition cannot have been Harald who was a contemporary of the tenth-century English king, *Athelstan, but he was very probably Olaf the White, king of Dublin and of Vestfold. Both Olaf and Ketil are mentioned in contemporary Irish sources dating from the third quarter of the ninth century, and Norse sources are insistent that Ketil's daughter, *Aud the Deep-Minded, was married to Olaf the White of Dublin. Ketil either accompanied Olaf on an expedition of conquest to the Scottish Isles, at which time the Orkney earldom was also established, or alternatively, Ketil conquered the Hebrides independently of the Norwegian king and was later forced to submit to him. Ketil appears in Irish annals as the leader of a renegade band of *Gaill-Gaedhel* ('Scandinavian-Irish') who were raiding in Ireland in 857, and who were associated with the Irish king, Cerball of Ossory, who died in 888. After Ketil's death, the influence of his family quickly collapsed in the Hebrides and northern Scotland, and his kin were forced to emigrate to Iceland. His daughter, Aud, and sons, Björn the Easterling and Helgi Bjólan, and son-in-law Helgi Magri, all hailed from the Hebrides and were remembered as key figures in the early settlement of Iceland.

BIBL. Smyth 1977a: 116-26

Kiritinus *see* **Curetan**

Knútr *see* **Cnut**

L

Laisran abbot of Iona *c.* 600–5

Laisran was the third abbot of Iona in succession to *Baithene. Laisran's father, Feredach or Fergus, was *Columba's first cousin. *Adomnán in his *Life of Columba* shows us Laisran in charge of a work-force of monks engaged in constructing a large building at Durrow in the Irish midlands. Laisran emerges from this anecdote as a man who, although initially a harsh task-master, later relented to become a caring leader. In another incident Adomnán shows us Laisran travelling in Columba's party 'through the rocky district of Ardnamurchan' in Argyll where he was conversing with *Diarmait, Columba's personal attendant. It is likely since Baithene's abbacy only lasted three years that Laisran had already become a permanent member of the Iona community in Columba's lifetime. He was succeeded by *Fergna and his festival was observed on 16 September.

BIBL. Anderson and Anderson 1961: 90 and text; Reeves 1857: 372

Laurence St, archbishop of Canterbury 604/10–19

Laurence was one of the original missionaries sent to Kent by Pope *Gregory the Great in 596. He was chosen by *Augustine to succeed him as archbishop of Canterbury. When, after the death of King *Æthelberht and the accession of the still-pagan *Eadbald, the mission seemed likely to collapse, Laurence contemplated returning to Frankish Gaul, as his companions, *Mellitus of London and *Justus of Rochester had done.

However, as *Bede tells us, he received a visitation from St Peter, who reproached him for cowardice, and, to emphasize his displeasure, beat him severely. The next morning Laurence displayed his bruises to the king, who was moved to consider what a lord who could so chastise his faithful servants might do to his enemies. He recanted his former beliefs, was baptized and became a zealous patron of the church.

BIBL. *HE* ii, 6: 154-5; Brooks 1984: 64-6

Leofgyth *see* **Lioba**

Leofric earl 1023/32–57

Leofric came from a wealthy and important east midland family; his father *Leofwine was made ealdorman of the Hwicce in 994. He seems to have begun his public career as sheriff of Worcestershire under Earl *Hakon (1018–30), and was promoted to the earldom of Mercia after his father died. In 1035, he was the chief supporter of *Harold I, son of *Cnut and *Ælfgifu of Northampton, against *Harthacnut, Cnut's son by *Emma of Normandy. His wife Godgifu (Lady Godiva) was probably from the same region as Leofric himself; she seems to have been connected with Lincolnshire. Leofric's son, Ælfgar, who eventually succeeded him as earl of Mercia, was also married to a woman from the Danelaw; her name was Ælfgifu and she was probably the daughter of the powerful thegn *Morcar, murdered in 1015. Leofric's office, land and family connections made him the most powerful figure in England after *Godwine of Wessex, and the rivalry between their families did much to shape the politics of the mid-eleventh century. He was a benefactor of Evesham abbey, and both he and his wife acquired a reputation for piety, based upon their foundation of Coventry Abbey and the minster of Stow St Mary, Lincolnshire. At Worcester, however, he was remembered as a despoiler of the lands of the abbey and bishopric, as were his brothers, *Edwin and Godric, and his nephew, Æthelwine.

BIBL. Williams 1986: 7-8, 13-15; Sawyer 1979: xli-iii

Leofsige ealdorman 994—1002

Leofsige may have been *Byrhtnoth's successor as ealdorman of Essex, but his sphere of authority seems to have extended to the shires of Middlesex, Hertford and Buckingham, for early in his tenure of office, he complained to King Æthelred II about the behaviour of the port-reeves of Buckingham and Oxford. They had allowed Christian burial to a group of thieves, who were killed in a fight over some stolen property. The king, however, took the part of the reeves against the ealdorman. In 1002, Leofsige was deputed to arrange a truce with the Danish host which had been ravaging in the south-west, a task which he accomplished successfully. Subsequently he became embroiled with another royal officer, the high-reeve, Æfic, and killed him 'in his own house, without warning'. For this crime, Leofsige was banished, and forfeited his property. His sister, Æthelflæd, who tried to help him, also suffered forfeiture of her land, which included Fen Stanton and Hilton, Huntingdonshire. Leofsige's estates at Norton and Oxhey, Hertfordshire, were given to St Alban's. What finally became of Leofsige and his sister is unknown. His career is of considerable interest, however, and in legal terms, as Stenton pointed out, the offences of *hamsocn* (attacking a man in his own house) and *flymenafyrmth* (harbouring fugitives), both known from law-codes, 'are shown for the first time in relation to an actual case'.

BIBL. *ASC* s.a. 1002; Sawyer 1968, nos. 883, 891, 926; Stenton 1955: 76-81; Hart 1987: 76-7

Leofwine ealdorman 994—1023/32

Leofwine was appointed ealdorman of the Hwicce in 994. His father's name was Ælfwine, but nothing is known of him, though the family seems to come from the east midlands. Little can be said of Leofwine's career until 1013, when he submitted to *Swein Forkbeard and gave hostages, one of whom was his grandson, Æthelwine, 'who had his hands cut off by the Danes'. The occasion was probably the return of Leofwine and the other western magnates to their allegiance to *Æthelred II in 1014, after Swein's death, for his son *Cnut mutilated the hostages given to his father at that time. In 1017, Leofwine's son, Northman, was killed on the orders of Cnut, but Leofwine himself was promoted by Cnut to be ealdorman of Mercia in succession to the murdered *Eadric Streona. Both Leofwine's surviving sons were given office in the west; *Leofric was sheriff of Worcestershire, and *Edwin held a similar position in Herefordshire. Leofwine's last signature to Cnut's charters is in 1023, and he probably died soon afterwards; by 1032, his son Leofric had succeeded to Mercia.

BIBL. Williams 1986: 7-8

Leuthere bishop 670-6

Leuthere or Lothar was a Frank, the nephew of *Agilbert. He became bishop of Wessex when King *Cenwealh expelled *Wine in 670, and ordained *Aldhelm, who was a close friend. He died in 676.

BIBL. *HE* iii, 7: 236-7; iv, 5: 350-1; v, 18: 514, note 1

Lioba (Leofgyth) St, abbess *d.* 782

Lioba was a kinswoman on her mother's side of St *Boniface, the 'apostle of Germany'. Lioba became a nun of Wimborne Minster in Dorset and subsequently studied under *Eadburh at Minster-in-Thanet. In 748 she joined her kinsman Boniface in Germany and became abbess of Tauberbischofsheim. One of her nuns was St *Walburh, sister of St *Willibald, and the house was home to many other English men and women who participated in the conversion of the peoples east of the Rhine. Lioba was a friend of the Frankish king Charlemagne and his wife Hildegarde. She died in 782, and was buried beside Boniface at Fulda. Her life was written, some 50 years after her death, by Rudolph of Fulda, but it is her letters, preserved with those of Boniface, which reveal most about her character and interests.

BIBL. Talbot 1954: 87-8, 141, 204-26; Farmer 1978: 246-7

Liudhard St *d. c.* 603

Liudhard was the Frankish chaplain of *Bertha, who accompanied her to England when she married *Æthelberht of Kent. With the king's permission, Liudhard restored the church of St Martin, Canterbury, for the queen's use; traces of Roman and early Saxon work are still visible in the present fabric. The dedication to the Gallo-Roman saint, Martin of Tours, may be due to Liudhard, but could have been the original dedication, when the church served the British community. Liudhard was still alive when the mission of St *Augustine arrived in Kent, but played no recorded part in the conversion of the English.

BIBL. *HE* i, 25-6: 72-9; Farmer 1978: 248

Llywarch Hen British prince *fl.* sixth century

Though not mentioned among the sixth-century bards in the early ninth-century *Historia Brittonum* (see under *Nennius), a Llywarch Hen appears in the genealogies of the Men of the North (North Britain) in a context which would place him in the second half of the sixth century, and a later poem lamenting the death of *Urien of Rheged is attributed to him. His name is associated also, however, with a cycle of verse concerning *Cynddylan of Powys, a seventh-century figure, and with a series of

171

laments for the deaths of his own sons against the English in what has come to be regarded (perhaps unjustifiably) as a ninth-century context. Llywarch appears to have been adopted by a number of poets as the central figure in a complex of probably originally quite separate cycles of verse and his historicity obscured.

BIBL. Williams, I 1953; Williams I 1980; Ford 1974; Jarman 1981: 70ff.; Rowland 1989

Llywelyn ap Seisyll king of Gwynedd *d*. 1023

Llywelyn appears as an intruder into dynastic politics who may have been descended from *Anarawd ab Rhodri, king of Gwynedd, but only on his mother's side. Seisyll's ancestry is unknown and some have seen Llywelyn as primarily a prince of Deheubarth. He certainly married Angharad, daughter of *Maredudd ab Owain, and he was deeply involved in the affairs of Deheubarth, vanquishing a certain Rhain in 1022 who was supported by Irish troops and claiming to be a son of Maredudd ab Owain. It is not certain whether Aeddan ap Blegywryd, whom Llywelyn slew in 1018 with his four sons, was a prince of Gwynedd or Deheubarth. The Welsh annals call Llewelyn king of Gwynedd. When he died in 1023 Iago ab Idwal, great-grandson of *Idwal ab Anarawd, restored the native dynasty in Gwynedd but *Rhydderch ab Iestyn, another intruder, came to power in Deheubarth. Llywelyn's son, *Gruffudd, subsequently revived his family's dynastic aspirations.

BIBL. Lloyd 1911, vol. I: 346-7; Davies 1982: 107

Lul St, archbishop of Mainz *d*. 786

Lul was a West Saxon and a kinsman of St *Boniface, whom he joined as a missionary in Germany. He succeeded Boniface as archbishop of Mainz in 754, but was buried at Hersfeld, and his life was written by Lambert, a monk of that house. Lul was one of Boniface's most ardent supporters, and their letters to each other are of prime importance in understanding the origin and development of the church in Germany.

BIBL. Farmer 1978: 252

Lulach king of Scotland 1057-8

Lulach was proclaimed king of Scotland by the followers of *Macbeth when the latter was slain by Malcolm III Canmore on 15 August 1057. He is described as the 'nephew of the son of Boite' being the son of *Gruoch and her first husband Gillacomgain. Although only the stepson of Macbeth, Lulach was descended from the two royal houses of Scotland. Through his father, Gillacomgain, he was of the line of the tribal kings of Moray, and through his mother he was a descendant of *Kenneth III. It was therefore imperative for Malcolm to slay this successor of Macbeth if he were to secure his position in Scotland. Lulach was defeated and slain by Malcolm on 17 March 1058 at Essie in Strathbogie in the heart of Macbeth's dynastic territory in Aberdeenshire. Lulach's nickname of 'Fool' (*Fatuus*) was no doubt accorded him by his enemies. His burial in Iona suggests that, like his stepfather, Lulach was regarded by his followers as a legitimate Scottish king. His genealogy appears under the heading *Kings of Scotland* in the reliable early twelfth-century Irish genealogical collection in the Rawlinson manuscript B502 in the Oxford Bodleian Library.

BIBL. Anderson 1922, vol. 1: 603-4; Skene 1886-90, vol. 1: 411

Lyfing bishop 1038—46

Lyfing's career began in *c*. 1009, when he was appointed abbot of Tavistock, but his further advancement was due to the patronage of King *Cnut. He accompanied Cnut on the latter's pilgrimage to Rome in 1027, and on his return received the bishopric of Crediton, which included both Devon and Cornwall; Lyfing's uncle, Brihtwold, had previously held the Cornish see. In the disputed succession to the throne which ensued upon Cnut's death in 1035, Lyfing supported the claims of *Harold I, who rewarded him with the bishopric of Worcester in 1038. His connection with Harold nearly ruined him when the king's half-brother and rival, *Harthacnut, came to the throne. In 1040, Lyfing and his friend, Earl *Godwine of Wessex, were accused of complicity in the murder of the ætheling *Alfred, and Lyfing was deprived of his see, which was given to his accuser, *Ælfric Puttoc, archbishop of York. He was restored the following year, but the deposition of their bishop probably played a part in the refusal of the Worcestershire thegns to pay the heregeld in 1041, and their murder in that year of the king's housecarls, *Feader and Thorsteinn, who were sent to collect it. Not surprisingly, Lyfing was one of the prime supporters of Edward the Confessor, who prevailed upon Harthacnut to share the kingship with him in 1041. Lyfing died on 23 March 1046.

BIBL. Barlow 1963: 73-4, 213-14, 226-7

M

Macbeth king of Scotland 1040–57

Macbethad ('Son of Life') was a member of a Scottish dynasty who ruled in Moray, north of the Mounth, in eleventh-century Scotland. His ancestors may have claimed descent from the Scottish kings of Cenél Loairn in Argyll, who in the Viking Age migrated from the west up the Great Glen to occupy the territory of the Picts in Moray. Macbeth's father, *Findlaech (Finlay) was a hereditary *mórmaer* of Moray who is styled 'king of Scotland' in the contemporary *Annals of Ulster*. Macbeth may have been *Maelbaethe*, one of a pair of northern kings who submitted to *Cnut along with Malcolm II in 1032. In that case, Macbeth was already ruling as a king in Moray prior to his slaying of Duncan in 1040. Macbeth's wife was *Gruoch, grand-daughter of *Kenneth III, a Scottish king of the ruling dynasty of *Kenneth mac Alpín. Macbeth's marriage to Gruoch helped to unite rival segments of his own Moray dynasty and to unite the house of Moray with that of Kenneth III which was in turn bitterly opposed to the dynasty of the ruling Scots king, *Duncan I. Macbeth slew Duncan near Elgin in Moray, on 14 August 1040, thereby making himself king of Scotland. Duncan's infant sons then fled the realm — Malcolm Canmore going first (according to Fordun) to Cumbria and later to his maternal uncle, *Siward earl of Northumbria, while his brother, Donald Bán, fled to the Isles. It was about this time that *Orkneyinga Saga* tells of a war between Earl *Thorfinn the Mighty of Orkney and a Scottish king called *Karl Hundason, for control of Sutherland and Caithness. There is good reason to identify Macbeth with the otherwise mysterious Karl. According to the saga, Karl was defeated by the Norsemen who secured their hold over Caithness and raided eastern Scotland as far south as Fife. Meanwhile Macbeth was preoccupied with other enemies in the south. In 1045 he defeated and slew *Crinan, the abbot of Dunkeld who was Duncan's father. Shakespeare's reference to Birnam Wood may relate to this event, since Birnam is very close to Dunkeld. In 1052, Macbeth received Norman exiles from the English court. Two years later, Siward of Northumbria launched an invasion of Macbeth's country in an attempt to place his nephew, Malcolm Canmore on the Scottish throne. Siward lost a son and a nephew in a bloody but indecisive battle fought near Scone on 27 July. Macbeth was forced to yield territory to Malcolm as a result of this invasion — Malcolm being now in control of Lothian, or more likely of Perth and Fife, and with Macbeth confined to Moray and his hereditary lands north of the Mounth. Malcolm won his final victory over Macbeth in 1057, when on 15 August he defeated and slew his enemy at Lumphanan in Mar. On the death of Macbeth, his followers recognized *Lulach, Macbeth's stepson, as king of Scots, in opposition to Malcolm III. The popular and Shakespearian image of Macbeth as a villainous usurper and a tyrant has little or perhaps no historical justification.

He was clearly seen by himself and his followers as a king in the male line of the dynasty of Moray which was perhaps as old as that of the house of Kenneth mac Alpín in the south. Macbeth's usurpation of the kingdom from Duncan was a normal part of succession struggles in the early Middle Ages, particularly in Celtic society. By the standards of the time, Duncan's claim to the kingship through his mother was peculiarly weak. Macbeth may even have been regarded as a popular and successful king — his 17-year reign was remembered as a time of plenty. He was pious, too, going on pilgrimage to Rome in 1050 where he 'scattered money like seed' to the poor of that city. Such a pilgrimage could never have been undertaken had not Macbeth exercised a secure hold over the Scottish realm. He was a friend of the Church. He and his queen, Gruoch, made generous grants of land to the Culdees of Loch Leven 'with the utmost veneration and devotion'. Macbeth was buried on Iona — yet another indication that he was regarded by his followers and perhaps even by his enemies as hailing from a traditional and ancient line of Scottish kings.

BIBL. Anderson 1922, vol. 1: 580-602; Duncan 1975: 90-100; Skene 1886—90, vol. 1: 404-11; Crawford 1987; 71-4

Mac Durnan *see* **Máelbrigte mac Tornáin**

Máelbrigte mac Tornáin (Mac Durnan) abbot 888—927
Máelbrigte was a distant member of *Columba's royal kindred, belonging to the Cenél mBógaine branch of the Cenél Conaill in Donegal. Two of his cousins were also leading churchmen in Columba's *paruchia*. One, Dubhthach (*d*. 938), succeeded Máelbrigte as abbot of Iona in Ireland and Scotland; the other, Caencomhrac (*d*. 929), ruled as abbot and bishop of Derry and was steward of the tribute which accrued from enforcing the Law of *Adomnán. Máelbrigte was probably based throughout his ecclesiastical career at Armagh, where he succeeded to the abbacy in 888. He did not combine the rule of Armagh with that of Iona until the death of Abbot Flann of Iona in 891. This arrangement reveals the disarray in which the Iona community found itself in the tenth century due to persistent Viking atrocities. Iona itself was almost certainly unoccupied at this time. In 893 Máelbrigte intervened decisively to suppress a tribal battle at Whitsuntide in Armagh by imposing a fine of 630 cows and having four Ulstermen hanged. In 913, Máelbrigte travelled south into Munster 'to ransom a pilgrim of the Britons' — most likely another victim of the Viking chaos. Mac Durnan's Gospels in Lambeth Palace library are a set of four gospels compiled and illuminated in Ireland and which, according to a Latin poem by an English scribe, were presented to Christ Church Cathedral, Canterbury, by the English king and bibliophile, *Athelstan (*d*. 939). The note associates the gospels with *Maeielbrithus mac Durnan*, who may have initially presented the work to Athelstan. Máelbrigte, 'successor of Patrick and Columba rested in happy old age' on 22 February 927.

BIBL. Herbert 1988: 74-5; Kenney 1929: 644-5; Reeves 1857: 392-3

Máelciaráin Ua Maighne abbot of Iona 986

Máelciaráin became the successor or *comarba* of *Columba in 980 on the death of his predecessor, Mugrón. While it is uncertain whether the superior of the entire Columban community resided in Ireland or on Iona at this time, it is clear that Iona by now housed a permanent monastic community and had recovered from the worst of the Viking wars. *Olafr Sigtryggson, former Norse king of York and Dublin, died on Iona 'after penance and a good life' soon after his arrival there in 981. In 986 three Danish longships arrived on the coast of Scottish Dál Riata and 60 of their crew were executed and others sold. It was this piratical band or another associated with it, which fell upon Iona on Christmas night, 986, slaying the abbot and 15 of his community. The later Annals of the *Four Masters* claim that Máelciaráin Ua Maighne, the successor of Columba, suffered 'red martyrdom' at the hands of Dublin Vikings in this year. Máelciaráin was almost certainly the abbot who lost his life on Iona on Christmas night 986. His family, the Ua Maighne, were a branch of the Irish Cenél Conaill, to which dynasty Columba also belonged. Máelciaráin was succeeded by Dúnchad Ua Robocáin in the abbacy of Iona, but there is some evidence to suggest that Dúnchad may have resided at Raphoe in Donegal rather than on Iona.

BIBL. Reeves 1857: 395-6

Maelgwn king of Gwynedd *d.* 549

The genealogies present Maelgwn as the great-grandson of *Cunedda, though according to the early ninth-century *Historia Brittonum* (see under *Nennius) he was Cunedda's great-great-great-grandson. He figures prominently in Welsh medieval tradition as Maelgwn Gwynedd, and according to *Gildas he was distinguished from other British rulers by the extent of his kingdom. Gildas characterized him as the 'island dragon' (a reference to Anglesey) and condemned him for the murder in his youth of his uncle, the king, and more recently of his nephew and first wife. Maelgwn had spent some time in a monastic community and it was to Gildas' regret that he had returned 'like a dog to his vomit', to secular life, preferring the panegyrics of his bards — Gildas calls them 'Bacchanalian revellers' — to the melodious praises of God. He is said to have died during a plague, and the annals place his death in 547, to be corrected to 549, when a great plague is known to have afflicted the British Isles, but the precise date of Maelgwn's death is not certain.

BIBL. Lloyd 1911, vol. I: 130; Bromwich 1961: 437-41; Alcock 1973: 124-8; Jackson 1982: 34-5; Dumville 1984a; Williams 1984

Máelrubai founder and first abbot of Applecross 673–722

Máelrubai was a member of the Irish dynasty of Cenél nEógain located in the modern counties of Derry and Tyrone. His mother was believed to have been a kinswoman of Comgall, the founding abbot of Bangor in Co. Down, and Máelrubai most likely began his monastic career at that centre in north-eastern Ireland. His sailing to Britain is recorded in the *Annals of Ulster* in 671 and the record of his foundation of a monastic community at

Applecross two years later shows that contemporary chroniclers viewed the beginning of his ecclesiastical career in Scotland as an event of great importance. Máelrubai's choice of Applecross suggests he deliberately set out to rebuild on the ruins of *Donnán's missionary labours among the northern Picts, as does the fact that ecclesiastical dedications to Máelrubai in northern Scotland broadly coincide with those of Donnán. Máelrubai is commemorated in the place-names Clachán Ma-Ruibhe on Loch Carron and Eilean Ma-Ruibhe on Loch Maree (Loch Ma-Ruibhe), as well as numerous other possible dedications on Skye and elsewhere on the mainland of northern Scotland. It is notable that the distribution of dedications to Máelrubai are mutually exclusive to those associated with *Columba's earlier activities which suggests that we are dealing with quite separate and independent monastic *paruchiae*. It is also significant that *Adomnán, who was his contemporary, makes no mention whatever of Máelrubai or his mission to the Picts in his *Life* of Columba. Máelrubai lived to a great age, dying in his eightieth year on 21 April 722. The later Scottish record of his festival on 27 August has no early authority to support it. Máelrubai's monastic community had a relatively short life, since Applecross fell an early victim to the Viking onslaught in the early ninth century.

BIBL. Anderson 1922, vol. 1: 219-20; Smyth 1984: 109-11

Malcolm I king of Scots 943—54
Malcolm I, the son of *Donald II, succeeded his cousin *Constantine II when the latter abdicated the Scottish throne in 943. The politics of his reign were dominated by the final stages in the struggle between the kingdoms of Wessex and Dublin for control of Scandinavian York. Malcolm supported the Dublin king, *Olafr Sigtryggson, in opposition to the kings of Wessex and *Eirikr Bloodaxe, the exiled king of Norway. *Edmund of Wessex invaded Cumbria in 945, driving out Olafr Sigtryggson and recognizing Malcolm as overlord of Strathclyde-Cumbria, in return for Malcolm's defence of north-west England from Viking attack. Malcolm's cousin and successor in the Scottish kingship, *Indulf, held Strathclyde-Cumbria as Malcolm's sub-king, but Scottish overlordship in this region was already well established before the time of Edmund of Wessex. Malcolm led a raid into England as far south as the Tees in 948—9 in support of Olafr Sigtryggson who regained his York throne at that time. Malcolm was slain by the men of Moray at Fetteresso near Dunnottar in 954 and was buried on Iona.

BIBL. Anderson 1922, vol. 1: 449-54; Smyth 1984: 221-5

Malcolm II king of Scots 1005—34
Malcolm was the son of *Kenneth II and a Leinster princess from the Liffey Plain in Ireland. While he inherited a dynastic feud, he also made a major contribution to it by slaying his predecessor, *Kenneth III, at Monzievaird in Perthshire, in 1005. Ultimately that action led to the slaying of Malcolm's grandson, *Duncan I, by *Macbeth. He began his reign with an 'inaugural raid' on Durham in 1006 with a view to displaying his overlordship in English Bernicia, but he was repulsed with heavy

losses by the Northumbrian earl, *Uhtred. In *c*. 1008 he gave his daughter in marriage to *Sigurd the Stout, Norse earl of Orkney, and when Sigurd was slain in 1014, his son *Thorfinn, then only five, was reared at Malcolm's court and supposedly appointed ruler of Sutherland and Caithness. There is evidence to suggest that Malcolm allied with the Norsemen of the Isles in an attempt to curb the power of the Scots dynasty of Moray represented by *Findlaech and his son, Macbeth. This feud between Malcolm's house and the kings of Moray may lie behind the burning of Dunkeld in 1027. Malcolm produced no known male heir, but his daughter, Bethoc, married *Crinan, abbot of Dunkeld, whose son, Duncan, succeeded Malcolm in 1034. In 1018, at Carham on the Tweed, Malcolm won a great victory with the help of his sub-king, *Owen the Bald of Strathclyde. The Scottish army defeated Earl *Eadulf's forces, inflicting heavy losses on the English between the Tweed and the Tees, and immediately afterwards Malcolm bestowed booty on the church. Malcolm was not, as has often been supposed, striving to annex Lothian, which had been in Scottish hands before the time of the English king *Edgar and of *Kenneth II, who met in 973. Malcolm was bent on the overlordship of Bernicia, and the church which benefited from his patronage was most likely Durham which had been founded in 995. *Cnut invaded Scotland in 1031−2 reaching perhaps as far as the Tay, when he forced Malcolm to submit along with two other kings, *Maelbaethe* (Macbeth) and a certain *Iehmarc*, perhaps a *mórmaer* of Argyll. Malcolm's submission had little effect, but Cnut's campaign did secure Bernicia for England and it is from Malcolm's reign that the Scottish Border took on its permanent appearance. Malcolm's control over his rivals within Scotland may have been weakened by Cnut's invasion, and since he was leaving no male heir, the succession struggle resurfaced with a vengeance. In 1033 Malcolm slew a great-grandson of Kenneth III in an effort to leave the way open for his own grandson, Duncan. When Malcolm died at Glamis on 25 November 1034, he was indeed succeeded by Duncan who would eventually fall a victim to Macbeth. Malcolm was clearly a powerful and able king who was remembered in Gaelic poetry as 'the Battler', 'the Aggressor', a 'Destroyer of Foreigners', 'Voyager of Islay and of Arran', while contemporary annalists described him as 'the honour of all the West of Europe'. The contemporary Irish chronicler, Marianus Scotus, described him as king of *Scotia*, that being the first time the word was used for the territory of Scotland in place of the older *Alba*. Malcolm was buried in Iona. His death marked the end of an era in Scottish history, being the last in the direct line of male descendants of *Kenneth mac Alpín.

BIBL. Anderson 1922, vol. 1: 525-75; Duncan 1975: 97-100; Skene 1886−90, vol. 1: 384-99

Malcolm son of Donald, king of the Strathclyde Britons 973−97 *see* **Donald** son of Owen

Manne *fl.* first half of the eleventh century
  Manne and Svenne are commemorated on the runestone at Valleberga (Skane) in Sweden: 'May God help their souls well. And they lie in

London'. The inscription indicates that they were Christians, probably seamen and warriors of the royal fleet maintained by the English kings between 1012 and 1051, which was stationed at London. Two runestones have been discovered there, one in St Paul's churchyard, and the Danes (that is, presumably, the shipmen) had a cemetery there, where *Harold I was eventually buried.

BIBL. Jansson 1962: 51-2

Maredudd ab Owain king of Deheubarth *d.* 999

Maredudd was a grandson of *Hywel Dda and the brother of *Einion ab Owain, following whose death in 984 he emerged as the dominant figure in Deheubarth. Styled in the Welsh annals at his death in 999, 'the most praiseworthy king of the Britons', he is said to have ruled Dyfed, Ceredigion, Gower and Cydweli, his territories subject to attack in 991 and 994 by his nephews, Edwin and Tewdwr ab Einion. Maredudd distinguished himself by extending his authority into north Wales, for he slew Cadwallon ab Ieuaf, king of Gwynedd, in 986, and seized his kingdom. When Vikings, led by Godfrey, son of Harald, ravaged Anglesey the following year, Maredudd resettled those who had not been captured by them in Ceredigion and Dyfed and in 989 paid either tribute or ransom to the Vikings, who may have established a real presence in Gwynedd at that time, of one penny for each person; but this does not necessarily mean that his authority in Gwynedd had been terminated. Only on Maredudd's death in 999 does a native king of Gwynedd re-emerge in the person of Cynan ab Hywel ab Ieuaf (1000−3). In 992 Maredudd attacked Morgannwg with a force of Irish Vikings but this expedition appears to have had no lasting political consequences.

BIBL. Lloyd 1911, vol. I: 345-7; Davies 1982: 106-7; Davies 1990: 57-9

Mark *see* **Cunomor**

Mellitus St, archbishop of Canterbury 619−24

Mellitus was a member of the second mission sent to Kent by *Gregory the Great to assist St *Augustine, in 601. In 604 he became bishop of the East Saxons, with his see at London, in the church of St Paul, built by *Æthelberht, king of Kent. Mellitus fled from his see after the death of King *Sæberht of Essex in 616, and the apostasy of Sæberht's sons. They were unbaptized pagans, and when Mellitus refused their demand for the 'white bread' which he had given their father (that is, the Eucharistic host) they drove him out. He went with *Justus, bishop of Rochester, to Gaul, but returned to Kent when his colleague, Archbishop *Laurence, converted the Kentish king *Eadbald. Eadbald did not have the same authority as his father Æthelberht, and Mellitus was unable to return to his East Saxon see. In 616 he succeeded Laurence as the third archbishop of Canterbury and died in 624.

BIBL. *HE* i, 29: 104-5; ii, 3: 142-3, 5: 148-55; Brooks 1984: 9, 11-13

Merewalh king of the Magonsæte *d.* 685

The territory of the Magonsæte lay in the Herefordshire and Shropshire area, and was roughly co-terminous with the medieval diocese of Hereford. Its first king, Merewalh, may have been a son of *Penda of Mercia, who is thought to have established the kingdom as a Mercian dependency. Merewalh's name, however, means 'illustrious Welshman' and may indicate an origin in the local Anglo-British aristocracy of this border region. He was converted to Christianity by a Northumbrian priest, Eadfrith, about 660, and founded the church of Leominster for his mentor. In 679/80, Archbishop *Theodore established a bishopric for the kingdom, at Hereford. Merewalh married a princess of the Kentish line, *Eafa, who bore him three daughters, all of whom entered religion (see *Mildrith, *Mildburh) and a son, Merefin. Merewalh was succeeded by his sons from a previous marriage, Merchhelm and Mildfrith, and after them the province sank into obscurity.

BIBL. Finberg 1961d; Pretty 1989

Merfyn ap Gwriad king of Gwynedd 825—44, and founder of the Second Dynasty of Gwynedd

Following the death of Hywel ap Caradog, king of Gwynedd, in 825 after a period of civil war between Hywel and Cynan ap Rhodri, both of whom claimed descent in the male line from *Cunedda, and at a time when Vikings were active in the Irish Sea and the Saxons had temporarily conquered the adjacent kingdoms of Rhufuniog in 816 and Powys in 822/3, the Welsh annals and genealogies show that royal power passed to the Second Dynasty of Gwynedd in the person of Merfyn Frych ('the Freckled') ap Gwriad. Merfyn, who did not claim to be a direct descendant of Cunedda, was a prince of Powys, with Manx connections, whose father, Gwriad, had married Esyllt, daughter of Cynan ap Rhodri. Merfyn was the founder of the Second Dynasty of Gwynedd. His position was probably strengthened by his own marriage to Nest, sister of *Cyngen ap Cadell, king of Powys, and though the hold of Merfyn and his family on Gwynedd may have been insecure at first, the kingdom of Powys also eventually passed to Merfyn's son, *Rhodri, or to his sons. A new dynastic force had entered Welsh history.

BIBL. Lloyd 1911, vol. I: 323; Kirby 1976a: 97; Davies 1982; 104-5

Merlin (Myrddin) seer *fl.* traditionally sixth century

A late interpolation in one version of *Aneirin's poem, the *Gododdin*, refers to the 'blessed inspiration' of Myrddin, the prophetic poet who emerged in the twelfth century in Geoffrey of Monmouth's *History of the Kings of Britain* in an Arthurian setting as Merlin and associated with Carmarthen on the basis of a false etymology of Carmarthen as 'city of Merlin'. In bardic tradition Myrddin lost his sanity after the slaughter of his lord, *Gwenddolau, in north Britain at the battle of *Arfderydd* (Arthuret) — which is a motif also found in the *Life of Kentigern* about a certain Lailoken — and when Geoffrey subsequently wrote a *Life of*

Merlin he portrayed Merlin as a Wild Man of the Woods in the Caledonian forest.

BIBL. Jarman 1960; Clarke 1973; Jarman 1978

Mildburh (Mildburg) St, abbess *d*. 727/30
Mildburh was one of the daughters of *Merewalh of the Magonsæte and his Kentish wife, *Eafa. She became a nun at Much Wenlock, a house founded by her father, under the direction of the Frankish abbess, Liobsynde of Chelles, whom she succeeded in office.

BIBL. Finberg 1961c

Mildrith (Milthryth) St, abbess *d*. after 732
Mildrith was a daughter of *Merewalh of the Magonsæte and his Kentish wife, *Eafa. She was educated at the Frankish monastery of Chelles, and joined her mother when the latter retired into the monastery which she had founded at Minster-in-Thanet. On Eafa's death in 694, Mildrith succeeded her as abbess. She died after 732, and her remains were translated into a new church by her successor as abbess, *Eadburh; she quickly became venerated as a saint. In 1035, her relics were transferred to St Augustine's, Canterbury, which had acquired the lands of Minster-in-Thanet.

BIBL. Rollason 1982

Morcar thegn *d*. 1015
Morcar and his brother *Sigeferth were two of the leading noblemen of eleventh-century Northumbria. They seem to have been connected with the ætheling *Athelstan, son of *Æthelred II, whose mother was the daughter of *Thored, earl of Northumbria; both Morcar and Sigeferth were beneficiaries under the terms of the ætheling's will. Morcar married Ealdgyth, a niece of another Northumbrian ealdorman, *Ælfhelm, and of the Mercian thegn *Wulfric Spot. He was thus a cousin by marriage of *Ælfgifu of Northampton, daughter of *Ælfhelm, who married *Cnut in about 1013. Morcar and his brother were among those nobles of the north who accepted Cnut's father, *Swein Forkbeard, as king in 1013 and it was probably this act which led to their downfall after the death of Swein and the return of Æthelred II in 1014. The brothers were murdered at the kings's court in the winter of 1015, by *Eadric Streona, ealdorman of Mercia. This incident provoked a fatal breach between the king and his son *Edmund Ironside (see Sigeferth).

BIBL. Williams 1986: 5; Sawyer 1979: xlii-iii

Morgan ab Owain king of Gwent and Glywysing *d*. 974
Morgan Hen ('the Old') was a son of Owain ap *Hywel, king of Gwent, whose submission to *Athelstan, king of the West Saxons, in 927 is recorded in the *Anglo-Saxon Chronicle*. Morgan had succeeded his father by 931, in which year he attended Athelstan's court in the company of *Hywel Dda and *Idwal the Bald. He continued to be present on occasion

at the West Saxon court into the 950s. It was probably Morgan ab Owain rather than the much earlier Morgan ab Arthrwys in the late seventh century who gave his name to Morgannwg, signifying the now united former kingdoms, Gwent and Glywysing.

BIBL. Lloyd 1911, vol. I: 274, 338; Bartrum 1966: 139; Davies 1978: 92; Davies 1982: 103

Morgenau bishop of St David's 984—99

Morgenau was bishop in the reign of *Maredudd ap Owain at a time when the churches of Deheubarth suffered the attacks of Irish Vikings, and in 999 he was slain by them. According to Gerald of Wales he introduced meat into the diet at St David's, thereby breaking with the tradition of a strict vegetarian diet supposedly established by St *David so that his death acquired retributive overtones.

BIBL. Lloyd 1911, vol. I: 352

Mungo *see* **Kentigern**

N

Nechtán (Nectu) grandson of Verb, Pictish king *c*. 602–21

The precise genealogical details relating to this king, and indeed the identification of his dynasty remain uncertain. Bannerman has identified Nechtán or Nectu grandson of Verb as being also a grandson of *Gartnait (*c*. 584–602) his predecessor in the Pictish kingship. Nechtán is accorded a reign-length of about 20 years in the Pictish king-lists which would identify him with Nechtán son of Cano, who died, according to the *Annals of Ulster*, in 621. Since Gartnait, son of *Áedán mac Gabhráin, is said in the *Senchus Fer nAlban* to have had a son called Cano, then Nectu grandson of Verb, and Nechtán son of Cano, son of Gartnait, would indeed seem to be the same person. It is possible that he was the same person as Neithon son of Guithno of the Strathclyde Britons, who must also have flourished in the period 600–30. Whichever parentage we ascribe to Nectu of the Pictish king-lists, it does appear that the Picts were ruled in his time either by a king of Dál Riata extraction, or by a king of the Strathclyde Britons.

BIBL. Anderson 1973: 63, 93, 116, 154, 248, *n*.105; Bannerman 1974: 92-4

Nechtán son of Derile, Pictish king 706–24

Nechtán succeeded his brother *Bruide in the Pictish kingship in 706. Hostilities continued between the Picts and Northumbrians into Nechtán's reign. In 711 a slaughter of the Picts in the plain of Manaw (in Lothian) is recorded. But soon after this incident, Nechtán seems to have entered into a peace-treaty with the English which was still in effect at the time when *Bede was writing his *Ecclesiastical History*. Bede also informs us that Nechtán sent emissaries to *Ceolfrith, abbot of Monkwearmouth and Jarrow, seeking advice on the question of the Roman *versus* the Celtic reckoning of the date of Easter. Nechtán was also understood by Bede to have asked for masons to build a stone church 'in the Roman fashion'. This church may eventually have been built at Restenneth in Angus. In 717 Nechtán expelled the *familia* of Iona from their Pictish monasteries and sent them back across 'the Spine of Britain' to Argyll. The monastic community on Iona itself had accepted the Roman Easter in 716, under the persuasive influence of *Ecgberht, and those monks expelled by Nechtán may have only been the recalcitrant supporters of the 'Celtic' party from Iona. Nechtán had almost certainly joined the Roman party under the influence of *Adomnán, a former abbot of Iona who spent the period 688–704 travelling in Pictland and elsewhere, promoting the idea of the righteousness of the Roman Easter. It was Bishop Ecgberht, however, who completed the conversion process to Roman ways not only on Iona but also at Nechtán's court. The legend of *Curetan *alias* Boniface in the Breviary of Aberdeen shows Nechtán befriending Curetan of Rosemarkie, a bishop who belonged to Adomnán's Romanizing party within Scotland.

The only sign of political unrest in the first part of Nechtán's reign is the record of his taking his brother, Talorg son of Drustán, captive in 713. Nechtán himself retired to a monastery in 724, a move which signalled a period of anarchy and incessant dynastic warfare within the Pictish kingdom. It would seem that Nechtán had been forced into monastic retirement by his successor, *Drest, in 724, since he re-emerged two years later only to be taken captive by Drest. Between 726 and 729 the Pictish kingship was disputed by no less than four rival claimants, until *Óengus I finally established himself as victor. During this time, Nechtán did succeed in regaining the kingship for a brief period in 728 after crushing one of his rivals, Alpín, in a battle at Crathie (Caislen Credi). But Óengus won a final victory over Nechtán in the battle of Monith Carno in 729, after which Nechtán most likely retired back to his monastery. He died in 732.

BIBL. Anderson 1973: 85-9, 173-8; Duncan 1981: 20-36; Smyth 1984: 73-6, 137-8

Neithon son of Guipno, king of the Strathclyde Britons *c*. 600—30 *see* **Nechtán** grandson of Verb

Nennius scholar *fl.* early ninth century

Five medieval manuscripts of the *Historia Brittonum* (*History of the Britons*) assign the text to Nennius (or Ninnius), who describes himself in a prologue as a disciple of *Elfoddw. Elfoddw, styled 'archbishop' of Gwynedd in the annals, died in 809 and the first edition of the *Historia Brittonum* appeared in the fourth year of *Merfyn ap Gwriad in 829/30. The prologue, however, is probably of mid-eleventh-century date. Nennius appears to have been the name of a British scholar, known by 817 as the inventor of an alphabet, but how correctly the *Historia* was attributed to him is uncertain. The *Historia Brittonum* belongs to the genre of national history. Though it contains material on *Germanus and *Patrick, it is concerned with the origin-legend of the Britons and seemingly more with secular than ecclesiastical traditions, particularly those of the fifth century and early sixth concerning the coming of the Anglo-Saxons to Britain, the British leaders — *Vortigern, *Ambrosius Aurelianus and *Arthur — and the kings of the Anglo-Saxons. The *Historia Brittonum* was re-edited several times in the ninth and tenth centuries.

BIBL. Chadwick 1958b: 37ff.; Dumville 1975—6; Dumville 1986

Ninian (Nynia) bishop of Whithorn *c*. 500—50

Ninian is stated by *Bede in his *Ecclesiastical History* to have been a Briton who evangelized the Southern Picts (south of the Mounth) 'a long time before' *Columba laboured among the Northern Picts. Ninian was a diocesan bishop who built a stone church, called *Candida Casa* ('The White House') which was dedicated to St Martin and which is correctly identified with Whithorn in Galloway. Attempts to make Ninian a contemporary of St Martin of Tours are based on a twelfth-century *Life* of Ninian by Ailred of Rievaulx, but neither Bede nor the late eighth-century Latin poem (*Miracula Nynie Episcopi*) make such a claim. Bede's testimony on British and Pictish affairs has been overrated by historians. Columba did not convert the Northern Picts, who remained pagan into the early seventh century, and Ninian's missionary career is now more plausibly dated to the sixth century rather than to the fifth. He is stated in the *Miracula* to have been exiled by a wicked local ruler called *Tuduael* identified by Macquarrie with Tutagual or Tudwal, father of *Riderch Hen, a Strathclyde British king who ruled *c*. 580–612 and who was a friend and contemporary of St *Kentigern. The *Life* of Kentigern claims that when that saint came to settle at Glasgow, he found there a cemetery which had been consecrated by Ninian, suggesting some degree of continuity between the two men. The *Miracula* poem alleges that Ninian visited Rome where he was consecrated a bishop. Such a journey was possible but unlikely, and it was in Bede's interest to emphasize Ninian's 'regular training' in Rome as part of his support for the pro-Roman party within Pictland and as part of his outspoken antagonism towards British Christianity. The location of Ninian's mission among the Picts has been variously identified as south of the Forth or among the fictional 'Picts of Galloway'. The proper location would seem to be in Fife and Perthshire. Ninian's Pictish territories or their inhabitants are called the *Naturae* who were probably the same as the *Niuduera* of Fife mentioned in the anonymous *Life* of *Cuthbert. Accepting that *Candida Casa* is indeed Whithorn, then if Ninian was buried there as Bede claimed, it is difficult to reconcile this final phase of Ninian's career with that of his earlier episcopal authority among the Picts of Fife. Duncan believed that Ninian's mission was located among the Britons south of the Forth and perhaps based at Peebles. Ninian was believed to have died on 16 September. His medieval cult is demonstrated in place-names as far apart as the Isle of Man and the Shetlands. One of the earliest dedications — St Ninians near Stirling — goes back to the twelfth century.

BIBL. Duncan 1981: 31-3; Macquarrie 1987; MacQueen 1961; Radford 1957

Nothhelm (Nunna) king of Sussex *d. c*. 725
The early history of Sussex is poorly documented, but a series of charters in the name of Nothhelm, or Nunna, has been preserved, dating from the late seventh and early eighth centuries. Nothhelm is said to have been a kinsman of *Ine of Wessex, whom he accompanied on the campaign against the Britons of Dumnonia in 710. He gave to his sister Nothgyth land for the foundation of a monastery, but its site is unknown.

BIBL. Stenton 1971: 58, 73

Nothhelm archbishop of Canterbury 735–9
Nothhelm, a priest of London, was a friend and correspondent of *Bede, for whom he searched the archives of both Canterbury and Rome for material relating to the conversion of the English and the history of the English church. He became archbishop of Canterbury in 735.

BIBL. *HE* Preface: 2-7; Brooks 1984: 80-3

Nunna *see* **Nothhelm** king of Sussex

O

Oda St, archbishop of Canterbury 941—58

Oda was of Scandinavian origin; his father had been a warrior in the army of *Ivarr, who had settled in England. Oda himself was brought up by an English thegn (and a Christian) called Æthelhelm and entered the church. In c. 926 he was made bishop of Ramsbury and rose to be an important man in the counsels of King *Athelstan. He was one of the ambassadors sent to Hugh, duke of the Franks, in 936, to negotiate the restoration of Athelstan's nephew, Louis d'Outremer, as king of the Franks. It was probably during this visit to Frankia that Oda became a monk, for he is known to have made his profession of obedience at the reformed house of Fleury-sur-Loire, with which Duke Hugh was closely associated. In 941, Oda became archbishop of Canterbury. The first Code of King *Edmund, largely ecclesiastical in content, may be his work. Oda was a reformer of great determination, particularly interested in the east midlands and East Anglia, both areas which had at one time been under Danish control. In the 950s the bishopric of Elmham was re-established, with a new cathedral and extensive endowments. Oda also maintained contact with the continental movement for ecclesiastical reform, sending his nephew, *Oswald (later archbishop of York), to study at Fleury. He acquired the site of the defunct monastery of Ely from King *Eadwig in 957, presumably intending to re-establish regular life there, but in 958 he quarrelled with the king, and the project was left for others to complete. The dispute was occasioned by Eadwig's marriage to his kinswoman, *Ælfgifu, whom Oda forced him to repudiate on the grounds of consanguinity. The real reason was probably that Eadwig's marriage threatened the position of his younger brother, *Edgar, as heir to the West Saxon kingdom. In the same year, 958, Oda died on 2 June and was buried at Canterbury.

BIBL. Brooks 1984: 222-37

Odhrán (Oran) St, monk of Iona c. 570

Odhrán is alleged to have offered himself as a foundation sacrifice to *Columba and to be the first of the community to be buried in the monastic cemetery on Iona. In return for his self-sacrifice (it is not told how he died), Columba decreed that 'no prayer shall be granted to anyone at my grave, unless he first make it to thee'. The foundation of the monastery on Iona followed. Arguments against the authenticity of this tale from the Old Irish *Life* of Columba are strong, it being scarcely credible that such a barbarous and pagan rite could survive the introduction of Christianity. There is confusion in the early Irish calendars between this Odhrán of Iona and others of the name. Odhrán is not mentioned in *Adomnán's *Life* unless we accept that he is the same monk as an unnamed Briton, whom Adomnán believed was the first of the community to have died on Iona, and whom Columba blessed in his last moments but did not wait in his cell to see him actually die. Odhrán's name does not occur in the early list of the 12 initial followers of Columba, but since Columba founded Iona some years after his arrival in Britain (in 563), it is possible that Odhrán joined the community later, in time for the foundation of Iona. It is difficult to dismiss the cult of Odhrán altogether. His name appears in the *Martyrology of Óengus* (*c*. 800) but the notes associating him with Iona and with Reilig Odhráin ('Odhrán's Cemetery') there, may derive from a much later time. The tale of Odhrán's death was most probably invented to explain the name of the monastic cemetery on Iona. Odhrán's festival was kept on 27 October.

BIBL. Anderson 1922, vol. 1: 45-6; Reeves 1857: 202-3, 417-18

Óengus I son of Fergus (Onuist son of Urguist) Pictish king 729–61

Óengus I came to power in Pictland during the anarchy which marked the closing years of the reign of *Nechtán son of Derile. Óengus appears for the first time in 727 when he defeated a rival, *Drest, in no less than three battles. Óengus defeated another rival, *Alpín, in the following year, slaying his son, in a battle at Moncrieffe, after which Alpín was defeated at Crathie by Nechtán and forced to fly to Dál Riata. Óengus emerged as the ultimate victor in 729 when he defeated Nechtán in the battle of Monith Carno and on 12 August he defeated and slew his old rival Drest in the battle of Druim Derg Blathuug. Óengus was now the undisputed overlord of the Picts, and his reign which lasted for more than 30 years shows him to have been one of the most powerful and successful Pictish kings. He turned his hostilities against the Scots of Dál Riata early in his reign. In 736 he wasted the territories of Dál Riata and stormed Dunadd, one of its chief fortresses, capturing *Dúngal son of *Selbach and his brother, two leaders of the Cenél Loairn. Óengus's brother, Talorgen, followed up this victory in the same year by defeating Muiredach, the king of Cenél Loairn (a cousin of Dúngal), in the battle of Cnoc Coirpre in Calathros.

Óengus seems to have ruled as overlord not only of the Picts, but of Scots Dál Riata as well, from 736 until 'the ebbing of his sovereignty' in 750. In 741 we read of the 'smiting of Dál Riata by Óengus son of Fergus', while in 739 that same king drowned Talorgen son of Drustán, the Pictish tribal king of Atholl, who had been captured and bound in an incident near Dunolly in Cenél Loairn territory back in 734. It is thought that the boar symbol displayed on a rock carving at Dunadd may date from this period of Pictish domination in Dál Riata. Óengus's overlordship of Picts and Scots began to 'ebb' in 750 when his army, led by his brother, Talorgen, was heavily defeated by the Strathclyde Britons, ruled at this time by *Teudebur map Bili. Talorgen, brother of Óengus, lost his life in that encounter and it is probable that *Áed Find managed to free Dál Riata from Pictish domination as a result of this Northern British victory over the Picts in 750. Óengus continued to reign in Pictland until his death in 761 when he was succeeded by his brother, *Bruide.

BIBL. Anderson 1973: 86-8, 96-9, 182-9; Smyth 1984: 73-5, 177-8

Óengus II son of Fergus, king of Scots and Picts 820–34

Óengus succeeded his brother *Constantine as king of the Picts where he appears in Pictish king-lists as *Unuist* son of *Uurguist*. As a king of Dál Riata he belonged to the main line of descent from Fergus of the Cenél Gabhráin, and his rule over the Picts in succession to his brother suggests the continued growth of Scottish domination over Pictland. The reign of Óengus experienced the continued ferocity of Viking attack in the west of Scotland and the consequent shift in Dál Riata power from Argyll east into Perth and Fife. Óengus is said to have refounded St Andrews as a new cult centre of that saint.

BIBL. Anderson 1973: 97-9, 192-3; Smyth 1984: 177-80, 186-7

Œthelwald king of Deira, *d*. 655 see **Æthelwold**

Offa St, king of Essex *d*. 709

Offa, son of *Sighere of Essex, became king of the East Saxons about 707, but abdicated and went to Rome in 709, where he became a monk. He died soon afterwards.

BIBL. Yorke 1985: 22-3

Offa king of Mercia 757–96

Offa came to power after the murder of his kinsman, *Æthelbald of Mercia, in 757. He had first to defeat a rival claimant to the Mercian kingship, Beornred, of whom nothing is known but the name, and in this struggle, the Mercian supremacy over the other south English kingdoms, established by Æthelbald, was lost. It was Offa's achievement to rebuild this overlordship. The methods which he used are obscure, due to the general lack of contemporary sources for his reign, but it is clear that military conquest played a large part in Mercian success. It is also clear that this success was limited. The Kentish kingdom, which was in Offa's power by 764, rose in revolt in 776, when Mercians and Kentishmen fought together at the battle of Otford. For some ten years, until 785, Kent was effectively independent of Mercia. For the remaining southern kingdoms, even less evidence survives, but Offa was overlord of Sussex and Essex, and probably East Anglia, whose king, *Æthelberht, was killed on his orders. In Wessex, Mercian influence was not so strong; Offa defeated King *Cynewulf at the battle of Bensington in 779, but it was only when *Beorhtric succeeded in 786 that Mercian control was established in Wessex, and Beorhtric married Offa's daughter, *Eadburh. In the 770s, when his power was greatest, Offa was acknowledged Bretwalda and at this time at least, occasionally used the title *rex Anglorum* (king of the English). Outside England, Offa negotiated with the most powerful European ruler, Charlemagne, king of the Franks (and, from 800–14, emperor of the West). In 796, the two kings concluded a trading agreement, and a marriage alliance was proposed, but came to nothing. The papacy also regarded Offa as the most important king in England. It was to his court that the papal legates, George of Ostia and Theophylact of

Todi, were despatched in 786, and their legatine council was held in Mercia, under Offa's auspices.

In many ways, Offa's policies were those of a king of the English, rather than a king of Mercia. His reform of the coinage, based upon the reorganization carried out in Frankia by Charlemagne, produced the first silver pennies used in England; this not only became common currency throughout eighth-century England, but remained the standard coinage of England until the thirteenth century. His other lasting monument was Offa's Dyke, the great earthwork which delineated the boundary between English and Welsh. The building of this dyke left some formerly English territory on the Welsh side, as well as some Welsh lands on the English side, and must have been the result of negotiations with the Welsh rulers. The organization and manpower required for its construction give some idea of the efficiency of Offa's administration. Unfortunately the Code of laws which he is known to have issued has not survived, or at least has not yet been identified. It is possible that the *Tribal Hidage*, a tribute-list of the lands subordinate to a Mercian king, dates from his time, but it could belong to the reign of Æthelbald or to that of *Wulfhere; all that can be said is that it gives some picture of the material resources available to a Mercian ruler of the seventh or eighth centuries.

Offa's power, though great, was limited. The Kentish revolt of 776 was ultimately unsuccessful, but even after Mercian rule was re-established, Kentish hostility was strong. Its focus was *Jænberht, archbishop of Canterbury, and it was in order to diminish Jænberht's power that Offa persuaded the papacy to grant archiepiscopal status to the Mercian see of Lichfield in 787. This was, in effect, an admission of Mercian inability to command Kentish sympathies. It was the archbishop of Lichfield, *Hygeberht, and not Jænberht, who consecrated Offa's son, *Ecgfrith, in 787, as king of the Mercians. Offa stands as the greatest English king before Alfred, but in spite of his occasional use of the title, he did not succeed in making himself 'king of the English'.

BIBL. Stenton 1971: 206-25; Brooks 1984: 1: 11-21

Ohthere (Ottar) merchant traveller *fl.* second half of the ninth century
Ohthere was a Norwegian from the region of Tromso (Halgoland), who visited the court of King *Alfred in Wessex, and supplied the king with material about the northern world, which was incorporated into the Old English translation of the *History against the pagans* of Orosius. Ohthere described to King Alfred, whom he refers to as his lord, a voyage around the north of Norway into the White Sea, and the region known as Bjarmaland. He also told of his journey to *Sciringesheal* (Kaupang, in Oslofjord) and thence to Hedeby (Schleswig) in Denmark. It is not entirely clear what Ohthere was doing in England. He presented the king with some walrus-ivory, and it is most likely that he was a merchant, and therefore under Alfred's protection, rather than a permanent member of the king's household. (See also *Wulfstan.)

BIBL. Lund 1984

Oisc see **Hengest** and **Iurminric**

Olaf son of Indulf, king of Scots *c*. 971−7

Olaf's rule as king of Scots is in some doubt but he is styled 'King of Scotland' (Rí Alban) at his death in 977 in the *Chronicum Scotorum* and in the *Annals of Tigernach*. If Olaf's rule in Scotland is accepted, then he was clearly reigning in opposition to *Kenneth II (son of *Malcolm I) whose reign over the Scots extended from 971 to 995. By slaying Olaf in 977 Kenneth II sought to exclude the descendants of *Constantine II from the Scottish kingship and to confine the succession within his own branch of the dynasty. Olaf bore a Norse name, as did his father, *Indulf, and his brother *Culen Ring.

BIBL. Anderson 1922, vol. 1: 484-6; Smyth 1984: 210, 221, 224

Olafr ball *d. c*. 915

Olafr *ball* was one of the followers of *Ragnall, king of York. In 914 he was given some of the lands of the community of St *Cuthbert, much against their will, and when they remonstrated with him, committed the serious error of insulting the saint in his own church:

'What', he said, 'can this dead man, Cuthbert, do to me that he should threaten me every day? I swear by my powerful gods, Thor and Odinn, that from this hour, I shall be the most terrible enemy of you all.'

Bishop Cuthheard and his priests then fell upon their knees and called upon the saint, who responded in the approved fashion. As Olafr, 'that son of the devil' attempted to leave the church, 'when he had one foot across the threshold, he felt as if his other was impaled on iron. The pain pierced his devilish heart, he fell, and the devil thrust his sinful soul into hell.'

BIBL. Arnold 1885: 196-214 (The history of St Cuthbert); translated in Whitelock 1955, no. 6: 262

Olafr Gothfrithson king of Dublin 934−41, York 939−41

Olafr succeeded his father *Gothfrith as king of the Vikings of Dublin in 934. In 937 he allied with *Constantine II, king of Scots, in an attempt to secure the kingdom of York also, but was defeated by King *Athelstan of Wessex at the battle of *Brunanburh*. A second, successful attempt was made on the death of Athelstan in 939. In the following year, Olafr attacked Mercia also, sacking Tamworth, and seizing the Five Boroughs (Leicester, Lincoln, Stamford, Nottingham and Derby). He died in 941, and was succeeded by his cousin, *Olafr Sigtryggson.

BIBL. Smyth 1979: 31-106

Olafr Helgi, the Stout king of Norway 1014/15−28, *d*. 1030

Numerous English churches are dedicated to Olafr Helgi (St Olave), whose first appearance in these islands was with the 'immense raiding-army' of *Thorkell the Tall in 1009. When Thorkell in 1012 changed sides and entered the service of *Æthelred II, Olafr moved off to Frankia and by 1013 is found at the court of Duke Richard II of Normandy, Æthelred's brother-in-law. Here he became a Christian, under the duke's sponsorship, and seems to have entered Æthelred's employ, returning with him to England in 1014. It was perhaps his earnings from the king of England which financed his expedition to Norway in 1014 or 1015, in which he drove out the pro-Danish earls of Hladir, Sveinn and *Hakon, and established himself as king. His main ambition was the conversion of Norway, begun by his namesake *Olafr Tryggvason, which was accomplished with the help of missionaries from England. In 1028, Olafr was driven from his kingdom by King *Cnut, and fled to Russia. He returned in 1030, but was killed at the battle of Stiklarstadir. Miracles quickly began to be reported around his tomb and his body, which was found incorrupt, was translated to his own foundation of St Clement's at Nidaros, where his bishop, Grimkell, declared him a saint. In 1035, his son Magnus was fetched from Kiev, and the Norwegians rebelled against Danish suzerainty and accepted him as king.

BIBL. Jones 1968: 374-84; Campbell 1949: 76-82

Olafr Sigtryggson (Cuaran) king of Dublin 945−80, York 941−3, 949−52, *d*. 981

Olafr, nicknamed Cuaran ('sandal') was the son of *Sigtrygg Caech. He succeeded his cousin *Olafr Gothfrithson as king of York in 941. In the following year, King *Edmund of Wessex overran the Five Boroughs which Olafr Gothfrithson had conquered. Olafr Cuaran made peace with Edmund and accepted baptism in 943, but by the end of the same year had been driven from York; whether by West Saxon pressure, or by Scandinavian rivals is unclear. By 945, he had gained acceptance in Dublin, but not until 949 was he able to regain his position in York, apparently with the aid of King *Eadred of Wessex, who had managed to oust *Eirikr Bloodaxe from York in the previous year. In 952, Olafr was once again driven from York and Eirikr returned. Olafr went back to Ireland and ruled in Dublin until 980, when he retired as a monk to Iona. He died in 981. His son, Sigtrygg Silkenbeard, founded Christchurch cathedral, Dublin.

BIBL. Smyth 1979: 107-25

Olafr Tryggvason king of Norway 995−1000

Much has been written concerning Olafr Tryggvason, most of it legendary. He was a grandson of King Harald Finehair of Norway, and spent his childhood in exile, probably in Russia. He appears in English history as a sea-raider in the 990s, and it is most likely he who led the Viking force which fought and killed Ealdorman *Byrhtnoth of Essex at Maldon in 991. He was certainly attacking London in 994, but in the same year accepted King *Æthelred's offer of Danegeld, made peace and accepted baptism, with Æthelred as his godfather. The ceremony took place at Andover, and 'Olafr gave him his word, and kept it too, that he would never again come to England as an enemy'. In 995 he used his English loot to finance a successful bid for the kingship of Norway. Five years later, he was overthrown by his enemies at the great sea-battle of Svold; when all was lost, King Olafr, in his scarlet cloak, leapt from the deck of his mighty warship, 'Long Snake', and 'never again returned to his kingdom in Norway.'

BIBL. Jones 1968: 131-40

Onuist son of Urguist *see* **Óengus I**

Oran St, *see* **Odhrán**

Ordgar ealdorman 964-70

Ordgar, a Devonshire thegn, was the father of *Ælfthryth who married, first, Æthelwold, ealdorman of East Anglia, and after his death, King *Edgar, who made Ordgar ealdorman of Devon. His authority probably extended over Cornwall, and perhaps Somerset and Dorset as well. His son, *Ordwulf, was the founder of Tavistock Abbey, and the family remained prominent in the West Country throughout the eleventh century, until the Conquest of 1066.

BIBL. Finberg 1943; Finberg 1964c

Ordwulf thegn *d.* after 1005

Ordwulf son of *Ordgar was the brother of *Ælfthryth, queen and wife of *Edgar. He and his wife, Ælfwynn, founded the abbey at Tavistock, Devon, in 981. Ordwulf held high office during the reign of his nephew, *Æthelred II and was perhaps high-reeve of Lifton hundred, Devon, in which the abbey of Tavistock lay. From about 993, he was one of the king's most prominent advisors, but retired in 1005, perhaps entering Tavistock as a monk. He was a literate and cultured man, for *Ælfwold, bishop of Crediton, left two books to him in his will, a martyrology and a volume of the works of the Frankish scholar, Hrabanus Maurus (780-856). He died on 18 December, in an unknown year, and his descendants were still important local local men in the period down to the Norman Conquest.

BIBL. Hart 1975: 352-3; Keynes 1980: 188-9, 192, 209; Finberg 1951: 1-5

Osbald king of Northumbria 796 *d.* 799

Osbald, who was briefly king of Northumbria in 796, seems to have been an adherent of King *Æthelred, who was expelled from the kingdom in 778/9 by *Ælfwald. This is the inference to be drawn from the fact that Osbald soon afterwards was implicated in the murder of Ælfwald's *patricius*, Beorn. After Æthelred's restoration to the kingship in 790, Osbald was promoted to the rank of *patricius* himself, in 793, and on Æthelred's murder in 796, he was 'appointed to the kingdom by some nobles'. He held power for only 27 days, before the royal household and the Northumbrian nobles deserted and attacked him. Osbald went to Lindisfarne, where he seems to have had supporters, for when he fled to the land of the Picts, some of the Lindisfarne monks accompanied him. In a letter addressed to Osbald after his deposition, *Alcuin reproached him for breaking his vow to enter the religious life, and accused him of complicity in Æthelred's murder. He urged Osbald not to 'pile sin upon sin by ravaging the land', but to fulfil his vow and become a monk. Osbald took his advice, dying in 799. He was buried at York.

BIBL. Simeon of Durham, *Historia Regum*, trans. in Whitelock 1955, no. 3: 245, 248, 250; Thacker 1981: 216-17; Whitelock 1955, no. 200: 785-6

Osburh wife of King Æthelwulf, *d*. before 855

Osburh was the first wife of King *Æthelwulf of Wessex, and mother of his sons, *Athelstan, *Æthelbald, *Æthelberht, *Æthelred I and *Alfred, and his daughter, *Æthelswith. Osburh was a Kentishwoman, whose father Oslac was the king's butler (*pincerna*); he is said to have been descended from *Stuf and Wihtgar, the semi-legendary Jutish conquerors of the Isle of Wight in the fifth century. *Asser presents Osburh as a woman of some accomplishment, who took pains over the education of her children. She promised a book of English heroic poems to whichever of her sons should learn to read it first; needless to say, the feat was accomplished by her youngest, Alfred. She must have been dead by 856, when Æthelwulf married his second wife, *Judith, daughter of the Frankish king, Charles the Bald.

BIBL. Keynes and Lapidge 1983a: 13-4, 68, 75

Oscytel archbishop of York *c*. 955−71

Oscytel was the uncle of *Oswald, his successor as archbishop of York, and of Thurcytel, abbot of Bedford and of Crowland. His name, and that of Thurcytel, suggests that he was of Danish extraction (like Archbishop *Oda of Canterbury, who was also an uncle of Oswald). This hypothesis is to some extent confirmed by Oscytel's tenure of land in Leicestershire, which lay within the Danelaw. He was bishop of Dorchester-on-Thames by 951 (and possibly as early as 949), which served the whole of the east midland area once part of the diocese of Leicester. In about 955, he became archbishop of York, after the disgrace and imprisonment of his predecessor, *Wulfstan. It is probable that he continued to hold Dorchester-on-Thames, for he was buried at Thame, a manor belonging to Dorchester.

BIBL. Hart 1975: 353-5

Osgod Clapa staller *d*. 1054

Osgod Clapa ('coarse, rough') may have been one of the Danish followers of *Cnut, but it is also possible that he came from the family of *Theodred, bishop of London, established in England in the mid tenth century. He was certainly in Cnut's service, for he is described as a staller ('placeman'), someone with an office in the royal court. He may have commanded the royal fleet. He held land in Norfolk, Suffolk and Essex, and his daughter, Gytha, married another Essex magnate, *Tovi the Proud, in 1042. In 1046, he was exiled by King Edward the Confessor and fled to Flanders; it was probably there that he died, 'suddenly, in his bed', in 1054.

BIBL. *ASC* s.a. 1042, 1046, 1049, 1054; Nightingale 1987; Williams 1988: 333-6

Osgyth *see* **Osyth**

Oslac ealdorman 963–75

Oslac was appointed ealdorman by King *Edgar in 963. At first his authority was confined to southern Northumbria, the old Danish kingdom of York, but by 966, he was senior ealdorman of all Northumbria, including the territory of the high-reeves of Bamburgh. His name (Aslakr) is Norse, suggesting that he came from a Danelaw family, and his son, *Thored, held land in Cambridgeshire. Oslac was banished for unspecified reasons after the death of Edgar in 975. The *Chronicle* describes the 'grey-haired hero, wise and sage in counsel' being driven into exile 'over the turmoil of the waves'. Though it also calls him 'the famous Earl Oslac' his fame has not lasted. Even the date of his death is unknown.

BIBL. Whitelock 1959: 76-9

Osred king of Northumbria 705–16

Osred, son of King *Aldfrith of Northumbria, became king at the age of eight, against the opposition of *Eadwulf. Osred's cause was supported by his aunt, *Ælfflæd, abbess of Whitby, his *patricius* *Beorhtfrith and his foster-father, St *Wilfrid. *Bede hailed Osred as a new Josiah, but his later conduct was bitterly criticized by St *Boniface, who described him as 'driven by the spirit of wantonness'. *Æthelwulf, in his *De Abbatibus*, accused him of killing many of the Northumbrian nobles and forcing others into exile, or compelling them to become monks. Perhaps because of these deeds, Osred was murdered in 716. Despite the strictures of St Boniface and other churchmen, he was remembered favourably at the church of Beverley.

BIBL. Kirby 1974a: 1-34

Osred king of Northumbria 788–90

Osred son of *Alhred succeeded his murdered kinsman *Ælfwald as king of Northumbria in 788 or 789. In 790 he was 'deceived by the guile of his nobles, taken prisoner and...tonsured in the city of York'. Banished from his kingdom, he fled to the Isle of Man. In 792, he attempted to stage a coup against his supplanter, *Æthelred, but was betrayed and killed. He was buried at Tynemouth. His brother, St *Alhmund, was murdered in 802.

BIBL. Simeon of Durham, *Historia Regum*, trans. in Whitelock 1955, no. 3: 246-7

Osric king of the Hwicce *c.* 675–85

Osric, king of the Hwicce, and his brother Oshere (679–93) are remembered chiefly as patrons of the emergent church in the west. It was in their time that a bishopric for the Hwicce was established at Worcester, in 679 or 680, and at about the same time, Osric established the monastery of St Peter at Gloucester, with the assent of his overlord, *Æthelred of Mercia. Simultaneously, his brother Oswald founded Pershore Abbey, Worcestershire. Osric had already, in 675, founded a monastery at Bath, a double-house presided over by an abbess with the Frankish name of

*Bertha. Oshere established minsters at Ripple, Worcestershire, in 678, at Inkberrow, Gloucestershire, in the period 693−9, and at Withington, in the same shire. Very little is known of these smaller churches, but Cuthswith, abbess of Inkberrow, was a woman of cultured tastes, and a friend of St *Boniface.

BIBL. Finberg 1961b: 167-8; Sims-Williams 1976

Osric king of Northumbria 718−29
Osric, who succeeded *Cœnred as king of Northumbria in 718, was probably a son of King *Aldfrith, and brother of King *Osred. He died in 729, appointing Cœnred's brother, *Ceolwulf, as his heir.

BIBL. Kirby 1974a: 1−34

Osthryth St, queen *d*. 697
Osthryth, daughter of *Oswiu of Northumbria, married *Æthelred of Mercia, in one of a series of marriages between the Northumbrian and Mercian royal kindreds (see *Peada, *Alhfrith). The intention was presumably to establish peace between the two nations, but this aim was not achieved. Osthryth and Æthelred founded the monastery at Bardney, in Lindsey, to which the queen translated the relics of her saintly uncle, King *Oswald. At first the community refused to accept the remains of Oswald, who had conquered Lindsey and attached it to Northumbria, and only a heavenly light which stood all night above his corpse persuaded them to admit him. The hostility between Mercians and Northumbrians was manifested in 697, when Osthryth herself was murdered by the Mercian nobles. She was buried at Bardney, to which her husband eventually retired as abbot.

BIBL. *HE* iii, 11: 244-51; Farmer 1978: 304

Osulf high-reeve of Bamburgh before 934−63
Osulf, son of *Ealdred, was hereditary high-reeve of Bamburgh, that is, northern Northumbria. He attests charters of the West Saxon kings, *Athelstan, *Edmund and *Eadred, and after the fall of the last king of Viking York, *Eirikr Bloodaxe, in 954, became ealdorman of Northumbria under West Saxon lordship. His family continued to hold power in Bamburgh throughout the tenth and eleventh centuries.

BIBL. Whitelock 1959: 76-9

Oswald St, king of Northumbria 634−42
Oswald, son of *Æthelfrith, was exiled, along with his brothers, Eanfrith and *Oswiu, during the reign of their rival *Edwin as king of Northumbria (616−33). Oswald and Oswiu, with their sister *Æbbe, were baptized among the Irish. On Edwin's death in 633, Eanfrith seized his father's kingdom in Bernicia, but within the year he was killed by *Cadwallon of Gwynedd, as was Osric of Deira. Oswald then rallied the rest of the Bernicians, and succeeded in killing Cadwallon and putting his army to flight at the battle of Heavenfield, near Hexham. As a result of this

victory he seems to have been accepted as king not only of Bernicia, but of Deira as well, and the year of confusion, when Cadwallon had ravaged Northumbria and its kings had apostasized, was added to the reign of this king 'beloved of God'. *Bede maintains that Oswald was Bretwalda as well as king of Northumbria, but few details of the events of his reign, or the limits of his power, survive. His influence in Wessex is shown by the fact that he was godfather to *Cynegils, whose daughter, Cyneburh, he married. From Bede's standpoint, his most important act was to send for Irish missionaries to establish the church in Northumbria. They were led by St *Aidan, a monk of Iona, who established his bishopric on the island monastery of Lindisfarne. Since Aidan was not proficient in the English tongue, King Oswald, who had learnt Gaelic in exile, frequently acted as his interpreter. Oswald was finally killed by *Penda of Mercia at the battle of *Maserfeld* (Oswestry) and his sanctity was revealed when a horse suffering from colic was cured by contact with the earth on the spot where he fell; a most appropriate first miracle for an English saint. His remains were translated to Bardney, in Lindsey, by his niece, *Osthryth, and in 909, removed again to St Oswald's, Gloucester, by *Æthelflæd of Mercia. His head, however, was preserved at Lindisfarne, in the coffin of St *Cuthbert, which is why that saint is often shown carrying the head of Oswald.

BIBL. Stenton 1971: 81-6; Farmer 1978: 304-5

Oswald St, archbishop of York 971–92

Oswald was of Danish origin; one of his uncles, St *Oda, was the son of one of *Ivarr's Norse followers, and the other, *Oscytel, has a Danish name. Oswald became a priest at Winchester, but his ambition was to take monastic vows. He spent six years at the Cluniac house of Fleury-sur-Loire, one of the centres of reform on the continent. In 958 he returned to England, and entered the household of Oscytel, now archbishop of York. In 961, he himself was promoted to the episcopate, and received the see of Worcester. Oswald built a new church there, dedicated to St Mary, with the idea of transforming the secular chapter into a monastic establishment, a transformation which was effected only very gradually. Monks for the new cathedral chapter were trained at Westbury-on-Trym, by Oswald's Frankish helper, *Germanus. In 971, Oswald, with the help of his close friend, *Æthelwine, ealdorman of East Anglia, re-established a monastery at Ramsey, and transferred the Westbury community there, while Germanus became abbot of Winchcombe. In the same period, Oswald attempted to reform Pershore, though with only temporary success. With *Dunstan and *Æthelwold, Oswald was one of the chief movers of the monastic reform in England. His see at Worcester was the mainspring of his efforts, and by the patronage of King *Edgar, it became the centre of a great liberty, the triple hundred of Oswaldslow, a ship-soke, whose tenants were responsible only to the bishop, and which was withdrawn from the jurisdiction of the ealdorman of Mercia and his officials. Oswald's close connection with the king, coupled with the wealth of Worcester, made him an ideal candidate for the archbishopric of York, when his uncle Oscytel died in 971. The northern see was poorly endowed and the wealth of Worcester was used for the upkeep of the archbishop's household; moreover it was useful, in a separatist province like Northumbria, that the archbishop should be the king's man. Oswald was an excellent administrator, as well as a pious and religious man. A long series of leases survive from his time, showing how the land of Oswaldslow was governed and exploited, and how the bishop provided for his men, and for the discharge of his secular obligations. He produced a memorandum (known as the *Indiculum*) which lays down in details the obligations and services of those who held tenancies of the bishopric of Worcester. The archives of York are less well preserved than those of Worcester, but include a list of lands which Oswald had recovered for the use of the church.

The creation of Oswaldslow aroused the animosity of the ealdorman of Mercia, *Ælfhere, upon whose rights it impinged. After the death of Edgar in 975, this hostility showed itself in attacks on some of the houses refounded and reformed by Oswald, though not on the episcopal see itself. Similar rivalries and encroachments were to characterize episcopal relations with the lay officials in Mercia down to the Norman Conquest.

BIBL. Sawyer 1975: 84-93, 228; John 1966

Oswine St, king of Deira 644−51
On the death of *Edwin of Northumbria in 633, the Northumbrian kingdom split into its two constituent parts, Bernicia going to Eanfrith son of *Æthelfrith, and Deira to Edwin's cousin, Osric son of Ælfric. Both were killed within the year, and Northumbria was united under Eanfrith's brother, *Oswald. Oswine, Osric's son, spent the next few years in exile in Wessex, but after the death of Oswald in 642, he returned to Deira, and was accepted as king, though perhaps under the suzerainty of *Oswiu of Bernicia, who was married to Edwin's daughter, *Eanflæd. As Oswiu's power grew, however, he determined to rid himself of Oswine. In 651, an outright conflict blew up. Oswine refused battle and took refuge with one of this thegns, but was betrayed and murdered. His kinswoman Eanflæd insisted that her husband founded a monastery at Gilling in expiation of this crime, where Oswine was buried and venerated as a saint; its first abbot, Trumhere, was a kinsman of Oswine, the last king of the Deiran line.

BIBL. *HE* iii, 14: 254-61

Oswiu king of Northumbria 642−70
Oswiu, son of *Æthelfrith, became king of Northumbria after the death of his brother, St *Oswald, in 642. It seems to have taken some little time for him to establish his position, and it was not for a year that he was able to recover his dead brother's body, which had been dismembered and displayed on the battlefield of *Maserfeld* (Oswestry) by *Penda of Mercia. He had also to conciliate the Deirans, which he did by marrying *Eanflæd, daughter of *Edwin, and allowing her kinsman, *Oswine, to rule Deira from 644 to 651, when he had him murdered. In place of Oswine, Oswiu made his own nephew Æthelwold, Oswald's son, king of Deira. Æthelwold

subsequently rebelled against his uncle, and in 655 fought against him, in alliance with Penda, at the battle of the *Winwæd*. This was the turning-point of Oswiu's fortunes; he and his son *Alhfrith defeated and killed Penda, and scattered his forces. It was probably from this point that Oswiu was acknowledged as Bretwalda of the southern English. Penda's son, *Peada, was killed the next year, and for three years, Mercia itself was governed as a Northumbrian province, until the advent of *Wulfhere, who restored its independence. Æthelwold was killed at the *Winwæd*, and Deira was given to Alhfrith as under-king. He too rebelled against his father, though no details are known, and is not heard of after 664.

In Oswiu's reign the question of the affiliations of the Northumbrian church became critical. Edwin had brought missionaries from Kent, who followed Roman customs, and though most fled the country on his death, a small core remained at York, around *James the deacon. Oswald and Oswiu, however, had been converted in Ireland, and it was from Iona that Oswald had fetched St *Aidan who established the monastery and bishopric of Lindisfarne. Oswiu's marriage with Eanflæd, who was brought up among her mother's people in Kent, exacerbated the position, for she followed Roman ways. The major problem was the reckoning of the movable feast of Easter, the most important feast of the Christian church. Different systems of calculation were used by Irish and Roman churchmen, which could result in a difference of a month in the chosen date, so that, as *Bede says, 'it sometimes happened that Easter was celebrated twice in the same year, so that the king had finished the fast and was keeping Easter Sunday, while the queen and her people were still in Lent'. To prevent this happening a synod of the Northumbrian church was held at Whitby in 664, under Oswiu's presidency. It plumped for Roman custom. When in the same year, *Deusdedit, archbishop of Canterbury, died, it was Oswiu, in conjunction with *Ecgberht of Kent, who sent his chosen successor to Rome, and when that successor, Wigheard, died at the papal court, it was to Oswiu 'king of the Saxons' that Pope Vitalian wrote to break the news. But already Oswiu's star was setting. Wulfhere of Mercia was establishing his authority amongst the southern English; it was his bishop, Jaruman, who was sent to Essex when King *Sighere apostasized, to recall the province to its faith. Oswiu's overlordship was probably already ended when he died in 670, the first king of Northumbria recorded to have died of illness, rather than in battle. His son *Ecgfrith succeeded him.

BIBL. Stenton 1971: 81-8, 120-2, 232-3

Oswulf king of Northumbria 758–9

The abdication of *Eadberht of Northumbria in 758 seems to have given rise to a bitter feud between the members of the Northumbrian royal line and their more powerful nobles. Eadberht commended his kingdom to his son, Oswulf, but within the year, Oswulf was murdered by his own household (a shocking breach of the code of loyalty) on 24 July 759. On 5 August following, the nobleman *Æthelwold Moll was chosen king in his place. It is not specifically stated that Æthelwold was involved in the king's murder, but it must be regarded as a possibility. In 765,

Æthelwold was driven from Northumbria by Oswulf's kinsman, *Alhred, and Oswulf's son, *Ælfwald, drove out Æthelwold's son *Æthelred in 779; these incidents suggest a long-standing feud between the two families.

BIBL. Simeon of Durham, *Historia Regum* trans. in Whitelock 1955, no. 3: 241-4; Kirby 1974: 1-34

Ottar *see* **Ohthere**

Osyth (Osgyth) St *d. c.* 700
Osyth was the daughter of *Frithuwold of Surrey and his wife Wilburh, sister of *Wulfhere of Mercia. She is said to have been born at her father's palace of Quarrendon, Buckinghamshire, and brought up by her maternal aunt, St Edith, at Aylesbury. Another aunt, St Eadburh, gave her name to Adderbury, Oxfordshire ('Eadburh's fortified place'). Osyth married *Sighere, king of Essex, but left him to become abbess of Chich (St Osyths), Essex.

BIBL. Yorke 1985: 20; Blair 1989: 106-7

Owain ap Hywel king of Deheubarth *d.* 988
When their father died in 950, the Welsh annals show that the three sons of *Hywel Dda, Rhodri, Edwin and Owain were hard-pressed by the sons of *Idwal who recovered power in Gwynedd. Rhodri died in 953 and Edwin in 954, and Owain turned to a consolidation of his position in Deheubarth — he never attempted to annex Gwynedd as his father had done. Though Owain's reign witnessed a considerable amount of learned and historical activity — the writing and collecting of the Harleian genealogies and the compilation of annals — very little is recorded about him. An attack on Morgannwg's most westerly cantref of Gorfynydd in 960 may reflect a redirection of attention away from Gwynedd to this important southern principality but the annals do not indicate persistent campaigning in this area. The quiet undramatic extension of the influence of the leading men of Deheubarth into western Morgannwg seems to have been a more characteristic feature of the late tenth and eleventh centuries. Though he lived until 988, Owain's sons, first *Einion and then *Maredudd, appear to have replaced him in effective power from the early 980s.

BIBL. Lloyd 1911, vol. I: 344-5

Owen king of Strathclyde *c.* 925–37
Owen was the son of *Donald II, king of Scots, and he held the kingship of the Strathclyde Britons under the overlordship of his cousin *Constantine II who had succeeded Donald to the Scottish throne in 900. Owen is consistently seen acting in alliance with Constantine II in their dealings with King *Athelstan. Owen was present at the treaty of Penrith in 927 when the Scots agreed to renounce the Scandinavian alliance against Wessex; he joined Constantine in breaking that treaty in 934 and again by his participation in the battle of *Brunanburh* in 937. He may have been slain at *Brunanburh* since there is no evidence to suggest he was alive after 937.

BIBL. Smyth 1984: 201-4, 229

Owen map Bili (Eugein map Beli) king of the Strathclyde Britons *c*. 642

Owen was one of the more powerful kings of Strathclyde in the tradition of his remote predecessor, *Riderch Hen. In 642 he defeated and slew the Scots king, *Domnall Brecc, in the battle of Strathcarron in Stirlingshire, a victory which signalled the temporary eclipse of Dál Riata power in northern Britain. Owen's brother, *Bruide mac Bili, became overlord of the Picts in the period 672−93, slaying *Ecgfrith, king of Northumbria, in 685 and destroying his army which had invaded Pictland. Clearly, Strathclyde had re-emerged as a dominant power in northern Britain in the seventh century. The date of Owen's death is unknown, but he had presumably died by 658 when the obituary of a certain Guret, king of Strathclyde, is recorded.

BIBL. Jackson 1955: 84; Kirby 1962: 82-3

Owen the Bald king of the Strathclyde Britons, *fl*. 1018

Owen the Bald was the son of *Donald son of Owen who had earlier ruled in Strathclyde and who died in Rome in 975. Owen's brother, Malcolm, had submitted to *Edgar at Chester in 973 in his capacity as 'king of the Cumbrians'. The *Historia Regum* claims that Owen the Bald fought alongside *Malcolm II of Scotland in the Scottish victory over the Bernicians at Carham south of the Tweed, in 1018. The presence of the Strathclyde king in the Scottish army conforms to a well-established tradition of alliance between Owen's father and grandfather on the one hand, with the kings of the Scots on the other. Owen the Bald is the last known king of the Strathclyde Britons, but he may have been succeeded in the Strathclyde kingdom by the future *Duncan I, grandson of Malcolm II of Scotland.

BIBL. Anderson 1922, vol. 1: 550, 577; Smyth 1984: 220, 227, 229, 233

P

Palladius bishop *fl.* early fifth century

The contemporary chronicle of Prosper of Aquitaine records that it was at the urging of the deacon, Palladius, that Pope Celestine sent *Germanus, bishop of Auxerre, to Britain to combat the Pelagian heresy in 429, and that Palladius was himself ordained first bishop of the Irish who believed in Christ in 431. It is not known whether Palladius was a deacon at Auxerre or Rome or what became of him after 431, but Prosper praised Pope Celestine (422–32) for converting the Irish and the relation of Palladius's appointment to the missionary work of *Patrick among the Irish remains unresolved. His Easter Table, however, may lie behind early Irish computistical texts.

BIBL. Hanson 1968: 47, 52ff.; Thomas 1985: 300ff.; Cróinín 1986

Pallig *d.* 1002

In 1001, a Danish host ravaging in the western shires was joined by Pallig, a Dane in the service of King *Æthelred II, who deserted his lord 'in spite of all the pledges which he had given him (and) the great gifts...in estates and gold and silver' which he had received. It is to be presumed that Pallig's English lands lay in Devon, the shire which the Danes had attacked. Later writers make Pallig the brother-in-law of King *Swein Forkbeard of Denmark, and claim that he, his wife Gunnhildr and their son, were among the Danes killed in the massacre of St Brice's Day (13 November) 1002, ordered by the enraged Æthelred. The massacre was real enough, and it is quite possible that the treasonable behaviour of Pallig in 1001 was one of the factors which led Æthelred to believe in a Danish 'fifth column' in England. Whether Pallig came from Scandinavia, or from one of the shires of the English Danelaw, and whether he was Swein's brother-in-law, it is difficult to say.

BIBL. *ASC* s.a. 1001; Williams 1986

Patrick St, missionary bishop *fl.* fifth century

Anxious to protect his converts from the depredations of slavers and to defend himself against what he regarded as unjust criticisms of his work as a missionary bishop among the Irish, alone of fifth-century British figures Patrick has left some account of himself, firstly in his letter to Coroticus (*Ceretic), a British chieftain who had plundered in Ireland, and secondly in his *Confession*, detailing the difficulties and dangers of his episcopate. Patrick reveals himself as a Briton, captured in his youth by tribal raiders and spending several years as a slave in Ireland before returning to convert the Irish to Christianity, eventually as a bishop. If the Sayings of Patrick, found in the early ninth-century *Book of Armagh* — in the first of which Patrick claims to have travelled extensively in Gaul and Italy and among the islands of the Tyrrhenian sea (between Corsica and Sardinia and the Italian mainland) — are not certainly genuine (and they are not), there is no early evidence to support late seventh-century claims that he did so or indeed that he visited Auxerre. There is nothing in the Latin of Patrick's genuine writing to suggest that he had received an education outside Britain. The continuing involvement of the Church in Britain with his mission is implied by the *Confession*, in which Patrick refutes accusations of extravagance and embezzlement. There is no unanimity among scholars as to the date of Patrick — whether the first or the second half of the fifth century — but there is an increasing conviction that he cannot have been the first or the only missionary to the Irish. The contemporary chronicle of Prosper of Aquitaine records that the deacon *Palladius, ordained by Pope Celestine, was sent as first bishop to the Irish who believed in Christ in 431. Unless Patrick worked in Ireland before 431, there must have been some Christian communities in Ireland (perhaps southern Ireland) when he began his mission. Whereabouts in Ireland he worked is also unclear, but though Armagh came afterwards to be regarded as Patrick's principal foundation, Patrick describes in his *Confession* how in a vision it was the people of the 'wood of Foclut' (in Tirawley, Co. Mayo) 'beside the western sea' who begged him to return and preach in Ireland; so that the scene of his activities could have been rather Connaught among the Uí Néill and in their dependent and newly conquered territories to the east. Tradition locates his burial, however, at Downpatrick.

BIBL. Binchy 1962; Hanson 1968; Thomas 1985: 307ff.; Thompson 1985

Paulinus St, bishop 625–44

Paulinus was a member of the missionary band which arrived in Kent in 601. When *Edwin of Northumbria married *Æthelburh, sister of *Eadbald of Kent in 625, Paulinus was sent north with the bride to attempt the conversion of Northumbria. With the support of Edwin, Paulinus met with success; Edwin, his nobles, and 'a vast number of the common people' were baptized in 627. Paulinus became bishop of Northumbria and established his see at York. He worked in Bernicia as well as Deira, and is said to have spent 36 days at the royal vill of Yeavering (Northumberland), baptizing converts in the River Glen. In the south, he built a church at Campodunum (near Dewsbury, Yorkshire), and another, in stone, at Lincoln, in which *Honorius was consecrated as archbishop of Canterbury. *Bede preserves a description of Paulinus, derived at second-hand from a man who had been baptized by him in the River Trent, near Littleborough:

'He was tall, with a slight stoop, black hair and a thin face, a slender aquiline nose, and he was at the same time both venerable and awe-inspiring in appearance.'

Paulinus' mission ended with the death of Edwin in 633. He returned to Kent with Queen Æthelburh, where the bishopric of Rochester was then vacant. It was given to Paulinus, who held it until his death on 10 October 644.

BIBL. *HE* ii, 9-20: 162-207

Peada king of the Middle Angles *d.* 656

Peada was a son of *Penda, king of Mercia, who was made king of the Middle Angles at some time between 651 and 654. He wished to marry Alhflæd, daughter of *Oswiu of Northumbria, but the price was baptism, which Peada accepted at the urging of his brother-in-law, *Alhfrith. Peada and his followers were baptized at Wallbottle by *Finán, bishop of Northumbria. He returned to the Middle Angles with a group of four Northumbrian priests, trained in the Irish customs, of whom the leader was St *Cedd. Though Peada's father, Penda, was a resolute and principled pagan, he did not prohibit the preaching of Christianity and under Cedd's guidance the Middle Angles accepted Christianity. In 655, Penda made his final attack upon Northumbria and was killed by Oswiu at the battle of the River *Winwæd*. Peada was at first allowed to hold southern Mercia as a sub-kingdom under Oswiu's overlordship, but in the following year was murdered, allegedly through the treachery of his wife.

BIBL. *HE* iii, 21: 278-81; 24: 288-95

Penda king of Mercia ?626–55

It is with the reign of Penda, son of Pybba, that the history of Mercia emerges into daylight. It is not certain when he became king; it could have been as early as 607, and he was certainly in power by 628, when he defeated the West Saxon kings, *Cynegils and Cwichhelm at Cirencester, and thereby acquired the territory of the Hwicce (Gloucestershire, Worcestershire and part of Warwickshire). Penda's whole career was one of aggressive warfare, in which he extended the frontiers of Mercia north, east and south. The *Historia Brittonum* (a ninth-century compilation, see under *Nennius) says that it was Penda who separated the Mercians from Northumbria, and this may be so; it would account for his implacable enmity to the Northumbrian kings, *Edwin, *Oswald and *Oswiu. Indeed Edwin, when in exile, had married Cwenburh, daughter of *Cearl, Penda's predecessor as king of Mercia and probably his rival. In 633, Penda, in alliance with *Cadwallon of Gwynedd, attacked Northumbria, and killed Edwin at the battle of Hatfield Chase. He had Welsh allies also when he defeated and killed Oswald at the battle of *Maserfeld* (Oswestry) in 642; his own brother and co-king, Eowa, was also killed in this engagement. In the time of *Aidan (d. 651) he was raiding deep into Northumbria, for he attempted to burn down the royal fortress of Bamburgh. By the 650s, he was probably overlord of the southern English. His son *Peada was king of the Middle Angles, and another son, *Merewalh, ruled the Magonsæte (roughly Herefordshire and Shropshire). *Æthelhere of East Anglia and *Æthelwold of Deira were in alliance with him in 655, when he led an army of 30 'legions', led by 'royal commanders' against Oswiu of Northumbria. This was his last campaign, for he was defeated and killed at the battle of the *Winwæd*.

Penda fathered a numerous progeny. His queen, Cynewise, whom he left in charge of Mercia in 655, was probably the mother of Cyneburh, wife of *Alhfrith of Deira and abbess of Caistor, Northamptonshire,

203

and of her sister Cyneswith, who also became a nun. Wilburh, wife of
*Frithuwold of Surrey, and her sisters, SS Edith of Bicester and Eadburh
of Adderbury, Oxfordshire, are also said to have been Penda's daughters.
Penda's sons included, besides Peada, the Mercian kings *Wulfhere and
*Æthelred, and perhaps Merewalh of the Magonsæte. All were Christians
but Penda remained a pagan to the end of his days, though he allowed
Christian missionaries to preach in his territories. *Bede relates Penda's
views on those who were baptized and subsequently abandoned their
faith:

'he said that they were despicable and wretched creatures who scorned
to obey the God in whom they believed'.

BIBL. *HE* ii, 20: 202-5; iii, 16: 262-3; 21: 278-80; 24: 288-94; Davies 1977;
Brooks 1989b: 159-70

Plegmund archbishop of Canterbury 890−923

Plegmund was an ecclesiatic from Mercia, who is said to have lived for
several years as a hermit at Plemstall, Cheshire, which preserves his name
(*Plegmundes stowe*, 'the holy place of Plegmund'). He was made archbishop
of Canterbury by *Alfred of Wessex, who attracted to his court many
English and continental scholars in an attempt to raise the standards of
learning in ninth-century England. Plegmund reorganized the diocesan
structure of Wessex, previously divided between Sherborne and Winchester;
Sherborne became the see for Dorset, with Wells for Somerset and Crediton
for Devon and Cornwall, and Ramsbury was established for Wiltshire and
Berkshire, Winchester being confined to Hampshire and Surrey. In his
time also, the standards both of writing and Latinity at Christchurch were
much improved, marking the beginning of the scholastic revival of the
tenth century.

BIBL. Brooks 1984: 152-4, 209-14

R

Rædwald king of East Anglia *c*. 599–*c*. 625

Rædwald of East Anglia is not well-documented, and neither the date of his accession nor that of his death is known with accuracy. He befriended the exiled *Edwin of Northumbria, and in 617 defeated his rival, *Æthelfrith, at the battle of the River Idle, enabling Edwin to make himself king of Northumbria. It was perhaps this victory which secured Rædwald's acceptance as Bretwalda of the southern English, on the death of *Æthelberht of Kent, for *Bede tells us that even before Æthelberht's death, Rædwald had been 'gaining the leadership for his own nation'. Rædwald had in fact been baptized in Kent, but experienced difficulties in converting his wife and his nobles. Bede maintained, on the authority of Ealdwulf of East Anglia (d. 713), that Rædwald kept a temple in which both pagan and Christian altars were served, and which Ealdwulf had seen as a boy. It was only very gradually that Christianity made headway in East Anglia, for Rædwald's son and successor, Eorpwald, was killed by a pagan, and the whole province apostasized. The lack of written material for this region is balanced by the discovery, in 1939, of the great ship burial at Sutton Hoo, near Rendlesham, which was the main seat of the East Anglian kings. It is one of the richest deposits ever unearthed in Europe, though typically it is still not possible to decide with certainty which of the East Anglian kings it commemorates. Rædwald himself must, however, be a strong contender for the owner of this splendid treasure.

BIBL. *HE* ii, 5: 148-9; 12: 174-83; 15: 188-91; Evans 1986

Ragnall king of York 910–20

Ragnall, one of the grandsons of *Ivarr the Boneless, was expelled from Dublin in 902, and for the next few years roamed the western seas, harrying the kingdoms of Strathclyde and Scotland until the defeat of the Danes at York in 910, by *Edward the Elder of Wessex, at the battle of Tettenhall. This disaster gave Ragnall an opening; he seized power in York and became king at some time between 910 and 914. In the latter year he attacked *Ealdred of Bamburgh and seized a large part of English Northumbria, at least as far as the River Tyne. An army raised against him by *Constantine II of Scotland was defeated the same year at the first battle of Corbridge. From 917–18, Ragnall was operating in Ireland, in support of his brother, *Sigtrygg Caech, and in his absence, *Æthelflæd of Mercia assembled a coalition of Mercians, Strathclyde Britons and Scots against him. By 918, she was intriguing with disaffected factions within York itself, but her death in the same year meant the end of this activity. Ragnall was able to defeat the army of Constantine II at the second battle of Corbridge, and in 919 overcame the opposition in York. He died in 920, and was succeeded by his brother, Sigtrygg Caech.

BIBL. Smyth 1975: 93-116

Ragnarr Lothbrok, *fl.* ninth century

Ragnarr Lothbrok, ('hairybreeks'), 'a famous but unidentifiable Dane' is so enmeshed in heroic legend that his historical deeds are impossible to discern. He is said to have been the father of (*inter alia*) *Ivarr the Boneless and *Halfdan, who led the 'Great Army' in its assault upon England in 865, allegedly in revenge for the murder of their father by *Ælle of Northumbria. Ragnarr was captured by Ælle while raiding in Northumbria, and cast into a snake-pit, whose denizens stung him to death. 'The young pigs would grumble if they knew what the old one is suffering' he said, prophetically.

BIBL. Smyth 1977b; Jones 1968: 485-6

Ragnhild wife of several earls of Orkney *c.* 954–70

Ragnhild was the daughter of *Eirikr Bloodaxe, king of Norway and later king of York, and his Danish queen, Gunnhildr. Eirikr was slain on Stainmore in Northumbria in 954 along with his allies, Arnkel and Erlend, earls of Orkney and the sons of *Torf Einar. After this debacle Eirikr's queen abandoned York and retreated with the survivors of Eirikr's household to Orkney. Ragnhild, Eirikr's daughter, settled on Orkney and is remembered in *Orkneyinga Saga* as a powerful and scheming woman who dominated the politics of the Northern Isles in the late tenth century. She was married first to Earl Arnfinn, son of *Thorfinn Skull-splitter, whom she had slain at Murkle in Caithness, and on Arnfinn's death she married his brother, Havard, who succeeded to the earldom. She next incited Einar, a nephew of Havard's, to slay her latest husband, which crime was duly carried out at Stenness on Mainland, Orkney. Ragnhild's last recorded husband was Ljot, yet another son of Thorfinn Skull-splitter who succeeded his brother Havard in the earldom.

BIBL. Pálsson and Edwards 1978: 32-5; Laing 1961: 90

Ranig (Hrani) earl 1016–after 1041

Ranig was a Dane in the following of *Cnut, who received an earldom based on Herefordshire in 1016. He took part in the ravaging of Worcestershire ordered by *Harthacnut in 1041, but nothing is known of his career after this point. He must have been dead by 1044, when Herefordshire became part of the earldom of Swein son of *Godwine.

BIBL. Williams 1986

Rhain ap Cadwgan king of Dyfed *fl.* second half of eighth century

When *Seisyll, king of Ceredigion, conquered Ystrad Tywi, the kingdom of Dyfed was much diminished in extent and became known as Rheinwg, named probably after the first king King Rhain of Dyfed to face the reconstruction of a dismembered territory. This is generally thought to have been Rhain ap Cadwgan but Rhain ap Maredudd, who died in 808, is a possibility.

BIBL. Lloyd 1911, vol. I: 262

Rhodri ap Merfyn king of Gwynedd *d.* 878

It is not known when Rhodri Mawr ('the Great') became king of Gwynedd and it was not necessarily on the death of his father, *Merfyn ap Gwriad, but the Irish annals show that he was king by 856 when he slew the Viking leader, Horm, at a time of intensified Scandinavian assault on Britain and renewed Saxon attack on Powys and Gwynedd. The poet Sedulius Scottus wrote one poem certainly, and perhaps another two, in praise of a king, Roricus, who is probably to be identified with Rhodri Mawr. Rhodri was the son of Nest, sister of *Cyngen, king of Powys, and either Rhodri or his sons established themselves as rulers of Powys. He married Angharad, sister of Gwgon ap Meurig, king of Ceredigion, who was regarded by later genealogists as the mother of most of his sons, and either he or his sons acquired control of Ceredigion. But Rhodri remained militarily vulnerable. In 877 the Vikings drove him in flight to Ireland and the following year he was slain by the Saxons, almost certainly the Mercians under *Ceolwulf II.

BIBL. Lloyd 1911, vol. I: 342ff.; Chadwick 1958b: 79ff.; Dumville 1982; Davies 1982: 105-6

Rhydderch ab Iestyn king of Deheubarth 1023–33

A period of dynastic obscurity in Deheubarth followed the death of *Maredudd ab Owain but the indications are that the sons of *Einion ab Owain, Edwin and Cadell, held royal power in the early tenth century until the ascendancy of *Llywelyn ap Seisyll in the period *c.* 1020. At the same time in Morgannwg, the eclipse of the family of *Morgan ab Owain allowed new dynasties to come to power. Rhydderch ab Iestyn was among those who emerged in Gwent in the early tenth century. In 1023 on the death of Llywelyn ap Seisyll he even established himself as king in Deheubarth, and, though he appears as a dynastic intruder, the claim was subsequently made for him that he was a descendant of *Owain ap Hywel Dda. He was slain in 1033 and succeeded by Hywel and Maredudd, sons of Edwin ab Einion ab Owain, who thereby restored the native dynasty, but his son, *Gruffudd, was to resurrect his father's involvement at a later date.

BIBL. Lloyd 1911, vol. I: 347; Davies 1982: 103, 107-8; Davies 1990: 36

Riderch Hen (Rhydderch Hael) king of the Strathclyde Britons *c.* 580–612

The early ninth-century historian *Nennius (drawing on sources from Strathclyde of the seventh century) names Riderch Hen ('the Old') as one of three British kings who fought alongside *Urien of Rheged against Hussa, king of Bernicia (585–92). The northern British kings had besieged the Bernician Angles on Lindisfarne island. Riderch's father, Tutagual appears in the Welsh source *Bonedd Gwyr y Gogledd* as 'Tutagual of the people of Clyde' (*Tutwal Tutclyt*). Joceline's late twelfth-century *Life of Kentigern* claims that Riderch had been baptized in Ireland and was responsible for establishing *Kentigern within his kingdom. The same source names Riderch's queen as *Languoreth*. Riderch is associated in

Welsh literature with a Strathclyde prophet who turns up later in Arthurian literature in the character of *Merlin. *Adomnán, in an important anecdote on Riderch, shows the king consulting *Columba and drawing on that saint's powers as a prophet. Riderch is described by Adomnán as an insecure king, 'who can never know at what hour he is to be killed by enemies'. One of those enemies was also a friend of Columba — *Áedán mac Gabhráin, king of Scots Dál Riata. Áedán led an attack on Strathclyde in Riderch's time. Riderch Hen is also known in Welsh tradition as Rhydderch Hael ('the Generous'). According to Joceline, Riderch was succeeded by his son, *Constantine, who was later regarded as a saint. But Riderch's direct descendants do not seem to have succeeded to the Strathclyde kingship, which passed to his cousin, *Neithon son of Guipno and to Neithon's grandson, *Owen map Bili.

BIBL. Anderson 1922, vol. 1: 134-9; Anderson and Anderson 1961: 238-9; Jackson 1955: 82-3

Rögnvaldur Brúsason earl of Orkney c. 1037–46

Rögnvaldur was the son of Earl Brúsi of Orkney and the nephew of Brúsi's younger brother *Thorfinn the Mighty. The Norwegian king, *Olafr Helgi (Haraldsson) appointed Brúsi as his agent in the Northern Isles of Scotland in 1021 and set him, in effect, over Thorfinn. Meanwhile Brúsi's infant son, Rögnvaldur, was placed at Olafr's court partly as a hostage who in time became a loyal friend of the Norwegian king. When *Cnut the Great seized power in Norway, Rögnvaldur followed Olafr into exile in 1028 and returned to fight alongside his king at the battle of Stiklarstadir in 1030. Olafr was slain at Stiklarstadir, but Rögnvaldur rescued a future king of Norway, Harald Sigurdarson, who was wounded in the battle. Rögnvaldur next fled to the court of King Onund of Sweden and from there he and Harald went on to live under the protection of Jaroslav at Novgorod in Russia. Rögnvaldur eventually returned to Norway in the company of Magnus the Good, whom the Norwegians accepted as their king in 1035 in opposition to the son of Cnut. When Rögnvaldur heard of the death of his father, Brúsi, in Orkney and that Thorfinn had seized all the Orkney earldom for himself, he sailed west to claim his father's patrimony in the Scottish Isles (c. 1037). For eight years, Rögnvaldur managed to share the earldom amicably with his uncle, Thorfinn, whom he accompanied on Viking raids against the English, Scots and Irish. Eventually Thorfinn demanded one third of the islands for himself (in addition to his own territories in Caithness). He defeated Rögnvaldur in a naval battle in the Pentland Firth, after which Thorfinn moved his residence to Orkney, and Rögnvaldur fled back to King Magnus in Norway. Rögnvaldur returned with one ship in the winter of that same year to surprise Thorfinn in his hall, which was ambushed and burnt. Thorfinn barely escaped death, retreating to Caithness, while Rögnvaldur now occupied Kirkwall for the remainder of the winter. While staying on Papa Stronsay where he was collecting malt for Christmas ale (in 1047), Rögnvaldur was attacked in his house by Thorfinn and his men. The house was set alight and Rögnvaldur escaped, disguised in the robes of a

208

Christian deacon. He was soon discovered among rocks by the shore and slain, it is thought, by Thorkel the Fosterer, one of Thorfinn's most trusted companions. Rögnvaldur's body was taken to Papa Westray for burial. He was remembered in Norse tradition as a popular and gifted ruler, and as a handsome man with fine golden hair. Contemporary skaldic verses in praise of Rögnvaldur survive from the poets *Arnór Jarlaskáld ('Earls' Poet') and from Óttarr Svarti ('the Black'). The latter refers to Rögnvaldur in a praise poem on King Olaf of Norway — 'Shetlanders will serve you,...overlord of Orkney'.

BIBL. Anderson 1922, vol. 1: 584-7; Pálsson and Edwards 1978: 56-71

Rögnvaldur of Moer Norwegian earl *c.* 850

Rögnvaldur, earl (or *jarl*) of Moer in western Norway, was the father of *Torf Einar the first *historical* earl of Orkney and of Rollo, or Hrólfur, the founder of Normandy and ancestor of William the Conqueror. According to Snorri Sturlason's *Heimskringla*, Rögnvaldur accompanied the Norwegian king, Harald Finehair, on an expedition to the British Isles in the ninth century, when he was granted Orkney and Shetland by Harald as compensation for the death of Ivarr, one of Rögnvaldur's sons, on that expedition. Rögnvaldur did not however settle in the Northern Isles, which he immediately granted to his brother, *Sigurd the Powerful, who is regarded as the first earl of Orkney. The Norwegian king who granted Orkney and Shetland to Rögnvaldur and his descendants cannot have been Harald Finehair. Rögnvaldur is more likely to have received the isles from Olaf the White, king of Norse Dublin.

BIBL. Anderson 1922, vol. 1: 332-4; Smyth 1977a: 70-2

S

Sæberht king of Essex, *d.* 616/17

Sæberht was the son of Ricula, sister of King *Æthelberht of Kent, and was converted to Christianity by his uncle's persuasion. At this period, Essex was clearly a Kentish dependency; it was Æthelberht who founded the see of London, at St Paul's, for bishop *Mellitus, in 604. Sæberht's three sons, who succeeded him, were pagans, who expelled Mellitus because he refused them the 'white bread' which he had given their father 'Saba'; that is the Eucharistic host. They were killed in battle against the West Saxons, *c.* 623.

BIBL. Yorke 1985: 17-18

Samson St, abbot and bishop, *fl.* sixth century

The first *Life* of Samson of Dol in Brittany, perhaps written in the first half of the ninth century but possibly earlier — it may incorporate a seventh-century kernel, is the earliest *Life* of a saint to relate to Wales. Samson is said to have been educated in the monastery of *Illtud at Llanilltud Fawr before seeking a more austere life with a community on Caldey island, of which he became abbot before eventually crossing to Brittany to become abbot and bishop of his own foundation at Dol. The historicity of these traditions is uncertain, but the *Life* provides a valuable glimpse of how some Welsh religious communities were seen in the ninth century if not earlier, and the Samson of the *Life* may be the Samson who witnessed the acts of a council of Paris between 556 and 573.

BIBL. Taylor 1925; Chadwick 1969: 250ff.; Poulin 1977; Chédeville and Guillotel 1984: 144ff.; Henken 1987: 115-20

Seaxburh queen 672−3

Seaxburh, wife of King *Cenwealh of Wessex, is said to have ruled the West Saxons for a year after her husband's death in 672. Though it is unusual to find women exercising independent regal powers, it does sometimes occur; see, for another example, *Æthelflæd of Mercia. The West Saxon custom was obviously rather different in the seventh and eighth centuries than in the ninth, for by that time they did not have queens (see *Judith).

BIBL. *ASC* s.a. 672

Seaxburh (Sexburg) St, queen and abbess *d. c.* 700

Seaxburh was one of the saintly daughters of King *Anna of the East Angles. She married *Eorcenberht, king of Kent, and founded the monastery of Minster-in-Sheppey, to which she retired as abbess on her husband's death in 664. When in 679 her sister St *Æthelthryth died, Seaxburh succeeded her as abbess of Ely, and her own daughter

Eormenhild, widow of *Wulfhere of Mercia, became abbess of Minster-in-Sheppey. On Seaxburh's death, Eormenhild became abbess of Ely.

BIBL. Farmer 1978: 355-6

Seaxwulf bishop 675−92

Seaxwulf was the first abbot of *Medeshamstede* (Peterborough) Abbey and probably its founder, though later tradition gives that honour to *Peada, king of the Middle Angles and his overlord, *Oswiu of Northumbria. The traditional foundation date is 654. The house lay in the territory of the North Gyrwe, a Middle Anglian district under Mercian control, and in 675, Seaxwulf became bishop of the Mercians, in succession to the deposed *Winfrith; his see was probably at Leicester. By 692, St *Wilfrid was acting as bishop of Leicester, and Seaxwulf must therefore have been dead. Peterborough Abbey was a strong force in the spread of churches in the midlands; *Hædde, abbot of Breedon and later bishop of Lichfield, was one of its monks, as was *Cuthbald, Seaxwulf's successor as abbot, who founded Brixworth, Northamptonshire.

BIBL. Stenton 1933

Sebbi St, king of Essex 663−93/4

Sebbi and his kinsman *Sigehere succeeded to the kingdom of Essex on the death of Swithhelm in 663. Sigehere and his people abandoned the Christian faith, but Sebbi remained constant. *Bede praises his piety and says that he would have preferred the cloister to the kingship, but that his wife refused to be separated from him (the consent of the spouse was required for a married person to enter religion). Towards the end of his life, when he was ill, he resigned his royal office and made his monastic profession to *Wealdhere, bishop of London. He died in 693 or 694, and was buried in St Paul's, London. His sons, Sigeheard and Swæfred, succeeded him.

BIBL. *HE* iii, 30: 332-3; iv, ll: 364-9; Yorke 1985: 20-2

Ségéne abbot of Iona 623−52

Ségéne son of Fiachna, was the successor of Abbot *Fergna, and he was the first abbot of Iona who had not served as a monk during *Columba's lifetime. But Ségéne was a close kinsman of Columba being the nephew of *Laisran, the third abbot. Ségéne played a crucial role in the transmission of stories relating to Columba which eventually found their way into *Adomnán's *Life* of that saint. It was Ségéne who personally heard King *Oswald of Northumbria relate his tale of a vision of Columba which the king had experienced on the eve of his battle with *Cadwallon near Hexham in 634. Oswald would undoubtedly have met Abbot Ségéne during his earlier exile among the Scots, but this meeting must have occurred between 634 and the death of Oswald in 642. Abbot Ségéne was the recipient of a letter written by Cummian, a leading Irish ecclesiastic, in 632−3, exhorting Ségéne and his Iona community to abandon the Celtic dating of Easter. Ségéne along with other leading clerics from the northern half of Ireland wrote to Pope Severinus, presumably after holding a synod to discuss the question of their adherence to the Celtic rite, and the reply from Rome, issued by John IV, pope-elect (who succeeded Severinus in August 640) survives in part in *Bede's *Ecclesiastical History*. It is addressed (among others) to the abbot of Armagh and to *Segenus* of Iona, described as 'priest'. In spite of the admonitions of John IV, Ségéne and his Iona community stuck to their guns over Celtic liturgical practices. During Ségéne's abbacy, the ecclesiastical power of Iona reached its zenith. Ségéne was invited by Oswald of Northumbria to establish the Christian church in Northumbria, and in 634–5, Bishop *Aidan was despatched with a number of companions from Iona who settled on Lindisfarne. For the remainder of his abbacy, Ségéne must have exercised immense influence on the infant Anglo-Saxon church through the bishopric of Lindisfarne. He established a church on either Rathlin or Lambay Island off the Irish coast in 635, and when his vast jurisdiction over Irish, Pictish, Scottish and English houses is taken into account, it is clear that in his lifetime he was the most influential ecclesiastical leader in the British Isles. Ségéne died in 652, one year after his bishop, Aidan, died at Bamburgh. Ségéne's festival was observed on 12 August, and he was succeeded by *Suibhne in the abbacy of Iona.

BIBL. Anderson and Anderson 1961: 90-1 and text; Herbert 1988: 40-3; Kenney 1929: 220-3; Reeves 1857: 373-5

Seisyll ap Clydog king of Ceredigion, *fl.* second half of eighth century
    Probably in the second half of the eighth century, Seisyll, king of Ceredigion, conquered Ystrad Tywi, on his southern border, from the kings of Dyfed and forged a new political creation which became known as the kingdom of Seisyllwg and embraced Cardiganshire and much of Carmarthenshire.

BIBL. Lloyd 1911, vol. I: 257

Selbach king of Scots Dál Riata 700–23
    Selbach was the brother of *Ainbcellach who seized the kingship of Dál Riata for only a year in 697. As members of the Cenél Loairn dynasty, these brothers were newcomers to the kingship of Dál Riata. Their dynastic homeland lay on either side of Loch Linnhe and the Firth of Lorn. Selbach took the kingship of Dál Riata on the death of his predecessor, Fiannamail, in battle in 700. During this time Selbach met with opposition not only from the Cenél Gabhráin dynasty of hereditary kings of Dál Riata but also from rival factions within his own Cenél Loairn. Dunolly, a fortress of the Cenél Loairn, was burnt in 698 and attacked by Selbach yet again in 701, while the same king restored the fort in 714. In 719 Selbach defended his kingship against his brother Ainbcellach, whom he defeated and slew at Findglen, probably near Loch Avich. In the same year he was defeated in a sea battle by the Cenél Gabhráin who were led by a certain Dúnchad Bec 'king of Kintyre' in Cenél Gabhráin territory. Selbach held on to his kingship until 723 when he abdicated in favour of his son *Dúngal and 'entered into religion'. Selbach tried unsuccessfully to regain

the kingdom in 727 when, on the expulsion of his son, he sallied forth from monastic retirement to challenge the Cenél Gabhráin in battle. He died in 730.

BIBL. Anderson 1973: 180-2

Serf St, bishop *c.* 695–700

The thirteenth-century *Life* of this saint contains more fantastic tales than most other examples of medieval hagiography. Serf's parents are named as Obeth, king of Canaan, and Alpia, an Arabian princess. Serf is alleged to have studied in Alexandria, to have become a Canaanite bishop, to have ruled as Patriarch of Jerusalem and to have been elected pope. He is said to have crossed the Alps and to have walked dry-shod over the Red Sea and the Straits of Dover. He arrived in Scotland in the time of *Adomnán with 7000 followers and came to Culross in Fife, where he eventually persuaded the reigning Pictish king, *Bruide son of Derile (*Dargart* in the *Life* of St Serf), to grant him that place to found a monastic community. Finally, with Adomnán's help he founded another community on an island in Loch Leven in Kinross. Other places associated with Serf in his *Life* are a cave at Dysart on the northern shores of the Forth and a cell at Dunning in Strathearn, where he is said to have died on (his festival day) 1 July. While the Near Eastern origins of Serf may appear wild in the extreme, they can be compared with very similar traditions relating to *Curetan (Boniface), and emanated from the pro-Roman party in Pictland in the aftermath of the Easter Controversy. Some Scottish traditions associated with the saint have more to recommend them than has recently been supposed. An early Irish tract on the mothers of the saints attributed to Óengus the Céli Dé (*c.* 800) names Serf's parents as Alma the daughter of a king of the Picts, and (quite fantastically) Proc, a Canaan or Egyptian father. This source adds: 'he is in Culross [and] in Strathearn [and] in the Comgells between the Ochill Hills and the Sea of Forth (*Muir nGiudan*)'. Serf's association with the contemporaries Adomnán and Bruide son of Derile appears reasonable and can be compared with Curetan's association with *Nechtán son of Derile and also with Adomnán. Skene cites a memorandum in a St Andrews cartulary which mentions the granting of the island in Loch Leven to St Servanus and to the Keledei (Céli Dé) anchorites, while in the eleventh century, *Macbeth and his queen, *Gruoch, both granted lands to Serf's church on Loch Leven and to the community of Culdees or Céli Dé which he founded there. The *Life* of *Kentigern makes Serf the older contemporary of the late sixth-century Kentigern and a disciple of the early fifth-century *Palladius — all of which can be dismissed as a nonsense.

BIBL. Anderson 1922, vol. 1: 127-9, 130; Skene 1886-90, vol. 2: 255-9

Sexburg *see* **Seaxburh**

Sigeberht king of East Anglia 630/1–*c.* 635

Sigeberht was the son of *Rædwald, and brother of Rædwald's successor as king of East Anglia, Eorpwald. During his brother's reign, Sigeberht was exiled in Frankish Gaul, where he was baptized. On becoming king, c. 630, he established *Felix, a Burgundian priest, as bishop of the East Angles, and gave Burgh Castle, in Suffolk (the site of an old Saxon Shore fort) to the Irishman *Fursa, to build a monastery. Sigeberht resigned his kingdom to his kinsman Ecgric in order to become a monk. When, however, East Anglia was invaded by the Mercians under their king, *Penda, Sigeberht was compelled to leave his monastery and lead the East Anglia host, 'to inspire the army with confidence'. He went into battle unarmed, with only a staff of office in his hands, and both he and King Ecgric were killed. *Anna succeeded to the kingdom. The precise date of the fatal battle is unknown.

BIBL. Stenton 1959

Sigeberht Sanctus king of Essex d. c. 653

Two kings called Sigeberht ruled the East Saxons in the seventh century, Sigeberht Parvus ('the Little') and Sigeberht Sanctus ('the Saint'), who succeeded him. Sigeberht Sanctus was a close friend of *Oswiu of Northumbria, whom he used to visit frequently, and it was Oswiu who persuaded him to abandon paganism and become a Christian; he was baptized at Wallbottle by *Finán, bishop of Northumbria. Sigeberht re-established Christianity in Essex, after the pagan reaction which had followed the death of *Sæberht in 616/17, and *Cedd became the first bishop of Essex since the expulsion of *Mellitus. Sigeberht was murdered 'because he was too ready to pardon his enemies', by two of his thegns. His successor, Swithhelm, was baptized by Cedd at Rendlesham on the urging of his friend, Æthelwold of East Anglia; he died in 664.

BIBL. *HE* iii, 22: 280-5; Yorke 1985: 18-19

Sigeferth thegn d. 1015

Sigeferth and his brother *Morcar were among the leading nobles of the Danelaw (Northumbria and the Five Boroughs). They seem to have been connected with the sons of *Æthelred II by his first wife, *Ælfgifu, daughter of Earl *Thored of Northumbria, for the ætheling *Athelstan remembered them in his will. He left to Sigeferth an estate at Hockliffe, Bedfordshire, a sword, a horse and a shield. Morcar was related by marriage to the family of *Ælfhelm, ealdorman of Northumbria, and his brother, *Wulfric Spot. In 1013, the northern nobles were the first to submit to *Swein Forkbeard, king of Denmark, as he moved through England driving out King Æthelred. Swein was accepted as king of England, but died in February 1014, and the English nobles, setting aside the claims of his son, *Cnut, renewed their allegiance to Æthelred. It was probably in revenge for their former submission to Swein that Æthelred had Sigeferth and Morcar murdered at the royal court in 1015. Sigeferth's widow was seized and imprisoned at Malmesbury, and the brother's property was confiscated. The ætheling *Edmund Ironside, Athelstan's full brother, rescued Sigeferth's widow from captivity, married her, took over the property of her dead husband and his brother, and, as a result, received the submission of the northern nobles.

BIBL. Williams 1986

Sigeric archbishop of Canterbury 990−4
   Sigeric was a monk of Glastonbury, who rose to become first, abbot of St Augustine's, Canterbury, then, in 985−6, bishop of Ramsbury and finally, in 990, archbishop of Canterbury. His archiepiscopate coincided with the expedition to England of *Olafr Tryggvason and his raiding-army. When this force inflicted a disastrous defeat on the English at Maldon in 991, Sigeric was one of those who negotiated a truce. He is said to have advocated the payment of tribute to the Viking raiders, and this, coupled with the fact that he had to buy off the same force in 994 to prevent the sack of Canterbury, earned him the (posthumous) nickname of 'Sigeric Danegeld'. In order to raise the sum demanded in 994, Sigeric had to borrow from Bishop Æscwig of Dorchester-on-Thames, pledging the manor of Monks Risborough, Buckinghamshire, as security. He died the same year.

BIBL. Brooks 1984: 278-87

Sigfrid St, bishop *d. c.* 1045
   Sigfrid, a monk of Glastonbury, was sent by King *Æthelred II to *Olafr Tryggvason, king of Norway, to help in the evangelization of the north. After Olafr's death in 1000, Sigfrid moved to Sweden, under the rule of Olafr Skotkonung, and was established at Vaxjo (Ostrabo), of which he became bishop, and where he finally died, after a life spent in preaching and baptizing in all three Scandinavian kingdoms, Denmark as well as Norway and Sweden. He died on 15 February, but the year is unknown; he is said to have lived to a great age, perhaps even into the 1060s.

BIBL. Farmer 1978: 357; Oppermann 1937: 56-97

Sighere king of Essex 663−88
   Sighere was co-ruler of Essex with *Sebbi, but he and his people apostasized during the great plague of 664, and had to be re-converted by Jaruman, bishop of Mercia. Sighere seems to have conquered Kent, perhaps in alliance with Mul, brother of *Cædwalla of Wessex. He was dead by 689, when Swæfheard, son of Sebbi was king of Essex, in conjunction with Oswine. Sighere was the father of *Offa of Essex, by the Mercian princess, St *Osyth.

BIBL. Yorke 1985: 20

Sigtrygg Caech king of York 920−7
   Sigtrygg Caech (Squinty) brother of *Ragnall, was one of the grandsons of *Ivarr the Boneless. In 917, with his brother's aid, he established

215

himself as king of the Dublin Vikings, When Ragnall died in 920, Sigtrygg relinquished Dublin to another of Ivarr's grandsons, *Gothfrith, and took up the Danish kingdom of York. In 926 he made terms with *Athelstan of Wessex, at Tamworth; he accepted baptism, and took the king's sister, Eadgyth, as his wife. Soon, however, he renounced both his bride and his faith. In 927 he died, and Athelstan was able (temporarily) to seize York.

BIBL. Smyth 1979: 1-17

Sigurd I the Powerful earl of Orkney c. 850—70

Sigurd the Powerful (inn ríki) was the brother of Earl *Rögnvaldur of Moer in western Norway. Rögnvaldur is said in Norse sagas to have been granted the Northern Isles of Scotland by King Harald Finehair of Norway and to have passed them on immediately to his brother Sigurd who settled down as first jarl or earl of those islands, holding his title, according to Heimskringla, from the king of Norway. Sigurd allied himself with *Thorstein the Red, son of the Norse king, Olaf the White of Dublin, and together they campaigned on the Scottish mainland conquering Caithness and Sutherland. Sigurd slew a Scottish ruler, Máelbrigte or Melbrikta Tönn, near the Dornoch Firth in Sutherland. The victorious Sigurd cut off Máelbrigte's head and hung it from his saddle, but the teeth from the severed head grazed the leg of the Viking and the wound, turning septic, proved fatal. Sigurd was buried in a mound on the banks of the Oykel in south Sutherland perhaps at a place called Cyder Hall or Sydero (Sigurdar haugr). He was succeeded by his son, Guthorm, who died soon afterwards without heirs.

BIBL. Anderson 1922, vol. 1: 332-4, 370-2; Pálsson and Edwards 1978: 26-8

Sigurd II the Stout earl of Orkney c. 985—1014

Sigurd the Stout (digri) was the son of Hlödvir and grandson of *Thorfinn Skull-splitter, Norse earls of Orkney. His mother was Eithne, the daughter of an Irish king, Cerbhall. Sigurd was one of the greatest of the Orkney earls whose rule and influence extended far beyond the Northern Isles over Scotland and the Irish Sea as far as Man. Sigurd married the daughter of a Scottish ruler, Malcolm, identified either as *Malcolm II of Scotland or alternatively as a Scottish king or mórmaer of Moray. Sigurd gave his sister, Svanlaug, in marriage to the Norse earl, Gilli, who ruled the Hebrides as Sigurd's man, from Coll or Colonsay. Sigurd successfully defended Caithness from Scottish encroachments on his territories, defeating a Scottish ruler, Finnleik (or Findlaech) in a battle at Skitten Myre near Duncansby in Caithness. This seems to be the same battle as that described in Njáls Saga in which Sigurd, aided by the sons of Njál from Iceland fought near Duncansby in Caithness, in defence of Sigurd's Scottish mainland territory. Sigurd's Scottish lands are described in that source as consisting of Ross and Moray, Sutherland and the Dales. The latter are taken to mean either the Dales in Caithness or further to the west and south in Argyll. Sigurd's nominal conversion to Christianity is described in Orkneyinga Saga and Heimskringla which state that he was forcibly baptized by the Norwegian king, *Olafr Tryggvason, when Olafr landed on Orkney in 995. The encounter between the two rulers took place at Osmundwall in south Hoy. Sigurd is alleged to have accepted Christianity at the sword's edge and to have submitted to the Norwegian king, giving him his son, Hvelp (baptized Hlödvir) as a hostage. When Hvelp died soon afterwards in Norway, Sigurd withdrew his allegiance and we may assume also that he renounced his Christianity. In 1014, Sigurd was persuaded by Sigtrygg Silkenbeard, king of Norse Dublin, to join him in a great alliance against the Irish highking, Brian Boru. Sigurd fell fighting against the armies of Brian on Clotarf strand near Dublin on Good Friday, 23 April 1014. *Njáls Saga* claims he fell wrapped in his magic raven banner, woven for Sigurd (according to *Orkneyinga Saga*) by his mother in order to gain victory from the Norse war-god, Odin. The famous and much-travelled Norse skaldic poet, Gunnlaug Ormstunga ('Snakestongue'), is said to have composed a praise-poem on Sigurd the Stout during a visit to Orkney. The poem has not survived.

BIBL. Anderson 1922, vol. 1: 495-511, 528-41; Crawford 1987: 64-71

Sigvatr Thordarson *fl.* first half of the eleventh century

Sigvatr Thordarson was an Icelandic *skald* (poet) in the service of *Olafr Helgi, for whom he composed the *Vikingavisur*, a series of verses celebrating Olafr's battles. Perhaps the most interesting concerns the battle of Ringmere in 1010, also recorded in the *Anglo-Saxon Chronicle*:

'Yet again Olafr gave battle in Ulfkell's country — it was the seventh time, as I relate. All the English stood on Hringmaraheithr, when the heir of Haraldr caused strife — there was loss of life in battle'.

'Ulfkell's country' is East Anglia, governed by *Ulfkell Snilling, who, according to the *Anglo-Saxon Chronicle*, 'gave the Danes harder handplay' than the other English leaders. Sigvatr's comment seems to bear out his assessment.

BIBL. Campbell A 1971

Siward Digera (the Stout) earl *c.* 1033—55

Siward's origins are unclear, but he is usually assumed to be a Dane in the following of *Cnut. By 1033 he was earl of Northumbria, that is to say, of York. In 1041 he added Bamburgh to his territory by killing the high-reeve, Ealdorman *Eadulf, and marrying Eadulf's niece, Ælfflæd. By a previous marriage he had a son, Osbeorn, who was killed in battle with *Macbeth, king of Scots, in 1054, as was Siward's sister's son and namesake. Siward himself died in 1055, and was buried in the church of St Olave (*Olafr Helgi) at Galmaho (York), which he himself had built. His son by Ælfflæd, Waltheof, was too young to succeed, and his earldom was given to Tostig, son of Earl *Godwine of Wessex. A later legend tells how Siward, feeling death approach, called for his mail and his battle-axe, so that he could arm himself and thus avoid suffering the ultimate disgrace for a Viking hero, to expire in his bed.

BIBL. Hart 1975: 143-50, 359; Kapelle 1979: 27-49

Sléibíne abbot of Iona 752–67

Sléibíne succeeded *Cillene Droichtech as fifteenth abbot in succession to *Columba. He was of the tribe of Cenél Loairn which had come to dominate Dál Riata politics in the first half of the eighth century. Since Sléibíne's father is given as Congal, it is likely that the Cillene son of Congal who died on Iona in 752 was a brother of the abbot. Sléibíne spent much of his time going back and forward to Ireland enforcing the ecclesiastical *Law* of Columba on his far-flung *paruchia*. The *Law* of Columba was enforced for Sleíbíne by Domnall Mide, the Southern Uí Néill overking in 753. Domnall's interest in the Columban church is further indicated by that king's burial in Durrow in 763. Sléibíne went to Ireland in 754, personally enforced the *Law* of Columba there in 757, and returned to Iona in the following year. Sléibíne's co-adjutor, *Suibhne, travelled back to Ireland yet again in 766 in the year prior to Sléibíne's death. This increased interest in the Irish *paruchia* may reflect the waning of Iona's influence in the kingdom of the Picts since the expulsion of some of its monks during the reign of *Nechtán son of Derile. Sléibíne's travels were not confined to Ireland. According to the early ninth-century *Nennius's *History of the Britons*, Abbot Sléibíne visited Ripon in Northumbria to consult its monastic archive. Sléibíne was succeeded by *Suibhne, and his festival was kept on 2 March.

BIBL. Anderson and Anderson 1961: 100; Reeves 1857: 385-6

Stuf king of the Isle of Wight, *fl.* first half of the sixth century

Stuf and Wihtgar are said to have accompanied their kinsman *Cerdic to Britain, and to have received from him the Isle of Wight, in 534. Wihtgar's death is recorded under the year 544 in the *Anglo-Saxon Chronicle*. According to *Bede, writing in 731, the Isle of Wight and the area of Hampshire immediately proximate to it were settled, like Kent, by Jutes, and this information is repeated by *Asser, who also claims that *Osburh, mother of *Alfred the Great, was a descendant of Stuf and Wihtgar.

BIBL. Stenton 1971: 20-4; Yorke 1989

Suibhne abbot of Iona 652–7

Although Suibhne presided over what was in his time the most powerful ecclesiastical empire in the British Isles, nevertheless his rule on Iona was overshadowed by political events in the reign of his powerful contemporary, *Oswiu of Northumbria. After his victory over the Mercians in 655, Oswiu set about the domination of the Picts and Scots. Oswiu's nephew and puppet king, *Talorgen son of Enfret, slew the king of Dál Riata in a battle at Srath Ethairt in 654. Although Oswiu had first encountered Christianity during his exile on Iona, and although he was sympathetic to the Celtic liturgy, nevertheless growing opposition to the Celtic rite developed in Northumbria during the last years of Suibhne's rule as abbot of Iona. Suibhne was the sixth abbot in succession to *Columba and his festival was observed on 11 January. His name is given in the *Annals of Ulster* at 657 as 'of the tribe of *Urthri*'. His origins are unknown and he is the first among few early abbots of Iona who may not have belonged to Columba's royal kindred.

BIBL. Anderson and Anderson 1961: 91; Reeves 1857: 375

Suibhne abbot of Iona 767—72

Suibhne's pedigree is unknown which is unusual for an Iona abbot, who in pre-Viking times virtually all belonged to *Columba's royal kindred. Suibhne had already taken charge of the Iona community by 766 at the latest when as sixteenth abbot he visited Ireland one year before the death of his predecessor, *Sléibíne. Suibhne was almost certainly the monk of that name mentioned by Dicuil, the Irish Carolingian scholar and geographer, as his former teacher. Dicuil informs us that he was present when Suibhne received a monk who had visited the Holy Land some time before 767. Suibhne's festival was kept on 2 March.

BIBL. Reeves 1857: 386; Kenney 1929: 545-8; Smyth 1984: 167-8

Swein Forkbeard king of Denmark c. 986—1013

Swein was the son of King Harald Bluetooth, 'who won for himself all Denmark and Norway and made the Danes Christian', as his runestone at Jellinge proclaims. Swein's relations with his father were not easy and it was as a result of a rebellion that he succeeded Harald in about 986. In the 990s, he was operating in England in company with *Olafr Tryggvason. Olafr returned to Scandinavia in 994, and so probably did Swein. He had, however, found some support in England, or so it was believed, for at least one Essex thegn was accused of plotting to make Swein king (see *Æthelric of Bocking). In 1003 (if not before) he was raiding England once more; later Scandinavian legend claims he was seeking revenge for his sister Gunnhildr and her husband, *Pallig, murdered in the massacre of St Brice's Day, 1002. He was back in 1004, and again in 1006, when his army 'proceeded along the Berkshire Downs to Cuckhamsley Knob, and there awaited the great things that had been threatened, for it had often been said, that if ever they got as far as Cuckhamsley Knob, they would never again reach the sea'. Nothing happened and they 'went back by another route'. A truce was arranged with King *Æthelred II and a huge Danegeld paid, and Swein returned to Denmark in 1007. His third English campaign began in 1013. By this time the kingdom was in disarray after the ravages of *Thorkell the Tall and his 'immense raiding-army'. Swein's landing in the Humber in August 1013 brought him the almost immediate submission of the northerners. Crossing Watling Street, his men 'did the greatest mischief that any host was capable of', with the result that East Anglia and Wessex submitted also. Foiled at London, where Æthelred lay with Thorkell's fleet, he moved off to Bath, to receive the submission of the Mercians, and the far south-west. Finally the Londoners gave in to the inevitable and 'the whole nation accepted him as full king'. At Christmas, Æthelred followed his wife and their children to Normandy. Swein enjoyed his triumph for barely a month; he died at Candlemas (2 February) 1014.

BIBL. Lund 1986

T

Taliesin bard *fl.* sixth century

Taliesin was a British bard whom the early ninth-century *Historia Brittonum* (see under *Nennius) dates to the sixth century. He became a figure of legend and many relatively late poems were attributed to him and preserved in the late thirteenth-century manuscript known as the Book of Taliesin. A few, which extol the praises of *Cynan ap Brochfael, king of Powys, and *Gwallawg, ruler of Elmet, and in particular, *Urien of Rheged, have been regarded as possibly authentic sixth-century compositions. The poet is at times concerned for the fate of those he represents as his patrons − 'I would not be glad if Urien were slain': at others he celebrates particular victories − the battle of Gwen Ystrad ('the fair valley') to which 'the men of Britain came in hosts', and Argoed Llwyfein ('the wooded region') where 'the ravens were crimson because of the warfare of men'.

BIBL. Williams 1960; Williams 1968; Bromwich 1961: 509-11; Dumville 1977: 178-9; Jarman 1981: 21ff., 101ff.; Pennar 1988

Talorgen son of Enfret (Eanfrith), Pictish king 653−7

Talorgen's father was Eanfrith son of *Æthelfrith, king of Northumbria. Æthelfrith ruled from 592 until 617 after which Eanfrith was forced into exile among the Picts, remaining thus a fugitive in northern Britain until 633. He returned as king of Bernicia in 633−4 but was slain very soon afterwards. Eanfrith presumably married a Pictish princess during his sojourn in the north. Talorgen may well have claimed the Pictish kingdom through his mother, but equally he ruled the Picts at a time when his powerful uncle, *Oswiu, reigned in Northumbria. Oswiu is said by *Bede to have subdued 'the greater part of the Pictish race', hence it is no coincidence that his nephew, Talorgen, was ruling Pictland from 653. Talorgen won a victory over Dál Riata in 654 when he slew its king, *Dúnchad son of Conaing in battle at Srath Ethairt, probably in the same year as his uncle, Oswiu, was victorious over the Mercians. This victory of Talorgen may have been part of a traditional *crech ríg* or 'inaugural raid' which Celtic kings carried out against their hostile neighbours to mark the beginning of their rule. Talorgen was succeeded on his death in 657 by Gartnait son of Donuel and later by Gartnait's brother, *Drest.

BIBL. Anderson 1973: 169-72; Bannerman 1974: 93-4, 103

Talorgen son of Fergus, Pictish ruler *see* **Óengus I** son of Fergus

Talorgen son of Óengus, Pictish king *fl.* 782

Talorgen appears in the Pictish king-lists as Talorgen son of *Onuist*, and he was very probably the son of *Óengus I son of Fergus who died in 761. Óengus I had a brother called Talorgen (*d.* 750) and the family probably belonged to the tribal dynasty of Fortriu in the Strathearn region. This in turn makes it likely that Talorgen son of Óengus was the same person as *Dubtholarg* 'king of the Picts on this side of the Mounth', who died according to the *Annals of Ulster* in 782. Talorgen son of Óengus was succeeded in the Pictish kingship by *Conall son of Tadg.

BIBL. Anderson 1973: 166, 187-8, 191; Smyth 1984: 67, 69, 73, 75

Taran son of Entifidich, Pictish king 693−7
  Taran succeeded the powerful *Bruide mac Bili in the Pictish kingship in 693. His parentage and origins are unknown. His father's name may be derived from the Old Irish *Ainbtech*. His own name, given as *Taran* in Pictish king-lists and as *Tarachin* and *Tarain* in contemporary Irish annals, may be related to that of *Taranis*, the Gaulish thunder god. *Tarain* was also the name of a prehistoric king or ancestor-god of the Picts. The historical Taran was expelled from his kingdom after a short reign in 697, while two years later he fled to Ireland. His successor in the Pictish kingship was *Bruide son of Derile.

BIBL. Anderson 1973: 175-6, 178; Anderson 1922, vol. 1: 201-2, 206

Teilo St, abbot and bishop *fl.* sixth century
  Traces of the cult of St Teilo, traditionally regarded as a bishop and abbot, are widespread throughout south Wales, but its principal centre was Llandeilo Fawr (Carmarthenshire) where the Book of St Chad, a Gospel text now at Lichfield, once resided and in which were entered records of transactions involving the church of Llandeilo in the ninth and tenth centuries. No details are known, however, of Teilo's life, and the *Life of Teilo*, written in the twelfth century after Llandaff had established itself as Teilo's principal church, is devoid of historical value.

BIBL. Bowen 1954: 56ff.; Evans 1971: 162ff.; Henken 1987: 128-34

Teneu (Thaney) mother of St *Kentigern *c.* 530
  Teneu is said in the twelfth-century *Lives* of Kentigern to have been the daughter of Leudonus, a king of the Votadini or Gododdin, a British tribe occupying territory south of the Firth of Forth. Teneu's genuine Cumbric name and her association in the *Lives* with Dumpelder or Traprain Law, an ancient hill-fort of the Votadini, suggest that she and Kentigern did belong to an aristocratic line, perhaps of the Gododdin. The remainder of the details told of Teneu and her infant son in the *Lives* of Kentigern form part of a wilder and unverifiable hagiographical genre. She is said to have been raped, and subsequently punished by her father, being finally cast adrift in the Firth of Forth in a coracle which eventually landed at Culross in Fife, delivering Teneu into the caring hands of St *Serf.

BIBL. Anderson 1922, vol. 1: 127-30; Jackson 1958

Teudebur (Teudubr) map Bili king of the Strathclyde Britons 722−52
  Teudebur probably succeeded his father, Bili (or Beli) son of Elfin, as king of Strathclyde in 722. Teudebur's reign coincided with the powerful

rule of *Óengus I, son of Fergus, the Pictish king who from 736 until 750 ruled as overlord of Scots Dál Riata as well as king of the Picts. It was the Britons of Strathclyde, under their king, Teudebur, who broke the hold which Óengus exercised over northern Britain in 750. The Britons defeated the Picts at Mygedawg, perhaps at Mugdock on the borders of Stirling and Dunbartonshire, and slew Talorgen, brother of Óengus son of Fergus. Talorgen had been the able ally of Óengus from as early as 736. As a result of this British victory over the Picts in 750, we read of the 'ebbing of sovereignty of Óengus' in the same year. Teudebur died in 752, at which time *Eadberht, king of Northumbria, annexed the region of Kyle in south-west Scotland, which suggests that it had been included within the Strathclyde kingdom up to the end of Teudebur's reign. Teudebur was succeeded by his son, *Dumnagual.

BIBL. Anderson 1922, vol. 1: 239-40

Thaney see **Teneu**

Theodore archbishop of Canterbury 668–90

Theodore was born about 602, at Tarsus, in Syria, of Greek extraction. He became a monk, and probably removed to the west after Tarsus fell to the invading Arabs in 660. He seems to have sought refuge at Rome, and when in 668 the archbishop-elect of Canterbury, Wigheard, died at the papal court, Pope Vitalian appointed Theodore to take his place. He gave Theodore as a companion the African abbot, *Hadrian, lest he should introduce 'Greek customs which might be contrary to the true faith' into the English church. The context for this reservation is perhaps that Pope Vitalian's predecessor, Martin (649–53) had been deposed and banished by the Emperor Constans II for opposing imperial attempts to enforce obedience to Monothelitism, which was regarded as heretical in the west. Theodore and Hadrian ran into some difficulties in their journey through Frankia and were detained by the mayor of the palace, Ebroin, on suspicion of being imperial spies. It was not until May 669, a year after his consecration on 26 March 668, that Theodore finally reached Canterbury. He found a church inadequately staffed, suffering the ravages of the great plague of 664 which had killed many of its leaders, with a chaotic diocesan structure, and conflicting customs and usages. It was Theodore who, despite his advanced age, created the English church as a coherent whole. He and Hadrian established at Canterbury a school which taught Greek as well as Latin, Roman law, poetic metre, astronomy and the computus (ecclesiastical mathematics) as well as scriptural studies. His students included *Aldhelm, who has preserved for us a description of Theodore's pedagogical style, disputing with his Irish students 'like a boar surrounded by a pack of snarling hounds'. Theodore's energy extended to making a tour of his province, the first undertaken by an archbishop of Canterbury, 'wherever the people of the English were settled'. In 672, he called the first general synod of the English church, which met on 24 September at Hertford. Theodore's main concern was to reorganize the episcopal structure of the English church, breaking up the huge 'tribal' dioceses into smaller and more coherent units. He restored *Wilfrid to the Northumbrian see, deposing *Chad, but when in 678, Wilfrid fell out with King *Ecgfrith and was driven from Northumbria, Theodore took the opportunity to divide the see into three, with bishoprics at York, for Deira, Lindisfarne, for Bernicia, and Lincoln, for Lindsey. Wilfrid appealed to Rome against this division, and the papal curia compromised; the division was recognized, on condition that Wilfrid was restored to York with the right to choose his co-bishops. In fact Theodore's nominees remained in office, Bosa at York and *Eata at Lindisfarne. In Mercia, Theodore's path was smoother. Chad was removed to Lichfield as bishop of the Mercians, while the sees of Worcester and Hereford were created, for the Hwicce and the Magonsæte respectively. When the Mercians reconquered Lindsey, Eadhæd, its bishop, was established at Ripon, a further subdivision of the Northumbrian see, and a bishopric at Abercorn was established for the Picts under Northumbrian rule. Theodore styled himself 'Archbishop of the island of Britain and of the city of Canterbury', which well represents both his claims and his effective power. He died on 19 September 690.

BIBL. Brooks 1984: 71-6

Theodred bishop *c.* 926—51/3
   Theodred, who became bishop of London about 926, was probably of German extraction. His extant will shows that he held Hoxne, Suffolk, and he was probably bishop of Suffolk as well as London. He held estates in Norfolk, Essex and Cambridge as well as Suffolk, and one of the legatees, Osgod son of Eadwulf, was perhaps the ancestor of the rich eleventh-century thegn, *Osgod Clapa. It is probable that Theodred was one of the reforming clerics from the continent who contributed to the development of the English movement for monastic reform.

BIBL. Whitelock 1955, no. 106: 510-11; Whitelock 1975; O'Donovan 1973

Thored ealdorman 979—92
   Thored, who became ealdorman of Northumbria in 979, may have been the son of Earl *Oslac, banished in 975, but it has also been suggested that he is identical with Thored son of Gunnar, who ravaged Westmorland in 966. He was in any event probably the father of *Ælfgifu, the first wife of *Æthelred II. Thored led the English fleet against the raiding-army of *Olafr Tryggvason in 992, with disastrous results and is not heard of afterwards; his successor, *Ælfhelm, was holding Northumbria in 993. Thored's son, Athelstan, was killed at the battle of Ringmere in 1010.

BIBL. Whitelock 1959: 79-80

Thorfinn I Skull-splitter earl of Orkney *c.* 950—60
   Thorfinn Skull-splitter (*hausakljúfr*) was the son of *Torf Einar who succeeded his father in the Norse earldom of Orkney. Thorfinn's wife was Grelaug the daughter of a Scottish 'earl', Dungadr of Caithness. According to *Orkneyinga Saga*, Thorfinn was ruling on Orkney when Gunnhildr, the queen of *Eirikr Bloodaxe of York, led the remnants of her husband's household to Orkney after the slaying of Eirikr on Stainmore in 954. Thorfinn seems to have shared the earldom initially with his brothers

Arnkel and Erlend who fell fighting alongside Eirikr on Stainmore. When Gunnhildr retreated to Orkney, her sons took over the rule of the Northern Isles from Earl Thorfinn, suggesting in the minds of later saga compilers, at least, that the Orkney earls held their territories directly from the Norwegian overlord. Eventually, Gunnhildr and her sons left Orkney for the Danish court of Harald Gormsson, after which Thorfinn resumed his rule over the Orkney earldom. Gunnhildr married her daughter, *Ragnhild, to Thorfinn's son and successor, Arnfinn. According to *Orkneyinga Saga*, Thornfinn Skull-splitter died in his bed and was buried at Hoxa in North Ronaldsay.

BIBL. Anderson 1922, vol. 1: 462-7; Pálsson and Edwards 1978: 32-3

Thorfinn II the Mighty earl of Orkney *c*. 1014−65

Thorfinn was a boy of five when his father, Earl *Sigurd the Stout, was slain in Ireland at the battle of Clontarf in 1014. The Orkney earldom was then first divided between three of Sigurd's sons, Sumarlidi, Brúsi and *Einar Falsemouth. The infant Thorfinn was reared under the protection of his maternal grandfather, who was probably *Malcolm II, king of Scots, who invested Thorfinn with the earldom of Caithness and Sutherland. On the death of Sumarlidi, Einar appropriated his dead brother's share of Orkney, refusing to allow Thorfinn a portion of the inheritance. This led to the slaying of Einar by Thorkel, the fosterer of Thorfinn, at Sandwick in *c*. 1020. Competition for Orkney was now confined between Thorfinn and his surviving brother, Brúsi, and in 1021 (Icelandic annals) the two earls sailed on separate expeditions to Norway where they offered their submissions to King *Olafr Helgi Haraldsson. Meanwhile, Thorfinn (who had been raiding on his own account since the age of 15), became embroiled in a war with the new Scottish king, *Karl Hundason, who has been tentatively identified by some historians with *Macbeth. Thorfinn emerged triumphant from this struggle in which he established his claim to Caithness and Sutherland, and on the death of his brother, Brúsi, he took over sole rule of Orkney *c*. 1035. At this time also he seems to have extended his influence south and west across the Hebrides and into the Irish Sea at the expense of the Norse kingdom of Dublin. Meanwhile *Rögnvaldur son of Brúsi, who had been in exile in Norway, returned to claim his father's inheritance *c*. 1037−8. Peace was established between Thorfinn and his nephew for eight years, during which time Thorfinn lived in Caithness and Rögnvaldur in Orkney. During Thorfinn's repeated raiding in the Irish Sea, he brought fire and sword on a punitive raid against England 'south of Man' *c*. 1042. Eventually, he quarrelled with Rögnvaldur Brúsason whom he defeated in a naval battle in the Pentland Firth. In the struggle that followed, Thorfinn narrowly escaped death as he carried his Norwegian wife, Ingibjörg Finnsdóttir, from the flames of their burning hall on Mainland, Orkney. Thorfinn eventually triumphed when he had Rögnvaldur slain on Papa Stronsay sometime before Christmas in 1046, and thereafter he ruled as sole earl of Orkney until his death. Soon after Rögnvaldur's assassination, Thorfinn sailed to Norway in a vain effort to be reconciled with King Magnus the

Good whose men Thorfinn had slain in his struggle with Rögnvaldur. Thorfinn had probably been brought up a Christian on the Scottish mainland under the influence of his Scottish kin, but he lived as a pagan Viking until late in life when he had established himself on Orkney against all rivals. In *c*. 1050 he set off on a grand pilgrimage to Rome, sailing first to the court of Harald Hardrada of Norway; then on to that of Swein Ulfsson at Aalborg in Denmark; next to the German Emperor, Henry III in Saxony; and finally to Rome where he was received by the pope. His final turning to Christianity also prompted Thorfinn to establish *Thorolf as the first bishop of Orkney. Thorfinn lived into old age, turning to law-making and peaceful rule at his court at Birsay where he died *c*. 1065. He was buried in the Christ's Kirk which he himself had built at Birsay and was remembered in Norse tradition as the greatest of all Orkney earls. During his long life he had visited the Norwegian court on several occasions; he was feared and respected by Olafr Helgi, Magnus the Good, and by Harald Hardrada. His deeds were celebrated by his poet, *Arnór Earls' Poet, who remembered Thorfinn as 'the raven feaster' who ruled the seas with a rod of iron from 'Dublin to the Thursasker' or Muckle Flugga rocks off furthest Shetland. Icelandic tradition remembered him as an ugly man — tall, strong and dark-haired, with a big nose and bushy brows.

BIBL. Anderson 1922, vol. 1: 551-67, 584-87; vol. 2: 1-9; Pálsson and Edwards 1978: 38-76

Thorkell the Tall earl 1018−21, *d*. after 1023
   Thorkell Havi, 'the Tall', was the leader of 'the immense raiding-army which we called Thorkell's army', which fell upon England in August 1009. This force, which surpassed anything yet experienced in size and organization, ravaged southern England for the next three years, and was joined by contingents under *Eilaf and *Olafr Helgi. The rank and file came not only from Denmark but from Sweden (see *Ulv of Borresta) and probably Norway as well; when it disbanded in 1012, it 'dispersed as widely as before it had been concentrated'. It was this army which fought against *Ulfkell Snilling at Ringmere in 1010; the English dead included Athelstan, King *Æthelred II's brother-in-law. The campaign culminated in the sack of Canterbury in 1012, in which many leading ecclesiastics were captured, including *Ælfheah (St Alphege), the archbishop. Most were ransomed, but Ælfheah refused to allow ransom to be paid for him and was martyred in the Viking camp at Southwark. This killing seems to have been opposed by Thorkell, for it was after this that he offered his services to King Æthelred; he brought with him 45 ships and 'promised to defend this country' in return for food and supplies; and, of course, money. The tax raised to pay for Thorkell's fleet, the heregeld, was first levied in 1012 and remained an annual impost, for the support of a mercenary fleet, until 1051. It was in Thorkell's ships that Æthelred escaped to Normandy when the English submitted to *Swein Forkbeard, king of Denmark, in 1013. Thorkell was no more a friend of the Danish kings than was Æthelred. After the king's death in 1016, however, he

made common cause with *Cnut, and was made earl of East Anglia when Cnut established himself as king of England in 1018. In 1021 he and Cnut fell out, and Thorkell was banished from England. A reconciliation was effected in 1023, and Thorkell was made regent of Denmark; it was agreed that he should foster Cnut's son *Harthacnut, and that his own son should be brought up by the king. Whether this arrangement was ever implemented is doubtful, for Thorkell is not heard of after 1023. However his son *Haraldr did marry Cnut's niece *Gunnhildr, at some time after 1030. Thorkell's wife, Edith, bore an English name and may have been the widow of *Ulfkell Snilling.

BIBL. Campbell 1949: 73-6; Williams 1986; Lund 1986

Thorolf Norse bishop of Orkney c. 1050

The Old Icelandic *Orkneyinga Saga* claims that the Orkney earl, *Thorfinn the Mighty, built a church at Birsay on Orkney and established the first bishop there. This was late in Thorfinn's reign, following on his expedition to Scandinavia and pilgrimage to Rome c. 1050. Adam of Bremen (writing c. 1070) records that the first bishop of Orkney was called Thorolf; that he was appointed in the time of Archbishop Adalbert of Hamburg (1042−72) and that his seat was at *Blascona* on Orkney. According to Adam, Thorolf was appointed 'by order of the pope' on the request of legates from Orkney. Since Earl Thorfinn visited the pope on his Rome pilgrimage, and since he most likely called in on Hamburg *en route* from Denmark to Saxony, it seems probable that Thorfinn personally requested the appointment of the bishop. Thorolf's Norse name (Thórólfr) would suggest that he was Thorfinn's appointee, if not indeed a close relative. The ruined remains of an apsidal church discovered at the Brough of Birsay on Orkney very probably mark the site of Thorolf's and Thorfinns's eleventh-century cathedral church of Christ's Kirk.

BIBL. Anderson 1922, vol. 2: 7-10; Pálsson and Edwards 1978: 74-5

Thorstein the Red Norse king in Scotland c. 855−75

Thorstein the Red (*raudr*) was the son of *Aud the Deep-Minded and King Olaf the White of Dublin. Through his father he was descended from the royal line of Vestfold kings, while his mother, Aud, was the daughter of *Ketil Flatnose, Norse ruler of the Hebrides. Although Thorstein is known only from later Icelandic sources, his historicity is in little doubt. The reign of his father in Dublin is dated in contemporary Irish annals to the period 853−71, and Thorstein's wife, Thurídur, was the grand-daughter of the Irish king, Cerball of Ossory, who died in 888. Thorstein allied himself with *Sigurd the Powerful, earl of Orkney, and carved out a kingdom from territories of the conquered Picts in northern Scotland. The Icelandic *Landnámabók* and *Laxdœla Saga* claim that Thorstein made himself king over half of Scotland, but *Heimskringla* more accurately places the southern boundary of his realm at Strath Oykel west of the Dornoch Firth in Sutherland. Thorstein's kingdom consisted of Caithness, eastern Sutherland and perhaps the southern shores of the Moray Firth. When Thorstein was slain by the Scots, his family fortunes collapsed, and his mother, Aud, by then divorced from King Olaf of Dublin, was forced to emigrate to Iceland. She took with her Thorstein's son, Olaf Feilan, who settled in Laxárdal in western Iceland and was the founder there of a line of chieftains.

BIBL. Smyth 1977a: 123-4, 151-2; Smyth 1984: 160-3

Thorstein housecarl *d.* 1041, *see* **Feader** and **Thorstein**

Thurbrand the Hold, *d.* 1019
   Thurbrand the Hold was a Northumbrian magnate, prominent among the Anglo-Danish families of York. In 1016, with the connivance of *Cnut, he murdered *Uhtred of Bamburgh, and was himself killed by Uhtred's son, *Ealdred, in 1019. The circumstances are obscure, and are usually represented as the opening moves of a blood-feud, which continued to the end of the century. Thurbrand's title, however, implies that he held some kind of public office in the north, and he was probably the leader of the York Anglo-Danes, who supported Cnut in 1016, as Uhtred supported Cnut's rival, *Edmund Ironside. The enmity between his family and that of the high-reeves of Bamburgh represents the political hostility between York and Bamburgh which surfaces frequently in eleventh-century England.

BIBL. Kapelle 1979: 17-26; Hart 1975: 361

Thurferth earl 917−34
   In 917, Earl Thurferth and the holds and 'all the army which belonged to Northampton, as far north as the Welland' submitted to the rule of *Edward the Elder, king of Wessex. Thurferth, who had presumably been subordinate to the Viking kings of York, became the man of the West Saxon kings, and maintained his position as earl of Northampton until 934, when, presumably, he died. From *c.* 930, he was subordinate to *Athelstan Half-king.

BIBL. Hart 1973: 122

Thuri earl 1038−44
   Thuri, earl of the 'middle peoples', was one of those who took part in the harrying of Worcestershire in 1041, ordered by *Harthacnut as a punishment for the murder of two of his housecarls. He was in office by 1038 and was presumably dead by 1044, when his office passed to Beorn, nephew of Earl *Godwine of Wessex. The 'middle peoples' were the inhabitants of the east midlands. Thuri's origins are unknown; he has been assumed to have been a Dane in Cnut's or Harthacnut's entourage, but his appointment as earl seems to date from the reign of *Harold I, and he is more likely an Anglo-Dane from the east midlands.

BIBL. Williams 1986

Tjalve warrior *fl.* first half of the eleventh century
   Tjalve is commemorated on the runestone at Landeryd (Ostergotland) in Sweden: 'Væring raised this stone in memory of Tjalve his brother, the

dreng (warrior) who served with Cnut'. He was thus presumably one of those who served with *Cnut in the conquest of England in 1016.

BIBL. Jansson 1962: 50-1

Tondberht ealdorman *c*. 652/9

Tondberht, the first husband of St *Æthelthryth, was ealdorman of the South Gyrwe, a people living on the western edge of the Fens; the North Gyrwe inhabited a territory probably co-terminous with the original endowment of Peterborough Abbey. Both provinces were probably subject to the East Anglian rulers; Æthelthryth was the daughter of *Anna, king of the East Angles, and Thomas, who succeeded *Felix as bishop of the East Angles, was a man of the Gyrwe. By the 650s, the area was passing into Mercian control, and formed part of the kingdom of Middle Anglia ruled by *Peada, son of *Penda. Crowland, where the Mercian prince *Guthlac established his hermitage, lay in the land of the Gyrwe. The *Tribal Hidage*, a tribute-list drawn up for a Mercian ruler in the seventh or eighth centuries, assigns 600 hides each to the North and South Gyrwe.

BIBL. Stafford 1985: 31-2; Hart 1977: 50-1; Whitelock 1972

Torf Einar (Einar I) earl of Orkney *c*. 900

Einar was the youngest and illegitimate son of *Rögnvaldur of Moer in Norway. He persuaded his father to grant him the Orkney earldom after his older brother, Hallad had failed to clear the Northern Isles of Scotland of Viking marauders. Rögnvaldur agreed and Einar established himself in Orkney, clearing the Isles of troublesome Vikings who harried Norway in the summer months and who preyed on local farmers in the spring and autumn. He earned his nickname *Torf-Einar* being remembered as the Orkney earl who exploited the peat (*torf*) deposits of northern Scotland and the Isles. *Orkneyinga Saga* claims that Einar's rule extended as far south in Scotland as Tarbat Ness in Easter Ross. He can be regarded as the first historical earl of Orkney. His rule there was challenged by Halfdan Highleg, supposedly the son of Harald Finehair of Norway, but more likely the son of an earlier Norwegian king. Halfdan had slain Einar's father, Rögnvaldur, back in Norway, and later led an expedition against Orkney. Einar defeated Halfdan in battle and later put him to death on North Ronaldsay as a sacrifice to the war god, Odin. Eventually, Torf Einar was reconciled to Halfdan's father, paying the Norwegian king the necessary compensation for the slaying of his son. According to Snorri Sturlason's *Heimskringla*, Einar was an ugly man and blind in one eye.

BIBL. Anderson 1922, vol. 1: 373-7, 388-91; Pálsson and Edwards 1978: 28-32; Smyth 1984: 153-4

Tovi the Proud staller *d*. *c*. 1043/4

Tovi the Proud, who makes his first appearance in 1018, was probably a Dane of *Cnut's following. It was on his estate of *Lutgaresbury* (Montacute), Somerset, that the Black Rood of Waltham was discovered, in honour of which Tovi founded the church of Holy Cross at Waltham, Essex. With the great rood were found a smaller cross, a bell 'like a cow-bell' and a gospel-book; presumably the treasure of some small community buried long before, during the Viking raids, and forgotten. When the treasure was loaded onto an ox-cart the beasts refused to move; Tovi then recited the names of all his estates, and when he got to Waltham, they immediately set off. A hall, which may date from Tovi's time, has recently been excavated at Waltham Abbey.

Tovi was a rich and powerful man, a staller, with an office in the king's household. During the reign of Cnut, he is found attending the shire-court of Hereford on the king's business. In 1042, he married Gytha, daughter of *Osgod Clapa, who was probably his second wife. His son, Athelstan (who cannot have been Gytha's child), forfeited his lands for treason, though some of his estates passed to his son Esger or Ansgar the staller, who held them in 1066. The patronage of Holy Cross was taken over by Earl Harold, son of *Godwine of Wessex, who greatly enlarged the foundation. Tovi is not heard of after 1043, and probably died about that time.

BIBL. Stubbs 1861; Williams 1988; Huggins 1976

U

Uhtred ealdorman 930−*c*. 949

In 926, King *Athelstan confirmed to his 'faithful man' Uhtred, land at Hope and at Ashwell, both in Derbyshire, which Uhtred had 'bought with his own money' at the order of King *Edward the Elder, and Ealdorman *Æthelred; that is between 899 and 911. The comparative rarity of Uhtred's name suggests that he was Uhtred son of *Eadulf of Bamburgh. This suggestion is supported by the fact that another charter, of the same date and couched in similar terms to the one which granted Hope and Ashwell to Uhtred, confirms an estate at Chalgrave, Bedfordshire, to *Ealdred, for Uhtred son of Eadulf had a brother of just this name. The existence of these two charters has been taken to indicate a preliminary 'softening-up' process, whereby thegns were encouraged to acquire land in the areas of Danish settlement which their lord the king intended to re-conquer. If, however, the recipients of these charters are indeed the sons of the ruler of Bamburgh, they are also evidence of West Saxon attempts to win the support of the English of Northumbria for the coming campaign against the Danish settlers. The arrival on the scene of *Ragnall, who seized the kingdom of York in 910, interrupted this rapprochement, and in 914, Ealdred and Uhtred were actually driven from Bamburgh. Ealdred sought the aid of *Constantine II of Scotland to retrieve his position, and in 920 the brothers made submission to Edward the Elder. Uhtred witnesses charters of Athelstan as ealdorman (perhaps of north Mercia) between 930 and 934, and those of *Eadred between 946 and 949; in the latter year, he received a gift of land at Bakewell, Derbyshire, where he established a religious community. Uhtred *cild*, described as *pedisequus* of Eadred (that is, a member of the royal household), and the recipient of a grant of land at Chesterfield, Derbyshire, in 955, is probably a kinsman of Ealdorman Uhtred.

BIBL. Hart 1975: 362; Sawyer 1979, no. 3: 5-7

Uhtred ealdorman 995−1016

Uhtred, son of Waltheof, belonged to the family which had ruled Bamburgh since the ninth century. His father was ealdorman of Bamburgh in 994, but in the following year it was Uhtred who took the initiative in the establishing of an episcopal see at Durham, whither the community of St *Cuthbert moved from Chester-le-Street. Uhtred's connections with the new see were strengthened when he married Ecgfrida, daughter of Bishop *Ealdhun. She brought him a substantial dowry of land attached to the church of Durham. In 1006, when Durham was besieged by *Malcolm II of Scotland, Waltheof's age caused him to leave the defence to Uhtred, who proved more than equal to the task. It was probably as a result of this successful action that *Æthelred II appointed Uhtred ealdorman of Northumbria in 1007, in succession to the murdered *Ælfhelm. Perhaps in order to consolidate his position in southern Northumbria, Uhtred repudiated his wife, the bishop's daughter, and married Sige, daughter of a rich citizen of York, Styr Ulfson. This marriage, however, brought Uhtred into conflict with Styr's enemy, *Thurbrand the Hold. In 1013, when *Swein Forkbeard landed his army in the Humber, Uhtred and the northern nobles submitted to him. When, after Swein's death in 1014, Æthelred II returned to his kingdom, he seems to have attempted to win over Uhtred by offering him his daughter, Ælfgifu, in marriage, an offer accepted by Uhtred, who divorced Sige in Ælfgifu's favour. When in 1015, Swein's son *Cnut made his bid for the crown, Uhtred supported his new brother-in-law, *Edmund Ironside, against the Danish host. Cnut, however, made alliance with Uhtred's enemy Thurbrand. Uhtred, under a safe-conduct, attempted to negotiate his position, but was murdered by Thurbrand with Cnut's connivance. Uhtred's brother, *Eadulf Cudel, succeeded to Bamburgh, but the earldom of Northumbria went to Cnut's ally, *Eirikr of Hlathir.

BIBL. Hart 1975: 143-50, 362-3; Kapelle 1979: 14-21

Ulfkell Snilling thegn *d.* 1016

Ulfkell Snilling ('the Bold') was one of the leading thegns of East Anglia, and from 1004 to 1016 exercised the power, even if he had not the title, of ealdorman of East Anglia. He defended the province against *Swein Forkbeard in 1004, and though he lost the battle, the Danes themselves said 'that they had never met with harder hand-play in England than Ulfkell gave them'. In 1010 Ulfkell and his men were pitted against the 'immense raiding-army' of *Thorkell the Tall at the battle of Ringmere, which Scandinavian sources describe as being in 'Ulfkell's land' (see Sigvatr). As well as being a great warrior, Ulfkell was a pious man and a benefactor of Bury St Edmunds. He was killed at the battle of Ashingdon in 1016. His widow is said to have married Thorkell the Tall; she was probably not, as sometimes claimed, a daughter of *Æthelred II.

BIBL. Hart 1975: 363; Campbell 1949: 76, 89

Ulfr earl *d. c.* 1028

Ulfr and *Eilaf were the sons of Thorgils Sprakaleg; Ulfr was the brother-in-law of *Cnut, whose sister Estrith he married, and his own sister, Gytha, was the wife of Earl *Godwine of Wessex. Ulfr himself seems never to have held land or office in England. His career is difficult to reconstruct, as a result of the legendary material that gathered around his name. He may have been regent of Denmark after the demise of *Thorkell the Tall *c.* 1023. He was opposing Cnut, however, at the battle of Holy River in 1027, and although they were reconciled, Cnut had Ulfr murdered soon afterwards. He was buried at Roskilde. By Estrith he left two sons; one, Beorn Estrithson, became an earl in England, and was murdered in 1049 by Swein son of Earl *Godwine, and the other, Swein Estrithson, became king of Denmark.

BIBL. Campbell 1949: 82-7

Ulv of Borresta *fl.* first half of the eleventh century

Ulv of Borresta was an important landowner in Uppland, Sweden, commemorated on the Yttergarde runestone, raised by his sons, Karse and Karlbjorn:

'Ulv took in England three gelds. That was the first which Toste paid. Then Thorkell paid. Then Cnut paid.'

Toste's expedition is not mentioned by that name in any English source; it presumably took place before 1009, for the Thorkell of the stone must be *Thorkell the Tall. Toste may have been one of the leaders of the host which was operating in the west in the years 997–1002. If Ulv, as seems likely, was a member of Thorkell's 'immense raiding-army', it is possible that he followed his leader into Cnut's service after the death of *Æthelred II, and was paid off in 1018.

BIBL. Jansson 1962: 53-5; Lund 1986: 117-18

Urien ruler of Rheged *fl.* sixth century

Urien appears in the genealogies of the Men of the North (North Britain) in a context which would place him in the second half of the sixth century, but it is the early ninth-century *Historia Brittonum* (see under *Nennius) which locates him most precisely in time as the leader of a British coalition, embracing *Riderch Hen, king of the Strathclyde Britons, and *Gwallawg, ruler of Elmet, against the Angles under their king, Theodric (*c.* 572/3–79/80) during the besieging of whom on the island of Lindisfarne he was slain by a rival British chieftain, Morcant, possibly a prince of the Votadini. The early bardic poems of *Taliesin locate him geographically as ruler of Rheged with his centre at Lyvennet in the Eden valley. 'Golden king of the north', sings the bard, 'I will praise your deeds'. One of the Taliesin poems laments the death of Urien's son Owain — 'a vivid man above his many-coloured trappings'.

BIBL. Williams 1960; Williams 1968; Bromwich 1961: 516-20; Jarman 1981: 21ff.

Urk housecarl *d.* 1058/66

Urk was a Danish member of the military retinue of *Cnut (a housecarl), from whom he received grants of land at Portesham, Dorset, in 1024 and at Abbotsbury. He entered the service of Edward the Confessor, from whom he received land at Abbots Wootton, also Dorset. He was the founder of Abbotsbury Abbey, to which most of his land eventually passed, and also of the Abbotsbury Guild of St Peter. The purpose of this association, like others of its kind, was to provide for the mutual support of its members, in life and death. Urk probably died in the late 1050s or early 1060s. His wife, Tole, gave her name to Tolpuddle, Dorset.

BIBL. Harmer 1952: 120-3, 576; Keynes 1989: 207-43

V

Virgno *see* **Fergna Brit**

Vortepor king of Dyfed *fl.* first half of sixth century

The grey-haired Vortepor (Gwrthefyr), called 'tyrant of the Demetians' (the men of Dyfed), is among the kings denounced by *Gildas, accused of immorality (including incest) and murder. He appears in the earliest genealogies of the kings of Dyfed as the son of Aircol, a descendant of Eochaid, son of Artchorp. Eochaid was said to have led the people of the Déisi from southern Ireland to south-west Wales (probably *c.* 400–50). These kings of Dyfed, therefore, were of Irish extraction. The inscription MEMORIA VOTEPORIGIS PROTICTORIS ('memorial of Vortepor, Protector') is found on a stone which formerly stood at Castell Dwyran in Dyfed and implies that Vortepor was invested by contemporaries with a pseudo-Roman status.

BIBL. Jackson 1982: 31-2; Alcock 1971: 122; O'Cathasaigh 1984; Davies 1982: 87ff.

Vortigern British ruler *fl.* fifth century

Known to Welsh tradition as Gwrtheyrn Gwrthenau (Vortigern the Thin), Vortigern appears to have been a fifth-century Romano-British ruler who was said to have employed Germanic troops (according to *Bede those commanded by *Hengest and Horsa) against the threat of a Pictish and Scottish attack only to find himself assailed by his rebellious allies who overwhelmed and defeated him. Gildas refers to Vortigern, whose name means 'overlord', as 'the proud tyrant', which suggests that he occupied a position of considerable power. Much material hostile to his memory circulated in Wales and found a place in the early ninth-century *Historia Brittonum* (see under *Nennius), but the kings of Gwrtheyrnion (Radnorshire) in the early ninth century claimed descent from a Vortigern who was probably understood to be the fifth-century figure, as did *Cyngen ap Cadell. In later hagiographic legend incorporated in the *Historia Brittonum*, he was depicted as a fugitive within Wales from the wrath of St *Germanus who hounded him to death at *Caer Guorthigern* (Craig Gwrtheyrn) on the Teifi, but it would be unwise to use this material to reconstruct the career of the historical Vortigern, or even to suppose that Vortigern incurred the hostility of Germanus of Auxerre as a Pelagian heretic at the time when Germanus came to Britain to combat Pelagianism.

BIBL. Kirby 1968; Dumville 1977; Jackson 1982: 35-40

Vræ staller, *fl.* first half of the eleventh century

Vræ is commemorated on a runestone at Savsjo (Smaland), in Sweden, erected by his daughter, Tova:

233

'Tova raised this stone in memory of Vræ her father, Hakon Jarl's staller.'

Vræ's lord was perhaps *Hakon, son of *Eirikr of Hlathir, who became earl of Worcestershire. One of Vræ's brothers died in England, but presumably Vræ returned to Sweden.

BIBL. Jansson 1962: 58-60

Wærburh (Werberga) St *d. c.* 700

Wærburh, daughter of *Wulfhere of Mercia, became a nun at Ely, ruled by her great-aunt, St *Æthelthryth. Her uncle *Æthelred of Mercia recalled her to found several monasteries in his kingdom, including Weedon, Northamptonshire, Hanbury, Staffordshire and Threckingham, Lincolnshire, where she died. She was buried at Hanbury, but her remains were later removed to Chester, where her cult developed in the church dedicated to her.

BIBL. Farmer 1978: 401

Wærferth bishop 872−914/5

Wærferth, bishop of Worcester, was one of the scholars recruited from Mercia by King *Alfred in his programme of educational reform. *Asser says it was Wærferth who translated the *Dialogues* of Pope *Gregory the Great from Latin to English; Book II of this work is in effect a biography of St Benedict, father of monasticism in the west. The Old English version of *Bede's *Ecclesiastical History*, translated at the same time, is in the Mercian dialect, and Wærferth may have had a hand in it. Alfred also had translated Gregory's *Pastoral Care*, a work on the duties of bishops, copies of which were distributed around all the English sees. Of the two copies which survive from Alfred's time, one is that sent to Wærferth of Worcester.

BIBL. Keynes and Lapidge 1983a: 23-41

Walburh (Walburga, Walpurgis) St *d.* 779

Walburh was the sister of SS *Willibald and Winnebald, and a kinswoman of St *Lioba. She was trained as a nun at Wimborne, Dorset, and went, like both her brothers, to join the English missionaries in Germany. She entered the double-monastery of Tauberbischofsheim, of which Lioba was abbess, but after two years removed to Heidenheim, as abbess, in succession to her brother Winnebald, the former abbot, who died in 761. His relics were translated to Eichstatt in 776, and when Walburh died three years later, her remains were sent to the same place. Her feast-day was 1 May, and her cult became confused with the pagan spring-festival celebrated at the same time, which became known as *Walpurgisnacht*.

BIBL. Levison 1946: 79-81; Farmer 1978: 395

Wiglaf king of Mercia 827−9, 830−c. 838

After the death of *Beornwulf of Mercia, the kingdom was ruled by one of Beornwulf's ealdormen, Ludeca. He died in 827, and Wiglaf took power. At this time the West Saxons under *Ecgberht were launching a bitter attack on their old enemies, the Mercians, and in 829, Wiglaf was expelled from his kingdom. He regained his position in 830. Since he was not a member of the Mercian royal line, he attempted to consolidate his position by marrying his son Wigmund to *Ælfflæd, daughter of King *Ceolwulf I. By 831 he was in control of Middlesex, and an assembly at Croft, Leicestershire, in 836 was attended by the archbishop of Canterbury and all the bishops of the southern province. There is no indication, however, that Wiglaf ever succeeded in restoring the Mercian overlordship destroyed at the battle of *Ellendun* (Wroughton) in 825. He probably died about 838, and was succeeded by Wigmund, but on his death in 840 Mercia went to a rival dynasty with the succession of *Beorhtwulf.

BIBL. Stenton 1971: 232-5

Wigstan (Wistan, Wystan) St *d*. 849

Wigstan, grandson of *Wiglaf of Mercia, was the son of Wigmund and of *Ælfflæd, daughter of *Ceolwulf I. In 849, he was murdered at Wistowe, Leicestershire ('the holy place of Wigstan'), by Beorhtfrith, son of King *Beorhtwulf. The alleged reason was that Wigstan had refused to allow his widowed mother's re-marriage to Beorhtfrith. Wigstan was buried with his father and grandfather at Repton, a house associated with Mercian royalty since the seventh century; it was there that St *Guthlac had received the tonsure, and it was the burial-place of King *Æthelbald. Wigstan rapidly became the object of veneration, and the extensive re-modelling of the church of Repton which took place at about this time, including the provision of a corridor-crypt for the display of relics, is probably connected with the development of his cult. The canonization of Wigstan had a political element; it kept alive the memory of his kindred's claim to be rulers of Mercia. Repton was occupied by the Vikings in 874, an event which led to the flight of King *Burgred, and his replacement by *Ceolwulf II, who was probably related to Wigstan.

BIBL. Rollason 1983

Wihtgar *see* **Stuf**

Wihtred king of Kent 690–725

Wihtred son of *Ecgberht became king of Kent in 690, after it had fallen under the rule of 'various usurpers and foreign kings', among whom may be counted *Cædwalla of Wessex and *Sighere of Essex. Wihtred had to accept the co-rule of Swæfheard, son of King *Sebbi of Essex, but by 695 he could issue a law-code (still extant) in his sole name. He died on 23 April 725 and was succeeded by his three sons, *Æthelberht, Eadberht and Ealric.

BIBL. Stenton 1971: 62; Whitelock 1955, no. 31: 362-4 (Wihtred's Law-Code); *HE* iv, 26: 430-1; Yorke 1985: 21

Wilfrid St, bishop of 664–709/10

Wilfrid was born about 633, into a noble Northumbrian family. When in his early 'teens he wished to enter on his independent career, his father sent him to Queen *Eanflæd, wife of *Oswiu of Northumbria. Finding him interested in the religious life, she sent him to Lindisfarne in attendance on one of her retainers who wished to end his life there. Wilfrid then decided to travel to Rome, and went to Canterbury, where he spent a year. He finally set out for the continent in the entourage of *Benedict Biscop, but at Lyons there was a quarrel and Wilfrid left the party. He spent three years at Lyons, in the household of its bishop, Aunemundus, before proceeding to Rome. On his return to Northumbria, he gained the frienship of *Alhfrith, king of Deira, who gave him the monastery of Ripon, and had him ordained a priest by *Agilbert, the Frankish bishop of Wessex. At the Synod of Whitby in 664, Wilfrid was chosen as spokesman for the Roman party. It was of course for Roman custom that the synod decided, and when Bishop *Colmán of Lindisfarne preferred to resign his see and return to Ireland rather than accept the Roman Easter, Wilfrid was chosen bishop, with his see at York. He went to Paris for his consecration, which was performed by Agilbert, then bishop of Paris, and 12 Frankish bishops. While he was absent, Oswiu chose *Chad as bishop of the Northumbrians. It is not quite clear that Chad was actually intruded into Wilfrid's see (though Wilfrid seems to have believed this); it is possible that Wilfrid's see was intended to be Deira, with Chad in charge of Bernicia. However, Archbishop *Theodore, on his arrival in England in 669, deposed Chad, and confirmed Wilfrid as bishop of Northumbria. Oswiu's son and successor, *Ecgfrith, was at first favourable to Wilfrid, and gave him the land to found a monastery at Hexham. Wilfrid's encouragement of Ecgfrith's wife, St *Æthelthryth, in her determination to leave her husband and enter religion soured relations, and in 678 there was an outright quarrel; Wilfrid was driven from Northumbria. Theodore took advantage of this situation to divide the Northumbrian diocese, appointing Bosa, a monk of Whitby, as bishop of York, and *Eata, abbot of Lindisfarne, as bishop for Bernicia, with the choice of Lindisfarne or — to add insult to injury — Wilfrid's monastery at Hexham for his see. Eadhæd was appointed as bishop for the province of Lindsey. Wilfrid went to Rome to appeal to the papal court against this action. In 679, Pope Agatho approved the division of the see but ordered that Wilfrid should be restored to York, with the right to choose his co-bishops. This judgement was resisted by a Northumbrian synod which met in 680, and Wilfrid was first imprisoned and then expelled. He went to *Æthelwalh of Sussex, accomplished the conversion of the South Saxons, and founded a monastery at Selsey. He had already been involved in missionary work on his return journey from Rome in 679, when he preached in Frisia. When in 685, Æthelwalh was killed by *Cædwalla of Wessex, who overran Sussex, Wilfrid persuaded Cædwalla to give him a quarter of the Isle of Wight, in order to convert its inhabitants. In the meantime the division of the Northumbrian see was proceeding apace; a bishopric was established at Hexham in 681, and Eadhæd, who had been driven from Lindsey by the Mercian reconquest of 679, was established at Wilfrid's monastery of Ripon. The death of Ecgfrith in 685 opened the way for a reconciliation. Wilfrid and Theodore met at London and came to an agreement; Theodore urged the new king of Northumbria, *Aldfrith, to accept Wilfrid. Of the new sees created by Theodore, only Ripon was vacant, and there Wilfrid was established, though he also administered the see of Lindisfarne after the death of *Cuthbert in 687. In 690 Theodore died. It is possible that Wilfrid hoped to be made archbishop of Canterbury; he certainly tried to gain acceptance as bishop of all Northumbria. This led to a breach with King Aldfrith, and Wilfrid was once more expelled from Northumbria. The Mercian king, *Æthelred, was a personal friend, and for the next few years, Wilfrid administered the bishopric of the Middle Angles, probably from Leicester. In 699 he appealed by proxy to Pope Sergius I, who ordered a Northumbrian and English synod, at Austerfield, in 702, which failed to agree, and another journey to Rome by Wilfrid in person produced no effective remedy. Only after the death of Aldfrith was he restored to his property. He espoused the cause of Aldfrith's infant son, *Osred, in the succession-struggle which followed the king's death, and at the Synod of the River Nidd, in 706, he was reinstated. *John of Beverley, who was then bishop of Hexham, was moved to York, and Wilfrid was installed at Hexham (the see of Ripon was now defunct). He died on 12 October, either in 709 or 710, at the monastery which he had founded at Oundle.

Wilfrid's career is vividly recounted in his *Life*, composed by *Eddius Stephanus. He exemplifies the many facets of the seventh-century English church, as bishop, founder of monasteries, missionary, pilgrim and politician. He introduced the pure Benedictine Rule at Ripon and Hexham, the first to do so, and it was at Ripon that the missionary *Willibrord received his early training. Wilfrid's appeals to the jurisdiction of Rome are important in the development of the papal court in the west. He was a great builder, though all that is left of his efforts now are the crypts of the two great churches at Ripon and at Hexham.

BIBL. Colgrave 1927; Kirby 1974a

Willehad St, bishop d. 789

Willehad was a product of the school of York and a friend of *Alcuin. In 766 King *Alhred of Northumbria despatched him to Frisia, to join the English missionaries working there. Charlemagne sent him to Saxony, but the Christian religion was too closely associated with Frankish political control for him to make much headway there, and the Saxon revolt of 782 ended his endeavours. After a visit to Rome, he settled for a while at Echternach, but in 787 returned to Saxony as bishop of Bremen. He died on 8 November 789.

BIBL. Farmer 1978: 204-5

Willibald St, bishop d. 786−7

Willibald was a West Saxon, who, with his brother Winnebald, and his sister *Walburh (Walburga), went as a missionary to Germany in the wake of *Willibrord and *Boniface. He undertook a pilgrimage to Jerusalem and the Holy Land, which is described in detail in the *Hodoeporicon of St Willibald*, composed by the nun *Huneberc, from Willibald's own account. He travelled via Sicily and Cyprus, taking the sea-route, was arrested as a spy in Emesa, and visited Damascus, Nazareth, Mount

Tabor, Tiberias and Caesarea as well as Jerusalem itself, where he fell ill, but was healed at the spot where Jesus cured the paralytic. On the way home, he purchased some balsam, and in order to evade the duty thereon, concealed it in a gourd, into which he inserted a hollowed reed, filled with crude petroleum. The customs-officers at Tyre were deceived by the smell of petroleum, which hid the fragrance of balsam. On his way home, Willibald spent two years at Constantinople, and some time at St Benedict's monastery of Monte Cassino, but Pope Gregory III sent him, at the request of Boniface, to Germany. There he founded Eichstatt, of which he became bishop in 742, and the double-monastery of Heidenheim ruled first by his brother Winnebald, and after his death, by his sister Walburh (Walburga). Willibald died in 786 or 787.

BIBL. Talbot 1954: 153-80

Willibrord St, archbishop of Utrecht *d.* 739

Willibrord, a Northumbrian by birth, received his early training at Ripon, but when *Wilfrid was expelled from Northumbria in 678, he left the monastery and went to Ireland. He studied some years with *Ecgberht the Englishman, who in 690 despatched him as a missionary to Frisia. He gained the support of Pepin II, mayor of the palace, and the real ruler of Frankia, and in 695 was consecrated bishop of Utrecht, at Rome. In 698, he founded the monastery of Echternach (in Luxembourg), a centre for the training of both English and indigenous clergy for the new churches east of the Rhine. He even began to extend his preaching activities into Denmark. Willibrord died at Echternach in 739, at the age of 81.

BIBL. Levison 1946: 53-69

Wine (Wini) bishop 660–75

In or about 660, Wine was made bishop of the West Saxons by *Cenwealh, thus encroaching upon the rights of Bishop *Agilbert, with whom Cenwealh had quarrelled. In 670, Wine too fell out with the king, and left Mercia. He then bought the vacant see of London from King *Wulfhere of Mercia, an act of simony (trafficking in ecclesiastical benefices) for which he was shunned by more principled clerics, and castigated by *Bede. It was however Wine, as bishop of Wessex, who consecrated *Chad, with the assistance of two British bishops, in 664, since the plague had killed so many English churchmen that he was the only English bishop who had been canonically ordained.

BIBL. *HE* iii, 7: 234-5; 28: 316-17

Winfrith bishop 672–4

Winfrith was the fourth bishop of the Mercians, succeeding on the death of *Chad, whose deacon he had been. In 674 he was deposed by Archbishop *Theodore, probably because he objected to the latter's plans for the division of the Mercian diocese. *Eddius describes how Winfrith was attacked on his way to Rome by envoys of Ebroin, mayor of the palace of Theodoric, king of the Franks, in mistake for Bishop *Wilfrid, and it is probable that Winfrith was going to Rome to protest against his deposition. If so, he was unsuccessful, for he was never restored to his see, and retired into the monastery of Barrow-in-Furness, where he died. The Mercian see was divided into the two dioceses of Lichfield and Leicester in the time of his successor, *Seaxwulf.

BIBL. *HE* iv, 3: 346-7; 6: 354-5; Colgrave 1927: 50-1

Wistan see **Wigstan**

Wulfheard the Frisian *d.* 896

Wulfheard is named with two compatriots, Æbba and Æthelhere, among the casualties of a naval battle against the Vikings in 896. They were Frisians in the employ of King *Alfred of Wessex, and were killed along with Lucuman, the king's reeve, and Æthelfrith, the king's *geneat*; in all, 62 English and Frisians, and 120 Danes lost their lives. The presence of Frisians is connected with Alfred's rebuilding of the West Saxon fleet 'neither on the Frisian nor the Danish pattern, but as it seemed to him himself that they could be most useful'. His use of Frisian craftsmen and warriors is perhaps connected with the alliance with Flanders cemented about this time by the marriage of Alfred's daughter *Ælfthryth with Baldwin II, count of Flanders.

BIBL. *ASC* s.a. 897

Wulfhere king of Mercia 658−75

After the battle of the River *Winwæd* in 655, in which *Penda was killed, Mercia remained for three years under the domination of Northumbria. In 658, the Mercian nobility rallied to Wulfhere, Penda's son, who became king. He re-established the domination of Mercia south of the Humber. By 665 he was recognized as overlord of Essex, and could sell the bishopric of London to *Wine in the 670s. He conquered the Isle of Wight, giving it, with the area of Hampshire nearest to it, to *Æthelwalh of Sussex, and *Frithuwold of Surrey was his subordinate. By 670, if not before, Wulfhere was probably in the position of an overlord. He overreached himself when he invaded Northumbria in *c.* 674, and he died in the next year, succeeded by his brother *Æthelred. Wulfhere married Eormenhild, daughter of *Eorcenberht of Kent and *Seaxburh. She bore him two children, *Cœnred and St *Wærburh.

BIBL. Stenton 1971: 84-5; Stenton 1981: 433-52

Wulfred archbishop of Canterbury 805−32

Wulfred was a native of Middlesex, holding land at Hayes. He entered the household of *Æthelheard, archbishop of Canterbury, becoming archdeacon, and succeeded to the archbishopric on Æthelheard's death, in 805. He reformed the cathedral chapter, re-instituting the common refectory and dormitory which had been abandoned since the early days of the church; though the clergy still owned their own property, they lived a communal life. This reorganization necessitated a re-arrangement of the see's estates to provide for the needs of the Canterbury *familia*. Wulfred, following his predecessor Æthelheard, took every opportunity to consolidate the community's holdings, exchanging outlying estates for properties in Kent and the south-east. The lands of Canterbury Cathedral were organized into large estates administered from central manor-houses where dues and services were rendered; 'a glimpse of the process of manorial formation and growth'. Wulfred was also concerned with abuses in the church at large, and in particular with the existence of 'proprietary churches' in the hands of powerful lay nobles and their families. He was concerned with the rights such nobles had to nominate abbots and abbesses for such houses and at the Synod of Chelsea, 816, the bishops were given sole authority to appoint abbots and abbesses to the religious communities within their dioceses. It is doubtful if this edict really affected the problem, and 'secular domination' of religious foundations was a bone of contention right down to the twelfth century. Wulfred himself was anxious to wrest control of the Kentish houses of Minster-in-Thanet and Reculver from the royal house of Mercia, which embroiled him with King *Cœnwulf, and led to his temporary deposition from the archiepiscopate in 817−21. He finally made peace with Cœnwulf's heir, Abbess *Cwœnthryth, in 826.

BIBL. Brooks 1984: 132-42, 155-60, 175-97

Wulfric Spot thegn *d*. 1002/4
   Wulfric Spot was a rich thegn of Mercia, the son of *Wulfrun. His brother *Ælfhelm was ealdorman of Northumbria from 993 to 1006. One of his nieces, Ælfhelm's daughter, *Ælfgifu of Northampton, became the first wife of *Cnut, and another, Ealdgyth, married *Morcar, one of the leading thegns of Northumbria. Wulfric was the founder of Burton Abbey, and his will, appended to the abbey's foundation charter, reveals the extent of his landed wealth, which reached into ten shires from Yorkshire to Gloucestershire.

BIBL. Sawyer 1979

Wulfrun noblewoman *fl*. second half of the tenth century
   Wulfrun was a rich noblewoman of Mercia, who founded the minster of St Mary, Wolverhampton; a town which preserves her name ('Wulfrun's chief settlement'). She is the only hostage whose capture is recorded when *Olafr Gothfrithson took Tamworth in 940, and her land seems to have lain chiefly in Staffordshire. She was married, although the name of her husband is unknown, and the fact that her son, *Wulfric Spot, is also known as Wulfric son of Wulfrun probably indicates that she was of higher rank than her spouse. Her other son, *Ælfhelm, became ealdorman of Northumbria in 993.

BIBL. Sawyer 1979

Wulfstan merchant *fl*. second half of the ninth century
   Wulfstan was a Scandinavian merchant of Hedeby (Schleswig) who described to King *Alfred his journey to Truso, on the River Vistula, for inclusion in the Old English version of Orosius's *History against the*

pagans. His account of the north Baltic lands, and the customs of the Slavonic tribes who inhabited the area, is one of the earliest sources for the history of the region (see *Ohthere).

BIBL. Lund 1984

Wulfstan archbishop of York 931—52, *d*. 955

Wulfstan became archbishop of York in the reign of King *Athelstan of Wessex, at whose court he was consecrated. Althelstan was at that time attempting to strengthen the ties between the church in the north and the West Saxon monarchy. In 934, he gave to the church of York the whole district of Amounderness, which he had bought from the 'pagans', that is, the Viking settlers in the area. By 939, however, Wulfstan seems to have come to terms with the Viking kings of York. In 940, he accompanied *Olafr Gothfrithson on his campaign against the Five Boroughs, and it was Wulfstan and Archbishop *Oda of Canterbury who arranged the subsequent truce between Olafr, and Athelstan's successor, *Edmund. Wulfstan also played a prominent role in the submission of the Danes of York to King *Eadred of Wessex in 947. In the same year, however, he and the northern nobles submitted to the rule of *Eirikr Bloodaxe, and Wulfstan supported Eirikr again in 954. In that year, the archbishop was arrested on King Eadred's orders, 'because accusations had often been made to the king against him'. He was not released until 954, when Eirikr was finally expelled from York, and killed at Stainmore. Even then, it is far from clear that he was allowed to return to his see. He died at Oundle, in the diocese of Dorchester-on-Thames, on 26 December 955. Wulfstan had stood for the independence of York from West Saxon control and subsequent archbishops of the northern province were chosen for their fidelity to the West Saxon kings.

BIBL. Hart 1975: 376-7

Wulfstan Uccea *fl.* second half of the tenth century

Wulfstan *Uccea* ('toad-like') was a thegn of the east midlands in the middle of the tenth century; he held estates at Ailsworth and Kettering, Northamptonshire, and at Haddon, Yaxley and Conington, Huntingdonshire. Ailsworth had been the possession of a widow and her son, who apparently had some grudge against Wulfstan's father, Ælfsige; they had made an image of him and stuck pins in it, 'and it was discovered and the deadly image dragged out of her room'. Mother and son were tried for witchcraft; she was drowned in the Thames at London Bridge, and he escaped and became an outlaw. Their land at Ailsworth was forfeited and given to the injured party, Ælfsige. This is the only known trial for witchcraft in the whole period before 1066.

BIBL. Robertson 1956, no. 37: 68-9

Wulfstan Lupus archbishop of York 1002—23

Wulfstan, also known by his (self-given) nickname *Lupus* ('wolf'), was one of the most influential figures in the reigns of both *Æthelred II and *Cnut. His origins are obscure but he probably came from the east midlands; his career very likely began in one of the Fenland monasteries, perhaps Ely where he was eventually buried, and much venerated. By 996 he was bishop of London, but in 1002 was translated to Worcester, which he held in plurality with the archbishopric of York until 1016, when he appointed Leofsige as his suffragan in Worcester. He was a great preacher and moralist who was also skilled in both secular and ecclesiastical law. It was Wulfstan who composed the later codes of Æthelred II (V–IX Æthelred) and the codes of Cnut (I–II Cnut), as well as a number of private legal collections. He was in constant attendance on Æthelred, and senior archbishop in the time of Cnut; it was he who consecrated the church which Cnut founded on the site of the battle at Ashingdon in 1020, for the souls of all those killed in the conflict.

Wulfstan's national importance did not mean that he neglected the affairs of his own dioceses. He seems to have provided the canons of St Paul's church at London with a new rule, and to have reorganized their estates. A list of the men who contributed to the manning of the ship owed by St Paul's to the king's service may date from his time. The earliest cartulary of Worcester, the first produced in England, dates from his episcopate, and is annotated in his own hand, as is the memorandum of St *Oswald on the estates of the archbishopric of York. Nor did Wulfstan concern himself solely with his own houses. He reformed St Peter's, Gloucester, replacing the secular clerks with monks in 1022, but much of his energy was directed towards the training and organization of the secular clergy, who had been largely ignored by the monastic reformers of the tenth century. It was for them that he produced the collection of rules known as the *Canons of Edgar*, between 1004 and 1008. The *Northumbrian Priests' Law*, written for the clergy of York Minster, may date from his time or a little later. Much of his writing, especially his sermons or homilies, relate to the duties of parochial and minster clergy. This interest is linked with his ambitions for the moral reform of the laity. In the *Institutes of Polity*, Wulfstan lays down the duties of all the orders of society, beginning with the king. This aim comes out clearly in the most famous of his works, the *Sermon of the Wolf to the English*, preached in the dark days of 1014. Its theme is the sins of the English of all walks of life, for which the Danish invasion and conquest is God's punishment.

Wulfstan is an example of a great Christian statesman. Doubts have been expressed about his Latinity, but much of his writing is in the vernacular, in a prose style highly individual, forceful and direct, even in translation into modern English. Two poems in the *Anglo-Saxon Chronicle* are thought to be from his hand: one a panegyric on Edgar (s.a. 959) and another on the reaction after Edgar's death (s.a. 975). They reflect a deep nostalgia for the 'Golden Age' of Edgar, when Wulfstan's ideal of a theocratic monarchy, in which king, church and people were fused into one Christian polity, found expression.

BIBL. Whitelock 1942

Wystan *see* **Wigstan**

References

Alcock, L 1971 *Arthur's Britain: history and archaeology AD 367–634*. London

Alexander, M (trs) 1973 *Beowulf*. Harmondsworth

Allen, J R and J Anderson 1903 *The Early Christian Monuments of Scotland*. Edinburgh

Anderson, A O (ed) 1922 *Early sources of Scottish history AD 500–1286*. 2 vols. Edinburgh

Anderson, A O and M O Anderson (eds) 1961 *Adomnan's life of Columba*. London and Edinburgh

Anderson, M O 1973 *Kings and kingship in early Scotland*. Edinburgh and London

Arnold T (ed) 1885 *Symeonis monachi opera omnia*. Rolls series, London

Auden, W H and P B Taylor 1981 *Norse poems*. London

Backhouse, J 1981 *The Lindisfarne Gospels*. Oxford

Bannerman, J 1974 *Studies in the history of Dalriada*. Edinburgh and London

Barber, R 1979 *The Arthurian legends*. Woodbridge

Barley, M W and R P C Hanson (eds) 1968 *Christianity in Britain 300–700*. Leicester

Barlow, F 1963 *The English Church 1000–1066*. London

Barlow, F 1970 *Edward the Confessor*. London

Barrow, G W S 1973 *The kingdom of the Scots: government, church and society from the eleventh to the fourteenth century*. London

Barrow, G W S 1978 'Some problems in twelfth- and thirteenth-century Scottish history — a genealogical approach.' *The Scottish Genealogist* 25.4: 97–112

Barrow, G W S 1981 *Kingship and unity: Scotland 1000–1306*. London

Bartrum, P C 1966 *Early Welsh genealogical tracts*. Cardiff

Bassett, S (ed) 1989a *The origins of Anglo-Saxon kingdoms*. Leicester

Bassett, S 1989b 'In search of the origins of Anglo-Saxon kingdoms.' *in* Bassett, S (ed) 1989a: 3–27

Bates, D 1987 'Lord Sudeley's ancestors: the family of the counts of Amiens, Valois and the Vexin in France and England during the eleventh century.' *in* Manorial Society of Great Britain *The Sudeleys, Lords of Toddington*, Thetford: 34–48

Biddle, M and B Kjølbye-Biddle 1985 'The Repton stone.' *Anglo-Saxon England* 14: 233–292

Binchy, D 1962 'Patrick and his biographers.' *Studia Hibernica* 2: 7–173

Blair, J 1989 'Frithuwold's kingdom and the origin of Surrey.' *in* Bassett, S (ed) 1989: 97–107

Blunt, C E, B H I H Stewart and C S Lyon 1989 *Coinage in tenth-century England from Edward the Elder to Edgar's reform*. Oxford

Bowen, E G 1954 *Settlements of the Celtic Saints in Wales*. Cardiff

Bromwich, R 1961 *Trioedd Ynys Prydein: The Welsh Triads*. Cardiff

Bromwich, R 1972 *Armes Prydein: The prophecy of Britain*. Dublin

Bromwich, R and R B Jones (eds) 1978 *Astudiaeth ar yr Hengerdd: Studies in old Welsh poetry*. Cardiff

Brooks, N 1984 *The early history of the church of Canterbury*. Leicester

Brooks, N 1989a 'The creation and early structure of the kingdom of Kent.' *in* Bassett, S (ed) 1989a: 55–74

Brooks, N 1989b 'The formation of the Mercian kingdom.' *in* Bassett, S (ed) 1989a: 159–170

Butler, L A S and R K Morris (eds) 1986 *The Anglo-Saxon church: papers in honour of Dr H M Taylor*. London

Cameron, M L 1983 'Bald's leechbook: its sources and their use in compilation.'

Anglo-Saxon England **12**: 153–182

Cameron, M L 1988 'Anglo-Saxon medicine and magic.' *Anglo-Saxon England* **17**: 191–215

Campbell, A (ed) 1949 *Encomium Emmae reginae.* Camden Society, third series 72

Campbell, A (ed) 1962 *The chronicle of Æthelweard.* London

Campbell, A (ed) 1967 *De abbatibus.* Oxford

Campbell, A 1971 *Skaldic Verse and Anglo-Saxon history.* Dorothea Coke Memorial Lecture in Northern Studies. London

Campbell, A (ed) 1973 *Charters of Rochester (Anglo-Saxon charters 1).* London

Campbell, J 1986 'Asser's *Life of Alfred.*' *in* Holdsworth, C and T Wiseman *The inheritance of historiography.* Exeter: 115–35

Campbell, M 1971 'Cnut the Great's women: Queen Emma and Ælfgifu of Northampton.' *Medieval Scandinavia* **4**: 66–79

Chadwick, H M 1949 *Early Scotland: the Picts, the Scots and the Welsh of Southern Scotland.* Cambridge

Chadwick, N K (ed) 1954 *Studies in early British History.* Cambridge

Chadwick, N K (ed) 1958a *Studies in the early British church.* Cambridge

Chadwick, N K 1958b 'Early culture and learning in North Wales.' *in* Chadwick, N K (ed) 1958a: 29–120

Chadwick, N K 1958c 'Intellectual life in West Wales in the last days of the Celtic church.' *in* Chadwick, N K (ed) 1958a: 121–182

Chadwick, N K 1963a *Celt and Saxon: Studies in the early British border.* Cambridge

Chadwick, N K 1963b 'The conversion of Northumbria: a comparison of sources.' *in* Chadwick, N K (ed) 1963a: 138–166

Chadwick, N K 1963c 'Bede, St Colman and the Irish abbey of Mayo.' *in* Chadwick, N K (ed) 1963a: 186–205

Chadwick, N K 1969 *Early Brittany.* Cardiff

Charles-Edwards, T M 1978 'The authenticity of the *Gododdin*: an historian's view.' *in* Bromwich, R and R B Jones (eds) 1978: 44–71

Chédeville, A and **H Guillotel** 1984 *La Bretagne des saints et des rois Ve-Xe siècle.* Rennes

Clapham, A W 1930 *English Romanesque architecture before the conquest.* Oxford

Clarke, B 1973 *Life of Merlin: Geoffrey of Monmouth's* Vita Merlini. Cardiff

Clemoes, P (ed) 1959 *The Anglo-Saxons: studies in some aspects of their history and culture presented to Bruce Dickins.* London

Colgrave, B (ed) 1927 *The Life of Bishop Wilfrid by Eddius Stephanus.* Cambridge

Colgrave, B (ed) 1940 *Two lives of Saint Cuthbert.* Cambridge

Colgrave, B (ed) 1956 *Felix's life of Saint Guthlac.* Cambridge

Colgrave, B (ed) 1968 *The earliest life of Gregory the Great.* Cambridge

Colgrave, B and **R A B Mynors** (eds) 1969 *Bede's* Ecclesiastical History *of the English people.* Oxford

Cooper, J 1970 *The last four Anglo-Saxon archbishops of York.* Borthwick Papers, 38, York

Cowan, I B and **D E Easson** 1976 *Medieval religious houses: Scotland.* London

Cramp, R 1977 'Schools of Mercian sculpture.' *in* Dornier, A (ed) 1977a: 191–223

Crawford, B E 1987 *Scandinavian Scotland.* Leicester

Crawford, S J (ed) 1966 *Byrhtferth's manual.* Early English Texts Society, old series 177, London

Croínín, D 1986 'New light on Palladius.' *Peritia* **5**: 276–283

Dales, D 1988 *Dunstan, saint and patron.* Cambridge

Davidson, H E 1964 *Gods and myths of Northern Europe.* Harmondsworth

Davies, R R 1987 *Conquest, coexistence and change: Wales 1063–1415.* Oxford

Davies, W 1977 'Annals and the origins of Mercia.' *in* Dornier, A (ed) 1977a: 17–29

Davies, W 1978 *An early Welsh microcosm.* London

Davies, W 1982 *Wales in the early middle ages*. Leicester

Davies, W 1990 *Patterns of power in Early Wales: The O'Donnell Lectures in the University of Oxford, 1983*. Oxford

Dornier, A (ed) 1977a *Mercian Studies*. Leicester

Dornier, A 1977b 'The Anglo-Saxon monastery at Breedon-on-the-Hill, Leicestershire.' *in* Dornier, A (ed) 1977a: 153–168

Dumville, D N 1975–6 '"Nennius" and the *Historia Brittonum*.' *Studia Celtica* **X/XI**: 78–95

Dumville, D N 1977 'Sub-Roman Britain: history and legend.'. *History* **62**: 173–192

Dumville, D N 1982 'The "six" sons of Rhodri Mawr: A problem in Asser's life of King Alfred.' *Cambridge Medieval Celtic Studies* **4**: 5–18

Dumville, D N 1983 'Brittany and "Armes Prydein Vawr".' *Études Celtiques* **20**: 145–159

Dumville, D N 1984a 'Gildas and Mælgwn: problems of dating.' *in* Lapidge and Dumville (eds) 1984: 51–60

Dumville, D N 1984b 'The chronology of *De Excidio Britanniæ*.' *in* Lapidge and Dumville (eds) 1984: 61–84

Dumville, D N 1986 'The historical value of the *Historia Brittonum*.' *Arthurian Literature* **6**: 1–26

Dumville, D N 1988 'Early Welsh poetry: problems of historicity.' *in* Roberts, B F (ed) 1988: 1–16

Dunbabin, J 1985 *France in the making, 843–1180*. Oxford

Duncan, A A M 1975 *Scotland: the making of the kingdom*. Edinburgh

Duncan, A A M 1981 'Bede, Iona and the Picts.' *in The writing of history in the Middle Ages: Essays presented to R W Southern*. (eds) R H C Davis and J M Wallace-Hadrill. Oxford: 1–41

Dykes, D W 1976 *Anglo-Saxon coins in the National Museum of Wales*. Portsmouth

Enright, M J 1979 'Charles the Bald and Æthelwulf of Wessex: the alliance of 856 and the strategies of royal succession.' *Journal of Medieval History* **5**: 291–302

Evans, A C 1986 *The Sutton Hoo ship burial*. London

Evans, D S (ed) 1971 *Lives of the Welsh saints* by G H Doble. Cardiff

Evans, D S 1988 *The Welsh life of St David*. Cardiff

Farmer, D H 1974 'Saint Wilfrid.' *in* Kirby, D P (ed) 1974a: 35–59

Farmer, D H 1978 *The Oxford dictionary of saints*. Oxford

Farmer, D H (ed) 1983 *The age of Bede*. Harmondsworth

Fell, C 1971 *Edward, King and Martyr*. Leeds

Fell, C 1984 *Women in Anglo-Saxon England and the impact of 1066*. London

Finberg H P R 1943 'The house of Ordgar and the foundation of Tavistock Abbey.' *English Historical Review* **58**: 190–201

Finberg, H P R 1951 *Tavistock Abbey*. Cambridge

Finberg, H P R 1961a *Early charters of the west midlands*. Leicester

Finberg, H P R 1961b 'The princes of the Hwicce.' *in* Finberg, H P R 1961a: 167–172

Finberg, H P R 1961c 'St Mildburh's Testament.' *in* Finberg, H P R 1961a: 197–216

Finberg, H P R 1961d 'Princes of the Magonsæte.' *in* Finberg, H P R 1961a: 217–224

Finberg, H P R 1964a *Lucerna*. London

Finberg, H P R 1964b 'Sherborne, Glastonbury and the expansion of Wessex.' *in* Finberg, H P R 1964a: 95–115

Finberg, H P R 1964c 'Childe's Tombe.' *in* Finberg, H P R 1964a: 186–203

Fletcher, E 1981 *Benedict Biscop*. Jarrow Lecture, Jarrow

Forbes, A P 1872 *Kalendars of Scottish Saints with personal notices of those of Alba, Laudonia and Strathclyde*. Edinburgh

Ford, P K 1974 *The poetry of Llywarch Hen*. Berkeley and London

Foster, I Ll 1965 'The emergence of Wales.' *in* Foster, I Ll and G Daniel (eds)

Prehistoric and Early Wales. London: 213—235

Galbraith, V H 1964 'Who wrote Asser's *Life of Alfred?*' in *An introduction to the study of history.* London: 88—128

Geary, P J 1988 *Before France and Germany: the creation and transformation of the Merovingian world.* Oxford

Gneuss, H 1972 'The origins of Standard Old English and Æthelwold's school at Winchester.' *Anglo-Saxon England* **1**: 67—112

Godman, P (ed) 1982 *Alcuin: The bishops, kings and saints of York.* Oxford

Gœtinck, G 1988 'Lifris and the Italian connection.' *Bulletin of the Board of Celtic Studies* **35**: 10—13

Greenaway, G 1980 'Saint Boniface as a man of letters.' in Reuter T (ed) 1980: 31—46

Grierson, P 1940 'Grimbald of St Bertin's.' *English Historical Review* **55**: 529—561

Gruffydd, R G 1978 'Canu Cadwallon ap Cadfan.' in Bromwich R and R B Jones (eds) 1978: 25—48

Gruffydd, R G 1982 'Marwnad Cynddylan.' in Gruffydd, R G (ed) *Bardos* Cardiff: 10—28

Hanson, R P C 1968 *Saint Patrick: his origins and career.* Oxford

Harding, A 1986 'Legislators, lawyers and lawbooks.' in Charles-Edwards, T M, M E Owen, and D B Walters (eds) *Lawyers and laymen* Cardiff: 237—257

Harmer, F E (ed) 1914 *Select English historical documents of the ninth and tenth centuries.* Cambridge

Harmer, F E (ed) 1952 *Anglo-Saxon writs.* Manchester

Harper-Bill, C, C Holdsworth, and **J L Nelson** (eds) 1989 *Studies in Medieval History presented to R Allen Brown.* Woodbridge

Hart, C R 1966 *The early charters of eastern England.* Leicester

Hart, C R 1973 'Athelstan "Half-King" and his family.' *Anglo-Saxon England* **2**: 115—144

Hart, C R 1975 *The early charters of northern England and the north Midlands.* Leicester

Hart, C R 1977 'The kingdom of Mercia.' in Dornier, A (ed) 1977: 43—61

Hart, C R 1982 'Byrhtferth's Northumbrian Chronicle.' *English Historical Review* **97**: 558—82

Hart, C R 1987 'The Ealdordom of Essex.' in Neale, K (ed) *An Essex tribute: essays presented to Frederick G Emmison.* Chelmsford: 57—84

Hehir, B O 1988 'What is the *Gododdin?*' in Roberts, B F (ed) 1988: 57—95

Heighway, C and **R Bryant** 1986 'A reconstruction of the tenth-century church of St Oswald, Gloucester.' in Butler, LAS and RK Morris 1986: 188—95

Henderson, I 1967 *The Picts.* London

Henken, E R 1987 *Traditions of the Welsh saints.* Cambridge

Herbert, M 1988 *Iona, Kells and Derry: The history and hagiography of the Monastic Familia of Columba.* Oxford

Heslop, T A 1980 'English seals from the mid ninth century to 1100.' *Journal of the British Archaeological Association* **133**: 1—16

Hood, A B E 1978 *St Patrick: his writings and Muirchu's life.* London

Hooper, N 1989 'Some observations on the navy in late Anglo-Saxon England.' in C Harper-Bill *et al.* (eds) 1989: 203—213

Hoskins, W 1970 *The westward expansion of Wessex.* Leicester University Department of Local History Occasional Papers no. 13. Leicester

Huggins, P J 1976 'The excavation of an 11th-century Viking hall and 14th-century rooms at Waltham Abbey, Essex.' *Medieval Archaeology* **20**: 75—133

Hughes, K (ed D Dumville) 1980 *Celtic Britain in the early Middle Ages.* Woodbridge

Jackson, K H 1945/6 'Once again Arthur's battles.' *Modern Philology* **43**: 44—57

Jackson, K H 1953 *Language and history in early Britain.* Edinburgh

247

Jackson, K H 1955 'The Britons in southern Scotland.' *Antiquity* **29**: 77–88
Jackson, K H 1958 'The sources for the life of St Kentigern.' *in* Chadwick, N K (ed) 1958a: 273–357
Jackson, K H 1959 'The Arthur of history.' *in* Loomis, R S (ed) 1959: 1–11
Jackson, K H 1969 *The oldest Scottish poem: The Gododdin*. Edinburgh
Jackson, K H 1982 'Gildas and the names of British princes.' *Cambridge medieval Celtic studies* **3**: 30–40
James, J W 1967 *Rhigyfarch's life of St David*. Cardiff
Jansson, S B F 1962 *The runes of Sweden*. London
Jarman, A O H 1960 *The legend of Merlin*. Cardiff
Jarman, A O H 1978 'Early stages in the development of the Myrddin legend.' *in* Bromwich R and R B Jones (eds) 1978: 326–349
Jarman, A O H 1981 *The Cynfeirdd: early Welsh poets and poetry*. Cardiff
Jarman, A O H 1988 *Aneirin: Y Gododdin*. Llandysul
Jenkins, D 1986 *The law of Hywel Dda*. Llandysul
John, E 1966 'The king and the monks in the tenth-century reformation.' *in* John E *Orbis Britanniae*. Leicester: 154–180
Jones, G 1968 *A history of the Vikings*. Oxford
Jones, T 1964 'The early evolution of the legend of Arthur.' *Nottingham Medieval Studies* **8**: 3–21
Kapelle, W E 1979 *The Norman conquest of the North*. London
Kenney, J F 1929 *The sources for the early history of Ireland: ecclesiastical*, reprinted 1979. Dublin
Keynes, S 1980 *The diplomas of King Æthelred 'the Unready' 978–1016*. Cambridge
Keynes, S 1989 'The lost cartulary of Abbotsbury.' *Anglo-Saxon England* **18**: 207–43
Keynes, S and M Lapidge (trs) 1983 *Alfred the Great: Asser's Life of King Alfred and other contemporary sources*. Harmondsworth
Kirby, D P 1962 'Strathclyde and Cumbria: a survey of historical development to 1092.' *Cumberland and Westmorland Antiquarian and Archaeological Society*. n.s **lxii**: 77–94
Kirby, D P 1967 *The making of early England*. London
Kirby, D P 1968 'Vortigern.' *Bulletin of the board of Celtic studies* **23**: 37–59.
Kirby, D P 1971 'Asser's *Life of Alfred*.' *Studia Celtica* **6**: 12–35
Kirby, D P (ed) 1974a *Saint Wilfrid at Hexham*. Newcastle-upon-Tyne
Kirby, D P 1974b 'Northumbria in the time of Wilfrid.' *in* Kirby (ed) 1974a: 1–34
Kirby, D P 1976a 'British dynastic history in the pre-Viking period.' *Bulletin of the board of Celtic studies* **27**: 81–114
Kirby, D P 1976b 'Hywel Dda: Anglophil?' *Welsh Historical Review* **8**: 1–13
Kirby, D P 1977 'Welsh bards and the border.' *in* Dornier, A (ed) 1977a: 31–42
Kirby, D P 1983 'Bede, Eddius Stephanus and the *Life of Wilfrid*.' *English Historical Review* **98**: 101–14
Klæber, F (ed) 1951 *Beowulf and the fight at Finnsburg*. Boston and London
Laing, S 1964 *Snorri Sturluson, Heimskringla*, Pt 1 *The Olaf Sagas* (2 vols) revised J Simpson. London
Laing, S 1961 *Snorri Sturluson, Heimskringla*, Pt 2 *Sagas of the Norse kings*, revised P Foote. London
Lapidge, M 1975a 'The hermeneutic style in tenth-century Latin literature.' *Anglo-Saxon England* **4**: 67–111
Lapidge, M 1975b 'Some remnants of Bede's lost *Liber Epigrammaticum*.' *English Historical Review* **90**: 798–820
Lapidge, M 1981 'Some Latin poems as evidence for the reign of Athelstan.' *Anglo-Saxon England* **9**: 77–83
Lapidge, M 1982 'Byrhtferth of Ramsey and the early sections of the *Historia Regum* attributed to Simeon of Durham.' *Anglo-Saxon England* **10**: 97–122

Lapidge, M 1988 'A Frankish scholar in tenth-century England: Frithegod of Canterbury and Fredegaud of Brioude.' *Anglo-Saxon England* **17**: 45–65

Lapidge, M and **D Dumville** (eds) 1984 *Gildas: new approaches*. Woodbridge

Lapidge, M and **M Herren** (eds) 1979 *Aldhelm: the prose works*. Ipswich

Lapidge, M and **J L Rosier** 1985 *Aldhelm: the poetic works*. Cambridge

Levison, W 1946 *England and the continent in the eighth century*. Oxford

Lloyd, J E 1911 *A history of Wales from the earliest times to the Edwardian conquest 2 vols*. London

Loomis, R S (ed) 1959 *Arthurian literature in the Middle Ages*. Oxford

Lund, N (ed) 1984 *Two voyagers at the court of King Alfred: Ohthere and Wulfstan*. York

Lund, N 1986 'The armies of Swein Forkbeard and Cnut: *leding* or lith?' *Anglo-Saxon England* **15**: 105–118

Lutz, C E 1977 *Schoolmasters of the tenth century*. Hamden, Connecticut

McGatch, M 1977 *Preaching and theology in Anglo-Saxon England: Ælfric and Wulfstan*. Toronto

McKitterick, R 1983 *The Frankish kingdoms under the Carolingians, 751–987*. London

McNeill, P and **R Nicholson** (eds) 1975 *An historical atlas of Scotland c. 400–c.1600*. St Andrews

Macquarrie, A 1987 'The date of Saint Ninian's Mission: a reappraisal.' *Records of the Scottish Church history Society* **xxiii**: 1–25

MacQueen, J 1961 *St Nynia: a study of literary and linguistic evidence*. Edinburgh

Maund, K L 1985 'Cynan ap Iago and the killing of Gruffudd ap Llywelyn.' *Cambridge Medieval Studies* **10**: 57–66

Mayr-Harting, H 1972 *The coming of Christianity to Anglo-Saxon England*. London

Metcalf, D M 1977 'Monetary affairs in Mercia at the time of Æthelbald.' *in* Dornier, A (ed) 1977a: 87–106

Miller, M 1976/8 'The foundation legend of Gwynedd in the Latin texts.' *Bulletin of the board of Celtic studies* **27**: 515–532

Miller, M 1979a 'The dates of Deira.' *Anglo-Saxon England* **8**: 35–61

Miller, M 1979b *The saints of Gwynedd*. Woodbridge

Nelson, J L 1977 'Inauguration rituals.' *in* Sawyer, P I and I N Wood (eds) *Early medieval kingship*. Leeds: 50–71

Nelson, J L 1978 'Queens as Jezebels: the careers of Brunhild and Baltild in Merovingian history.' *in* Baker, D (ed) *Medieval Women*. Studies in church history, Subsidia 1, Oxford: 31–77

Nelson, J L 1986 '"A king across the sea": Alfred in continental perspective.' *Transactions of the Royal Historical Society* 5th series **36**: 45–68

Nicolaisen, W F H 1976 *Scottish place-names: their study and significance*. London

Nightingale, P 1987 'The origins of the court of Husting and Danish influence on London's development as a capital city.' *English Historical Review* **102**: 564-6

Nordenfalk, C 1977 *Celtic and Anglo-Saxon painting*. London

O'Cathasaigh, T 1984 'The Deisi in Dyfed.' *Eigse* **20**: 1–33

O'Curry, E 1861 *Lectures on the manuscript materials of ancient Irish history*. Dublin

O'Donovan, M 1972 'An interim revision of episcopal dates for the province of Canterbury.' Part I, *Anglo-Saxon England* **1**: 23–44

O'Donovan, M 1973 'An interim revision of episcopal dates for the province of Canterbury.' Part II, *Anglo-Saxon England* **2**: 91–114

Oppermann, C J A 1937 *The English missionaries in Sweden and Finland*. London

Padel, O J 1981 'The Cornish background to the Tristan stories.' *Cambridge Medieval Celtic Studies* **I**: 53–81

Pálsson, H and **P Edwards** (eds) 1978 *Orkneyinga saga: the history of the earls of Orkney*. Harmondsworth

REFERENCES

Pennar, M 1988 *Taliesin poems. Introduction and English translation*. Lampeter
Pitman, J H 1925 *The riddles of Aldhelm*. Yale Studies in English 67, reprinted Hamden, Connecticut 1970
Poulin, J-C 1977 'Hagiographie et politique: la première vie de Saint Samson de Pol.' *Francia* **5**: 1–26
Pretty, K 1989 'Defining the Magonsæte.' *in* Bassett, S (ed) 1989a: 171–183
Pryce, H 1986 'The prologues to the Welsh lawbooks.' *Bulletin of the board of Celtic studies* **33**: 151–187
Pugh, T B (ed) 1971 *Glamorgan county history* III. Cardiff
Radford, C A R 1957 'Excavations at Whithorn (Final Report).' *Transactions of the Dumfries and Galloway Natural History and Antiquarian Society* **xxxiv**: 131–94
Raraty, D G J 1989 'Earl of Godwine of Wessex: the origin of his power and his political loyalties.' *History* **74**: 3–19
Reeves, W (ed) 1857 *The life of St Columba, founder of Hy*. Dublin
Reuter, T (ed) 1980 *The greatest Englishman: essays on St Boniface and the church at Crediton*. Exeter
Richards, J 1980 *Consul of God: the life and times of Gregory the Great*. London
Ridyard, S 1988 *The royal saints of Anglo-Saxon England*. Cambridge
Ritchie, G and **A Ritchie** 1981 *Scotland: archaeology and early history*. London
Roberts, B F (ed) 1988 *Early Welsh poetry: studies in the book of Aneirin*. Aberystwyth
Robertson, A S (ed) 1956 *Anglo-Saxon charters*. Cambridge
Rollason, D W 1982 *The Mildrith legend, a study in early medieval hagiography in England*. Leicester
Rollason, D W 1983 'The cults of murdered royal saints in Anglo-Saxon England.' *Anglo-Saxon England* **11**: 1–22
Rollason, D W (ed) 1987a *Cuthbert, saint and patron*. Durham
Rollason, D W 1987b 'The wanderings of Saint Cuthbert.' *in* Rollason, D W (ed) 1987a: 45–59
Rowland, J 1989 *Early Welsh saga poetry: a study and edition of the Englynion*. Woodbridge
Savory, H N 1984 *Glamorgan County History II*. Cardiff
Sawyer, P H **(ed)** 1968 *Anglo-Saxon charters, an annotated list and bibliography*. London
Sawyer, P H 1975 'Charters of the reform movement: the Worcester archive.' *in* Parsons, D (ed) *Tenth-century studies*. Chichester: 84–93
Sawyer, P H (ed) 1979 *Charters of Burton Abbey* (Anglo-Saxon Charter 2). London
Scragg, D E (ed) 1981 *The battle of Maldon*. Manchester
Simpson, L 1989 'The King Alfred/St Cuthbert episode in the *Historia de Sancto Cuthberto*: its significance for mid-tenth-century history.' *in* Bonner, G, D Rollason and C Stancliffe *St Cuthbert, his cult and community to AD 1200*. Woodbridge: 397–411
Sims-Williams, P 1975 'Continental influence at Bath monastery in the seventh century.' *Anglo-Saxon England* **4**: 1–10
Sims-Williams, P 1976 'Cuthswith, seventh-century abbess of Inkberrow, near Worcester, and the Würzburg manuscript of Jerome on *Ecclesiastes*.' *Anglo-Saxon England* **5**: 1–21
Sims-Williams, P 1983 'The settlement of England in Bede and the *Chronicle*.' *Anglo-Saxon England* **12**: 1–41
Sisam, K 1932 'Cynewulf and his poetry.' *Proceedings of the British Academy* **18**: 303–331
Skene, W F (ed) 1867 *Chronicles of the Picts: chronicles of the Scots and other early memorials of Scottish history*. Edinburgh
Skene, W F 1886–90 *Celtic Scotland: a history of ancient Alban* 3 vols. Edinburgh
Smith, J B 1971 'The kingdom of Morgannwg and the Norman conquest of

Glamorgan.' *in* Pugh T B 1971: 4–5

Smyth, A P 1975 *Scandinavian York and Dublin: the history and archaeology of two related Viking kingdoms*. Vol. 1, Dublin

Smyth, A P 1977a *Scandinavian kings in the British Isles 850–880*. Oxford

Smyth, A P 1977b 'The Northumbrian snake-pit.' *in* Smyth, A P 1977a: 36–53

Smyth, A P 1977c 'The second invasion of East Anglia and the martyrdom of King Edmund.' *in* Smyth, A P 1977a: 201–213

Smyth, A P 1977d 'Guthrum and the second summer army.' *in* Smyth, A P 1977a: 240–254

Smyth, A P 1977e 'Halfdan, king of Northumbria.' *in* Smyth, A P 1977a: 255–266

Smyth, A P 1979 *Scandinavian York and Dublin: the history and archaeology of two related Viking kingdoms*. Vol. 2, Dublin

Smyth, A P 1982 *Celtic Leinster: towards an historical geography of early Irish civilisation*. Dublin

Smyth, A P 1984 *Warlords and holy men: Scotland, AD 80–1000*. London

Stafford, P 1978 'The reign of Æthelred II: a study in the limitations on royal policy and action.' *in* Hill D (ed) *Ethelred the Unready: papers from the Milleniary conference*. BAR 59, Oxford: 15–46

Stafford, P 1981 'Charles the Bald, Judith and England.' *in* Gibson, M and J L Nelson (eds) *Charles the Bald: court and country*. BAR 101, Oxford: 137–151

Stafford, P 1985 *The East Midlands in the early Middle Ages*. Leicester

Stenton, D M (ed) 1970 *Preparatory to Anglo-Saxon England*. Oxford

Stenton, F M 1933 'Medeshamstede and its colonies.' *from Historical essays in honour of James Tait*. Manchester, 1933: 313–26; *reprinted in* Stenton, D M (ed) 1970: 179–192

Stenton, F M 1936 'St Frideswide and her times.' *Oxoniensia* 1: 103–112, reprinted in Stenton, D M (ed) 1970: 224–233

Stenton, F M 1955 *Latin charters of the Anglo-Saxon period*. Oxford

Stenton, F M 1959 'The East Anglian kings of the seventh century.' *in* Clemoes, P (ed) 1959: 43–52, reprinted in Stenton, D M (ed) 1970: 394–402

Stenton, F M 1971 *Anglo-Saxon England*. 3rd Ed. Oxford

Stenton, F M 1981 'The supremacy of the Mercian kings.' *English Historical Review* 33: 433–452

Stubbs, W (ed) 1861 *The foundation of Waltham Abbey; the tract* De Inventione Sanctae Crucis. Oxford

Stubbs, W (ed) 1874 *Memorials of St Dunstan*. Rolls series, London

Stubbs, W (ed) 1887 *Willelmi Malmesberiensis Monachi De Gestis Regum Anglorum*. Rolls series 90, London

Swanton, M (ed) 1975 *Anglo-Saxon prose*. London

Talbot, C H (ed) 1954 *The Anglo-Saxon missionaries in Germany*. London

Taylor, A B 1936–7 'Karl Hundason "King of Scots".' *Proceedings of the Society of Antiquaries of Scotland* lxxi: 334–342

Taylor, A B (ed) 1938 *The Orkneyinga saga*. London and Edinburgh

Taylor, T 1925 *The life of St Samson of Dol*. London

Thacker, A T 1981 'Some terms for noblemen in Anglo-Saxon England, c. 650–900.' *Anglo-Saxon studies in archaeology and history* 2 BAR 92, Oxford: 201–236

Thomas, C 1971 *The early Christian archaeology of North Britain*. London and Glasgow

Thomas, C 1985 *Christianity in Roman Britain to AD 500*. London

Thompson, E A 1984 *St Germanus of Auxerre and the end of Roman Britain*. Woodbridge

Thompson, E A 1985 *Who was St Patrick?*. Woodbridge

Turville-Petre (E O) G 1967 *Origins of Icelandic literature*. Oxford

Victory, S 1977 *The Celtic church in Wales*. London

Vigfusson G and **F York Powell** (eds) 1883 *Corpus poeticum boreale: the poetry of the old Norse tongue* 2 vols, reprinted 1965. New York

Wainwright, F T 1942 'North-west Mercia.' *Transactions of the Historical Society of Lancashire and Cheshire* **94**: 3–56, reprinted in Wainwright, ed Finberg 1975: 63–129

Wainwright, F T 1948 'Ingimund's invasion.' *English Historical Review* **63**: 145–169, reprinted in Wainwright, ed Finberg 1975: 131–161

Wainwright F T (ed) 1955 *The problem of the Picts*. Edinburgh

Wainwright, F T 1959 'Æthelflæd, Lady of the Mercians.' *in* Clemoes, P (ed) 1959, reprinted in Wainwright, ed Finberg 1975: 305–324

Wainwright, F T (ed) 1962 *The Northern Isles*. Edinburgh and London

Wainwright, F T 1975a 'The battle at Corbridge.' *in* Wainwright, ed Finberg 1975: 163–79

Wainwright, F T 1975b 'Ingimund's invasion.' *in* Wainwright, ed Finberg 1975: 131–61

Wainwright, F T, ed **H P R Finberg** 1975 *Scandinavian England*. Chichester

Watson, W J 1926 *The history of the Celtic place-names of Scotland*. Edinburgh

Webster, B 1975 *Scotland from the eleventh century to 1603*. Cambridge

Welch, M 1978 'Early Anglo-Saxon Sussex: from *civitas* to shire'. *in* Brandon, P (ed) *The south Saxons*. Chichester, Phillimore: 13–35

Welch, M 1989 'The kingdom of the south Saxons: the origins.' *in* Bassett, S (ed) 1989a: 75–83

Wharton, Sir H (ed) 1691 *Anglia Sacra*. Oxford

Whitbread, L 1959 'Æthelweard and the Anglo-Saxon chronicle.' *English Historical Review* **74**: 577–580

White, S D 1989 'Kingship and lordship in early medieval England: the story of Cynewulf and Cyneheard.' *Viator* **20**: 1–18

Whitelock, D (ed) 1930 *Anglo-Saxon wills*. Cambridge

Whitelock, D 1942 'Archbishop Wulfstan, homilist and statesman.' *Transactions of the Royal Historical Society* fourth series **24**: 42–60, reprinted in Whitelock, D (ed) 1981

Whitelock, D (ed) 1955 *English historical documents, volume 1: c 500–1042*. London

Whitelock, D 1959 'The dealings of the kings of England with Northumbria in the tenth and eleventh centuries.' *in* Clemoes, P (ed) 1959: 70–88, reprinted in Whitelock, D (ed) 1981: 76–9

Whitelock, D 1968 *The genuine Asser*. Reading

Whitelock, D 1972 'The pre-Viking age church in East Anglia.' *Anglo-Saxon England* **1**: 1–22

Whitelock, D 1975 *Some Anglo-Saxon bishops of London*. Chambers Memorial Lecture 1974. London, reprinted in Whitelock, D (ed) 1981

Whitelock, D (ed) 1981 *History, law and literature in tenth to eleventh century England*. London

Whitelock, D, D C Douglas and **S I Tucker** (eds) 1961 *The Anglo-Saxon Chronicle*. London

Williams, A 1982 '*Princeps Merciorum gentis*: the family, career and connections of Ælfhere, ealdorman of Mercia, 956–983.' *Anglo-Saxon England* **10**: 143–172

Williams, A 1986 '"Cockles amongst the wheat": Danes and English in the western midlands in the first half of the eleventh century.' *Midland History* **11**: 1–22

Williams, A 1988 'An introduction to the Worcestershire Domesday.' *in* Erskine, R W H and A Williams, *The Worcestershire Domesday*. London: 1–31

Williams, A 1989 'The king's nephew: the family and career of Ralph, earl of Hereford.' *in* Harper-Bill, C *et al.* 1989: 327–343

Williams, I 1938 *Canu Aneirin*. Cardiff

Williams, I 1953 *Canu Llywarch Hen*. 2nd ed, Cardiff

Williams, I 1955 *Armes Prydein*. Cardiff (English version: *see* Bromwich 1972)

Williams, I 1960 *Canu Taliesin*. Cardiff (English version: *see* Williams, J E C 1968)

Williams, I 1980 'The poems of Llywarch Hen.' *in* Bromwich, R (ed) *The beginnings of Welsh poetry: studies by Sir Ifor Williams*. 2nd ed. Cardiff: 122–54

Williams, J E C 1968 *The poems of Taliesin*. Cardiff

Williams, J E C 1984 'Gildas, Maelgwn and the Bards.' *in* Davies, R R *et al* (eds) *Welsh society and nationhood*. Cardiff: 19–34

Wood, I 1984 'The end of Roman Britain.' *in* Lapidge, M and D Dumville (eds) 1984: 1–26

Wood, M 1981 *In search of the Dark Ages*. London

Wormald, P 1978 'Bede, "Beowulf" and the conversion of Anglo-Saxon aristocracy.' *in* Farrell, R T (ed) *Bede and Anglo-Saxon England*. BAR British series **46**: 32–95

Wright, C E (ed) 1955 *Bald's leechbook: British Museum Royal Manuscript 12, D xvii*. Early English manuscripts in facsimile **5** Copenhagen

Yorke, B 1985 'The kingdom of the East Saxons.' *Anglo-Saxon England* **14**: 1–36

Yorke, B (ed) 1988a *Bishop Æthelwold, his career and influence*. Woodbridge

Yorke, B 1988b 'Æthelwold and the politics of the tenth century.' *in* Yorke, B (ed) 1988a: 65–88

Yorke, B 1989 'The Jutes of Hampshire and Wight and the origins of Wessex.' *in* Bassett, S (ed) 1989a: 84–96